Sublime Thoughts /
Penny Wisdom

New Studies in American Intellectual and Cultural History

Thomas Bender, Series Editor

Without God, Without Creed: The Origins of Unbelief in America
James Turner

*From Colonies to Commonwealth; Familial Ideology
and the Beginnings of the American Republic*
Melvin Yazawa

*The Morality of Spending: Attitudes toward the Consumer Society
in America, 1875–1940*
Daniel Horowitz

Masters and Statesmen: The Political Culture of American Slavery
Kenneth S. Greenberg

*Scholarly Means to Evangelical Ends: The New Haven Scholars and
the Transformation of Higher Learning in America, 1830–1890*
Louise L. Stevenson

*The New Urban Landscape: The Redefinition of City Form
in Nineteenth-Century America*
David Schuyler

Intimacy and Power in the Old South: Ritual in the Lives of the Planters
Steven Stowe

The Republic Reborn: War and the Making of Liberal America, 1790–1820
Steven Watts

*Consciousness in New England: From Puritanism and Ideas
to Psychoanalysis and Semiotic*
James Hoopes

William James, Public Philosopher
George Cotkin

A Consuming Faith: The Social Gospel and Modern American Culture
Susan Curtis

Paradox Lost: Free Will and Political Liberty in American Culture, 1630–1760
Jon Pahl

*Sublime Thoughts/Penny Wisdom: Situating Emerson and Thoreau
in the American Market*
Richard F. Teichgraeber III

Sublime Thoughts/ Penny Wisdom

SITUATING EMERSON AND THOREAU
IN THE AMERICAN MARKET

Richard F. Teichgraeber III

THE JOHNS HOPKINS UNIVERSITY PRESS

BALTIMORE AND LONDON

© 1995 The Johns Hopkins University Press
All rights reserved. Published 1995
Printed in the United States of America on acid-free paper
04 03 02 01 00 99 98 97 96 95   5 4 3 2 1

The Johns Hopkins University Press
2175 North Charles Street
Baltimore, Maryland 21218-4319
The Johns Hopkins Press Ltd., London

ISBN 0-8018-5000-2

Library of Congress Cataloging-in-Publication Data will be found
at the end of this book.
A catalog record for this book is available from the British Library.

This book is dedicated to the memory of
George Armstrong Kelly (1932–1987)

Contents

Contents

Preface and
Acknowledgments

I

Part of my view of Emerson and Thoreau is evident in the words of my title. They come (in inverted order) from the famous address Emerson delivered at the Harvard Divinity School on July 20, 1838. In it, he declared: "For all our penny-wisdom, for all our soul-destroying slavery to habit, it is not to be doubted, that all men have sublime thoughts; that all men do value the few hours of real life; they love to be heard; they love to be caught up into a vision of principles."[1] Because this sentence could easily be mistaken for one written by Thoreau in the two opening chapters of *Walden* (1854), I highlight Emerson's terms to direct attention to an idiom that he shared with Thoreau. More important, the suggestive interplay of Emerson's terms also hints at a shared strategy of social criticism I explore at some length in parts 1 and 2 of this book. What Emerson had to say about the market in the Divinity School Address, at first glance, seems straightforward enough. "Penny wisdom"—the "soul-destroying" habit of looking at the world exclusively with a merchant's eye and calculating how to improve one's material lot—is apparently what dams up our "real life" and "sublime thoughts," blocking currents of creativity, independence, and nobility that Emerson believed flowed through every person. But notice that criticism

1. Ralph Waldo Emerson, "The Divinity School Address," in *The Collected Works of Ralph Waldo Emerson*, vol. 1, *Nature, Addresses, and Lectures*, ed. Robert E. Spiller and Alfred R. Ferguson (Cambridge, Mass., 1971), 90.

here comes wrapped in a qualifying proclamation of hope that suggests Emerson did not see himself as speaking from somewhere located entirely outside the market, or standing in a purely adversarial relation to its inhabitants. "Sublime thoughts" are not presented as an elitist alternative to "penny wisdom"; rather, Emerson appeals to them as shared values—"*all* men have sublime thoughts" and "love to be caught up into a vision of principles"—in an effort to persuade his contemporaries to live up to their own professed higher ideals and thereby remedy failings of character for which he believed the market ultimately could not be held accountable.

This was much the same stance Thoreau took in his criticisms of market practices and institutions. While he once described life in market society as a "life without principle," his disaffection was neither consistent nor free of paradoxes. There were radically antimarket implications in his account of his experiment in living at Walden Pond, but Thoreau stressed that this experiment was not to be taken as a guide to social or economic reform. He also recognized the paradox of poverty in the midst of economic progress in antebellum America, yet said that progress had done more to degrade the affluent than the poor. And finally, to name one more paradox, he railed against the "curse" of trade in American life, yet also— following Emerson's example—used the language of trade to convey the joys of an unspoiled natural life. The many-sidedness of Thoreau's response to the market, his shifting back and forth from criticism to grudging accommodation, is best understood as a stance of ambivalent attachment. Thoreau certainly did not believe the market was soil in which the greatness of individuals might flourish. Yet he also did not believe that life *with* principle dictated unqualified opposition to or complete withdrawal from the market. (He never advocated voluntary poverty; he suggested it was merely one possibility.) What Thoreau fashioned in writing *Walden* was an intellectual position that both echoed Emerson's views in the Divinity School Address and mirrored an actual place he had once made for himself at Walden Pond: a place partly outside and partly inside the market. Outside because Thoreau wanted to present himself as an arbiter of its value, yet inside too because he thought his contemporaries at least could acknowledge the need for an antipecuniary ethic to restrain their acquisitiveness and recognize that trade and commerce might become means to higher ends. The message of *Walden*, Thoreau wrote, was not that the materials of the market should be shunned altogether, but rather that "with a little more wit we might" use them "to become richer than the richest now are, and make our civilization a blessing."[2]

2

This study of Emerson and Thoreau deals sympathetically with the complexities and paradoxes that characterized their views of the market. Unlike numerous recent commentators who cast them as befuddled or coopted critics who owed more to the market than they knew or cared to acknowledge, I do not take them to task for hidden compromises or disordered thinking. I hope to suggest instead that we deepen, and in some respects usefully complicate, our understanding of Emerson and Thoreau by seeing their practice of assigning contrasting and shifting meanings to the market as consciously chosen. Both figures sought to establish their authority to criticize antebellum market practices and institutions, in other words, not by rejecting them out of hand, but by assigning them other and higher meanings, and then attempting to persuade their contemporaries to recognize those meanings as their own. Emerson and Thoreau were, in short, "connected critics" of the market.

In dealing sympathetically with Emerson and Thoreau, I hardly mean to suggest that we accept their views uncritically, but rather to provide a more adequate and historically well-grounded explanation of why the market appeared to them as it did. An important part of the explanation I offer derives from Michael Walzer, from whom I borrow the term "connected critic." Walzer himself has used that term for two somewhat different purposes. The first is to defend and exemplify a form of social criticism that is interpretive in method, here pursuing a philosophical project—showing the existing norms of a society contain the grounds for moral criticism—which is not important for my purposes.[3] Fundamental to my reading of Emerson and Thoreau, however, is Walzer's use of "connected

---

2. Henry D. Thoreau, *Walden*, in *Walden and Other Writings*, ed. Brooks Atkinson (New York, 1950), 36.

3. Michael Walzer, *Interpretation and Social Criticism* (Cambridge, 1987), and *The Company of Critics: Social Criticism in the Twentieth Century* (New York, 1988). For a helpful evaluation of Walzer's philosophical project, see Joseph Raz, "Morality as Interpretation," *Ethics* 101 (January 1991): 392–405.

critic" to account for a historical phenomenon: the work of a group of actual critics who were neither alienated nor detached from practices and institutions they criticized, but instead criticized from the inside by invoking what they took to be their society's shared values as the grounds for criticism. Walzer does not include Emerson and Thoreau on his list of connected critics (most of whom, in his view, have been twentieth-century European intellectuals), but I intend to show they represent two additional instances of the historical phenomenon he has discussed. Moreover, exploiting his account of critics who have been insiders has allowed me to explore the complexities and paradoxes of Emerson and Thoreau as something other than signs of confusion and timidity. I see them instead as evidence of the conscious efforts each made to maintain moral ties with the society they criticized, yet of which they also thought themselves to be members.

To those who protest that I am trying to persuade the reader to a point of view by disguising its distance from us in time, I have two preliminary answers. The first is that I am indeed interpreting Emerson and Thoreau in a way that enhances our ability to respect what they said about what they knew of the market. Yet I do not assume this is always an easy task. One well-known difficulty with the maxim of respectful interpretation is that it risks suggesting that the audience for the interpretation is only the interpreter herself, presented as an isolated individual. The interpretation I have constructed in this book, however, includes efforts to explain why the full range of Emerson's and Thoreau's speculations about the market has proved so difficult to take in. When I discuss the ways in which Emerson used the language of the market to articulate his ideals, for example, I argue that his vocabulary was quite deliberately chosen. Yet I recognize too that this choice invited half-readings that have seen his project as little more than an effort to "spiritualize" the antebellum marketplace. Sometimes connected critics stand too close to the society they criticize and are thereby misunderstood.

Regarding the question of historical distance, I understand why some would say that Emerson and Thoreau were largely uninformed about perhaps more complicated and troubling manifestations of the market that lay in the future. But to focus immediately on what Emerson and Thoreau did not anticipate—lamenting Emerson's apparent insensitivity to the crassness and injustice bred by the market, or saying Thoreau failed to see that in its way *Walden* prescribed a code of conduct as morally restricted as that of the marketplace—is to miss the great significance of extensive and radical changes to which they did respond. The market Emerson and Thoreau knew brought many of the transformations necessary to America's becoming a major economic power. Between 1815 and 1850 Americans built elaborate networks of canals, turnpikes, and early railroad lines; cleared wide areas of land for trade and settlement; and began to industrialize manufacturing, especially in the Northeast. In Southern states, the outstanding change was, of course, the rise of the Cotton Kingdom and the westward expansion of plantation slavery. America's first "market revolution" not only radically transformed the economic relationships of people, but also brought far-reaching political and cultural change. At one level, the spread of commerce created a hybrid political economy by introducing wage labor and widespread capitalist agriculture in the North, and by fostering a different slave-based order in the South.[4] Viewed from a different angle, the "market revolution" also can be said to have produced the deepening sectional confrontation that led to the Civil War, since opposition to slavery in Northern states came to center both in the fear that Southern states aimed to spread slavery to the rest of the country and the hope that slavery as an economic system was an anachronism destined to be replaced by the North's free-labor system. The expansion of the market at the same time transformed the culture of all antebellum Americans—displacing local networks of oral communication with a glut of printed information in newspapers, magazines, and books that became the essential means of mass communication and an increasingly dominant source of cultural activity. Technological innovations such as the cylinder rotary press also made for a dramatic increase in the productive power of American publishing, which in turn served to make book-publishing into a major industry that catered to the demands of new mass reading public. In short, while producing for the market had been widespread since the political revolution of 1776, during the antebellum period it came to characterize a greater range of activities than ever before in American history.

Emerson and Thoreau wrote during decades, then, which brought inno-

---

4. Sean Wilentz, "Society, Politics, and the Market Revolution, 1815–1848," in *The New American History*, ed. Eric Foner (Philadelphia, 1990), 51–71; also see Charles Sellers, *The Market Revolution: Jacksonian America, 1815–46* (New York, 1991).

vations conducive to continuous economic growth, as well as fundamental political and cultural transformations. Even more disruptive changes of course lay in the future, and taken together they account for some of the discrepancy between the market Emerson and Thoreau knew and the historical situation we confront today. I resist the view, however, that we have somehow lost most or all sense of what the market may have meant to them. The question of *our* stance regarding the writings of Emerson and Thoreau at the end of the twentieth century is a complicated matter, and I will return to it in the epilogue. Here I would say only that their works today are more intelligible to us than ever before, and that various efforts continue to be made to integrate them with recognized patterns of the history of their own time. The upshot, in my view, is that an increasingly accurate comprehension of what Emerson and Thoreau thought themselves to be doing can make more authentic (and capacious) thinkers available for use in contemporary debates. The authentic, historical Emerson and Thoreau are also the figures we must have if we intend to get right the cultural and intellectual history of the United States.

3

This book appears in the midst of a remarkable renewal of interest in Emerson and Thoreau, and it may be helpful at the outset to locate my concerns against the backdrop of a variously motivated revival. During the past two decades, my contemporaries have been writing about Emerson and Thoreau along two parallel lines. American literary critics, philosophers, and political theorists are again finding in Emerson and Thoreau ideas and modes of speculation resources that help meet current needs of cultural and political self-understanding. While both Emerson and Thoreau continue to have their detractors, efforts to shed stereotypes and to rehabilitate their reputations as original thinkers and cultural visionaries are widespread, and they have been fed by a variety of important concerns: the recognition that the label "Transcendentalist" has impeded efforts to understand the complex mix of impulses and voices that characterize both Emerson's and Thoreau's texts; the enlistment of those texts in the work of freeing American philosophy from the technical preoccupations of the academic mainstream; renewed effort to demonstrate the intricacy and depth of their shared commitment to the individualistic premises of American life, to name but a few.[5]

Second, as opposed to the reshapings of Emerson and Thoreau for the purposes of late-modern literary criticism, philosophy, and political theory, there has been renewed interest in the project I join in with this study: examining the ties they had with the culture and politics of their own time. Call the dominant recent trend here, for lack of a better term, the "new historicist" approach. It seeks to reinstate Emerson and Thoreau as "useful" thinkers, but typically does so by asking how their high cultural status was created and then maintained over time, and—more especially—with what consequences have they enjoyed that status. Although an imprecise term, new historicism currently serves as the byword for an approach that attempts to define terms for a new relationship with major figures in our literary past, primarily by way of conceptualizing literary discourse as an activity that has been pursued within particular political and economic orders. In this approach, writings traditionally isolated as "literary" (because they were once presupposed to give us access to underlying and therefore timeless truths about the human condition) are now resituated within a network of dominant political and economic institutions, and then explored as locales of unresolved (and at times unconscious) conflicts in beliefs and values. Here the primary work of historically minded interpretation has come to focus on questions of race, gender, class, and the market, which in turn are said to provide the fundamental syntax for understanding those conflicts. While many dispute the new historicist understanding of what our history has been, I see no reason to deny the importance and integrity of its underlying desire to make the writings of major literary figures available to a new generation of readers with questions and interests in obvious ways different from those of earlier interpreters.

Yet while I am sympathetic with those who find need to redefine our relationship to the cultural and literary past, the new historicist approach to Emerson and Thoreau is not without its problems. Two shortcomings,

---

5. Among several important works that explore one or more of these concerns, see Stanley Cavell, *The Senses of Walden* (San Francisco, 1981); B. L. Packer, *Emerson's Fall: A New Interpretation of the Major Essays* (New York, 1982); Richard Poirier, *The Renewal of Literature: Emersonian Reflections* (New York, 1987); Judith N. Shklar, "Emerson and the Inhibitions of Democracy," *Political Theory* 18 (November 1990): 601–14; and George Kateb, *The Inner Ocean: Individualism and Democratic Culture* (Ithaca, 1992).

in particular, bear directly on the concerns of this study. In practice, too much of recent new historicist scholarship has displayed a remarkably casual attitude toward the painstaking work of reconstructing the concrete historical situations within which the meaning of their writings was first established. The new historicists are right to suggest that both Emerson and Thoreau be viewed as figures entirely aware that their publications appeared at a time when the emergence of a market economy was creating a new kind of culture in which a growing mass audience of readers would come to acquire unprecedented authority over the terms of a writer's public identity. But recent studies of antebellum America's new "literary marketplace" have failed to examine what contemporary readers actually had to say about Emerson and Thoreau, and nowhere has any effort been made to explore personal and professional ties each figure had with editors and publishers who first helped bring their writings into the marketplace.[6]

I am also troubled by the related inability of the new historicist approach to move beyond what appears to be its guiding cliché: namely, the proposition that what might look like dissent or subversion in literary discourse always turns out to be, on closer inspection, a set of attitudes or ideas that a dominant political and economic order can appropriate to justify and sustain itself. There is no question that, in defending this view, new historicist scholars seek to answer essential questions. Why did Emerson and Thoreau never seriously consider the possibility that the flaws of the market pointed to fundamental contradictions in the American order? Why did each so often convey their idealistic visions of American culture in the language of trade and commerce? On both counts, new historicists properly counter the claim that in protesting against the ascendancy of the market Emerson and Thoreau refused to accept it as a defining characteristic in American life. Hence, they approach Emerson and Thoreau, roughly as I do in, as figures who belonged to the economic order they criticized. But does this also mean that the filiations with the market dis-

---

6. Among recent works that have either ignored or provided perfunctory accounts of the initial publishing and reception histories of Emerson's and Thoreau's writings, see Michael T. Gilmore, *American Romanticism and the Marketplace* (Chicago, 1985); R. Jackson Wilson, *Figures of Speech: American Writers and the Literary Marketplace, from Benjamin Franklin to Emily Dickinson* (New York, 1989); and Stephen Railton, *Authorship and Audience: Literary Performance in the American Renaissance* (Princeton, 1991). On the question of why studies linking literature and authorship to "the market" have proved so popular in recent years, see Brook Thomas, *The New Historicism and Other Old-Fashioned Topics* (Princeton, 1991), 19–23.

played in their writings ultimately served to obscure or vitiate their criticism? As a description of some of the unintended effects of Emerson's and Thoreau's positions, that argument has some merit. But it misses the intended point of their criticism altogether.[7] When Emerson and Thoreau questioned the value of the market, they typically were not considering the alternative of having no market transactions at all. That possibility is hard even to visualize. (As we shall see, the market, in various ways, enters into a remarkable number of the events Thoreau recounts at the outset of *Walden*.) Even in their most outspoken attacks, Emerson and Thoreau never simply recommended the cessation of market transactions. The choice they were considering was not—as new historicists apparently would have it—an all-or-nothing question, but instead a matter of "how much," "how unrestrained," and "how supplemented."[8] Rendering such questions plausible, without suggesting that Emerson and Thoreau were somehow in unwitting complicity with the market, is one of the central concerns of this study.

Finally, in this regard, my commitment to restore Emerson and Thoreau to their historical context has made for a book that is comparatively short on theory and long on efforts to allow Emerson and Thoreau to speak for themselves and to attend to the various ways in which their contemporaries understood their writings.[9] One consequence of this is a fairly generous supply of quotations. Another is, I believe, a sensitivity to questions of race, gender, and class that nonetheless resists their promotion to framing

---

7. See, e.g., David Leverenz, *Manhood and American Renaissance* (Ithaca, 1989), chs. 1 and 2. Leverenz argues that Emerson and Thoreau can be grouped with several other nineteenth-century American writers who contributed to a "cult of manhood" that obscured the incipient class conflicts of the market by constructing a gender ideology that cut across class lines. Yet this argument itself obscures the fact that Emerson and Thoreau thought the continuing presence of slavery in American life represented a disgrace that mocked the vaunted claims of harmony and progress often associated with "the market" in their time. As we shall see in pt. 2, Emerson and Thoreau alike could be scathing in denouncing the average white male's uninquiring tolerance of slavery.

8. I am indebted to Amartya Sen, "The Moral Standing of the Market," *Social Philosophy and Policy* 2 (Spring 1985): 1–19, for the distinction I underline here.

9. To say that Emerson and Thoreau can be understood as "connected critics" is not the same thing as saying they are systematic theorists of the development of the market. In Walzer's *Company of Critics*, two important instances of a connected critic—i.e., Randolph Bourne and George Orwell—are not theorists in the strict sense. I do not use Walzer's term, then, to suggest that Emerson and Thoreau are neglected theoretical virtuosos, but rather to provide a new framework within which we can better recognize and understand the characteristic ambivalence and diversity of their views of the market.

or governing the analysis developed here. Instead, I start with the writings and try to confront questions plainly posed by their own announced concerns and the manner in which they pursued those concerns. Doubtless some of what we consider important Emerson and Thoreau either excluded or understood in ways we no longer find acceptable. In our pursuit of current concerns, however, we risk sloppiness. There is nothing inherently misguided about a desire to discuss their writings in terms of our own cultural anxieties and needs, but I would say again that we should do so with a respectful interest in the differences that separate us from their texts. It is my hope that this book will sharpen that interest by building a structure that allows us to see the specific shape and distinctive features of their views of the market with greater clarity and understanding.[10]

4

The book does not pretend to discuss every aspect of how Emerson and Thoreau thought about or experienced the emergence of America's market economy. Its nine chapters (though written in the present order) are not intended as a complete or chronological canvassing of Emerson's and Thoreau's views. I deal primarily with the period between 1836 and 1862, years when Emerson and Thoreau published the writings for which they remain best known and when their literary careers directly overlapped. This also happens to have been a period bounded by two national traumas: the onset (in 1837) of a financial panic that ushered in the half-decade of America's first great economic depression, and the coming of the Civil War. I explore three themes in detail, each identified in the titles of the parts into which I have subdivided the chapters of the book. Part 1 develops the interpretation of Emerson and Thoreau as connected critics I sketched at the outset of this preface. That interpretation carries over into part 2, where I reopen the question of how they expressed their opposition to American slavery. As no other issue did, slavery tested their shared assumption that ideals internal to American society could be achieved

---

10. Scholars have noted, correctly, that Emerson and Thoreau differed from one another in important respects. So I do not employ the concept of connected critic to suggest a greater degree of homology between them than may be warranted. What is remarkable, in my approach, was that they shared a broad imperative to enlist their contemporaries in the task of self-criticism, and to bring them to understand that the current ills of American soci-

without sweeping institutional reform. For how could they repudiate slavery and not in some fashion also repudiate America itself? How could they sustain ties to political and social institutions they saw as deeply implicated in an abominable human practice? Emerson and Thoreau answered these questions in different ways at different times in their careers. Part 2 tries to locate their responses more clearly in the history of American abolitionist thought. It also tries to show that for Emerson and Thoreau the general question of what American slavery was quickly turned into several more specific questions: how to understand the relationship between efforts to end slavery and larger economic changes taking place during the antebellum period, and then how to interpret the North's continuing acceptance of slavery and how to alter Northern public opinion. While those questions provoked angry criticism of their contemporaries, they also dictated a strategy in which the argument about American slavery became an argument about the meaning of the North's way of life. The general question Emerson and Thoreau finally tried to answer, then, was not quite the one they asked at first. It had a crucial addition that again identified them—as well as the abolitionists whose views they often echoed—as connected critics: how to persuade fellow Northerners to recognize that the political and economic principles *we* embrace demanded the repudiation of slavery.

Part 3 provides a publishing and reception of the "classic" texts of Emerson and Thoreau that adds texture to the interpretation I offer in parts 1 and 2. Yet my three final chapters also make more limited use of the notion of connected critic. Some contemporaries certainly did see Emerson and Thoreau as figures who criticized American society from the inside, invoking shared values as the grounds for their criticism. (History would inscribe Emerson's name as a father of his country, Margaret Fuller proclaimed in 1844, because "he is one who pleads her cause against herself.") But most did not, and spelling out why seemed a less important (and less interesting) project than accounting for the disparate variety of things that were said about them. A shift of focus also seemed to me justified because in the vast scholarly literature on Emerson and Thoreau we have no systematic accounts of how their contemporaries actually viewed their ideas and writ-

---

ety were not inevitable or beyond repair. To posit a common design in their understanding of the market, however, is not to ignore their differences, nor to imply that they were less interesting than the similarities.

ings. Such accounts are missing, partly because most cultural and literary historians have read astonishingly little of the reviews and commentary that initially greeted their publications, partly because previous work in this area has been based on remarkably naïve assumptions regarding the transformation that the market brought to the production, circulation, and status of writing during the antebellum period. Part 3, then, turns to grapple with the question of how Emerson and Thoreau themselves *experienced* the antebellum literary marketplace. Here my primary concern is to show that their writings became known much earlier, reached a much broader audience, and embarked through a variety of institutional channels more numerous than has traditionally been recognized. It would be a mistake to press Emerson and Thoreau too close to the popular literary culture of their time, but their writings were by no means ignored or set aside as an elite supplement.

5

Two final points. This book is about two highly canonical figures. Each enjoys a starring role in most versions of the story of American culture, even when cast as irresponsible Northern intellectuals—"antiheroes"—whose shared stance of simple and harsh moral purity on the question of American slavery supposedly impeded efforts to accomplish its peaceful reform and thereby ushered in a national catastrophe.[11] Their personal and intellectual relationship itself also remains a frequent topic of official study. However, in view of the ongoing controversy as to whether any select group of writers can be said to speak for a culture as a whole, I want to stress that it is not my purpose to resecure the identification of Emerson and Thoreau with the presumed essence of nineteenth-century American culture. The concept of a shared national culture was (for reasons I attempt to make clear in chapter 7) every bit as elusive during the antebellum period as it is now—and not just because of political and economic differences that divided North and South. Fascination with Emerson and Thoreau requires no apology, but the America they knew and drew strength

---

11. See Stanley Elkins, *Slavery: A Problem in American Institutional and Intellectual Life* (New York, 1959), pt. 4; and George Fredrickson, *The Inner Civil War: Northern Intellectuals and the Crisis of the Union* (New York, 1965), ch. 1.

from had a rich variety of competing subcultures, no one of which was more representatively "American" than the others.

I would hasten to add, however, that while renewed interest in the process of canon formation has reminded us that canons ought not to be taken as neutral registers of literary and intellectual worth, it also has allowed us to see that canonization can throw up obstacles to adequate evaluation and understanding of "canonical" writers themselves. In Emerson's case, as Michael Lopez has pointed out, canonization until recently has meant "simplification, sanitizing, condescension, then denunciation, then an oddly begrudging and severely qualified defense" by scholars generally considered to be his friendly critics. Or as Richard Poirier has put it, while Emerson has been a pervasive presence in American culture for the past century and a half, his writings also make "claims upon us to which we have not yet sufficiently responded."[12] Much the same could be said of Thoreau, although in his case I would add that we do not as yet have an adequate account of how his writings were initially received within American culture. In this regard, it is striking that modern critics and biographers have not thought to explore the significance of the fact that *Walden* was published by Ticknor and Fields, now remembered as the Boston publishing house that during the 1850s assembled the canon of American literature that reigned until the 1920s. It is surprising, too, that scholars have not yet pursued an observation Frank Luther Mott made some forty years ago—namely, that *Walden's* status as a popular American classic was originally the result of cheap book-publishing programs that made it easily available to middle-class homes during the first decade of the twentieth century. The received account, in fact, continues to be that *Walden* achieved canonical status only within the past fifty years.[13] Clearly, my book will not fulfill all these needs; nor does it systematically address the general question of the place of Emerson and Thoreau in the history of American literary culture.[14] But it does address several neglected problems

---

12. Michael Lopez, "De-Transcendentalizing Emerson," *Emerson Society Quarterly* 34 (1988): 97; Poirier, *Renewal of Literature*, 78.

13. Frank Luther Mott, *Golden Multitudes: The Story of Best Sellers in the United States* (New York, 1947), 154–55; Robert Sattelmeyer, "The Remaking of *Walden*," in *Writing the American Classics*, ed. James Barbour and Tom Quirk (Chapel Hill, 1990), 75.

14. There is a large recent literature on this subject; see the references cited in Frederick Crews, "Whose American Renaissance?" *New York Review of Books*, October 27, 1988, 68–81 (rpt. as ch. 2 in Frederick Crews, *The Critics Bear It Away: American Fiction and the Academy* [New York, 1992]).

involved in pursuing the latter issue by taking some novel approaches to the question of how Emerson and Thoreau understood and experienced the emergence of America's market economy.

This book was written both to persuade other scholars in my field and to appeal to non-specialist readers. Parts 1 and 2 offer what I take to be a new interpretive account of Emerson's and Thoreau's stance as figures who were both inside and outside their culture. Part 3 draws on extensive primary research in antebellum magazines and newspapers to present what I believe are the first extended interpretive accounts of what their contemporaries had to say about their now "classic" writings. At the same time, this book will introduce nonspecialist readers to important recent work on Emerson, Thoreau, and antebellum culture. In this respect, my study can also be approached as an example of "integrative" scholarship that makes connections across disciplines, places more specialized research in a larger context, and then tries to interpret, draw together, and bring new insight to bear on the research of others. It is of course for my readers to decide if I have succeeded with this project.

Parts of this book made earlier and differently shaped appearances in *The Culture of the Market: Historical Essays* (Cambridge, 1993), which I introduced and co-edited with Thomas L. Haskell. I have drawn from this volume principally in this preface and in chapter 2—"'A Yankee Diogenes': Thoreau on the Market"—which revises and extends a paper I contributed to that collection of essays. I am grateful to the publisher for permission to reprint. I am also indebted to listeners at Rutgers, Vanderbilt, Rice, Texas, Harvard, and Tulane, where early drafts of some of these chapters were originally presented. Fellowship support at various early stages of research and writing was provided by the American Council of Learned Societies and the National Endowment for the Humanities. Summer grants from Tulane's Murphy Institute of Political Economy supported the final stages of my work.

Finally, I must thank by name several friends and scholars who read all or part of this book and offered valuable suggestions. Andrew Achenbaum, Thomas Bender, Thomas Haskell, James Hoopes, Robert Gross, Rebecca Carr Hawkins, George Kateb, Leo Marx, Wilfred McClay, and Teresa Toulouse offered helpful criticism of early drafts of the entire manuscript, as well as good advice on clarifying the main threads of my discussion. Others who read portions of the book in its preliminary stages include John Ferejohn, Matt Mancini, Sidney Maskit, Samuel Ramer, Jonathan Riley, Judith Schafer, Peter Schwartz, and David Steiner. Bonnie Honig and Thomas Haskell provided invaluable detailed comments on early drafts of chapters 1 and 2 and greatly helped refine their arguments and organization. My research assistants during the summers of 1990 and 1991—Phil MacLeod and Ben Maygarden—made it possible for me to begin to understand how Emerson and Thoreau initially became visible and gained authority in American culture. Finally, I am also deeply and happily indebted to Ruth Carter, who directly assisted in the production of this book from start to finish.

I

Connected Critics:
Emerson and Thoreau
on the Market

This time, like all times, is a very good one, if we but
know what to do with it.

—Emerson, "The American Scholar"

I do not propose to write an ode to dejection, but to brag
as lustily as Chanticleer in the morning, standing on his
roost, if only to wake my neighbors up.

—Thoreau, *Walden*

I

"Sublime Thoughts" and "Penny Wisdom": Emerson on the Market

FOR REASONS I have discussed in the preface, I consider recent new histor-icist readings of Emerson and Thoreau to be both foil and inspiration for part of this book, and there are several passages in parts 1 and 3 where I will address a few of these readings more directly. Yet my discussion begins by moving in other related directions, since I also aim to consider more long-standing accounts of how Emerson and Thoreau understood the market in light of what I believe to have been the intellectual coherence of their views.

If one takes the history of Emerson scholarship seriously, the project of interpreting Emerson as I do is made more interesting and more challeng-ing by the fact that his views of the market have regularly been repre-sented in two apparently different ways. On the one hand, cultural his-torians tell us that Emerson first became a household word during the late 1840s and 1850s, because the many audiences he addressed in lyceums, Mechanics' Associations, Literary Societies, Young Men's Societies, and Young Men's Mercantile Libraries across the country heard him as voic-ing support for values prized in America's new economic order.[1] On the

---

1. For three recent accounts, see John P. Diggins, *The Lost Soul of American Politics: Vir-tue, Self-Interest and the Foundations of Liberalism* (New York, 1984), 197–205; Mary Kupiec

other hand, most modern literary historians and social theorists have seen the books for which his contemporaries prized him—*Representative Men* (1850), *English Traits* (1856), and *Conduct of Life* (1860)—as intellectually slack and therefore inessential. Many have also dismissed them as superficially conservative in their attitudes toward American society, arguing that Emerson's best thinking occurred in *Nature* (1836) and his first collection of *Essays* (1841), where we also find him despising and lamenting the life of economic pursuits. Despite what new historicists consider substantial evidence to the contrary, influential recent studies continue to insist that the ideals Emerson championed in his early writings—self-reliance, imagination, intuition, nonconformity, the quest for a life close to nature—were presented both in censure of, and as alternatives to, market practices and values.[2]

It was of course Emerson himself who said that "a foolish consistency is the hobgoblin of little minds."[3] Yet the fact that his views of the market have managed to invite such different accounts does not mean that we should see them as foolishly inconsistent. This chapter insists that an accurate reading of Emerson begins with the recognition that there never was an "early" antimarket Emerson as against some "late" promarket apologist who banked critical fires that had burned in *Nature* and the first *Essays*. In recognizing that Emerson's views were always of a piece, we can see why contemporaries who heard him lecture and bought his books were not entirely deluded about his endorsement of their economic pursuits. From the outset of his career, I argue here, Emerson cast himself as an idealist who sought to define the terms of an accommodation between his own values and the different principles he knew governed daily life in the

Cayton, "The Making of an American Prophet: Emerson, His Audiences, and the Rise of the Culture Industry in Nineteenth-Century America," *American Historical Review* 92 (June 1987): 597–620; and Charles Sellers, *The Market Revolution: Jacksonian America, 1815–46* (New York, 1991), 375–80.

2. The view that there was an early "ascetic" Emerson who rejected the practices and institutions of the market has its origins chiefly in V. L. Parrington's *Main Currents of American Thought*, vol. 2 (New York, 1927), 386–99; also see *The American Transcendentalists: Their Prose and Poetry*, ed. Perry Miller (Garden City, N.Y., 1957), ix. Among recent reformulations of this view, see Quentin Anderson, *Making Americans: An Essay on Individualism and Money* (New York, 1992), chs. 1 and 2; and George Kateb, *The Inner Ocean: Individualism and Democratic Culture* (Ithaca, 1992), 96–97.

3. Ralph Waldo Emerson, "Self-Reliance," in *Essays: First Series*, vol. 2, *The Collected Works of Ralph Waldo Emerson*, ed. Joseph Slater, Alfred R. Ferguson, and Jean Ferguson Carr (Cambridge, Mass., 1979), 33.

marketplace. The mistake Emerson's contemporaries made, however, was one that the new historicists (with different motives) repeat today: not making adequate effort to understand the remarkable complexity of the accommodation Emerson tried to fashion and concluding that his views somehow represent a roundabout celebration of the market.[4] There is no reason to doubt the depth or seriousness of Emerson's dissatisfactions with the market, or to screen out evidence in his later writings showing that he never abandoned his critical stance. Yet in trying to render the complexity of his views plausible, we can also go on to discern in Emerson's texts what I argue in this chapter was his center of gravity as a "connected" social critic: a conscious determination to locate his ideals within social practices and institutions he criticized and then to persuade his contemporaries to recognize those same ideals as their own. Emerson was often severe in his criticism of the moral and cultural failings of the market. Yet he also wished to show that such failings did not preclude the possibility that the market could play an important role in realizing America's promise as a new and democratic nation, if only enough people would see it as a means to that higher end.

I

We should start where Emerson himself started: not with specific reflections on economic activity in his day, even though they figured significantly in his early self-education, but with his larger conception of America's promise. Emerson initially cast his lot with a select group of contemporary European poets and writers—particularly Goethe, Coleridge,

---

4. Here my general approach to Emerson and Thoreau resembles, in one respect, that of Sacvan Bercovitch. He, too, has warned against interpretations of Emerson and Thoreau that present them as "middle-class apologists" or reduce their writings "in any sense to ideology." But the warning is not one that Bercovitch has consistently managed to heed, since he also wants to argue that, for all our classic writers, "the sacral meaning of America functioned as an ancestral taboo, barring them from paths that led beyond the limits of middle-class culture" ("How the Puritans Won the American Revolution," *Massachusetts Review* 17 [1976]: 625–26). The problem with Bercovitch's approach, which identifies as culturally hegemonic any criticism that falls short of posing fundamental alternatives to market capitalism and middle-class culture, is that it inevitably *does* serve to reduce their writings to ideology. For on his account, any expression of dissent that falls short of leading us "beyond the limits of middle-class culture" can—by virtue of the radical social change it forestalls—be said to stabilize and reinforce the status quo. (See *The American Jeremiad* [Madison, 1978],

Wordsworth, and Carlyle—whose shared idealistic modes of thinking insisted on "the power of Thought and of Will, on inspiration, on miracle, on individual culture." Yet he also sought to distance himself from what he saw as a historically obsolete elitism that flawed their otherwise compelling cultural visions. In nineteenth-century America, Emerson insisted, something fundamentally new was beginning. "What is good that is said or written now lies nearer to men's business & bosoms than of old," he wrote in his journal during the same month that *Nature* was published. "What is good goes now to all. What was good a century ago is written under the manifest belief it was as safe from the eye of the common people as from the Tartars." Emerson was wedded to the idea that in America the currents of creativity, independence, and nobility flowed through every individual. Near the end of his life, he remarked that the idealistic New England writers of his generation had fashioned the uniquely American belief that all of the nation's cultural, economic, and political institutions "existed for the individual, for the guardianship and education of every man." This idea, Emerson insisted, was "a sword such as was never drawn before," and he could have added that, more than any other nineteenth-century American thinker, he had provided compelling reasons for drawing that sword.[5]

There can be no question that Emerson was aware of the forces that stood in the way of achieving his vision: within individuals, the ready ten-

---

preface and ch. 6.) For all its brilliance in drawing our attention to the complexity of Emerson's and Thoreau's views of the antebellum market, Bercovitch's work illustrates the inevitable tendency of an interpretation in the hegemonic mode to slip back into the reductionist ways of relating consciousness to social structure that it purportedly seeks to avoid. The approach developed in this study aims to provide some clarification for those still seeking a nonreductionist way of understanding Emerson and Thoreau as social critics.

5. "The Transcendentalist," in *The Collected Works of Ralph Waldo Emerson*, vol. 1, *Nature, Addresses, and Lectures*, ed. Robert E. Spiller and Alfred R. Ferguson (Cambridge, Mass., 1971), 201. *The Journals and Miscellaneous Notebooks of Ralph Waldo Emerson*, ed. William H. Filman et al., 16 vols. (Cambridge, Mass., 1960–82), 5:202–3; Emerson, "Historic Notes of Life and Letters in New England," in *American Transcendentalists*, 5. Amy S. Lang, *Prophetic Woman: Anne Hutchinson and the Problem of Dissent in the Literature of New England* (Berkeley, 1987), 142, reminds us that in speaking of "every individual" Emerson never managed fully to include women as equal participants in his vision of America's promise. In his lecture on "Woman" before the Woman's Rights Convention in Boston on September 20, 1855, for example, he declared his commitment to equal rights for women, but only after denying the possibility of their pursuing lives independent of men. That Emerson's individualism of necessity dictates such a view of women, however, remains very much open to question.

dency to succumb to doubt, fear, habit, conformity, and tradition; within society at large, the moral and material corruption that seemed an inevitable outcome of modern commerce and politics. He was troubled, too, by the professional timidity of his generation of American thinkers and writers, by "a destitution of faith" that he feared would lead them either to opt for success on the market's terms, or to withdraw from society to cultivate their private utopias. Emerson himself, however, remained confident that he at least could begin the work he most wanted to do: the breaking down of existing conventions of thought and feeling about public and private life he regarded as stultifying and unnatural. "Not he is great who can alter matter, but he who can alter my state of mind," he wrote in "The American Scholar." "They are the kings of the world who give the color of their present thought to all nature and all art, and persuade men by the cheerful serenity of their carrying the matter, that this thing which they do, is the apple which the ages have desired to pluck, now at last ripe, and inviting nations to the harvest."[6]

We can begin to see in this last passage why F. O. Matthiessen once observed that Emerson saw no cause to divorce his idealism from "the material facts" of his day. Emerson certainly knew of (and shared) the view that art and poetry provided access to crucial dimensions of human experience. Yet, unlike contemporary English Romantic poets and German Idealist philosophers, he refused to see art and literature as uniquely significant manifestations of, or exclusive routes to, higher truths. "The invariable mark of wisdom," he wrote in *Nature*, "is to see the miraculous in the common."[7] Emerson's egalitarianism led him to celebrate "that divine idea which each of us represents," and to insist that there was in fact a wider and disparate variety of human activity of potentially equal benefit to individuals.[8] He was determined to uncover and celebrate moments of vision

---

6. "The American Scholar," in *Nature, Addresses, and Lectures*, 64.

7. F. O. Matthiessen, *American Renaissance: Art and Expression in the Age of Emerson and Whitman* (New York, 1941), 11. *Nature*, in *Nature, Addresses, and Lectures*, 44.

8. "Self-Reliance," 28. Richard Poirier, *The Renewal of Literature: Emersonian Reflections* (New York, 1987), develops this side of Emerson's thinking in much greater detail. Poirier begins by asking why we have come to suppose that "literature" provides a means of cultural unity or salvation, particularly when so many of our major American literary figures—beginning with Emerson—have veered away from that position. (The most forceful brief statement of the egalitarian assumptions that informed Emerson's individualism remains the opening paragraph of "Self-Reliance.")

in the apparently mundane activities of ordinary individuals, in "this thing which they do" now. Even in the economic marketplace, as we shall see, he believed in and attributed positive significance to the apparently simple recognition that in their thoughts individuals were often elsewhere as they went about their tasks—seeing this not so much as a sign of alienation from work at hand, as of their latent powers of imagination and intuition. He was also keenly aware of a tendency toward obscurantism for which he and other idealist writers have often been faulted: to remedy it he recognized that his guiding democratic commitment to alter the "state of mind" of ordinary men required that his appeals at times be made in ordinary language. Emerson's confident vision of America's promise, in short, was based not on a rejection of its existing values and institutions, but rather on the belief that he could find ways to show that in America the spiritual side of individuals was already progressively fashioning their experience of the world.

Emerson first revealed this side of himself in *Nature*, and there also previewed how his larger sense of cultural purpose would affect his subsequent efforts to come to terms with the economic values and institutions of his day. Complex and difficult as it is, *Nature* taken in its entirety remains an exuberantly confident statement of Emerson's belief in the capacity of ordinary individuals "to look at the world with new eyes," and it displays an egalitarian ethos that he never afterward surpassed. In its final paragraph, he went so far as to say: "All that Adam had, all that Caesar could, you have and can do. Adam called his house, heaven and earth; Caesar called his house, Rome; you perhaps call yours, a cobbler's trade; a hundred acres of ploughed land; or a scholar's garret. Yet line for line and point for point, your dominion is as great as theirs, though without fine names. Build, therefore, your own world." In reading these lines we become acquainted with a thinker who, in urging his new faith in ordinary individuals, frequently chose to couch his hopeful account of their capacities in terms of their everyday economic pursuits. In fact, in chapter 2 of *Nature*, he had already acknowledged that the only one of a potential multitude of uses of the natural world that all individuals as yet apprehended—namely, that nature can be mastered so that it ministers to our needs for food, shelter, and material comforts—came under the general name of "commodity." Later he would also concede that at present his new Adam and new Caesar remained content to work "on the world with his understanding alone. He lives in it, and masters it by a penny wisdom; and he that works in it, is but half-man, and whilst his arms are strong and his digestion good, his mind is imbruted and he is a selfish savage."[9]

The difficulties such recognitions raise for Emerson were real enough. But how much weight should we assign them? Some commentators have concluded that the pervasive "penny wisdom" of antebellum culture amounted to a mercenary view of the natural and the human worlds that Emerson found altogether unacceptable and was, in *Nature* at least, determined to move beyond. Others have also suggested that his worries in this regard grew so emphatic they culminated in a devaluation of the external world as alien and debased precisely because the market had transformed it into an object of exchange. Yet the main problem in arriving at a satisfactory account of Emerson's economic views in *Nature*, in the end, lies not so much in registering the depth of his protest against the reigning ethos of penny wisdom, as in reconciling that protest with his overriding message of hope for much better things to come. The sense of exhilaration that permeates *Nature*, after all, was only attenuated, not undermined, by Emerson's occasional brooding over what we would call the materialism of American life, and its forceful resurfacing in the book's concluding paragraph invites us to explain why his strategy for overcoming the faulty perspectives bred in the market never seriously entertained the possibility of simply renouncing them.

Nature does not offer a systematic response to this question. Yet there are at least three general areas in which the book can be said to have sounded condensed versions of three themes that would receive more sustained exposition in subsequent writings. The first—a preliminary set of suggestions regarding the proper way in which an idealistic poet-philosopher ought to reflect on the market—stemmed, in part, from Emerson's view that criticism of the materialism of American life would never be enough. "All things with which we deal," Emerson insisted, "preach to us," and it is clear that the market was among those things "preaching" to him when he composed *Nature*. His final comments on the market, for example, faulted it as a realm in which individuals remain comfortable with only a partial mastery of nature. The chief shortcoming of the practitioners of penny wisdom turns out to be neither greed nor selfishness, but timidity—reluctance to take action upon nature with all the faculties they possess. In speaking of and to each individual's higher faculties, however,

---

9. *Nature*, 45, 11, 43.

it is arguable that Emerson thereby also cast himself—and, by implication, other like-minded idealistic intellectuals—as potential allies of individuals whose lives were governed by the workings of the market. The logic of his position here, in part, may have been this: if, as Emerson acknowledged at the outset of *Nature*, his contemporaries understood the external world only as commodity, then a blanket condemnation of self-interestedness would fall mostly on deaf ears. Moreover, even if the dismay with which idealistic poet-philosophers typically viewed the development of a market society was justified, it had to be linked to a larger conception of possibilities for improving that society. Emerson took seriously the notion that everything in the external world must have a moral and spiritual side; hence his considerable misgivings about the market plainly did not mandate the possibility of taking revolutionary steps against it. Instead, he was prompted by that belief to define and propagate new cultural ideals, independent of the market, yet somehow also concealed within it and thus somehow capable of giving its inhabitants instruction in the higher purposes of human life. Another way to put this is to say that Emerson rejected essentialist interpretations of the market, stressing that there was no single framework within which its new institutions and practices could be understood. What he offered instead, beginning with *Nature*, was a variety of overlapping appraisals that mixed criticism with hope.

The second theme in Emerson's effort to show individuals how they might rule, rather than be ruled by, the new wealth brought by the spread of market relations remains one of the most frequently misunderstood gambles in his thinking: his use of the language of the economic marketplace itself—particularly concepts such as commodity, property, profit, wealth, and price—to show how steps might be taken beyond the mere creation of wealth to what he would later call its "wise use." In *Nature*, this effort initially took shape in comparatively brief subversions of certain key categories of economic discourse—in Emerson's own words, the point was to "unfix" and "transfigure" them—in order that they might be employed to express purposes higher than mere production and exchange. We can see one example of this procedure at work in the chapter on beauty, where in the process of illustrating the ways in which nature can satisfy each individual's hunger for beauty, Emerson observed that "the universe is the property of every individual in it. Every rational creature has all nature for his dowry and estate." The strategy also recurs in his call for a "revolution in our notions of property" at the outset of *Nature*. Emerson certainly recognized that the market had created a world in which property was understood primarily as the right of individuals to the exclusive enjoyment of their land and goods. "The charming landscape which I saw this morning," he observed, "is indubitably made up of some twenty or thirty farms," each owned by separate people. But he immediately went on to insist that this by no means must exhaust our understanding of property.[10] For there was also "a property in the horizon which no man has but he whose eye can integrate all the parts, this is, the poet. This is the best part of these men's farms, yet to this their warranty-deeds give no title." Richard Poirier has recently cited this last passage as evidence of Emerson's belief that the human power to make imaginative use of language in voicing moral and spiritual concerns was greater than any economic power. It may be somewhat more accurate to say that what Emerson envisioned here was something more in the way of a fair fight between those two powers.[11]

Finally, in *Nature* Emerson at times also suggested how his idealistic aspirations were supported by, and in certain respects also prefigured in, the new technology of his time. Emerson embraced technology, in part, because he saw it as a powerful support for democracy. One of its greatest beneficiaries was "the private poor man," who now "hath cities, ships, canals, bridges, built for him," and as a result was freer than ever before to learn and to travel, and hence to make a life of his own choosing. Emerson also celebrated technological innovations as powerful new evidence of the individual's imaginative freedom. "To diminish friction, he paves the road with iron bars," Emerson wrote, and with "merchandise behind him, he darts through the country, from town to town, like an eagle or a swallow through the air."[12]

Yet it was not just the new technology of the antebellum period to which Emerson assigned higher meaning. A year before the publication of *Nature*, he had also found cause to commend the new personal wealth that technology had brought to some individuals: "There are two reasons why Wealth inspires respect in virtuous men; first, because wealth forms a strong will, which is always respectable. Second; because the rich man's

---

10. Ibid., 11, 26.

11. Ibid., 9; Poirier, *Renewal of Literature*, 33–35, 147–48.

12. *Nature*, 12. For Emerson's views of technology, see Leo Marx's classic *The Machine in the Garden: Technology and the Pastoral Ideal in America* (New York, 1964); and John F. Kasson, *Civilizing the Machine: Technology and Republican Values in America, 1776–1900* (New York, 1976).

state is a mockery of the true state of man. 'He speaks & it is done; he commands & it stands fast.'" Similar passages are scattered throughout his journals, and taken together they suggest that Emerson at times believed that, not unlike the new machinery that facilitated their pursuit and accumulation of personal fortunes, rich individuals themselves could be taken as symbols of an admirable human capacity for extraordinary action and effort. To be sure, what he actually said or suggested about the new wealth of antebellum America in *Nature* expressed far more in the way of misgiving than of praise. Yet even while criticizing the dominant ethos of penny wisdom in his day, Emerson never suggested that some irreparable loss of values and imagination had occurred. Nor did he locate the main cause of America's conformity and spiritual emptiness in the production and exchange of commodities and the pursuit of wealth. Emerson's quarrel was not with commerce or money-making per se, but with their tendency to become disproportionately preoccupying, so as to blind individuals to other avenues of self-expression and thus deprive them of their use of other higher faculties. Yet Emerson at the same time rejected any perspective that precluded the possibility that the actual workings of such faculties could be detected in the ordinary language and practices of the market itself. His purpose, in other words, was not simply to open other (nonmarket) avenues of self-expression, but to find a way of seeing daily market pursuits themselves as sites of individual self-expression.[13]

2

For the remainder of his life, these were the themes Emerson worked to clarify whenever he turned his attention to economic questions. Beginning as early as "The American Scholar" (1837), we can see that he was deeply concerned about what he called "the discontent of the literary class," and more specifically about the extent to which the idealism of his generation of American intellectuals seemed to be driven by little else

---

13. *Journals*, 5:46; for other early reflections on wealth, see 7:135–7, 329, 331, 519; 8:89, 255, 280. Also see Howard Horwitz, *By the Law of Nature: Form and Value in Nineteenth Century America* (Oxford, 1991), 62–83. Horwitz, too, shows that Emerson believed he could affect change and reform in a market culture only by means of his "inflection" upon already existing forms of language and practice available to his contemporary audiences. Horwitz builds on a point made earlier by Poirier, *Renewal of Literature*, 167.

than discontent with established social and economic institutions. While troubled by the "tyranny of trade," Emerson was arguably just as troubled by the related question of how America could ever hope to realize its promise if its best minds were skeptics and naysayers. As he put it in "Man the Reformer": "Americans have many virtues, but they have not Faith and Hope . . . and no class [is] more faithless than the scholars or intellectual men."[14]

Yet exactly how did Emerson attempt to restore "Faith and Hope" to the perspectives of American intellectuals fated to live in an increasingly commercial society? *Nature* provided a theoretical framework for responding to this question, but "The American Scholar" offered his first fully detailed answer. Emerson was hardly alone in drawing attention to the issue. The role of "scholars" in American society in fact had become the standard theme of Phi Beta Kappa Society addresses at Harvard at the time he was invited to speak in June 1837.[15] Events in the spring of that year, however, had given the question unprecedented urgency. Emerson's famous speech, delivered late in the summer, occurred only four months after the onset of a financial panic that ushered in the half-decade of America's first great economic depression, and there can be no question that he was deeply unsettled by the historical novelty of this development. It would be misleading, however, to so magnify the impact of the depression of 1837 as to suggest that "The American Scholar" be read as a complete rejection of America's emerging market order. If we compare his account of the political and social implications of the first great American depression with

---

14. Emerson, "American Scholar," 67; Emerson, "Man the Reformer," in *Nature, Addresses, and Lectures*, 156–57. There is now a large literature on the development and uses of the term "intellectual." See Peter Allen, "The Meaning of 'an Intellectual,' in Nineteenth- and Twentieth-Century Usage," *University of Toronto Quarterly* 55 (1986): 342–58. On the importance Emerson attached to his position in defining the proper role of "intellectual persons" in American culture, also see "The Fugitive Slave Law," in *The Selected Writings of Ralph Waldo Emerson*, ed. Brooks Atkinson (New York, 1940), 861: "My habitual view," he wrote there, "is to the well-being of students or scholars. And it is only when the public event affects them, that it very seriously touches me." I discuss this essay at greater length in ch. 4.

15. Oscar M. Voorhees, *The History of Phi Beta Kappa* (New York, 1945), 124–25, describes the subject of Emerson's 1837 address as one that had been a "conventional theme of Phi Beta Kappa orations ever since he was a boy." But we as yet have no careful account of the ways in which Emerson both drew upon and departed from those many earlier orations, some of which (like Emerson's) were immediately reprinted as pamphlets, others that remain in manuscript form in the Harvard University Archives.

those of other Transcendentalists (e.g., Orestes Brownson or Bronson Alcott), it is clear that Emerson never accepted their more radical view of the depression as the outcome of fundamental social conflicts inherent in the market.[16] Closer reading of the four early essays that addressed themselves most directly to cultural problems brought on by the depression— "The American Scholar," "Literary Ethics" (1838), "Man the Reformer" (1841), and "The Transcendentalist" (1841)—also shows that one of Emerson's chief goals was to help the "literary class" of his generation overcome despair and disillusionment by explaining how they might pursue their higher ambitions in the face of economic change and disorder.

This side of Emerson was evident at the very outset of "The American Scholar." Although now well-known, his lament about the human costs of specialization was relatively brief, and it is clear that the ever-increasing division of labor had at least one perhaps ironic benefit in his view: in a society based on a complete "distribution of functions," the scholar has little trouble in recognizing that he must play the part of "delegated intellect." His chief practical concern, in turn, must center on the question of how he will choose to play that role. Can he become distinctively original and autonomous, or will he succumb to the temptations of success in the market by becoming a mere propagandist, the parrot of other men's thinking and interests?[17]

Emerson's initial consideration of this question in "The American Scholar" gave rise to what remains his most exalted vision of intellectual life. In his account of the education and duties of "man thinking," the true intellectual is portrayed as a figure who will propound and embody the ideal "whole man" whose continued existence is threatened by the power of commerce. Yet that goal could be achieved, Emerson stressed, only if the intellectual combined the analytical and reflective sides of his nature with engaged action. This engagement is not political or social reform (as Emerson makes clear in his concluding plea for "patience"), but rather an all-encompassing curiosity about the world one lives in—"nature" in the broadest sense: "The world,—this shadow of the soul, or *other me*, lies wide around. Its attractions are the keys which unlock my thoughts and make

---

16. For a more detailed discussion of Emerson's efforts to find moral and social instruction in the panic, see Horwitz, *By the Law of Nature*, 79–82. On Brownson and Alcott, see Anne C. Rose, *Transcendentalism as a Social Movement, 1830–1850* (New Haven, 1981), 78–79, 90–92, 117–18.

17. "American Scholar," 53.

me acquainted with myself. I run eagerly to this resounding tumult. I grasp the hands of those next to me, and take my place in the ring to suffer and to work, taught by an instinct that so shall the dumb abyss be vocal with speech."[18]

Emerson justified the extraordinary demands he made on intellectuals partly in terms of the extraordinary rewards that he saw coming to anyone who took up an intellectual vocation as he defined it. In a society of experts and specialists, only the "man thinking" still had the opportunity to put forth "his total strength in fit actions." Yet Emerson also made it clear that a commitment to enter regularly into the world's "resounding tumult" remained essential if intellectuals hoped to have higher principles more powerfully influence the conduct of those who devoted their lives to more mundane concerns. He emphasized, for example, that while intellectuals may find in the ordinary world a language very different from their own, they must understand it and try to turn it to their own purposes: "If it were only for a vocabulary, the scholar would be covetous of action. Life is our dictionary. Years are well spent in country labors; in town—in the insight into trades and manufacturers . . . to the one end of mastering in all their facts a language, by which to illustrate and embody our perceptions."[19]

"The American Scholar" had no practical advice as to exactly how this mastering might be achieved. But the essay did go on to provide a broader definition of the social "duties" of intellectuals that explains why it was necessary in the first place, and thus why the "man thinking" must use the language of the market to bring life to his own aspirations. All the duties of an intellectual, Emerson argued, crystallized in the notion of "self-trust." The intellectual is above all a visionary, whose office is "to cheer, to raise, and to guide men by showing them facts amidst appearance." He must show ordinary individuals that, despite routines that appear to limit or to impoverish their lives, they are still composed of and experience what Emerson called high "spiritual causes":

I embrace the common, I explore and sit at the feet of the familiar, the low. Give me insight into to-day, and you may have the antique and future

---

18. Ibid., 59.

19. Ibid., 60–61. Also implicit in Emerson's message is the view that the interest of "true scholars" in the market goes beyond simply influencing others. Emerson urges intellectuals to run to the "resounding tumult" not simply to *preach* their privately revealed truths, but to uncover and appeal to internal principles already known to, and somehow remembered by, the people they hope to influence.

worlds. What would we really know the meaning of? The meal in the firkin; the milk in the pan; the ballad in the street; the news of the boat; the glance of the eye; the form and the gait of the body;—show me the ultimate reason of these matters;—show me the sublime presence of the highest spiritual cause lurking, as always it does lurk, in these suburbs and extremities of nature; let me see every trifle bristling with the polarity that ranges it instantly on an eternal law; and the shop, the plough, and the ledger referred to the like cause by which light undulates and poets sing.

He also insisted that a true intellectual must find ways of showing that an awareness of our spiritual nature not only should, but in fact does, progressively shape our activity in the world, even those pursuits that we take to be mercenary and self-interested: "Men, such as they are, very naturally seek money or power; and power because it is as good as money,—the 'spoils,' so called, 'of office.' And why not? for they aspire to the highest, and this, in their sleep-walking, they dream is highest. Wake them and they shall quit the false good and leap to the true." This paints the intellectual as a figure committed to awakening other men to their higher selves. But the more striking feature of the picture Emerson sketches is again the sense that the main project of "man thinking" was not so much to preserve his ideals against the forces of the market as to find ways of insinuating them into the market itself.[20]

Yet how would this more subtle project ever come to pass? How do intellectuals resist the powerful temptations of success on the market's terms, while still dwelling in and engaging the world of commerce and exchange? What assurance did Emerson have, for that matter, that principles "not marketable or perishable" remained important and intelligible in a society whose soul now seemed so entirely "subject to dollars"? These questions are raised but left unanswered by "The American Scholar." Emerson returns to give them further consideration, however, in "Literary Ethics," "Man the Reformer," and "The Transcendentalist."[21]

Emerson called "Literary Ethics" his account of "the daily life and code of conduct of the true American scholar," but that description fits the

---

20. Ibid., 62, 67–68, 65.

21. During Emerson's lifetime, these three essays were at least as well known as "The American Scholar." Initially presented as an address at Dartmouth College on July 24, 1838, "Literary Ethics" was first published as a pamphlet in Boston in September, and later included in *Nature, Addresses, and Lectures* (1849), as well as in several pirated British editions of Emerson's writings. "Man the Reformer" and "The Transcendentalist" first appeared

other two essays equally well. It also is true that all three essays initially appear to define the vocation of an intellectual in terms that dictate a complete rejection of the market for the sake of a rural life of almost ascetic self-sufficiency. "All vision, all genius," Emerson remarked, comes by "giving leave and amplest privilege to the spontaneous sentiment," and then maintained that such imaginative freedom could not be found in the market but required instead "silence, seclusion, and austerity." Furthermore, the true intellectual ought to "embrace solitude as a bride," and if "he pines in a lonely place, hankering for the crowd, for display, he is not in the lonely place; his heart is in the market; he does not see; he does not hear; he does not think." Emerson insisted that a "taste for luxury" was the deadly trap a market society sets for its intellectuals, precisely because conformity seems to be the inevitable outcome of a desire for success on the market's terms. Indeed, in both "Man the Reformer" and "The Transcendentalist," he explained that the idealism of his generation of New England intellectuals was based partly on the view that the market foreclosed all possibility of individual autonomy and excellence. For those with vision and high principles, there appeared to be no economic careers worth pursuing. The moral climate of commercial society celebrated selfishness and dissembling; it seemed little more than "a system of distrust, of concealment, of superior keenness, not of giving but of taking advantage."[22]

Yet any reading of these three essays that concludes Emerson himself intended to maintain that the proper relationship between intellectuals and the market should remain one of irresolvable antagonism would be very misleading. Emerson was a thinker who, as Richard Poirier has observed in another context, often interrogated views he seemed initially to endorse. Hence, while his criticism of the shortcomings of market society was in no sense superficial, it was not his last word on the subject. Other passages, toward the end of these essays, show that a complete estrangement of intellectuals from the market was hardly what he had in mind as a remedy. "Let our affection flow out to our fellows," he urged in "Man the Reformer." "It is better to work on institutions by the sun than by the wind." Similarly, in "The Transcendentalist," he cautioned "the good, the illumin-

---

in the *Dial*, and they too later reappeared in *Nature, Addresses, and Lectures* and in several pirated British editions. See ch. 8 for a more detailed history of the reception of Emerson's publications before 1850.

22. "Literary Ethics," in *Nature, Addresses, and Lectures*, 105, 109; "Man the Reformer," 148; also see "Transcendentalist," 210–12.

nated" not to "sit apart from the rest, censuring their dullness and vices, as if they thought that, by sitting very grand in their chairs, the very brokers, attorneys, and congressmen would see the error of their ways, and flock to them."

Such sentences suggest that Emerson was not simply more optimistic than the Transcendentalists. His aim was to challenge and modify their view of intellectual life as one of detachment, and it is precisely here that his own stance had much more in common with what Walzer has defined as that of a "connected" social critic. Emerson himself described it in "Man the Reformer" as that of "mediator between the spiritual and the actual world."[23] Exposing the false appearances of his society was one of the "mediating" intellectual's main tasks, but ultimately not the most important one. Emerson recognized that the intellectual's moral authority to criticize the status quo required withdrawal from "the common labors and competitions of the market and the caucus," yet he also warned against making complete detachment into a way of life. Both "Man the Reformer" and "The Transcendentalist" stressed detachment had its own considerable dangers, and that defiance alone was hardly a guarantee of insight. As defiantly marginal men in their societies, critical intellectuals themselves often were blind to their own "cant and pretensions," both forms of intellectual falseness that Emerson found as unacceptable as habit or conformity. Detached intellectuals wasted too much of their "strength and spirits" in mere "rejection." Their "solitary and factitious manners" also left them unable to pay decent respect to the concerns of their fellows: "See this wide society of laboring men and women. We allow ourselves to be served by them, we live apart from them, and meet them without a salute in the streets. We do not greet their talents, nor rejoice in their good fortune, nor foster their hopes. . . . Thus we enact the part of the selfish noble and king from the foundation of the world." Intellectuals must stand alone sometimes—perhaps most of the time—but not always, since in Emerson's view the "extravagant hope" that makes that characteristic stance possible in the end is not peculiarly their own. Pretending that they observe a separate code of values only serves to deprive intellectuals of popular support

23. Michael Walzer, *The Company of Critics: Social Criticism in the Twentieth Century* (New York, 1988), ch. 1, which I have borrowed from to characterize Emerson's stance; Emerson, "Man the Reformer," 159.

and understanding, leaving them open to well-founded "criticism and to lampoons, and as ridiculous stories will be to be told of them as of any."[24]

Two practical implications followed from Emerson's effort to distance himself from what he took to be the prevailing Transcendentalist view of idealistic intellectuals as America's odd-men-out. The first—apparent in the closing paragraphs of both "Literary Ethics" and "Man the Reformer"— was his call for alienated young intellectuals of his generation to broaden their conception of their role in society. Emerson saw no need for them to abandon the work of protest and criticism. Yet he also asked that they recognize that their authority as critics ultimately required something more than enmity or complete detachment. That surely is part of what Emerson meant in "Literary Ethics" when he urged "the good scholar" to have "a two-fold goodness," with Reason at one pole and Common Sense at the other. "If he be defective at either extreme of the scale," Emerson observed, "his philosophy will seem low and utilitarian; or it will appear too vague and indefinite for the uses of life." Similar sentiments appear in "Man the Reformer," where Emerson urged critical intellectuals to become "lovers" of their society, recognizing and accepting that "it is better to work on institutions by the sun than by the wind." There simply was no point to the enterprise of criticism unless it was informed by a sense of historical possibility. Whatever his "doubts and objections" in the present, the intellectual must believe in "a vast future," be "sure of more to come than is yet seen." Otherwise, why complain? He must recognize, too, that criticism works best when it harbors the hope that the conduct of ordinary men can conform more closely to ideal standards than it does now, and that in various settings all men therefore share in his "insatiable thirst for divine communications." In short, Emerson argued, the ultimate warrant for the intellectual's critical encounter with his society was an idealism latent in the ordinary activities of society itself, an idealism that in the end it must always be the chief purpose of the "mediator between the spiritual and the actual world" to invoke.[25]

Finally, Emerson concluded that if intellectuals would learn to stand closer to the social institutions they criticized, then society itself might come to show greater patience and tolerance for its "few persons of purer

---

24. "Man the Reformer," 158; "The Transcendentalist," 214–15.
25. "Literary Ethics," 113; "Man the Reformer," 158–60.

fire." This more sympathetic view of intellectuals would develop naturally out of the recognition that they were not so much enemies of the existing order as those "superior chronometers" by which ordinary men should verify their bearings. For all their naysaying, intellectuals must exist chiefly to hold open for others the possibility of reform and renewal. A "purer fire" may prompt their criticism of the existing order, but it is not a fire altogether different from that which burns in ordinary individuals.[26]

3

Emerson's instruction on the proper role of "scholars" and "intellectual persons" perhaps can be summarized simply as an attempt to balance his idealistic values with a realistic assessment of the historical possibilities for putting such values into practice. To read Emerson in this way is to stress his tendency in the early essays to give vent to his idealism, to criticize the market sharply, and then to move on to urge an alternative order of conduct that realizes values the market apparently seemed to inhibit or foreclose. A careful reading of these essays, however, points to a more nuanced alternative. Emerson's realism did regularly temper his discontent, yet it also revealed a concern for specifying the exact economic and political contexts within which he was attempting to establish his high principles. "I do not wish to be absurd and pedantic in reform," he remarked in "Man the Reformer." "I do not wish to push my criticism on the state of things around me to that extravagant mark, that shall compel me to suicide, or to an absolute isolation from the advantages of civil society."[27]

An appreciation of what Emerson himself called his practical idealism and his commitment to an engaged intellectual life also casts doubt on the familiar but misleading claim that an early, antimarket Emerson ultimately gave way to a later, supposed apologist for capitalism. (What we have seen in his early writings suggests that if we want to speak of "anti-" and "pro-" market sides of Emerson, we must consider them of a piece.) But Emerson's effort to reconcile his idealism with his realism is significant in a second respect. It also provides a neglected context in which

---

26. "Transcendentalist," 216.
27. "Man the Reformer," 155.

to explore more carefully an issue I have touched on briefly in examining *Nature*: his predilection for using economic language to express his "sublime thoughts." Now it may be that this side of his thinking poses no major problem for interpretation. Michael Gilmore, who has made much of Emerson's frequent resort to the language of the market, argues that it represents but another example of the pervasive commercialization of American life in the nineteenth century. Not unlike many of his nineteenth-century contemporaries, Gilmore asserts, Emerson was "unable to distinguish between natural law and the market regime."[28] This interpretation responds to an intriguing and until recently largely overlooked question about Emerson: Why would a supposed critic of the market so often use its language to voice his criticisms and his alternative ideals? But to argue, as Gilmore does, that Emerson made this choice unwittingly is to ignore a considerable body of evidence suggesting that Emerson's vocabulary was quite deliberately chosen. His predilection for economic categories grew naturally out of his continuing effort to find ways of insinuating his ideals into the market or of sometimes even finding them there. Or as Emerson himself proclaimed in "The American Scholar": "Life is our dictionary. Years are well spent in country labors; in town—in the insight into trades and manufactures; in frank intercourse with many men and women . . . to the one end of mastering in all their facts a language by which to illustrate and embody our perceptions."[29] If ordinary men and women need intellectuals to give voice to their latent idealism and creativity, intellectuals in turn need the language they routinely employ in "trade and commerce" to embody shared ideals.

Did Emerson ever think, however, that his effort to "illustrate and embody" his values in the language of "trade and manufactures" might be read simply as an idealistic legitimization of the market's values and practices? The question is important and complex. Let me begin by acknowledging that the tone of Emerson's venture in places is difficult to pin down, particularly in his multilayered references to property. Sometimes he appears remarkably unequivocal in his condemnation of the institution of private property, as in the famous lines from the "Ode Inscribed to W. H. Channing" (1846):

---

28. Michael T. Gilmore, *American Romanticism and the Marketplace* (Chicago, 1985), 30–31.
29. "American Scholar," 60–61.

Things are in the saddle
And ride mankind.

There are two laws discrete,
Not reconciled—
Law for man, and law for thing;
The last builds town and fleet,
But it runs wild,
And doth the man unking.

Here Emerson opposes economic activity and all that he values. Yet elsewhere in the poem and in the other essays, his criticism of property is considerably less hostile and more limited in its scope.[30] He distinguished between different forms of private property, often directing his criticism at inherited wealth, not private property tout court. In Emerson's view, property that did not represent a direct reward for individual efforts bred complacency and conformity.

While Emerson's sometimes hostile tone in discussing property has been treated as support for the view that at his best he was essentially a naysayer in his reflections on the market, he was never consistent in his hostility. Moreover, in various other ways Emerson used the market's language to illustrate and embody the values he cherished. He was never content to be a naysayer, and from the outset of his career was determined to establish a linguistic framework in which market activity potentially made some sort of idealistic sense. And it is precisely the results of Emerson's work here that must have accounted for the feeling among his contemporaries that the ideals he extolled were not extrinsic to their economic pursuits. While Emerson did complain that "the tradesman scarcely ever gives an ideal worth to his work," he also insisted that once the tradesmen had come to see an idealism latent in the very ways in which they talk about their preoccupations, they would act to remedy that problem.[31]

Emerson's habit of giving an idealistic twist to market language takes different forms. Sometimes his strategy is to try to restore or maintain a

---

30. "Ode Inscribed to W. H. Channing," in *Selected Writings*, 770. It is worth noting that the rest of "Ode" is entirely characteristic of Emerson in its mixture of criticism and hope. See David Bromwich's more extended discussion in "Emerson and the Ode to W. H. Channing," in *A Choice of Inheritance: Self and Community from Edmund Burke to Robert Frost* (Cambridge, 1989), 133–44.

31. "American Scholar," 53.

"premarket" understanding of certain words. Here he was concerned that his contemporaries not lose sight of the original significance of notions such as profit, economy, and labor. In *Nature*, for example, the observation that all parts of the external world "incessantly work into each other's hands for the profit of man" clearly had little to do with an excess of returns over expenditures in a financial transaction, but instead spoke of profit in the more long-standing sense of benefits that come with developing one's character. Similarly, in "Man the Reformer," when he urged his readers to "learn the meaning of economy," he asked—as Thoreau would in the opening chapter of *Walden*—that they remember what "economy" meant before the coming of the market: prudent management of a private household, the practice of a frugality that assured self-subsistence in basic needs. Essentially the same approach guided Emerson's early thinking about labor. He conceded that, in an economy based on an ever-increasing division of labor, mastering all the manual skills required to be self-subsistent is no longer possible or desirable for most individuals. But the same need not be true for what he portrayed as a traditional view of labor as activity primarily concerned with self-knowledge.[32]

Emerson's determination to use the language of the market for his own purposes also took the somewhat more complex form of resisting the market's restrictions on the meanings of its own key concepts. In places, that resistance assumed the shape of irony; as in his private description of his journal as a "savings bank"; or as in "The American Scholar," where he urges American intellectuals not to "trust the revenue of some single faculty" and to travel the globe when the time comes "to replenish their merchantable stock." Yet there are also instances of more open disputing. As we have already seen, in *Nature* Emerson deployed the term "property" in a way that resisted its signification merely as a right of exclusive possession. In "Self-Reliance" (1841), he goes on to speak of "living property"—as the wide range of experience, skill, and knowledge an individual must "acquire" if he hopes to determine his own fate. Similarly, in "The Transcendentalist," he remarked that in reflecting on the market an idealist ought "not respect labor, or the products of labor, namely property, otherwise than as a manifold symbol, illustrating with wonderful fidelity of details the laws of being."[33]

---

32. "Man the Reformer," 154.

33. "American Scholar," 60; "Self-Reliance," 50; "Transcendentalist," 203. An alternative reading might argue that Emerson used market language restoratively (or subversively)

The troping of market language so conspicuous in Emerson's early essays also figured prominently and abundantly in his later writings. In the chapter on "Wealth" in *English Traits*, for example, we are told that, while "the creation of wealth in England in the last ninety years is a main fact in modern history," England had yet to learn how to "rule her wealth" according to a higher standard Emerson spoke of as "the supreme wealth of nations." Furthermore, while he acclaimed the achievement of wealth in England as an example of human capacity and effort, he did not see this as grounds for unqualified homage. Emerson never celebrated Britain's accumulation of wealth as such, precisely because the "supreme wealth of nations" involved the noneconomic goals of culture, education, science, and charity—goals of which the British were in his view still only dimly aware.[34]

The later and more well-known essay on wealth in *Conduct of Life* repeats many of these points, but makes them even more forcefully. Again Emerson praises the accumulation of wealth in America as an example of successful human effort rather than as a valuable achievement in itself. And again he holds up an alternative measure of true wealth to judge America's current economic achievements: "Wealth requires, besides the crust of bread, and the roof—the freedom of the city, the freedom of the earth, travelling, machinery, the benefits of science, music and fine arts, the best culture and the best company. He is the rich man who can avail himself of all men's faculties." Emerson then makes it clear that, if one actually employs this standard to measure success in the market, money alone will never proclaim its possessor as a man of culture and character. For commerce is a game in which skill and chance play equal parts: "The art of getting rich [on the market's terms] consists not in industry, much less in saving, but in a better order, in timeliness, in being at the right spot. One man has stronger arms or longer legs; another sees by the course of streams and growth of markets where land will be wanted, makes a clearing to the river, goes to sleep and wakes up rich." Commerce does not directly reward the primary Emersonian virtues, like self-reliance, and that was its short-

---

in order to resist the market's appropriation of a rich language that preceded it and was more fecund than its current market incarnations would allow. But Emerson here at the same time may still be considered a "connected critic," since both his agendas would combine his overriding commitment to de-essentialize market institutions and language by keeping their histories alive and open to dispute.

34. Emerson, *English Traits* (1856), in *Selected Writings*, 609, 613.

coming. Morally, the best that can be said for success in money-making is that affluence relieves one of certain temptations, while "in failing circumstances no man can be relied on to keep his integrity." Men of means, in other words, have little excuse for not being self-reliant, for not availing themselves of all their faculties.[35]

Yet if Emerson linked self-reliance and economic success in this limited sense, he also insisted that he had "never seen a man as rich as all men ought to be." The drive for wealth Emerson commended in the *Conduct of Life*, as we shall see in more detail below, was rooted in an understanding of wealth and riches that consciously turned these words in directions that market societies had yet to encourage their inhabitants to go. And Emerson's message here clearly would repeat a theme initially sounded in "The American Scholar," where he first lamented that the "tradesman scarcely ever gives an ideal worth to his work."[36]

It would be misleading, however, to isolate these instances of Emerson quarreling with the language of the market as the only examples of his effort to turn that language to his own purposes. There are other passages that show he thought that market language might also be used to articulate his idealism much more directly, and at first glance, his goal appears to be the consummation of an unlikely marriage—in this case, infusing the market itself with a new kind of meaning (rather than simply disputing its narrowly defined self-conceptions) by bringing into alliance modes of perceiving the world that Emerson himself elsewhere seems to suggest are fundamentally different. At the end of "Man the Reformer," this is the final stroke in his portrait of the idealistic reformer:

> As the merchant gladly takes money from his income to add to his capital, so is the great man very willing to lose particular powers and talents, so that he gain in the elevation of his life. The opening of the spiritual senses disposes men ever to greater sacrifices, to leave their signal talents, their best means and skill of procuring a present success, their power and their fame,— to cast all things behind, in the insatiable thirst for divine communications. A purer fame, a greater power rewards the sacrifice.[37]

Lifted out of context, there appears to be nothing complicated about this analogy. The merchant and the idealist share a capacity to act prudently

---

35. Emerson, "Wealth," in *Conduct of Life* (1860), in *Selected Writings*, 696, 694.
36. Ibid., 699; "American Scholar," 53.
37. "Man the Reformer," 160.

for the sake of higher objectives. Both must defer gratification, unlike those *born* to wealth. Where the merchant exercises self-restraint in choosing to invest rather than consume his income, the idealist displays "a sublime prudence" in foregoing worldly success and pleasure for the sake of his cultural and spiritual values. In this fairly limited sense, then, it is fair to say that Emerson believed that the capitalist spirit mimicked a nobler "insatiable thirst for divine communications." Yet put back in its broader context this passage must also be seen as an instance of Emerson's commitment to show how his values might come to fit into market society, not merely stand out in criticism of it. It demonstrates, too, how market language might help articulate an otherwise ineffable ideal. It was, after all, simple enough to remind the inhabitants of such a society that they had forgotten or failed to recognize an idealism latent in the language they used to describe their values and activities. It was a different—and arguably more difficult—problem to show that they already knew how to put into practice those higher values and modes of consciousness that Emerson believed embodied a "supreme prudence."

"Compensation" (1841) provides what may be the most intriguing instance of this side of Emerson's thinking about the market. There he drew on a central maxim of the market—namely, "the doctrine that every thing has its price"—to illustrate his account of compensation as a philosophical dualism governing every aspect of nature and human life by way of a continual process of subversion and reconstruction, of opposition and renewal. Emerson's account initially takes shape as a sharp criticism of what he presents as the orthodox Christian view of the economic standard of success. He recounts the experience of having heard a minister preach on the doctrine of the Last Judgment in a sermon that portrayed this world as a place where only the wicked prosper materially, and yet also spoke of the world-to-come as a realm where "the good [who] are miserable in the present life" will receive just compensation for their sufferings by receiving, in Emerson's words, "the like gratifications another day,—bank-stock and doubloons, venison and champagne." At the outset, it is clear that Emerson wanted to ridicule the minister's account of compensation as an unconscious inverting of the economic standard of success. Yet his larger purpose in "Compensation" was to show that "men are better" than the minister's confused orthodox Christianity had allowed, and it was with that end in mind that he proceeded to single out the market as one of various "documents" that can show us "a ray of divinity" and "the present action of the soul" in the workings of the world.[38]

This specific linking of the market with the beneficial operation of a higher spiritual law has provoked a controversy in modern scholarly discussions of "Compensation." Perhaps the most familiar interpretation argues that the essay amounts to an unconscious parody of the accounting procedures of the marketplace, since Emerson "ultimately seems unable to distinguish between natural law and the market regime."[39] But there is a subtler way of describing his purposes. It is evident throughout the essay that Emerson wanted to avoid settling on any simple moral standpoint regarding success or failure in the market. So here, as elsewhere, money-making was seen as no better, but also no worse, than other forms of human activity. On this reading, Emerson faulted the preacher not so much to refine his moral estimate of money-making as to suggest that we have no reason to believe that the principles that inform the acquisitive logic of the market somehow preclude an understanding of the deeper workings of the human soul. The particular way in which the market allows for such understanding was shown most clearly roughly halfway through "Compensation" where, after exhorting his readers to see how fables illustrate the principle that "all things are double, one against another," Emerson went on to observe that proverbs "hourly preached in all markets and workshops" can be seen to underscore essentially the same philosophical point:

> The absolute balance of Give and Take, the doctrine that every thing has its price,—and if that price is not paid, not that thing but something else is obtained, and that it is impossible to get any thing without its price,—is not less sublime in the columns of a leger than in the budgets of states, in the laws of light and darkness, in all the action and reaction of nature. I cannot doubt that the high laws which each man sees implicated in those processes with which he is conversant, the stern ethics which sparkle on his

38. "Compensation," in *Nature, Addresses, and Lectures,* 67, 55–56.

39. See Gilmore, *American Romanticism and the Marketplace,* ch. 1, esp. 30–32. Gilmore's chapter has been reprinted in *Emerson: Prospect and Retrospect,* ed. Joel Porte (Cambridge, 1982), and *Modern Critical Interpretations: Ralph Waldo Emerson,* ed. Harold Bloom (New York, 1985). Also see Bercovitch, *American Jeremiad,* 184–85; and Richard Grusin, "'Put God in Your Debt': Emerson's Economy of Expenditure," *Proceedings of the Modern Language Association* 103 (January 1988): 35–44.

chisel-edge, which are measured out by his plumb and foot-rule, which stand as manifest in the footing of the shop-bill as in the history of a state,—do recommend to him his trade, and though seldom named, exalt his business to his imagination.

The last phrase in this passage echoes a theme sounded in "The Divinity School Address"—where Emerson first proclaimed the compatibility of "sublime thoughts" and "penny wisdom"—and it forms part of an argument designed to correct the preacher's facile Judgment Day sermon by observing that we can probe a familiar market proverb for support of our deeper intuitions about human life. In short, Emerson's criticism of the preacher was not merely that his vision of salvation had pandered to the "base estimates of the market of what constitutes manly success," but more important that he had ignored the fact that those who sought "success" in the market could and did look to maxims that guided their everyday experience in order to understand certain larger truths about the meaning of life in this world.[40]

Seen from this perspective, "Compensation" reveals no major new departure in Emerson's thinking. As with other essays we have examined above, it offers no apology for the market, at the same time as it rejects an essentialist view of its workings. "I do not wish more external goods," Emerson remarked near the end of "Compensation," "neither possessions, nor honors, nor powers, nor persons." Nowhere in the essay, however, did he simply denounce the market as a proper means of organizing economic experience, nor as a realm whose characteristic preoccupations and ways of talking resist transformation into metaphors for experience in general.[41] "Compensation" remains important, then, primarily as a sustained illustration of the frame of mind with which Emerson usually approached the market—a frame of mind whose guiding assumption can be said to lie in one of *Nature*'s proverbs: "All things with which we deal preach to us." That earlier claim reminds us that Emerson was a visionary first, a critic second, that he always sought to inspire more than alarm or unsettle. It reminds us, too, that from the start Emerson refused to believe that the differences between the spiritual values he championed and the commer-

---

40. "Compensation," 67.

41. Ibid., 71. Horwitz, *By the Law of Nature*, 68, also points out that such an attitude serves to define a fundamental difference between "idealistic" critics of the market such as Emerson and Thoreau and later "materialists" such as Marx and Lukacs.

cial values of the market were irresolvable, even while he remained keenly aware of those differences. His recurring effort to transform and elevate the language of the market—in "Compensation" as elsewhere—is best understood, then, as one of the characteristic devices he employed to realize one of his chief purposes as an intellectual: to carry his contemporaries beyond the values that market language embodied in its ordinary applications.

4

Emerson himself was the first to recognize that his thinking had something to do with the new economic activities and institutions of his day. He was also the first to insist that the relationship was anything but simple, and none of the themes we have explored thus far in this chapter suggests that it was. If Emerson was never wholly critical of the market, he was never blindly bound to it either. Thus, while it is important to understand why he urged intellectuals not to turn their backs to the market and how he used market language to articulate his idealism, this ought not blind us to the fact that he never gave up the effort to keep a critical distance from his "commercial times." Indeed, just two years before his death in 1882, he made one of his bluntest complaints: "The stockholder has stepped into the place of the warlike baron. The nobles shall not any longer, as feudal lords, have power of life and death over the churls, but now, in another shape, as capitalists, shall in all love and peace eat them up as before."[42]

Yet the fact remains that if Emerson's approach to the market represented a continuing internal argument, the criticism to be found in his later writings has hardly registered in modern scholarly appreciation of his thinking.[43] Especially when discussion turns to his essay on wealth in *Con-*

---

42. "Historic Notes of Life and Letters in New England," in *American Transcendentalists*, 6. It is worth adding here that while Emerson defined his primary cultural mission as the maintenance of faith and hope, he clearly also feared being dogmatic in his views, and that fear forced him (as his journals make clear) to change his mind—many times.

43. See Matthiessen, *American Renaissance*, 4; and more recently, Sacvan Bercovitch, "Emerson, Individualism, and the Ambiguities of Dissent," *South Atlantic Quarterly* 89 (Summer 1990): 645–55. This book was in production when David M. Robinson's *Emerson and the Conduct of Life: Pragmatism and Ethical Purpose in the Later Work* (Cambridge, 1993) appeared. The earlier appearance of this volume might have encouraged a sharper crystallization of certain points—especially with respect to the practical idealism and the commitment to an engaged intellectual life evident in Emerson's early essays. Robinson admirably

duct of Life, scholars tend to portray Emerson as a thinker overtaken by market forces and unable to sustain even a moderately critical stance. Suppressing his earlier instinctive distaste for the activities of America's new business classes, so Daniel Aaron has argued in what remains the most forceful version of this familiar interpretation, Emerson comes to see these same activities as "exemplifying divine principles." A thinker who had once led the way for others in setting himself against acquisitiveness and materialism now, without acknowledging what has happened, outlines "a rationale for the entrepreneurs of an industrial age." The practical upshot of this change, Jesse Bier has also argued along this line, is that Emerson himself thereby "unwittingly contributed to the debauchment of his thinking," as late nineteenth-century capitalists eagerly appropriated his thinking, often in the form of aphorisms from his work that were framed and hung up over their desks.[44]

It comes as no surprise that "Wealth" has been read in this way. There are sentences in which Emerson does come across as a blind champion of laissez-faire capitalism, speaking of America's new entrepreneurial class as "idealists" whose "speculative genius" had resulted in "the gain of the world." But a full understanding of Emerson's own intentions in writing "Wealth" requires something more than isolated quotations picked selectively from a long essay that also included praise for socialists, who have "done good service in setting men on thinking how certain civilizing benefits, now only enjoyed by the opulent, can be enjoyed by all."[45] Furthermore, if a celebration of entrepreneurial capitalism had now come to be Emerson's chief purpose, then his "early" thinking about the market certainly would stand as the embodiment of a view he abandoned in "Wealth." It should be clear by now, however, that what would have dropped from sight was not an "early" total hostility to commerce, but rather an attitude in which criticism and admiration of America's eco-

---

delineates what he calls the "pragmatic orientation" of Emerson's major later works, yet overlooks its presence in his earlier work. As I've tried to show in this chapter, Robinson is also mistaken in believing that it was only in his later works that "Emerson became a social critic" (6).

44. Daniel Aaron, "Emerson and the Progressive Tradition," in *Men of Good Hope: A Story of American Progressives* (New York, 1951), 3–40; Jesse Bier, "Weberism, Franklin, and the Transcendental Style," *New England Quarterly* 43 (June 1970): 179–92. The "debauchery" Bier speaks of surely took place, but it arguably is not one for which Emerson is responsible—nor one he courted.

45. "Wealth," 700.

nomic practices and institutions were closely interconnected. Everything more I shall have to say about "Wealth" in the extended analysis that follows is meant to show that this earlier and more complex attitude survived; indeed, it is plausible to read this "late" essay as a recapitulation of all the key Emersonian themes explored so far in this chapter, the very themes that he set out to clarify when he first turned his attention to the marketplace.

Emerson's essay on "Wealth" should be approached as he conceived it: as a statement that pursued two lines of inquiry, each with distinctive concerns. The first was wealth in the strictly economic sense, in the discussion of which Emerson offered his explanation of the human needs and wants that give rise to a realm of production and exchange. The other focused on wealth of a higher order, and here he held up his cultural ideal of America as a society in which all individuals might come to make full use of their creative faculties. Some of the confusion about this essay may lie in the fact that Emerson himself at times ran his two lines of inquiry so closely parallel, especially in the opening pages, that they seem indistinguishable. But keeping them distinct is critical to understanding this essay's overall purpose. In fact, once we move past the opening pages—something most modern commentators seem uninterested in doing—all the evidence suggests that wealth in its broader meaning dominates most of Emerson's attention and serves as the standard by which he passed a still largely critical judgment on America's economic prosperity.

It is also important to appreciate the way in which Emerson arrives at this judgment. We have seen already that one of his most persistent early traits was a determination not to set his social criticism in stark opposition to the dominant values of his age. Once again in "Wealth," it is precisely the stance of the connected critic that he adopts. He begins with characteristically Emersonian questions: How should a "whole man" make his living in a market society? Can he do so honestly? Yet in the second paragraph he makes it clear that he wants to establish his authority to ask such questions by addressing his audience with one of their characteristic ways of viewing the world: "Every man is a consumer, and ought to be producer. He fails to make his place good in the world unless he not only pays his debt but also adds something to the common wealth. Nor can he do justice to his genius without making some larger demand on the world than bare subsistence. He is by constitution expensive, and needs to be rich." However one chooses to interpret the particular claims of this passage, there can be little question it shows that Emerson saw no need to employ a specialized language of his own to make his message heard. His playing with words, for example, suggests that he meant to reassure his audience that, while he sought to be their critical conscience, he was also one of them. Indeed, it was precisely with a determination to stand close to his audience that he then set out to tell them about the double meaning of America's wealth. When confronted with the materialism of American society, Emerson insisted—in a thinly veiled reference to *Walden*—that Thoreau's way would not do: "It is of no use to argue the wants down: the philosophers have laid the greatness of man in making his wants few, but will a man content himself with a hut and a handful of dried pease? He is born to be rich." Both Emerson and Thoreau were critics of the materialism of their age. Yet where Thoreau judged from a distance, Emerson's critical style was to complain from within a world of things that he thought Thoreau mistakenly had tried to escape, because there clearly was no escape in Emerson's view.[46]

Yet what do we make of the observation that all men are "born to be rich"? Everything we know about Emerson's use of language tells us not to take it at face value. As "Wealth" unfolds, it becomes clear that this claim is hardly a simple endorsement of money-making or of a new entrepreneurial ethic. (In fact, as we shall see, in the essay's final paragraph Emerson comes to sound more like a follower of Thoreau than his critic.) Throughout "Wealth" what we encounter is a multilayered way of thinking about the market institutions and language that again can be traced back to his first writings. In *Nature* and "The American Scholar," we have seen already that Emerson's qualified admiration of America's economic prosperity was a by-product of his broader interest in elaborating and affirming what he took to be the new egalitarian ideals of American culture. There is no evidence to suggest that this project was abandoned in "Wealth." The overall design of the essay shows Emerson again driven to commend a desire to be rich in the narrow sense only because he felt he could demon-

---

46. Ibid., 694–95; on Emerson's sense of himself as a loyal critic of his society, also see "New England Reformers," in *Selected Writings*, 455: "It is handsomer to remain in the establishment better than the establishment, and conduct that in the best matter, than to make a sally against evil by some single improvement. . . . Do you complain of the laws of Property? It is a pedantry to give such importance to them. Can we not play the game of life with these counters, as well as with those? in the institution of property as well as out of it?" (In ch. 2 I try to show that Thoreau was much closer to Emerson's position here than he recognized.)

strate that this desire was triggered by spiritual motives—a desire for "riches" in the broadest sense—which eventually would supersede a simple appetite for things. Hence, while Emerson certainly did believe that the entrepreneurs of his time provided new instances of heroic effort and worthy performance, their activity still required interpretation; and the interpretation he offered in "Wealth" was a characteristic mix of limited approval and hopeful criticism.

What was it exactly about America's entrepreneurs that called forth Emerson's admiration? At first it appears that their accomplishments are about to come in for unqualified praise when he speaks of wealth as having "its source in applications of the mind to nature." But if entrepreneurs are thereby "idealists," they are so only in this very loose sense. Moreover, as we have seen already, Emerson's subsequent account of the specific skills that compose "the art of getting rich" continually warns against overestimating the range of their idealistic talents. Money-making was essentially a matter of patience, good timing, and—especially—good luck. There was no inexplicable magic about it; what there was of "genius" in the activity of entrepreneurs lay mostly in their skill as rhetoricians. They were, in Emerson's view, "the monomaniacs who talk up their project in marts and offices and entreat men to subscribe." The building of America's new factories and railroads was, therefore, simply the result of "the importunity of these orators who dragged all the prudent men" into their schemes.[47]

For Emerson, what mattered most about the "men of the mine, telegraph, mill, map, and survey" was not what they had already done in building new economic institutions, but rather what they might yet accomplish in helping America realize its promise as a democratic nation. Nowhere in "Wealth" did Emerson ever hold up the entrepreneur as a model others should emulate. He even warns his audience away from their example at one point: "Commerce is a game of skill," he observed, but also a game "which every man cannot play, [and] which few men can play well." We also miss the general drift of Emerson's argument if we fail to notice that the question that concerns him early in this essay—What are America's rich men for?—quickly becomes linked to a more central and longstanding concern in his thinking—What would America become? Here Emerson goes on to argue only that an important part of the answer turns

---

47. "Wealth," 694, 698.

on the practical matter of what wealthy Americans choose to do with their property, and he does not mince words in explaining how he thinks they ought to act. The man "rich as all men ought to be" will see that his private wealth is only a means to higher ends. The ideal entrepreneur will aim to help in the creation of a society in which the primary purpose of economic prosperity would be to foster universal civilization, "wealth" in the fullest sense as the cultural awakening of all men. If the entrepreneur had a moral raison d'être in Emerson's view, it rested entirely in the prospect of his using his private riches for cultural philanthropy. "Wealth" was hardly a celebration of the entrepreneurial ethic; it was meant to be the outline of an ideology of service Emerson hoped would supersede that of money-making.[48]

But what kind of demystifier of America's wealth was it who could also argue that "Wealth brings with it its own checks and balances. The basis of political economy is non-interference. . . . Do not legislate. Meddle and you sap the sinews with your sumptuary laws. . . . In a free and just commonwealth, property rushes from the idle and imbecile to the industrious, brave and persevering"? This looks rather like a blind proponent of laissez-faire, until we look more closely and see that Emerson was describing reigning nineteenth-century economic platitudes within and against which he was determined to express the larger aspirations of his nation. There also can be little question that the latter project was unthinkable had Emerson not believed that his countrymen aspired to other and more important forms of wealth apart from goods that were bought and sold in the marketplace. To be sure, in defending that belief Emerson was not prepared to challenge all the conventional economic wisdom of his day. But he also did not disguise the fact that many aspects of laissez-faire political economy left him unsatisfied and disgruntled. For example, it is clear that, while Emerson accepted economic inequality as an inevitable by-product of America's new prosperity, he did not for that reason believe that all forms of private property were sacrosanct. In "Wealth," Emerson tied ownership directly to the public responsibility of building "civilization": "They should own who can administer, not they who hoard and conceal; not they who, the greater proprietors they are, are only the greater beggars,

---

48. Ibid., 702, 699. It is plausible to see "Wealth" as signaling Emerson's recognition of the emergence of an antebellum commercial aristocracy. Yet in saying that only a few could play the game of commerce with skill and success, Emerson intended to put no particular moral value on that point.

but they whose work carves out work for more, opens a path for all." Property was not a reward for one's skill or one's labor; it was a "surplus product" whose owners must "animate" it for higher social purposes. Indeed, Emerson went on to say—in the same paragraph where he praises socialists for drawing attention to the same point he is stressing—that property owners unwilling to meet their public responsibilities ought not to retain title to their wealth if it takes the form of property in those products of civilization that rightly belong to all men.

If "Wealth" provides a rationale for the entrepreneur of an industrial age, it is ultimately a selective rationale that welcomes only those ready to join Emerson in the still undone work of giving all Americans "access to the masterpieces of art and nature," and of creating a society whose economic abundance would be used primarily to provide every one of its members "the means and apparatus of science and the arts." That in essence was Emerson's vision of the unique double meaning of America's "wealth": an egalitarian culture where the benefits of civilization, once reserved for an opulent few, would now be enjoyed by all. This vision lacks detailed practical directives, and Emerson displays noticeably little confidence that America's new rich men would join hands with him. Nonetheless, the philosophical foundation of that vision remained his long-standing belief that in America the currents of a creative, independent, and noble life flowed in every person.[49]

This belief was evident in all that Emerson had to say about (and to) America's entrepreneurs, but it found its full and forceful expression in the last third of "Wealth," where it has gone largely unnoticed. Here Emerson returned to answer the two questions he had posed at the outset. His five "measures of economy" explained how in a market economy ordinary men could become and remain "whole men." He began by stressing that a purposeful life can be accomplished in any occupation, so long as that occupation is chosen freely. Hence, the "wealthiest" of societies, in Emerson's view, will be that in which "every man does that which he was created to do." Once he has discovered his proper talent, the whole man must also establish his economic independence. In practical terms, this means he will learn what things he can live without, thereby rendering himself immune to the acquisitive ethos of the market. The market nurtures and depends on vanity, but he will act on pride. For where vanity takes us "a long

49. Ibid., 705, 700–701, 699.

way leading nowhere," pride by contrast "is handsome, economical; pride eradicates so many vices, letting none subsist but itself. . . . Pride can go without domestics, without fine clothes, can live in a house with two rooms." The whole man can be economically self-contained because he knows, too, what those pursuing larger incomes never grasp: "Want is a growing giant whom the coat of Have was never large enough to cover."[50]

Yet economic independence can no longer be the same thing as economic self-subsistence. Emerson conceded that the market had rendered that ideal unworkable, and in its place demanded specialization and—more important—an "incessant watching" of one's resources. Seen from one angle, the market may appear to be a realm of self-regulation. Yet seen from another, it is also a realm where the value of one's goods will always be "flowing like water," and the best one can hope for here in economic terms is to keep one's place amidst risk, flux, and fluidity. Keeping one's place in the market, however, does not preclude the possibility of realizing other nobler, noneconomic aims. That surely is part of what Emerson has in mind when he says that "there is no maxim of the merchant which does not admit of an extended sense." A "man raised to his highest power" will see that the merchant's economy remains only a "coarse symbol of the soul's economy." It is coarse because the merchant usually takes the meaning of the one rule that guides his life—*absorb and invest*—much too narrowly. For what lies behind the simple question he regularly asks himself— Will I spend my income, or will I invest?—is the larger question of what each person will do with his life. The merchant who sees his wealth simply as a means of pleasure is on the road to ruin. The one who invests, however, "climbs to higher platforms," because in that choice he attests to a desire for "higher results" and must have "courage and endurance" to attain his ends.[51]

John Diggins has described "Wealth" as "that intriguing document" in which "the American is taught how to seek profits without losing his soul."[52] But Emerson's lesson is more complex and intriguing than this characterization suggests. What we have explored here are the reflections

---

50. Ibid., 709, 711.

51. Ibid., 715–16.

52. Diggins, *Lost Soul of American Politics*, 200; also see Sellers, *Market Revolution*, 378–80, who claims that in "Wealth" Emerson came to exult over the triumph of "untrammeled capitalism."

of a thinker who saw wealth as a synonym for civilization seeking to give new direction to members of a society in which wealth was taken to be little more than a matter of having or making money. Seen in this perspective, the argument of "Wealth" hardly represents an effort to link the pursuit of profit directly to the search for salvation. One of its messages is precisely the opposite: being rich may not corrupt, but don't equate worldly gain (or loss) with spiritual standing; the entrepreneur's new wealth has no moral standing until it comes to serve his nation. Yet the essay is not so much a sustained indictment of the assumption that money is a sign of spiritual election, as it is yet another exhibit of Emerson's determination to uncover nobler purposes he felt certain were contained within "the demand to be rich." No one simple practical conclusion grows out of this effort. Emerson's purpose is by no means to provide an unabashed endorsement of free enterprise ideology. He urges the new entrepreneurial class to link its wealth to the cause of civilization, yet gives clear warning that America's "democratic institutions" will "step into the place of these proprietors" if they fail in this higher mission. He also cautions ordinary men to remember that the personal achievement of wealth in the narrow sense is by no means a prerequisite for the salvation of their souls: "The true thrift is always to spend on the higher plane; to invest and invest, with keener avarice, that he may spend in spiritual creation and not in augmenting animal existence. Nor is the man enriched, in repeating the old experiments in animal sensation; nor unless through new powers and ascending pleasures he knows himself by the actual experience of higher good to be already on the way to the highest."

There is no praise for a life of voluntary poverty here, but otherwise this reads like a précis of Thoreau's opening chapter on "Economy" in *Walden*. America is rich enough: if the nation's promise was simply a growing supply of material goods, Emerson plainly disavowed it, insisting that what was new in his nation had little to do with a proliferation of wants. Yet he clearly believed, too, that Americans remained capable of fashioning ways of living free of acquisitiveness precisely because the codes of conduct encouraged and rewarded in the market—the cult of "thrift" and the logic of investment—could be expanded to serve higher purposes. Hence, the financial metaphors with which Emerson concluded "Wealth" represent the same sort of didactic paradox that, as we shall see in the next chapter, colored the opening chapter of *Walden*. For Emerson, too, sought to explain his ideals in terms of a way of life they were in the end designed to transform, and he believed that the means of affecting that transformation were already at hand—in the very methods of commercial life itself.[53]

5

The account of Emerson's views of the market presented in this chapter doesn't match the stereotype of a thinker who celebrated worldly success as a sign of spiritual election. Nor does it match the stereotype of a fierce young critic of America's emerging business civilization, who somehow lost his bearings in the middle of his career. Those still familiar accounts do not represent willful distortions of his thinking; they of course would not be stereotypical had they failed to seize on important aspects of his work. But they remain stereotypes nonetheless, since the actual details of Emerson's thinking about the market are more interesting and complicated than either of these approaches suggests.

Two points that I have tried to establish in this chapter deserve emphasis in conclusion, and in stressing them again I also want to suggest briefly how they might help us understand why Emerson's views of the market have lent themselves to such divergent interpretations. On the most general level, this chapter has explored what I consider to be the chief ways by which Emerson challenged his contemporaries—especially fellow intellectuals and those directly engaged in commerce—to join him in imagining how life in a market society might come to serve purposes higher than the mere accumulation of material wealth. I have also stressed that a neglected but central theme in Emerson's work was his insistent claim that intellectuals who hoped to make their idealistic aspirations relevant in America had to be prepared to present those aspirations in a new way, transmuted into the language of a society where wealth, power, profit, and property now comprised what he called the reigning "theory of success." Because Emerson believed that the "demand to be rich" sprang from a deeper and more admirable desire to expand all of one's faculties, he concluded that advocates of moral principles and imagination had no cause to

---

53. "Wealth," 716.

reject out of hand the new values and institutions of the marketplace.[54] Indeed, it was precisely on this count that he often faulted fellow liberal intellectuals. In his view, they had only "got as far as rejection; not as far as affirmation"; they were simply "angry and railers," and so had "nothing new and memorable to offer." Unwilling to play the role of naysayer, Emerson by contrast cast his fate with an alternative vision of becoming the American thinker whose ideas would "correct" his nation's narrow theory of success. He aspired to be the "wise man" he once described in his journals: that figure who "would create in all the inhabitants a new consciousness of wealth by opening their eyes to the sparkle of half concealed treasures that lie in everybody's door-yard."[55]

It was the didactic urgency of Emerson's idealism, his overriding need to uncover the "half concealed treasures that lie in everybody's door-yard," which in time became the basis for much of his remarkable popularity during his lifetime. Others before (and after) him also observed that the coming of an industrial market economy had induced a fundamental shift in conceptions of knowledge and morality. Yet, where most have seen the immediate cultural impact of the market to be the fostering of a more empirical, rationally ordered style of thinking, Emerson was determined to show that it was actually encouraging a different and far more significant transformation—one that was releasing a creative energy he assumed to be bottled up in every person.[56] Emerson's well-documented impact on

---

54. It is worth noting that in his early journals Emerson at times attempted to explain and justify his "commercial times" more directly in terms of some ethical norm embedded in conduct required to attain wealth, although it appears he never succeeded in satisfying himself on this point. Emerson early learned something of the difficulties of finding "virtue" in the market from his reading of Adam Smith's *Theory of Moral Sentiments* (1759). In 1824, at the age of twenty-one, Emerson began to assemble his most comprehensive quotation book, whose first entry read: "[See] in Adam Smith the account of the advantages of Wealth, etc. Moral Sent. Part IV. C. I." Smith there told a complex parable explaining how admiration for the rich spurs an ambitious poor man's son to reorder his life to pursue wealth. But Smith's parable also tells this as a story of self-deception of the sort Emerson himself would warn of in his own later writings about wealth. *Journals*, 6:116; also see 4:262–63, 283, 321–22, 373.

55. "Culture," 717; *Journals*, 9:258.

56. There is a large literature on the ways in which "rationality" was enhanced by the expansion of market relations. For a recent account of how the extension of the marketplace aided in the spread of numerical proficiency during the antebellum period, see Patricia Cline Cohen, *A Calculating People: The Spread of Numeracy in Early America* (Chicago, 1982), chs. 4–6.

middle-class American culture after the mid-nineteenth century attests both to the appeal of that vision and to the attractiveness of the rhetoric he used to convey it. By proclaiming, and then trying to demonstrate, that "sublime thoughts" lurked behind the dominant "penny wisdom" of his day, Emerson dared his contemporaries to take themselves more seriously, challenged them to define what higher ends would be served by current successes in augmenting their "animal existence."[57]

Yet the fact remains that the full complexity of Emerson's challenge rarely has been understood exactly as he offered it, in his time or ours. So the actual shape of his career and the character of his influence on American culture in the end raise some hard questions about the fate of an intellectual determined to remain closely connected to institutions he also seeks to criticize. While Emerson may have become a household word in his own time, the historical evidence also suggests that most of his audience heard his approval and then ignored or overlooked his criticism. (Until quite recently, this process appears to have worked the opposite way around among modern commentators, at least when dealing with the "early" essays.) What, then, are we to make of the fact that the full range of Emerson's speculations about the market has always proved so difficult to take in? There is arguably something more complex at work here than continuing misunderstanding of Emerson's original intentions. Foreshortening and distortion, misreadings and half-readings are perhaps inevitable parts of the process by which all intellectuals and writers are canonized. But in Emerson's case it would be misleading to reduce that process, as Mary Kupiec Cayton has, to a matter of his having been systematically misconstrued from the start. In squaring Emerson's intentions with his impact, we would do better to consider why the potential for half-readings of his thinking was latent in his approach. And here the line of analysis pursued in this chapter provides some final brief suggestions about how future studies of Emerson might consider a question that remains inadequately explored.[58]

---

57. Cayton, "Making of an American Prophet"; Burton J. Bledstein, *The Culture of Professionalism: The Middle Class and the Development of Higher Education in America* (New York, 1976), 259–63.

58. Cayton, "Making of an American Prophet," has argued that in the process of becoming a cultural figure whose views were seen to embody the values of the professional and mercantile classes that flocked to his lectures after 1850, "Emerson's ideas were bled of any philosophical, political, and religious implications, and used as the basis for a secular faith

We know remarkably little about the initial phases of the process by which Emerson was put into place as one of America's "classic" authors, and the question of exactly how his contemporaries responded to the texts we have come to consider his most important works is one to which I'll return in chapters 7 and 8. Central to any adequate understanding of how Emerson became one of America's cultural "prophets," however, must also be a careful and sympathetic reconsideration of what he understood to be his own vision of America's promise. And that reconsideration must grow out of the recognition that Emerson's dream of America as the first nation where all men had equal access to the products of civilization assumed that "culture" in some manner stood outside of the market, separate from a realm which—as he put it in "Wealth"—was marked by "falsehoods and petty tricks which we suicidally play off on each other." Although he rejected their elitism, then, it is clear that on this point Emerson rejoined the English Romantics and the German Idealists in holding fast to the idea that culture was a transcendent realm whose higher meaning and values were, at best, only anticipated in the activities of ordinary social and economic life. This assumed separation of culture from the realm of production and exchange, however, in the end had an inescapably ambiguous practical significance. At first glance, the affirmative character of culture we find in Emerson's writings seems to provide a clear-cut critical attitude toward the market, since the market apparently must be either condemned as a lower order of experience (as in *Nature*) or faulted as an incomplete and unfulfilled mode of existence (as in *Conduct of Life*). However, those Emerson called on to embrace culture also remained free to transmute the critical tension between the ideal and the real, the meaningful and the material, into a simple distinction between an outer world of sometimes ugly facts and an inner world of harmony he also often spoke of as the realm of "the soul." And during the 1850s, when Emerson first actively sought a widespread public hearing for his views, that is exactly what appears to have happened: the higher satisfactions that he said the inner world provided—be they the masterpieces of art or the wonders of nature—

---

that focussed on materially defined progress, unlimited wealth, and conspicuous social achievement" (619). Yet this conclusion appears to contradict her opening claim that the story of the "popularization" of Emerson was not "necessarily one of simplification and homogenization of a complex determinate message for a non-expert audience" (602). That Emerson's message was simplified over time I have no doubt; that it was entirely misunderstood (or bled of all philosophical content) remains open to question.

were seen as justifications for an existing social and economic order, and the nobler values he attributed to culture and soul thereby turned out to provide an unintended but nonetheless reassuring apology for acquisitiveness, inequality, and exploitation.[59]

Was Emerson aware of the ambiguity present in his vision? How did he deal with the disappointment of winning admirers and converts who transformed his complaints about market practices and institutions into a confirmation of the principles that sustained them? Did he really believe his complex view of the market would gain full public understanding? Did he, in the final analysis, stand too close to a society whose conduct he sought to transform and improve? Such questions about Emerson's career have yet to be fully explored, partly because his vision of his role as a connected critic of American society has rarely been credited with its full complexity. There is little prospect of a more adequate understanding of Emerson's intentions, however, if we continue to work backward to him with the assumption that somehow he ought to have recognized that the market was the chief source of the problems he sought to overcome.[60] Viewed from this angle, his thinking will only continue to appear superficial and unwittingly apologetic. But if we try to work forward from Emerson's statement of his own visionary purpose, from a lifelong understanding that his primary mission, even as he often sharply criticized market practices and institutions, was to maintain faith and hope, there is still a figure here worth our close attention. It is time to give up the still familiar image of Emerson as a thinker who ignored the institutional arrangements of the early American Republic to "pursue wild thoughts of new human possibility."[61] Seeing him in such terms exaggerates the nebulous-

---

59. "Wealth," 705; "Culture," 717. My account of the ambiguity of culture as Emerson conceived it draws from John Brenkman, *Culture and Domination* (Ithaca, 1987), ch. 1. Emerson was of course hardly alone in his determination to separate culture from the realms of political and economic activity.

60. My reading of Emerson here again resembles that of Bercovitch to some extent. With a different explanation of the sources and motives of Emerson's social criticism, he has arrived at a somewhat similar conclusion: "What I'm suggesting is that capitalism meant far more in America than an economic system" ("How the Puritans Won the American Revolution," 610). My own interpretation suggests that although Emerson certainly did reject an essentialist view of market capitalism, Bercovitch exaggerates Emerson's radicalism and his penchant for substituting symbolic for social analysis—two modes of thought that in fact appear to go hand-in-hand in Emerson's way of viewing the world.

61. Irving Howe, *The American Newness: Culture and Politics in the Age of Emerson* (Cambridge, 1986), 20.

ness of his ideals. It also ignores what I have attempted to uncover in this chapter: his complicated determination to locate those ideals within the workings of the institutions of his day. Emerson wanted to build a culture commensurate with the economic as well as the political opportunities of his young nation, and the Emerson who still deserves our attention is the figure who refused to believe that his grand hopes might have been altogether different from those of his countrymen or beyond their understanding. Looking back, some might say this belief—the belief that identifies him as a connected critic of his society—was naïve. Yet this need not stop us from recognizing or pondering the intricacy of his efforts to prove it was true.

2

"A Yankee Diogenes":
Thoreau on the Market

THOREAU HAS BECOME central to the study of American culture because so many masks seem to fit him comfortably. In *Walden*, he remarked
that his own pages "admit of more than one interpretation," and the now
voluminous history of commentary and scholarship on his career and
work amply justifies that self-description (290).[1] In his own century, as
we shall see later in this book, Thoreau was recognized as an extreme
individualist, an unyielding critic of Christianity, a brilliant self-educated
naturalist, a radical abolitionist, and one of America's first conservation-
ists. Portraits by twentieth-century interpreters have included Thoreau
the pastoralist, the civic humanist, the democratic individualist, the romantic liberal, and the forerunner of both literary modernism and contemporary "deep ecological" thinking. Small wonder that one recent survey of his various political reputations concluded that Thoreau "seems to
be in everyone's camp"; he was almost as heterogeneous as America itself.[2]

---

1. Henry D. Thoreau, *Walden*, in *Walden and Other Writings*, ed. Brooks Atkinson (New
York, 1950). Page numbers in the text refer to Atkinson's still widely available edition.
2. Michael Meyer, *Several more lives to live: Thoreau's Political Reputation in America* (Westport, Conn., 1977), 3.

Thoreau's reflections on American economic activity and institutions have always loomed large in efforts to understand the variety of his meanings. Many of his contemporaries recognized immediately that his love of nature in some manner represented an alternative to the spirit of material acquisitiveness that seemed to permeate their age. An early reviewer of *Walden* for *Putnam's Magazine* called Thoreau "a Yankee Diogenes," and described the aim of his life as "a hermit on the shore of Walden Pond" to be "the very remarkable one of trying to be something, while he lived upon nothing; in opposition to the general rule of striving to live upon something, while doing nothing." But Emerson was arguably too polite in characterizing him simply as a man who "had no talent for wealth."[3] In some moods, Thoreau feared and despised America's new economic abundance more deeply than any other major nineteenth-century writer. Among many other things, *Walden* may be the greatest American contribution to a long-lived Western tradition of moral comment on the madness of money-making. Thoreau looked upon life in a market society as "life without principle," and his continuing opposition to America's emerging business civilization prompted what may be the single most astonishing piece of social commentary in his work:

> Let us consider the way in which we spend our lives. This world is a place of business. What an infinite bustle! I am awaked almost every night by the panting of the locomotive. It interrupts my dreams. There is no sabbath. It would be glorious to see mankind at leisure for once. It is nothing but work, work, work. I cannot easily buy a blank-book to write thoughts in; they are commonly ruled for dollars and cents. . . . I think that there is nothing, not even crime, more opposed to poetry, to philosophy, ay, to life itself, than this incessant business.[4]

Alfred Kazin has called Thoreau "a conscientious objector" to the world of unbridled profit and futile gain,[5] but it seems more appropriate to char-

---

3. *Putnam's Magazine* (October 1854): 443. Ralph Waldo Emerson, "Thoreau," in *Selected Essays*, ed. Larzer Ziff (New York, 1982), 395. Characterizations of Thoreau as Diogenes were commonplace during his lifetime, and dated back to early reviews of *A Week on the Concord and Merrimack Rivers* (1849). For more on this issue, see ch. 9.

4. "Life Without Principle," in *Walden and Other Writings*, 712. Also see *Walden*, 7, where in explaining what he meant in claiming that "the mass of men lead lives of quiet desperation," Thoreau at first appears to say that their desperation resulted from an abject surrender to the new demands of the economic marketplace.

5. Quoted in Jesse Bier, "Weberism, Franklin, and the Transcendental Style," *New England Quarterly* (June 1970): 185.

acterize this angry passage as the work of a figure determined to dispossess America of its material demons.

Yet any careful reader of his writings knows that Thoreau's disaffection was by no means consistent or free of paradoxes, was less conscientious than it appears at first glance. While there are radically antimarket implications in much of his social criticism, he made it clear that he never wanted to be taken as a guide to social reform. He recognized the paradox of poverty in the midst of America's economic progress, but often said this progress had done more to degrade the affluent than the poor. He railed against the commercialization of American life, but conceded that some of the new commercial activity and technology of his time spoke directly to higher spiritual and imaginative sensibilities. In fact, Thoreau frequently chose to convey the joys of a natural and spiritual life in the very language of business and commerce. And finally, to name one more seeming paradox, he was like other writers of his generation himself a tradesman—one of the "scribbling gentry," as he once put it—whose objects of exchange were his books, essays, poems, and reviews.[6] Thoreau's two years at Walden Pond were not in fact a time when "he lived upon nothing"; most of his waking hours there were probably devoted to writing he later brought for publication and sale in the new and growing literary marketplace of antebellum America.

It may be that Thoreau's students ultimately will provide us with keys that unlock each of these riddles individually. Some paradoxes may have been deliberate and open to easy resolution. It is plausible to see Thoreau's persistent efforts to describe his experience at Walden in economic terms as no more than a parody of the market's means of evaluation, a parody whose ultimate design is to "undermine our commitment to commerce." Yet there will always remain the obstinate fact that there are so many of these riddles, that a number of different paths lead into Thoreau's thinking about the market, that he shifted back and forth from criticism to grudging accommodation, that he had—in short—much greater variety in his response to the market than we have been taught to assume.[7]

---

6. *The Correspondence of Henry David Thoreau*, ed. Walter Harding and Carl Bode (New York, 1958), 442.

7. Judith P. Saunders, "Economic Metaphor Redefined: The Transcendental Capitalist at Walden," in *Modern Critical Interpretations: Henry David Thoreau's 'Walden,'* ed. Harold Bloom (New York, 1987), 67. Also see Stephen Railton, *Authorship and Audience: Literary*

In this chapter, I want to show that in the end this may well be the most important and interesting thing to accept about Thoreau. Rather than trying to decide whether he was finally for or against the market as he knew it, we should recognize that the variety of his attitudes remains our chief interpretive problem, and seek to make better sense of that. Thoreau's name has often been invoked to lend moral authority to protest against the dominance of the market in American life, and with good reason. But we should also acknowledge that a full understanding of his response to the market ultimately requires us to come to terms with his ambivalent attachment as well as with his fierce opposition. To insist on the importance of the question, "Given the many-sidedness of Thoreau's talk about the market, how should we characterize his attitude toward it?" may be our best guide to what he actually wanted to say.

I

One place to begin to ask that question is with the first three chapters of *Walden*. These were the chapters, as we shall see later in this book, which most interested Thoreau's contemporaries. They were also the place in which Thoreau made his most sustained effort to explain the relationship between his values and those of the marketplace. He introduces himself there as a self-sufficient man dedicated to the pursuit of a simple and independent life free of the "curse of trade" (63). Yet it quickly becomes apparent that the full story of his two years at Walden Pond involved a relationship with the market that became considerably more complex than a complete withdrawal. Recognizing the complexity of that lived relationship—as well as understanding why Thoreau sometimes disguised it—will give us an initial lead into the question of the variety of his views.

The story of Thoreau's settling at Walden Pond moves through two distinct stages. The first recounts the activity involved in building his modest house. Here Thoreau began by stressing that his experiment was not to be seen as any sort of angry retreat from modern society. It represented in-

---

Performance in the American Renaissance (Princeton, 1991), 62, which draws attention to the apparent paradox that while the initial subtitle of *Walden* presented it as a story, "Life in the Woods," the book itself "tells more about contemporary American society than almost any other major work from this period."

stead an effort to show that the material wealth of civilization, "though so dearly bought," could be put to much better use than his contemporaries chose to recognize. "It is certainly better to accept the advantages . . . which the invention and industry of mankind offer," Thoreau remarked, than to assume that moral regeneration required us to "live in a cave or a wigwam or wear skins." Although he addressed his experiment to those seeking higher purpose in their lives, then, his message was not that the materials of the market should be shunned altogether, but rather that "with a little more wit we might use" those materials "to become richer than the richest now are, and to make our civilization a blessing" (36).

This first statement of intentions is important in drawing our attention to the fact that the actual work of building a house at Walden Pond began not with a sudden, defiant act of withdrawal, but with the borrowing of tools from others, and that Thoreau's unhurried completion of his work ultimately occurred within a fairly elaborate network of social cooperation and economic exchange. First, there was an axe (borrowed from Bronson Alcott) that allowed him to cut and hew timber from the pond's hillside and to shape his studs and rafters, then yet other tools borrowed for the more intricate work of mortising and tenoning his beams. Thoreau started this work near the end of March 1845, and by mid-April—"for I made no haste in my work"—his house was framed and "ready for the raising" (38). Here he also notes in passing, however, that the house was not entirely the creation of his own hands. For while clearing the site for his home, Thoreau had purchased additional boards from James Collins, an impoverished Irishman who lived with his family in a shanty near the pond. By the beginning of May, the entire frame of his house had been set up. Thoreau comments that while he didn't need assistance from others to raise his modest structure, he nonetheless called on some of his Concord acquaintances for help, so as to "improve so good an occasion for neighborliness" (40). He moved in on the 4th of July, delaying completion of his chimney until the fall, while he turned to the more pressing task of tending the two and a half acres of beans he had planted to feed himself and help meet his expenses.

In many of its details, the first stage of Thoreau's experiment tells the story of a figure still ensconced in networks of mutual support and interest-driven reciprocity. (Indeed, Thoreau himself is arguably a representative of civilization, since in using the axe to make a place for himself at the pond, he employs—apparently without being aware of it—one of the chief symbols of civilization in antebellum America.) In the second stage, the variety and importance of these networks become even more apparent. His modest venture in commercial farming—in an effort to earn ten or twelve dollars, Thoreau had planted two and a half acres, chiefly with beans—at the outset required him to "hire a team and a man for the plowing" (49). Thoreau's cash crop ultimately does not bring in enough income to meet all his needs, and so by "surveying, carpentry, and day-labor of various kinds" in Concord he earns additional money to make ends meet (52). He also controls his "pecuniary outgoes" by returning to Concord to have his clothing washed and mended and occasionally to dine out as well (54). In short, while the hut at Walden Pond may have been Thoreau's residence for two years, it turned out to be less of a home and more of a headquarters for a figure who sought a measure of self-sufficiency, but not at the cost of complete isolation.[8] A determination to live his own life never prevented Thoreau from dividing and sharing some of the burdens of his existence, or from getting his living by working for wages.

Several details in the sometimes self-mythologizing story Thoreau tells about the establishment of his household remain open to question. Why the misleading suggestion at the outset of *Walden* that he built his house entirely by himself (3)? Why the misleading description of himself as "merely a squatter" (49)? (Thoreau's friend Emerson was the owner of the plot of land on which his hut stood.) Moreover, if Thoreau's self-sufficient "life in the woods" embodied a clear-cut alternative to the acquisitiveness of market society, why the sometimes self-mocking humor in his detailed description of his personal plan of living? Why the occasional concessions that his experiment had many of the markings of a tall tale? And, finally, why did Thoreau disguise the fact that the chief "private business" he went to Walden to transact had been his writing? It surely seems curious that an author who promised at the beginning of *Walden* to provide "a simple and sincere account" of his life should deliver a self-description so intricate (yet in some respects also incomplete and misleading) that it belies any neat précis (3).

The very intricacy of the story Thoreau provided may point the way to answering some of these questions. For among the things that his story

---

8. Barbara Novak, *Nature and Culture: American Landscape and Painting, 1825–75* (New York, 1980), 4; *Correspondence of Henry David Thoreau,* 167.

asks us to recognize is that Thoreau's search for an escape from the "curse of trade" led him not into a world-transcending economy, but one that permitted him to slip in and out of the network of economic exchanges. Indeed, it is Thoreau himself who shows us that he never managed to withdraw completely from the market, whatever his original intent may have been. What he came to fashion instead was a way of life perhaps best described as being set up on the margins of the market, almost entirely free of the material acquisitiveness it encouraged, yet also dependent upon it in several ways, as we have just seen, for achieving his quest for independence. The temporary embrace of a life of voluntary poverty did not eliminate all motives for exchange in Thoreau's case. Indeed, money transactions not only provided him with the land and some of the materials for his house; they also enabled him to purchase his solitude, since Collins and his family—apparently the only other people living close to the pond in the spring of 1845—departed once their shanty was bought by Thoreau.

It also turns out that Walden Pond itself was hardly a pristine landscape. To say that Thoreau unwittingly settled in a center of commercial activity would be an obvious exaggeration. But it is remarkable how often such activity intruded upon his existence. Thoreau noted privately in his journal that it was impossible to go walking in the Concord woods during the daylight hours in any season without hearing the sound of the axes, and wood-choppers were a frequent presence during his stay at Walden.[9] Even more conspicuous was the new Fitchburg railroad line, which passed so close to the pond that an arm of it was filled for a high rail embankment that could be seen from almost any point on the pond. Leo Marx has noted that there is scarcely a chapter in *Walden* where Thoreau did not mention seeing or hearing the engine, or walking "over the long causeway made for the railroad through the meadows." More significant, it also is clear Thoreau was often elated by the presence of a new invention whose promise in the end seemed to offset its dangers. There was nothing of a simple-minded Luddite hostility toward new industrial technology in *Walden*.[10] Thoreau did attack the popular illusion that the improvement of technology was an end in itself. But he held fast to the belief that more

---

9. Robert D. Richardson Jr., *Henry Thoreau: A Life of the Mind* (Berkeley, 1986), 136.

10. Leo Marx, *The Machine in the Garden: Technology and the Pastoral Ideal in America* (New York, 1964), 247.

extensive commercial activity made possible and encouraged the spread of culture and civility around the world. Indeed, Thoreau twice rehearsed—midway through "Sounds" and again in the last paragraph of "The Pond in Winter"—the already well-established view that commerce was a potentially civilizing process. On the one hand, its material benefits, if properly used, could make men and societies more gentle and refined. For by promoting leisure and travel, it allowed individuals to broaden their tastes and understanding. "I am refreshed and expanded when the freight train rattles past me," Thoreau wrote, "and I smell the stores which go dispensing their odors all the way from Long Wharf to Lake Champlain, reminding me of foreign parts, or coral reefs, and Indian oceans, and tropical climes, and the extent of the globe." On the other hand, commerce also militated against violence by encouraging individuals of different nations to trade rather than to war with one another. Thoreau of course had no desire to engage in international commerce, but he did say that sighting its objects being carried in a train on the shores of Walden Pond made him "feel more like a citizen of the world" (108).[11]

Now all these points might seem obvious enough if we could manage to restrict our attention exclusively to what Thoreau tells us about how and where he pursued his experiment. Yet we are not accustomed to thinking of him as a figure with any needs that were met directly (or indirectly) by market transactions. What, then, deflects our vision away from a fact that Thoreau himself was prepared to acknowledge? Part of an answer is that much of his energy in the opening chapters of *Walden* was spent in didactic and often angry criticism of a society that had come to believe that somehow *all* of its needs could be met by the market. Running parallel to his initial account of his experiment, then, is Thoreau's version of a familiar catalogue of follies that countless critics of the market before him had also found reprehensible. The morality the market teaches men is not self-re-

---

11. Also see the final paragraph of "The Pond in Winter" (*Walden*, 266), where Thoreau concludes his account of the work of ice-cutters at Walden Pond by speaking of their future customers as "the sweltering inhabitants of Charleston and New Orleans, of Madras and Bombay and Calcutta" who would also "drink at my well." The view that commerce, as an economic process, was central to the process of civilization was particularly widespread in late eighteenth-century and early nineteenth-century Western thought. Albert O. Hirschman, *The Passions and the Interests: Political Arguments for Capitalism before Its Triumph* (Princeton, 1977), has defined this view as the "*doux-commerce* thesis."

liance, but success in getting the better of one another, success that comes only by deceiving, supplanting, and betraying one another. Wealth is always created at the expense of some other person, and this means market societies must spawn radical forms of social inequality and dependency. The creation of wealth also depends on an ever-increasing division of labor, a process that produces more goods but at the cost of making human labor meaningless. The division of labor inevitably results in the division of man. Thoreau also often suggested that everything he understood to represent the promise of American life—that is, the commitments and values that were at the core of a democratic nation—was being undermined by the wickedness of the market. Indeed, those most in need of moral reform in Concord were those who had apparently succeeded in the market. The poor at least remained mobile, while the rich were weighed down both by possessions and by their complete dependence on others for the maintenance of their elaborate farms and households.[12]

The force of Thoreau's censure of the materialism of American life should never be underestimated. Yet here again there is no reason why acknowledgment of its power should blind us to the various ways in which Thoreau himself regularly muted or qualified his censure. There are reasons to wonder exactly where he finally stood in the confrontation between spiritual and material values. From the very outset of *Walden*, after all, he stressed that the market's ethic of acquisitiveness was not yet so pervasive that it had resulted in an irreparable loss of values. Nor did he ever locate the main cause of the conformity and spiritual emptiness of American life in the production and exchange of commodities. While obviously dismayed by the "curse of trade," Thoreau was arguably just as concerned to show that it was not too late to give up the worst of the "prejudices" market economies had created and sustained. One of his chief purposes in writing *Walden* clearly was to provide one example of how men remained free to cultivate the higher faculties of their inner selves, despite living in a society in which "trade curses every thing it handles" (63).

Put another way, close reading of the opening chapters of *Walden* tells us Thoreau was Janus-faced in his response to the market. Much of the time he seems to be looking backward, usually in anger and despair, to

---

12. "I also have in mind," Thoreau wrote at the outset of *Walden*, "that seemingly wealthy, but most terribly impoverished class of all, who have accumulated dross, but know not how to use it, or get rid of it, and thus have forged their own golden or silver fetters" (15).

simpler ways of living, free of the artificial needs of life in a market society. In fact, it is the extraordinary force of Thoreau's censure of the materialism of American life that suggests just how deeply rooted the hold of the market was, and how apparently incorrigible were the new habits of material self-indulgence it nurtured. Yet at the same time his fierce censure also suggests just how determined he was to protect his countrymen from the worst consequences of their own economic success. If America's promise was simply a growing supply of material goods, Thoreau obviously disavowed it. He also went on to insist, however, that there remained much that was new and promising about America, and here there surfaced a side of his thinking—usually unnoticed by students of his social and economic views—which took for granted the affluence of which he was often such a harsh critic. For in the three opening chapters of *Walden*, Thoreau's perspective sometimes shifts entirely from renouncing America's wealth to suggesting alternative better uses for it.

In the first two chapters, the clearest instances of this different attitude can be seen in his perhaps surprising concern for what he sees as the special plight of "the degraded rich." In Thoreau's view, his prosperous Concord neighbors were the "most terribly impoverished class of all"—not just because they were unable to imagine living full lives without their material goods, but also because they had failed to consider how their wealth might be put to far better use (15). They wasted their money not simply in the purchase of trivial things, the frivolous objects of luxury and fashion, but also because they had failed to seek out "work of *fine* art" instead. In the affluent homes of Concord, Thoreau complained, "There is not a nail to hang a picture on, nor a shelf to receive the bust of a hero or a saint" (33). This same complaint is later lodged against the town as a whole. Enough of the prosperity of Concord had been spent in conspicuous consumption for the chiseled stone of its new public buildings. Far better if its wealth could now find a way to provide for new "halls of free worship or free speech," where its citizens would take more pains "to smooth and polish their manners" and lose that "insane ambition to perpetuate the memory of themselves by the amount of hammered stone they leave" (51).

It is in the chapter on "Reading," however, that we see the fullest statement of this largely overlooked side of Thoreau's response to the market. There he provided a more detailed vision of Concord as a community that would use its wealth to become a cosmopolitan cultural center. Why had his prosperous village not yet seen that it now had in hand resources to "take the place of the nobleman of Europe," by also surrounding itself with whatever conduces to its culture: "genius—learning—wit—books—paintings—statuary—music—philosophical instruments, and the like" (99)? While still regarded mostly as an inveterate foe of all organized effort, Thoreau clearly did appreciate, as Robert Gross has shown, the possibilities of neighborly cooperation in the realm of culture.[13] It is important to recognize here, however, that he also appreciated that it was precisely America's economic progress that might help foster a more democratic culture. In Thoreau's view, while the production of wealth had yet to be joined to the production of meaning, the possibility of linking the two still remained open. "New England can hire all the wise men in the world to come and teach her," he insisted, "and board them round the while, and not be provincial at all. That is the *uncommon* school we want" (100). It seems fair to add that the successful establishment and maintenance of such a school also presupposed the continuing "uncommon" affluence of New England.

2

So far, what we have seen in the three opening chapters of *Walden* might be summarized as the grounds for accommodation within Thoreau's criticism of the market—an accommodation that was sometimes surprisingly hopeful, more often reluctant, but usually visible in either form. Thoreau was not wholly of the market, but he was in it, even during his years at Walden Pond. Or, putting it in his own language, to keep his "afternoons" free, Thoreau was willing to sell his "forenoons" in the marketplace. His aim was not to find ways of avoiding all work, but simply not to consume the greater part of his days in "getting his living." As with government, Thoreau could abide the workings of the market so long as he did not have to facilitate them or to be largely dependent upon them for his continuing existence. "I can do without," he boasted defiantly in "Resistance to Civil Government" (639). But it would be more accurate to say that he could do without, whenever he chose to do without. Thoreau didn't expect the market somehow to disappear. His goal was to pursue

---

13. Robert A. Gross, "Much Instruction from Little Reading: Books and Libraries in Thoreau's Concord," *Proceedings of the American Antiquarian Society*, vol. 97, pt. 1, 1987, 129–88.

ways of living that left him free to pick and choose the terms on which he would enter into the realm of economic exchange. Thoreau believed he was not corrupted by the market because he was just serving his basic needs, not pursuing his personal economic profit. Thus, one of the lessons of *Walden* was that "the market" had been made to serve Thoreau at the same time as Thoreau avoided serving "the market."

One result of adopting this perspective is that we can explain an important part of what Thoreau had in mind when he said that "the success or failure of the present economical and social arrangements" ultimately did not interest him (50). For we can now see more clearly why Thoreau felt his goals could be achieved without fundamental institutional reform. In the end, it was not in fact the market that accounted for the "lives of quiet desperation" led by his prosperous Concord neighbors (7). Their malaise was instead the outcome of the mistaken assumption that the market had created a world in which they were no longer free to choose to reform themselves and thereby to live fuller lives. It may be that the market is a realm of unnecessary and dangerous dependencies, but in Thoreau's view there was as yet no reason to believe that his contemporaries were somehow imprisoned by those dependencies. It "is never too late to give up our prejudices," he insisted, no matter how strong or misconceived they seem to be (8).

This recurring insistence on the possibility of self-reform is important, because it also provides a neglected context in which to understand Thoreau's predilection for using the language of the market to express his moral and spiritual values. Now it may be that this aspect of *Walden* really needs no careful analysis or explanation. If we accept the conventional view of Thoreau as entirely a naysayer in his response to the market, his purpose is perhaps not hard to divine. He deliberately appropriated the language of the market only to expose it. "What Thoreau is doing," Kenneth Lynn has declared in an early statement of this now familiar approach, "is to destroy the enemy with the enemy's own weapons."[14] But there are difficulties with this line of analysis. It turns, first of all, on a one-sided reading of Thoreau's views of the market. One question that arises here is: how are we to understand his frequent use of the categories of economic discourse—what Stanley Cavell has described as a "nightmare maze of

---

14. Kenneth S. Lynn, *Visions of America: Eleven Literary Historical Essays* (Westport, Conn., 1973), 14.

terms about money and possessions and work"—if the market turns out *not* to be his chief "enemy"?[15] This approach is also problematic because it apparently must ignore a great deal of textual evidence suggesting that, as with Emerson, Thoreau's predilection for economic categories figured centrally in his effort to show those who thought their lives were entirely determined by the workings of the market that they in fact remained free to redeem themselves. Indeed, it is arguable that the pervasiveness of economic language in *Walden* was less the outcome of Thoreau's desire to fault his contemporaries' values than an expression of his determination to show that, even while criticizing their values, he was in important ways still one of them. In this respect, again as with Emerson, Thoreau can be approached—especially in his recurring use of the language of the marketplace—as a thinker who exemplifies the practices of what Michael Walzer has called "the connected critic." He was, in other words, a writer who sometimes sought to earn his authority to criticize by arguing with his fellows in their own language, by adopting their characteristic ways of talking about the world to show them that this language could be used to express purposes nobler than mere production and exchange.[16]

To offer this as a key to Thoreau's meaning is by no means to suggest that it unlocks all doors into his thinking. The opening chapters of *Walden* remain exceptionally puzzling in some important respects, with a depth of irony that is hard to gauge and a tone that is astonishingly variable. Why did Thoreau so carefully contrast his experiment to the procedures and purposes of businessmen, if not to shame and embarrass them? Why cast his own spiritual quest as a cost-benefit analysis, replete with meticulously detailed statistics, if not to insist on the fundamental opposition of the spiritual to the material? Sometimes, as Cavell has argued so forcefully, it does appear that Thoreau's purpose was little more than a brutal mocking of commercial values, "by forcing a finger of the vocabulary of the New Testament" down our throats. For the latter text seems to be the obvious origin of his recurring use of economic imagery "to express, and correct, spiritual confusion: what shall it profit a man; the wages of sin; the parable

---

15. Stanley Cavell, *The Senses of Walden* (San Francisco, 1981), 88.

16. For Thoreau's interest in language more generally, see Michael West, "Charles Kraitsir's Influence upon Thoreau's Theory of Language," *Emerson Society Quarterly* 19 (Winter 1973): 262–74; Philip F. Gura, *The Wisdom of Words: Language, Theology, and Literature in the New England Renaissance* (Middleton, Conn., 1981); Richardson, *Thoreau*, 93–96.

of talents; laying up treasures; rendering unto Caesar; charity."[17]

Yet sometimes Thoreau commends—without any trace of sarcasm—the methods of commerce, even as he condemns its ends, and at the same time uses the language of the market to illustrate and embody his own values. "I have always endeavored to acquire strict business habits," he wrote, "they are indispensable to every man" (18). And he makes quite clear that those habits include the confidence to take risks, the habit of keeping careful records, and—more generally— a view of each person's life as consisting of a limited amount of energy and time, which may be saved, spent, conserved, employed, or squandered—much like one's money and property.[18]

The vagaries of tone at the outset of *Walden* undoubtedly will continue to give support to the familiar view that Thoreau was essentially a naysayer in his thinking about the market. It is arguable, however, that if we go to examine more carefully some of the various ways in which he employed the language of commerce, what we find is a thinker determined to show that while the market had created spiritual confusion, it had also provided some of its own correctives for that confusion. Thoreau obviously meant to challenge the goals of a market society, but he also wanted to do so in terms he thought would be readily comprehensible to its habitants; or, to state it more directly, he was often measuring the spiritual confusion of his age by internal standards, standards held up in the market itself. What made Thoreau a distinctively "Yankee" Diogenes, according to *Putnam's Magazine*, was that—not unlike his fellow New Englanders—he was "too shrewd not to comprehend the advantages of living in what we call the world."[19]

How did Thoreau, as a connected critic of antebellum economic values and institutions, assure the subjects of his criticism that he was one of them? One of his strategies has been explored recently by Richard and Jean Masteller in a careful demonstration of the ways in which the opening chapters of *Walden* parodied a new genre of house pattern books that

17. Cavell, *Senses of Walden*, 89. But also see Railton, *Authorship and Audience*, 71, who argues that Thoreau sometimes would draw from his contemporaries' Christian catechisms for words that he then redefined in passages testifying to nature's joy.

18. Saunders, "Economic Metaphor Redefined," 63. While I think Saunders assigned too narrow a meaning to Thoreau's use of economic terms, I am much indebted to her provocative analysis.

19. *Putnam's Magazine* (October 1854): 443.

had become popular in American culture in the 1840s and 1850s. Works in this genre—the most famous of which were authored by Andrew Jackson Downing (1815-52)—typically presented a variety of designs for domestic dwellings, including detailed cost estimates, recommendations of particular construction materials, and advice on choosing rural sites for new houses. They also recurrently stressed that building in the countryside would realize a necessary harmony between human beings and the natural world.[20]

There can be no question that *Walden* attacked and parodied many of the key assumptions of this new genre. Where Downing offered thirty-two possible designs for individual dwellings, Thoreau provided a single humble design: a drawing of his one-room dwelling that would appear on the title page of most editions of *Walden* published in the nineteenth century. Moreover, where the most inexpensive laborer's cottage in Downing's view was estimated to cost $330.00, Thoreau's itemized list of construction materials—itself a parody of another characteristic feature of the pattern books—amounted to a mere $28.00 and 12½¢. It is arguable, however, that *Walden* was not designed to subvert all of the central values of the genre. As the Mastellers show, the main element of continuity between Thoreau and previous authors of house pattern books lay in a shared assumption that the architectural beauty of a house ought to be the external manifestation of the inward good of its inhabitants. Even while sharply criticizing them on other grounds, Thoreau never quite abandoned this last central assumption. Indeed, he stressed that the issue that most divided him from other authors of house pattern books was a straightforward practical matter: "The cart before the horse is neither beautiful nor useful. Before we can adorn our houses with beautiful objects the walls must be stripped, and our lives must be stripped, and beautiful housekeeping and beautiful living be laid for a foundation: now, a taste for the beautiful is most cultivated out of doors, where there is no house and no housekeeper" (34). It

---

20. Richard N. and Jean C. Masteller, "Rural Architecture in Andrew Jackson Downing and Henry David Thoreau: Pattern Book Parody in *Walden*," *New England Quarterly* 57 (December 1984): 483–510. Also see Leonard N. Neufeldt, *The Economist: Henry Thoreau and Enterprise* (New York, 1989), who argues that *Walden* was designed, in part, to parody the widely popular conduct manuals and guidebooks published in America during the antebellum period. While I have returned in this study to some questions Neufeldt tried to resolve, I also consider various issues that apparently never got under his skin: Thoreau's persistent troping of market language for purposes other than parody, his occasional self-mocking humor, and the relationship between his views of the market and his opposition to slavery.

would be a mistake, however, to follow the Mastellers in reading this passage as a "dramatic explosion" of the house pattern genre.[21] If nature is the locus of Thoreau's higher values, his encouragement of others to pursue his values does not preclude their eventual return to the project of improving human civilization. The work of adorning houses with beautiful objects clearly remains to be done, and it requires no vision of American culture fundamentally different from that propounded by authors of the house pattern books. If their chief mistake was a matter of putting the cart before the horse, it plainly cannot be the entire cultural program of the genre that Thoreau is rejecting here. What he points to instead is the central confusion in how they hope to realize that program: the facile assumption that good domestic architecture was somehow a sure sign of an already refined, uplifted person. Yet the larger notion that good architecture could in fact be refining and uplifting, as well as the underlying assumption that America's continuing economic affluence might eventually provide for "beautiful objects," are never rejected out of hand. Like Emerson, Thoreau did not abandon the hope that the inhabitants of a market society could learn to rule their wealth for what he took to be higher purposes.

Another example of the way in which Thoreau remained a connected critic of his world can be seen in the ways in which he often turns his subtle humor back on himself. Here we also encounter a characteristic feature of his use of market rhetoric that most recent commentators have overlooked.[22] Thanks to modern biographers, we today know enough about all the circumstances surrounding Thoreau's experiment at Walden Pond—he remained within easy walking distance of his home; his mother and sisters visited with food every Sunday; he was a "hermit" who returned frequently to Concord—to say that there is something comical about his longstanding reputation as one of the company of rugged American woodsmen and loners.[23] But it was in fact Thoreau himself who first drew attention

---

21. Ibid., 507.

22. Neither Saunders nor Cavell, for example, has anything to say about Thoreau's humor. J. Golden Taylor, *Neighbor Thoreau's Critical Humor* (Logan, Utah, 1958), remains a useful introductory study. Also see David S. Reynolds, *Beneath the American Renaissance: The Subversive Imagination in the Age of Emerson and Melville* (New York, 1988), 484–85, 497–506. The humor in the opening chapters of *Walden* also suggests that Thoreau did not believe that the emergence of the market posed a deep cultural crisis in American life. Comedy typically is not part of a crisis mentality.

23. Leo Marx, *The Pilot and the Passenger: Essays on Literature, Technology, and Culture in the United States* (New York, 1988), 90.

to the sometimes very comic dimensions of his venture. Early in *Walden*, he describes himself punningly as engaged in "trade . . . with the Celestial Empire," and later says that his Concord friends had come to think of him as "a sort of real-estate broker" (73). If we ask about the purpose of such self-descriptions, it makes little sense to say they were designed to serve Thoreau's supposedly larger goal of brutally mocking his contemporaries' commercial values. If there is mockery in here, it is being playfully turned back on the critic, and his purpose in punning seems better described as an effort to ingratiate himself with the objects of his criticism by making fun of the sometimes wearyingly solemn story he is telling about himself.

It is arguable that this is also one of the main purposes informing the absurdly detailed statistics of the "Economy" chapter. Seen from one familiar angle, the elaborateness of Thoreau's statistics represents a parody of the bookkeeping mentality, an obviously satirical celebration of penny-pinching that outdoes anything to be found in Benjamin Franklin's *Autobiography*. There is a tall tale here that makes persistent fun of a mentality whose principles Thoreau knowingly takes to ludicrous extremes. Yet if Thoreau is often twitting both the disciples of Poor Richard and the readers of house-pattern books, he is also sometimes using his meticulous statistics to make fun of himself, and in the process again acknowledging the limits of his own success in becoming more self-reliant. The careful "account" of his household expenses, after all, shows plainly that Thoreau never gave up the small luxuries of dining out or of having his clothes washed and mended elsewhere. He even confesses, with self-mocking candor, that since all his wash was done at his mother's home in Concord he had no record of the bills for his laundry.

In short, the often absurdly meticulous bookkeeping in the first chapter of *Walden* suggests that Thoreau knew he had become one of the objects of the tall tale being told in *Walden*. That recognition is important because it appears to have been intended as a means to diminish some of the distance between Thoreau and his contemporaries. For while Thoreau's chief purpose in *Walden* may have been to show materialistic Americans how to discover and explore a world beyond the market, his satirical use of the statistics can be said to strip that spiritual quest of some of its mysteriousness, since he often defines his own spiritual quest in terms of one of their most characteristic forms of getting and spending, the accountant's ledger. Consider, for example, the paragraph that immediately follows his detailed description of the costs of various materials he used in building his house.

He crowed proudly: "I intend to build me a house which will surpass any on the main street in Concord in grandeur and luxury, as soon as it pleases me as much and will cost me no more than my present one" (44).

Thoreau of course did not intend to build his own mansion, but this tongue-in-cheek bragging is significant because it represents one of several examples in *Walden* of the way in which Thoreau was ready to devalue his own pretensions to greatness. If he remained determined not to get in step with his acquisitive Concord neighbors, he was also determined not to stop looking at himself with a skeptical and comic eye. Thoreau was—when he chose to be—a jester in his role as social critic. He was something of a kibitzer as well, since part of what made his criticism of his contemporaries credible was his ability to study himself in light of their own practices of getting and spending. And the sometimes self-mocking humor that emerged from such self-study showed that Thoreau's criticism of his world did not depend simply on detachment and enmity.[24]

Yet Thoreau's use of market language ultimately amounts to more than just parody and satire. It was also designed to serve the more serious and important purpose of showing how self-reform was possible within the confines of a market society. If Thoreau's puns made for self-parody, they also sometimes showed that some of the economic principles in the market could be expanded to serve purposes higher than the production and exchange of things. In the end, all the elaborate financial metaphors and detailed statistics of "Economy" make for what might be called a didactic paradox: Thoreau explains his experiment in terms of what it appears designed to escape, yet he also wants to show that a means of escape is readily at hand, in some of the very methods of commerce itself. Thoreau recognized that the market was in part an economic system that could never have flourished without an adequate supply of self-disciplined individuals, attuned to the promptings of economic relationships by inward-turning, self-monitoring habits of thought. Yet he insisted too—and this is precisely

---

24. Michael Walzer, *Interpretation and Social Criticism* (Cambridge, 1987), 61. It was Thomas Carlyle who perhaps first drew Thoreau's attention to the importance of humor in rendering abstract ideas accessible to the public at large; see Thoreau, "Thomas Carlyle and His Works," in *Early Essays and Miscellanies*, ed. Joseph Moldenhauer et al. (Princeton, 1975), 235: "We should omit a main attraction in these books, if we said nothing of their humor. Of this indispensable pledge of sanity, without some leaven of which the abstruse thinker may justly be suspected of mysticism, fanaticism, or insanity, there is a superabundance in Carlyle. Especially the transcendental philosophy needs the leaven of humor to render it light and digestible."

why his contemporaries were asked to think of him as a Yankee Diogenes—that such habits can be applied to better purposes. We ought to be as attentive to our lives as tradesmen are to their possessions. For if we wish to know better who we are, we, too, must keep careful records, always observing what comes in and what goes out. We should also get up at sunrise, not simply to get ahead, but because our lives consist of a limited amount of time and energy "which may be conserved, saved, spent, employed, squandered, or hoarded—just like property."[25]

In exploring this side of Thoreau's thinking, Judith Saunders has argued recently that his abundant use of the vocabulary of a Yankee capitalist in *Walden* represented an effort to take his audience's reigning ideological assumptions to their "logical conclusion."[26] But his purpose may be somewhat more complex than this view manages to suggest. For Thoreau's determination to use the language of the market for his own purposes took at least two distinct forms. Following Emerson's example, the first involved efforts to restore or maintain what might be called a premarket understanding of certain key concepts such as economy and profit. Remember what economy meant before the coming of the market, Thoreau insisted in the first chapter of *Walden*: the prudent management of a private household, and the practice of a frugality that assured self-subsistence in basic needs. Remember, too, he said in *Walden* and elsewhere, that the true profits of all one's activities are those benefits that accrue with the full development of one's character. This is not taking market ideology to a "logical conclusion," but rather an effort to *resist* that ideology's sharp containment of the meaning of its own key ideas.

It would be misleading to suggest, however, that Thoreau's play with market language was primarily conservative in its design. There are other passages that show that he—again like Emerson—also thought that market language might be manipulated to articulate his idealism more directly. One of the least discussed examples of this side of Thoreau's thinking occurs at the outset of the second chapter of *Walden*—"Where I Lived, And What I Lived For." There he briefly recounted an experiment in house-building that had antedated his venture at Walden Pond. His goal then had been the same—a largely "free and uncommitted" life (75)—but the means entirely different, since this earlier quest had taken the form of

---

25. Saunders, "Economic Metaphor Redefined," 62.
26. Ibid., 63.

an imaginative exercise that had required no actual physical labor or relocation.

The experiment unfolded in two related phases. In the first, Thoreau explained that, after having surveyed the countryside within a dozen miles of Concord, he decided to buy "in his imagination" all the farms he had visited. "For all were to be bought," he insisted, "and I knew their price" (73). This grand assertion was based in part on an implicit suggestion that there was no actual market price for what Thoreau sought to "own" of the Concord landscape. The highest pleasures he found in the natural world could never come to be the exclusive possessions of individual farm owners. Nor could those pleasures ever be enhanced by their improving labor. It was precisely Thoreau's proud refusal of the obligations of "actual ownership"—his discovery of "the number of things which he can afford to let alone" (74)—which in his own view made him richer than his friends. For unlike them, he managed to maintain a simple way of life that allowed him to see what was "real" in his estate.

For Thoreau, then, it appears that the chief price of owning what he thought most valuable was voluntary poverty, never having gotten his fingers "burned by actual possession" (74). Yet it clearly was not that alone, and arguably not necessarily that. In recounting the second phase of his earlier experiment, Thoreau shows that his goal had not been merely leaving things alone. Here in fact he admits that he had come very close to purchasing a farm—"the Hollowell place"—for himself. The owner changed his mind at the last moment, however, just before the time came to transfer the deed to his property. Thoreau also allowed him to keep his initial $10.00 tender offer, although he suggests in passing that he had good legal grounds for contesting Hollowell's last-minute refusal.

In looking back on the negotiations, Thoreau again concludes that he had managed to remain rich because the failure of his offer ultimately allowed him to maintain his poverty—in fact, given the loss of his tender offer, it clearly served to increase it. But here he also goes on to characterize his wealth in more detail:

I found thus that I had been a rich man without any damage to my poverty. But I retained the landscape, and I have since annually carried off what it yielded without a wheelbarrow. With respect to landscapes,—

"I am monarch of all I *survey*,
   My right there is none to dispute."

63

I have frequently seen a poet withdraw, having enjoyed the most valuable part of a farm, while the crusty farmer supposed that he had got a few wild apples only. Why, the owner does not know it for many years when a poet has put his farm in rime, the most admirable kind of invisible fence, has fairly impounded it, milked it, skimmed it, and got all the cream, and left the farmer only the skimmed milk. (74)

The passage illustrates the mastery and pleasures of "imaginative owner-ship" that Thoreau obviously means to distinguish from the drudgery of "actual ownership." It also might be read as a gloss of a brief passage in *Nature* (1836), in which Emerson earlier had called for a "revolution in our notions of property." Like Emerson, Thoreau knew very well that he lived in a society in which property typically meant little more than the right of individuals to the exclusive enjoyment of their lands and goods. Yet he, too, insisted that this simple definition had not exhausted all pos-sible understandings of the term. For there was also, as Emerson put it, "a property in the horizon which no man has but he whose eye can integrate all the parts, that is, the poet."[27]

Richard Poirier has taken Emerson's call for a revolution in our concep-tion of property as evidence for a belief that the human power to make new and imaginative use of language was finally greater than any economic power. It is plausible to read this belief into the story told at the outset of "Where I Lived, And What I Lived For."[28] (There can be little question that the "real-estate broker" is also an Emersonian poet.) But the message Thoreau finally conveys is too complex to be pinned down so definitively. At first glance, it does appear that market values and transactions stand opposed to all that Thoreau believes in. Yet in the paragraphs that con-clude the story of his earlier experiment, his criticism of the world of actual ownership seems to narrow significantly in its scope. He comments, for example, that he had not been unwilling to become a proprietor, con-ceding that he probably would have purchased Hollowell's farm had its owner not refused his offer at the last moment. More strikingly, he also makes it clear that in attempting to buy the farm he had not found himself in the position of being forced to choose between "actual" and "imagina-tive" ownership of land. Thoreau did not scorn private property per se, so

---

27. Emerson, *Nature*, in *Selected Essays*, 38.
28. Richard Poirier, *The Renewal of Literature: Emersonian Reflections* (New York, 1987), 131.

much as what he saw as a needless obsession with improving one's property. "I was in haste to buy" the Hollowell farm, he explained, "before the proprietor finished getting out some rocks, cutting down the hollow apple trees, and grubbing up some young birches which had sprung up in the pasture" (75). If all this is an example of a "revolution in our notions of property," it obviously speaks of a change in which the work of relishing and respecting nature takes precedence over the task of improving or mastering it. Yet Thoreau has also imagined here a world in which imaginative and actual ownership are compatible, so long as the first in practice takes precedence over the second. His deep misgivings about the market never allowed for the possibility of taking revolutionary steps against it. What they gave rise to was his determination to define the ideals of a new culture independent of the market, yet also capable of giving it instruction in the higher purposes of human life. And here Thoreau's play with the language of the market might be seen as an instance of his commitment to show how his values might come to fit into market society, not merely stand out in criticism of it.

3

One way of summarizing what we have uncovered in Thoreau's language is to say that, while he was always deeply critical of the materialism of American life, he joined Emerson and other idealistic intellectuals of his time in arguing that Americans could find ways to rule their wealth for higher purposes. Furthermore, whereas most of his countrymen still assumed there was more wealth to create, Thoreau adamantly insisted that they were already rich enough, and what they most needed now was "magnanimity and refinement" (99). In light of what we've explored in the previous section, there also can be little question that one of Thoreau's chief purposes in using commercial language was to drive these points home. It is true that he used the rhetoric of the market to mock it and to expose its failure, but he also used it to reveal alternative ways of thinking and acting—"buying" the world with imagination rather than with money. The strategy in his play with language was always double-edged: designed to broaden, as well as to expose, the meaning of the vocabulary of trade and wealth.

Yet again it is important not to claim too much for this line of analysis.

Thoreau's idealism was never quite so all-inclusive or self-confident as that of Emerson, whose views of the market were otherwise remarkably like his in many respects. Thoreau probably saw more clearly than his friend and mentor how difficult it would be to reconcile the different ambitions of the idealist and the materialist. (He once asked himself in his journal, "But what is the use of trying to live simply . . . when those to whom you are allied insanely want and will have a thousand other things which neither you nor they can raise and nobody else, perchance, will pay for? The fellow-man to whom you are yoked is a steer that is ever bolting right the other way.") Also by comparison to Emerson, the range of moods that informed Thoreau's practice as a connected critic was somewhat broader in its variety. He could be patriotic, elegiac, prophetic, scolding, sardonic, angry, and despairing, depending on where one chooses to dip into *Walden*.[29]

It is important to notice, too, that Thoreau was careful to point out that there were certain already established moral accommodations with the market that he found hypocritical and unacceptable. Philanthropy in particular represented a moral balancing act of which he wanted no part. Thoreau saw clearly that, for all the new wealth in antebellum America, a disturbingly large number of his contemporaries lived in poverty and misery. And during his two years at Walden Pond he continued to encounter that paradox, discovering that the area around Walden once had been where the poor Irish and blacks of Concord lived. Yet despite a genuine sympathy for the poor, Thoreau was no admirer of those who wanted to do more to provide for them. In his view, the profusion and generosity of charitable institutions in New England represented, in large part, what current historians would describe as an exercise in social control. Thoreau thought it naïve to see charity as an effort by those with wealth to honor their good fortune by sharing some of it with others. "Philanthropy is almost the only virtue which is sufficiently appreciated by mankind," he conceded, but then added quickly that "it is greatly overrated; and it is our selfishness that overrates it" (68). In Thoreau's view, the new "philosophy of the almshouse" had two main practical results. The first was to justify

---

29. *The Journal of Henry Thoreau*, ed. Bradford Torrey and Francis H. Allen, 14 vols. (Boston, 1906), 8:8. Robert Sattelmeyer, "The Remaking of *Walden*," in *Writing the American Classics*, ed. James Barbour and Tom Quirk (Chapel Hill, 1990), 61–63, suggests that *Walden* can be approached as two books. The early chapters betray a lineage in lecture material in various ways, the most obvious of which is a diversity of rhetorical styles. The later more introspective chapters draw more heavily from Thoreau's private journal.

material acquisitiveness by quieting the souls of the rich. The other was to encourage the dependency of the poor by encouraging them to believe their condition was unavoidable. Neither served to address what Thoreau saw as the chief affliction of poverty: the lack of self-respect among the poor themselves.

Thoreau argued that the aim of true reform was to create a society of individuals largely dependent upon themselves and therefore unencumbered by the material things produced for sale in the market. Here philanthropy obviously would be unnecessary. For the ideology of "doing-good" for the poor requires the economic inequality that comes with the production and exchange of commodities, and so the practice of charity within a market economy only serves to confirm and uphold the problem it pretends to remedy. If the chief affliction of poverty for the poor themselves was a lack of self-respect, this was entirely the by-product of living in a society where the pursuit of wealth was continually held up as the chief purpose of man's daily existence. When Thoreau discovered the starving and filthy family of John Field, an immigrant Irishman, living near Walden in a miserable hut, he recognized its complete degradation. Yet it clearly was the spiritual, not the material, impoverishment of John Field that troubled him. Thoreau observed that Field was an "honest, hard-working, but shiftless" man—shiftless precisely because he had come to America pursuing the illusion "here you could get tea, and coffee, and meat everyday," and despite the failure of all his efforts to realize that dream had yet to give it up (184–85). Thoreau never wrote about the poor to glorify the dignity of their poverty. What he stressed recurrently was that the question of poverty was inseparable from the larger question, What would America become? So long as the national purpose was seen to be the creation and accumulation of more wealth, Thoreau thought there could never be an effective social remedy for the indignity of poverty. "Superfluous wealth," he wrote, "can buy superfluities only" (293).

The reasons for Thoreau's dismissal of philanthropy as a moral restraint on material acquisitiveness seem straightforward enough: it was, more often than not, counterfeit virtue, rooted in self-righteous concern for the good opinion of others; it embraced the materialism of American life instead of calling it into question. It is precisely here, however, that some modern scholars want to locate what appears to be the most curious paradox in Thoreau's views of the market. He could say repeatedly that money brought more evil than good to America, and warn that riches were of no avail to those who wanted lives with spiritual purpose. Yet it is fair to ask if the apparent extremity of Thoreau's proposed alternative—embodied most famously in his concluding plea that all individuals seek only to "mind your own business" (290)—in the end also served to preclude any systematic effort to prescribe or govern manners for the sake of some higher public good. In fact, Thoreau's consistent refusal to draw a program of reform out of his criticism of the market has recently given rise to the view that he thereby came to demonstrate an "unwitting kinship" with the very behavior he deplored. The final image *Walden* leaves us with, Michael Gilmore has argued, is that of a solitary, self-absorbed individual, a figure utterly indifferent to the common good—and that image ironically enough seems to amount to a distorted "reflection of the laissez-faire individualist pursuing his private economic interest at the expense of the public welfare."[30]

Yet the argument that the Walden Pond experiment created a world as morally restricted in its way as that of the marketplace points to a paradox that dissolves upon close inspection. To begin with, this interpretation turns on a one-sided reading of Thoreau's intentions as a critic of the market that has been challenged throughout this chapter. It is a mistake to say that his views of trade and commerce were marked by absolute opposition or undifferentiated antagonism. Thoreau's experiment, as we have seen, put him a little to the side, not outside, of the market. Moreover, as we shall see, because Thoreau never presented his experiment as the foundation for a complete and self-contained alternative to the market, it makes little sense to approach them as entirely comparable realms of human experience.

The more important interpretive issue this reading raises, however, lies with the question of what practical implications we are entitled to draw out of Thoreau's venture. Here we ought at least to begin by taking seriously what Thoreau himself said were the *limits* of his accomplishments. He was, as we have noted already, explicit in urging his readers not to take *Walden* as a reformer's manual. (Here, too, is another major difference between *Walden* and the antebellum house-pattern genre: Thoreau insisted that his years at Walden Pond did not present a "pattern" for others to follow.) He was also explicit in reminding them that his text was a record of an experiment that had long since come to an end. From the outset of

30. Michael T. Gilmore, *American Romanticism and the Marketplace* (Chicago, 1985), 44. Also see Sacvan Bercovitch, *The American Jeremiad* (Madison, 1978), 187.

Walden, Thoreau made it clear that both of those points taken together cautioned that the importance of the practical details of his way of living at the pond ought not to be overestimated. "I would not have any one adopt *my* mode of living on any account," he wrote. "I desire that there may be as many different persons in the world as possible; but I would have each one be very careful to find out and pursue *his own* way, and not his father's or his mother's or his neighbor's instead" (64). It was, then, a democratic spirit of experiment—a cultural ethos of assertive individualism—which Thoreau championed, never the particular regimen of his days at the pond. Indeed, in his conclusion he explained that he had ended his experiment precisely when it threatened to become another confining routine of the sort he had gone to the pond to escape in the first place: "I left the woods for as good a reason as I went there. Perhaps it seemed to me that I had several more lives to live, and could not spare any more time for that one. It is remarkable how easily and insensibly we fall into a particular route, and make a beaten track for ourselves" (288). He then repeated that his life at Walden had never come to represent anything in the way of a utopian alternative to the acquisitiveness of the market. Husbandry surely was one way in which men might build lives characterized by greater self-reliance and minimal involvement in exchange, but it was by no means the only one. In fact, part of what Thoreau discovered at Walden Pond was that his own already chosen occupation as a part-time day laborer was "the most independent life of any," and it was that occupation he resumed when he returned to Concord (63).

What *Walden* affirmed, then, might be called Thoreau's democratic faith, his confidence that ordinary individuals had the resources to live fuller lives of their own making.[31] "I learned this, at least, by my experiment," he concluded, "that if one advances confidently in the direction of his dreams, and endeavors to live the life which he has imagined, he will meet with a success unexpected in common hours" (288). If every man is

---

31. George Kateb, *The Inner Ocean: Individualism and Democratic Culture* (Ithaca, 1992), 77–105, explores this side of Thoreau in much greater detail. On Kateb's account, Thoreau joins Emerson and Whitman as the greatest proponents of a theory of "democratic individuality" that expresses itself in three interrelated themes: (i) resisting encroachments of the state into new areas of life; (ii) admonishing and encouraging individuals to accept responsibility for themselves in their life projects; and (iii) defining a new relation to all experience, which may be called either a philosophical or poetical relation to reality. Kateb observes that economic activity and concerns have no important place in this theory. Here and in the previous chapter I am of course arguing against that view.

potentially his own hero, it surely is a mistake to read Thoreau's concluding plea to mind your own business as a prescription for retreat or withdrawal. In fact, if we look at the entirety of the plea he actually made—
something most modern commentators seem remarkably unable to do—
what we find is a considerably more complex and interesting message.

"Let every one mind his own business," Thoreau wrote, *"and endeavor to
be what he was made"* (290). It is fair to see this as a précis of *Walden* so long
as we don't overlook the fact that Thoreau was here repeating a point
already made—and perhaps made more clearly—at the outset of the book:
the possibilities of self-exploration and self-knowledge remain open to all
men, whatever their status or place in society. Minding your own business
in this setting means attending more carefully to the ordinary activity of
one's life, because its benefits potentially are as great as those Thoreau discovered with his deliberate life in the woods. The life of any individual can
mean more, wherever and however one may choose to live it.[32] There is an
often fiercely egalitarian sentiment at work throughout *Walden* that
rejects any view of life that would restrict access to the higher values in
imagination and heroic effort to a select, aristocratic few. Like Emerson
before him, Thoreau insisted that, in America at least, the possibilities of
a better life were within the grasp of all men. In urging "everyone to be
what he was made," however, faithful imitation of his example was hardly
what he had in mind. Thoreau never advocated voluntary poverty; he suggested it was merely one possibility.

Yet it is surely too simple to say that the final image *Walden* leaves us
with is that of a defiant egalitarian, too easy to replace the hermit with the
iconoclast, thereby only trading one cliché for another. Thoreau did urge
others to follow him in shaking off habit and convention. He refused to
believe that constraints imposed by institutions such as the market might
leave individuals powerless to shape their own destinies. "Shall a man go
and hang himself," he wrote, simply "because he belongs to the race of
pygmies, and not be the biggest pygmy that he can?" (290). But it would be
misleading to conclude from this that Thoreau's stance ultimately was designed to undermine the values and institutions of the marketplace. Thoreau himself insisted he had no interest in making his world over. While
he despised the materialism and inequality of antebellum America, his life-
project was not to create a different and more economically just world. The

32. Ibid., 89–90.

example of his Walden experiment was meant rather to inspire others to pursue more deliberate and thoughtful lives in the world that was given to them. "However mean your life is, meet and live it," he argued in his conclusion. "Do not shun it and call it hard names. It is not so bad as you are. . . . The faultfinder will find faults even in paradise. Love your life, poor as it is" (292).

Thoreau offered no clear way out for others, and he explicitly refused to posit his own ideal as a norm. Despite his own estrangement from his commercial times, that estrangement never dictated either complete withdrawal or unqualified opposition. Nor did it point toward concrete economic and social reforms. What Thoreau sought, in the end, might be described as an intellectual position that mirrored an actual place he had once made for himself at Walden Pond: a place both outside and inside the market—outside because Thoreau obviously wanted to present himself as an arbiter of its value, but inside too because the most he finally expected of his countrymen was acknowledgment of the need for an antipecuniary ethic to restrain their acquisitiveness and recognition that trade and commerce were "but means, and not the end."[33]

4

Gathered together, the various strands of this chapter provide what may be a surprisingly straightforward answer to the question raised at the outset: Why were there several sides to Thoreau's thinking about the market? The evidence explored here suggests that the variety of his attitudes, in the final analysis, reflected a readiness to compromise. Given Thoreau's long-standing and well-earned reputation as a slashing critic of the market, that may seem a preposterous claim. But only if we forget that compromise has two distinct meanings. There is compromise in the sense of giving up a single principle, in light of its inapplicability to life, which sounds, and is, wrong as a description of Thoreau's position. And there is compromise in the sense of recognizing that our principles conflict with one another, and cannot be realized at once, and this is a neglected side of *Walden* to which I've tried to draw more attention here. In fact, it is arguably the best way of making sense of that combination of fierce criticism

---

33. "Life Without Principle," 728.

and ambivalent attachment that marked his thinking about the market. Thoreau, it is true, found his age dull, materialistic, timid, and conformist. Yet while he detested many of the things he saw around him, he also refused to believe he lived in a disenchanted world. The market certainly was not the soil on which the greatness of individuals might blossom, but it was not quite poisoned soil either. Life *with* principle did not require that the market be overthrown, nor did it dictate complete withdrawal. Thoreau never said that he had gone off to Walden simply to show others that if they did not like their world they could move away. Cavell has observed correctly that the main task of *Walden* was "to discover how to earn and spend our most wakeful hours—whatever we are doing." But he ought to have italicized the last phrase.[34] Thoreau proposed neither retreat nor institutional reform, but instead the fashioning of new individuals who could manage the temptations of a market society—especially its ethic of consumption and its increasingly commercialized popular culture—without losing their bearings.

This view may not do full justice to certain other interesting and important aspects of Thoreau's thinking about the market—especially his understanding of the relationship between commerce and slavery, which I will consider separately in the next part of this book. It also may be that no single approach to Thoreau will ever provide a completely satisfactory interpretation of his views. For a growing number of modern readers, the resistance of *Walden* to simplification and straightforward analysis has become its chief claim on our attention.[35] Yet too much can be made of Thoreau's supposed inaccessibility. He did say that his pages admit of more than one interpretation; yet he also said he had no desire to be obscure. Thoreau may at times sound like the inhabitant of a separate world, but that finally was not what he meant to be. Those who insist *Walden* is a supremely difficult text inevitably lose sight of the writer determined to follow Emerson's lead in defining and interpreting the "newness" of America. Like Emerson, Thoreau never thought the ideals he championed were obscure. What he believed was that they were unrealized and yet still immanent in American life—immanent, it seems, mostly because he divided his

---

34. Cavell, *Senses of Walden*, 5.

35. See, e.g., Walter Benn Michaels, "Walden's False Bottoms," in *Modern Critical Views: Henry David Thoreau*, ed. Harold Bloom (New York, 1987), 79–95; and Gregory S. Jay, *America the Scrivener: Deconstruction and the Subject of Literary History* (Ithaca, 1990), 1–8.

nation by generations, not by social or economic classes. For all its flaws, Thoreau's "true America" remained young and therefore still a place of promise. There is nothing in *Walden* of the European Romantics' complaint of having been born too late, no longing for a past that seemed superior to the present. It was to the "young men" of Concord that Thoreau made a direct appeal at the outset of *Walden*. It was "old men" and their "old deeds" that invited some of his fiercest criticism. "My seniors," he proclaimed, " have told me nothing, and probably cannot tell me anything to the purpose" (8). They had lost sight of, perhaps never even had understood, the real promise of America, choosing dull routines and material comforts over a life dedicated to the free testing and measurement of all their capacities. Yet Thoreau did not see the betrayal of his elders as a closing off of all future opportunities to realize America's promise. At the end of *Walden*, he beckoned his readers to imagine a future America that was to be created in the spirit of his own life: egalitarian, adventurous, critical of established customs and institutions, and engaged with the diversity of nature and human society. The label "alienated" will not stick to Thoreau. For all his complaining, he was, in writing *Walden*, a man who had taken on a cultural mission: to provide—in the carefully recorded example of his own life—the stimulus for a clearer and stronger understanding of that ethos of democratic individualism by which his contemporaries claimed to live.

Finally, to approach Thoreau as a connected critic of American institutions also points to some largely unexplored questions concerning Thoreau's place in studying the history of American culture. We are not used to thinking of him as something other than a figure of neglected opposition. But this is a habit we ought to abandon, despite its sometimes distinguished pedigree. The most familiar account of Thoreau's career, dating back to Emerson's famous obituary essay, concludes that his reputation was a local matter and that his career as a writer was a story of hard times and failure that gave way to modest success late in his life. Assuming Thoreau's obscurity in his own time also fits neatly with the equally familiar view that, because of the extremity of his opinions, few of his contemporaries understood or wanted to hear what he had to say. In a society rushing headlong to embrace the market, it is no surprise to discover that a denigrator of the commercialization of American life failed to gain a popular audience. Recent scholarship, however, suggests that contemporary evaluation of Thoreau was considerably higher than the traditional account allows.[36] This chapter has tried to show that we also have something more complex and interesting in Thoreau's criticism of American economic life than the views of an iconoclast. Taken together, these revised portraits suggest that any approach that continues to come to Thoreau by way of Emerson's famous obituary risks at least two fundamental misunderstandings. For Emerson not only misrepresented the cultural standing of Thoreau's work during his lifetime; he also was misleading about Thoreau's general disposition as a social critic. The writer Emerson said "did not feel himself except in opposition" was never in absolute opposition to any of the American institutions of his day, except for slavery.[37] Any adequate understanding of Thoreau, then, must bring more clearly into view two closely related sides of his thinking that Emerson seemed remarkably unable to see: his determination to offer the inhabitants of a market society a good deal more than criticism, and his actual success in overcoming the critic's impulse to be no more than a faultfinder. Complaining may have been one of Thoreau's specialties, but he took no special pride in it. "The attitude of resistance," he once wrote, "is one of weakness, inasmuch as it only faces an enemy; it has its back to all that is truly attractive."[38] Tossed between his hopes and fears, Thoreau remained determined to pursue his hopes. In the end, he was unwilling to embrace the frequent pessimism of his own analysis of the condition of American society. It is that refusal—Thoreau's determination to outlast the defeat of his hopes, his insistence that those hopes did not embody exorbitant demands—not his more familiar complaints about the materialism of his age, which I have tried to make better sense of in this chapter.

---

36. Reynolds, *Beneath the American Renaissance*, 497–506. I offer my own account of the publication and initial reception history of *Walden* in ch. 8.

37. Emerson, "Thoreau," in *Selected Essays*, 396. It is astonishing how many things about Thoreau Emerson chose to leave out of his eulogy. As R. Jackson Wilson has recently observed, "anyone who read the published version of the eulogy would not have been able to tell that Thoreau had ever published anything." See Wilson, *Figures of Speech: American Writers and the Literary Marketplace, from Benjamin Franklin to Emily Dickinson* (New York, 1989), 215–16. On the immediate historical setting of the eulogy, see Gabrielle Fitzgerald, "In Time of War: The Context of Emerson's 'Thoreau,'" *American Transcendentalist Quarterly* 41 (Winter 1979): 5–12.

38. *Journal of Henry Thoreau*, 9:36.

2

A "Vexed and Disorganizing Question": Emerson, Thoreau, and American Slavery

So now, the arrival in the world of such men as Toussaint, and the Haytian heroes, or of the leaders of their race in Barbadoes and Jamaica, outweighs in good omen all the English and American humanity. The anti-slavery of the whole world is dust in the balance before this. . . . I esteem the occasion of this jubilee to be the proud discovery that the black race can contend with the white.

—Emerson, "Emancipation in the British West Indies"

. . . America, the most prosperous country in the Universe, has the greatest calamity in the Universe, Negro Slavery.

—Emerson, "The Fugitive Slave Law"

Much has been said about American slavery, but I think that we do not even yet realize what slavery is.

—Thoreau, "Slavery in Massachusetts"

3

Emerson and Thoreau in the
Historiography of American Slavery

DURING THE SECOND WEEK of December 1842, when it was announced at the Concord Lyceum that Wendell Phillips, having accepted an invitation sent to him by Henry David Thoreau, would lecture during the following week, a fearful curator named John Keyes immediately protested and moved as a resolution, "that as this Lyceum is established for social and mutual improvement, the introduction of the vexed and disorganizing question of Abolition or Slavery should be kept out of it." This motion was defeated, with Emerson joining Thoreau and a majority of the other members of the Lyceum in voting against it. But dissension over discussing the question of slavery resurfaced the following winter, when Phillips was given a second invitation to speak at the Concord Lyceum. Once more Keyes protested, now condemning Phillips's first speech as "vile, pernicious, and abominable," and calling a town meeting to censure him. Warned in advance by Thoreau, Phillips attended the meeting uninvited and responded successfully to the conservatives' criticism. The decisive confrontation in the Concord Lyceum, however, took place in the spring of 1845. Finding themselves outvoted when they again opposed extending an invitation to Phillips to speak on slavery, Keyes and two other like-minded curators resigned in protest on March 5, and then were replaced by Emerson, Thoreau, and Samuel Barrett, a local Unitarian minister. Not surprisingly, this group immediately issued the invitation and Phillips spoke on March 11. The next day Thoreau sent a letter to William Lloyd Garrison, proudly recounting the recent dispute at the Concord Lyceum and firmly defending Phillips's right to speak. The most interesting fact about Phillips's address, Thoreau wrote, was "The readiness of the people at large, of whatever sect or party, to entertain with good will and hospitality, the most revolutionary and heretical opinions." Not surprisingly, Garrison printed the letter in its entirety in the March 28, 1845, *Liberator*.[1]

The Emerson and Thoreau who emerge from this story—defenders of a passionate and committed abolitionist and champions of free speech at a time when "entertaining" abolitionists "with good will and hospitality" was widely recognized as serving the cause of abolition—contrast sharply with the figures to be found in more recent accounts. Many modern historians have assumed that Emerson and Thoreau did relatively little to promote effective opposition to slavery, and that their supposed unwillingness to do more than they did must somehow be explained, then justified or criticized. Criticism has been more plentiful than justification. Since the publication of Stanley Elkins's *Slavery: A Problem in American Institutional and Intellectual Life* in 1959, historians repeatedly have blamed them for a supposed shared refusal to conceive of slavery reform as anything more than a private moral concern—a question between the individual and his or her own conscience. Elkins dismissed Emerson and Thoreau (and several other prominent Concord intellectuals) as figures who sought to maintain "a simple and harsh moral purity" and thereby failed to seize on more concrete alternative approaches that might have achieved peaceful reform of the institutional supports of American slavery.[2] This criticism has been

---

1. My account of the controversy surrounding Phillips draws from F. B. Sanborn, *The Life of Henry David Thoreau* (Boston, 1917), 469–74, and Walter Harding, *The Days of Henry Thoreau: A Biography* (New York, 1962), 175–76. (While dated in several respects, these volumes are considerably more attentive to Thoreau's complex cultural identity than recent biographies.) Thoreau's letter to the *Liberator* is rpt. as "Wendell Phillips before Concord Lyceum," in *The Writings of Henry David Thoreau, Reform Papers*, ed. Wendell Glick (Princeton, 1973), 59–62.

2. Stanley Elkins, *Slavery: A Problem in American Institutional and Intellectual Life* (New York, 1959). The outlines of Elkins's approach to Emerson were anticipated in Arthur M. Schlesinger Jr., *Age of Jackson* (New York, 1945), and subsequently refined and expanded to include Thoreau in various works, among the best known of which are George Fredrickson,

qualified somewhat lately by scholars who, following the lead of Aileen Kraditor, argue that Emerson and Thoreau cannot be taken as accurate guides to what motivated the organized opponents of slavery, and as a result they have been relegated to the wings of historical study of the values and strategies of abolitionism. Yet the assumption that Emerson and Thoreau could have done more, and thought more deeply, about their opposition to slavery persists. Anne C. Rose, for example, has faulted Emerson for not sustaining the broad reforming impulse of his early writings, thereby managing to stay out of popular antislavery politics in the 1850s. But Rose's complaint sounds much like that first voiced by Elkins. While historians today tend to downplay the significance of what Emerson and Thoreau said and did, the consensus remains that their opposition to slavery was largely a matter of absolute moral intransigence. The best that can be said for them seems to be that, while their moral disgust with slavery made for strong rhetoric, it proved an ineffective alternative to the more urgent work of conceiving concrete strategies to end American slavery.[3]

I

Part 2 of this book aims to reverse this emphasis by focusing on aspects of Emerson's and Thoreau's understanding of slavery that have received too little systematic study. My primary purpose is to identify their views more precisely by continuing the line of interpretation I pursued in part 1, where Emerson and Thoreau were portrayed as connected or loyal critics of their society—thinkers who found fault with economic practices and institutions of their day, yet were never intent on being subversive in their criticism. Emerson and Thoreau saw their ideals as unrealized yet still immanent in American society; hence, their fault-finding was not designed

---

The Inner Civil War: Northern Intellectuals and the Crisis of the Union (New York, 1965), and Bertram Wyatt-Brown, "Stanley Elkins and Northern Reform Culture," in *Yankee Saints and Southern Sinners* (Baton Rouge, 1985), 13–41.

3. Aileen S. Kraditor, *Means and Ends in American Abolitionism: Garrison and His Critics on Strategy and Tactics, 1834–1850* (New York, 1967), ch. 2; Anne C. Rose, *Transcendentalism as a Social Movement, 1830–1850* (New Haven, 1981). No recent study of American abolitionism pays more than passing attention to Emerson or Thoreau, and they now seem at best marginal figures in recent histories of the antebellum period more generally. See, e.g., James McPherson's widely acclaimed *Battle Cry of Freedom: The Civil War Era* (New York, 1988), in which Emerson and Thoreau are mentioned only in passing in his account of John Brown.

to voice absolute opposition to antebellum American institutions. Slavery was, however, an inescapable exception to this rule. As no other issue did, it tested their shared assumption that the promise of American life could be defined without calling for fundamental reform. For how could they remain connected critics of political and social institutions they saw as deeply implicated in an abominable human practice? How could they repudiate American slavery and not in some fashion repudiate America as well?

Emerson and Thoreau answered those questions in different ways at different times, and I believe we have yet to grasp the full range of their responses, or to locate those responses clearly in the history of American abolitionist thought. Two preliminary examples will suffice here. It is well known that their public repudiations of slavery came slowly. Both distrusted the religious zeal that inspired and sustained the American abolitionist movement. Hence, they remained reluctant—even while defending John Brown—to identify themselves with collective efforts to end slavery. Emerson and Thoreau shared the shame of American slavery, but they resented that sharing and insisted their opposition to slavery was never a matter of expiating a personal sense of guilt or furthering a "holy enterprise." Less well known, however, is the fact that when they did speak out against slavery, neither appeared to have qualms about heightening the sectional self-consciousness and antagonism that made slavery such a politically volatile issue in America. Indeed, at the time the Civil War began, both Emerson and Thoreau believed the North would be morally better off without the South, and that the political union of the American states was no longer worth preserving.

It would be a mistake to say, however, that Emerson and Thoreau were simply spokesmen for the sectional interests of Northern states.[4] In the end, their opposition to slavery had less to do with the direct injustice and cruelty of Southern slavery than with what Thoreau called "the cowardice and want of principle in Northern men." Both Emerson and Thoreau believed the most irresponsible people in antebellum America were Northern judges and politicians who had chosen to ignore the steady expansion of slavery or to compromise whenever confronted with choices that might

---

4. Lewis E. Simpson, *Mind and the American Civil War: A Meditation on Lost Causes* (Baton Rouge, 1989), 48–49, presents Emerson as the most important voice of nineteenth-century "New England cultural imperialism." For reasons I discuss at the conclusion of ch. 6, I think Simpson's portrait is overdrawn. It should be said, however, that Emerson was a much-maligned figure in Southern literary journals. (See ch. 8.)

have blocked its expansion. It also is too simple to explain such sentiments, as Elkins did, as evidence pointing to cloistered Northern intellectuals standing aloof from the institutions of their society, opting to fight
"slavery in its universal relations" alone. Emerson's stress on the ways in
which the "forms" of American life—its courts, churches, legislatures, and
schools—had failed to correct the problem of slavery was a recurring
theme in his speeches and writings. And perhaps the most striking line in
Thoreau's antislavery writings—to which I'll return several times in chapter 5—was, in part, a criticism of abolitionists for failing to understand the
full strength of slavery's Northern institutional supports: "Much has been
said about American slavery," he wrote in 1854, "but I think we do not
even yet realize what slavery is."[5] Thoreau thought himself an exception,
but not simply because he saw more clearly than others how completely
slavery had subverted America's commitment to its founding moral principles. His point here was also a practical one. Northern abolitionists would
never accomplish their goal, he was suggesting, until they understood that
their chief task was to persuade their contemporaries to recognize and
then to remove the powerful political and cultural supports of slavery
within their own supposedly free states.

2

For both Emerson and Thoreau, then, the question of what slavery is
had three crucial additions that again served to identify them (as well as
other abolitionists whose views they shared) as connected critics. Two concerned questions of strategy: how to interpret the North's continuing
acceptance of slavery and how to alter public opinion in the North. It was
here that the argument about slavery became largely an argument about
the meaning of the North's way of life, with Emerson and Thoreau, like
other opponents of slavery, finding justification for their cause in the claim
that economic, moral, and political principles *all* Northerners shared
demanded abolition. They insisted too that ending slavery was essential to
removing certain fundamental incongruities in their country that had
been accepted by its founders. In this context it was also slavery, not abo-

---

5. Thoreau, "Slavery in Massachusetts," in *The Writings of Henry D. Thoreau, Reform
Papers*, ed. Wendell Glick (Princeton, 1973), 96.

litionism, which could be condemned as the chief source of continuing discord in America.

The third concern that identified Emerson's and Thoreau's opposition to slavery as connected criticism was somewhat broader in its scope: how to understand the relationship between current efforts to end slavery and larger economic changes taking place during the first half of the nineteenth century. What had caused the abolitionist movement to come into existence in the first place? And exactly what did its appeals have to do with the spread of market practices and institutions? In addressing such questions, Emerson and Thoreau again joined other abolitionists in attempting to provide their contemporaries a historical foundation for opposing slavery. In the process, they also touched on what has since become one of the central puzzles of modern Anglo-American historiography, and at the moment is the subject of a new and developing scholarly controversy that I will trace briefly here. The general course of debate thus far has focused mostly on two issues. The first is whether the abolitionists' single-minded concern with chattel slavery ought to be seen as a significant limitation. Did it somehow serve to turn attention away from historically new forms of exploitation occurring in the wage-labor systems of factories of the late eighteenth and early nineteenth centuries? Abolitionists are no longer charged—as they once were—with hypocrisy or conscious deception. But fundamental disagreement remains about what some historians maintain is the central puzzle surrounding the abolitionists' selectivity. Responding to this first question opens out onto the larger historical question of how we ought to define the primary moral and cultural effects of the early growth of "the market." At first glance, the parallel development of abolitionism with the emerging market economies of Britain and America seems antithetical because of an apparent divergence in the psychological motives in which each rested. Where the market encouraged self-interested behavior—precisely what Thoreau once condemned as "life without principle"—anti-slavery reformers by contrast sought to relieve the suffering of others. How, then, do we explain the historical concomitance of two such opposite tendencies? And what exactly did the appeals of abolitionists have to do with the spread of the market?

At the moment, we have at least three different ways of formulating a historical linkage. The first, associated chiefly with David Brion Davis, seeks to account for the unprecedented strength of abolitionist movements in Britain and America during the first half of the nineteenth century largely in the context of an emerging free labor economy. On Davis's account, abolitionism represented a highly selective response to labor exploitation that helped crystallize the values and ascendent capitalist "middle class" and inadvertently identify them with the interests of society at large. For in isolating slavery as an unacceptable form of labor exploitation, he has argued, abolitionists implicitly turned attention away from the exploitation of a new class of factory workers. Davis is careful to point out that abolitionists typically did not consciously intend to serve the needs and interests of a capitalist class concerned with labor discipline and the legitimation of novel economic practices. Yet the heart of his argument is that their single-minded concern with one kind of human exploitation appears to have sustained a language of social reform that offered considerably less critical perspectives on other forms of exploitation, particularly that of workers suffering through the transition to modern industrial capitalism.[6]

Few historians doubt the contention that the impulses behind the antislavery phenomenon somehow must be linked to the economic order from which they emerged. But some now argue that Davis's effort to define the link chiefly in terms of class interest has come to obscure a more important historical question about the abolitionist movement—namely, why did it come into existence in the first place? Attempts to answer that question have prompted two alternative accounts of what linked the capitalist market to the cause of abolition. Thomas L. Haskell has argued that the market provided a vital historical precondition for the emergence of the antislavery movement by serving to expand conventional limits of causal perception and moral responsibility. Whatever its other long-term influences in defining the ideas and values of an ascendent middle class, Haskell notes, the market had a more immediate impact in supporting abolitionist sentiment by promoting certain new habits of mind—particularly the keeping of contractual promises and attending to the long-term consequences of one's acts—which pressed outward on the existing conventions of moral judgment. The practical upshot of this change in attitudes, he concludes, was to compel certain exceptionally scrupulous individuals to attack slavery and to create circumstances where others were now prepared to listen

---

6. David Brion Davis, *The Problem of Slavery in the Age of Revolution* (Ithaca, 1975), esp. 346–62. Ronald G. Walters, *The Antislavery Appeal: American Abolitionism after 1830* (Baltimore, 1976), is perhaps the most systematic interpretation of the antislavery movement as a stalking horse of Northern market values and institutions.

and comprehend the abolitionist appeal. Haskell's central point is not that the market bred humane action, but rather that in the particular circumstance of late eighteenth-and early nineteenth-century Anglo-American culture the market happened to have been the force that pushed the causal perception of some individuals across a threshold that hitherto had made the misery of slaves seem a necessary evil.[7]

On somewhat different grounds, Howard Temperley has joined Haskell in exploring ways in which abolitionism can be linked to the market without having to suggest that "attempts to enlist sympathy for faraway slaves were designed, either consciously or unconsciously, to divert attention from other evils nearer to home." Temperley suggests that the supposed puzzle of abolitionist neglect of wage labor fades once we recognize that, despite some opposing principles, capitalism and antislavery thought were for a time "overlapping systems of belief." Both assumed, for example, that the most dramatic increases in economic wealth were occurring in free-labor societies. And that assumption in turn allowed opponents of slavery to join classical political economists in adding the charge of unnecessary anachronism to that of gross injustice. The same assumption also informed the abolitionists' association with another emerging cultural force of their time: nationalist sentiment. In America, for example, the movement to end slavery sparked a prolonged and angry debate about what was and what was not American, and in this debate abolitionists often cast themselves as prophets of a new national unity. They insisted that ending slavery was essential to removing certain fundamental incongruities in their country that had been accepted by its founders. And in this context it was of course slavery, not abolitionism, that could be condemned as the chief source of continuing discord in America. Indeed, it was the institution

---

7. See Thomas L. Haskell, "Capitalism and the Origins of the Humanitarian Sensibility, Part 1," *American Historical Review* 90 (April 1985): 339–61; "Capitalism and the Origins of the Humanitarian Sensibility, Part 2," *American Historical Review* 90 (June 1985): 547–66. A lengthy controversy has developed out of this article: David Brion Davis, "Reflections on Abolitionism and Ideological Hegemony," *American Historical Review* 92 (October 1987): 797–812; John Ashworth, "The Relationship between Capitalism and Humanitarianism," *American Historical Review* 92 (October 1987): 813–28; Thomas L. Haskell, "Convention and Hegemonic Interest in the Debate over Antislavery: A Reply to Davis and Ashworth," *American Historical Review* 92 (October 1987): 829–78. All these essays, with final responses from Davis and Ashworth, are now reprinted in *The Antislavery Debate: Capitalism as a Problem in Historical Interpretation*, ed. and intro. Thomas Bender (Berkeley, 1992). My account of Davis draws on Bender's introduction, 5.

that most stood out against all the still needed economic and political changes abolitionists associated with the progressive development of their country.[8]

While specialists have written extensively about the almost simultaneous development of antislavery sentiment and industrial market economies in Britain and America, they have not shown much interest in clarifying what Emerson and Thoreau had to say on this point. That lack of interest makes some sense, since there are sentences that seem to show that Emerson and Thoreau alike viewed the relationship between abolitionism and the market in terms modern historians no longer find acceptable. Emerson's early opposition to slavery did represent, in part, an extension of the nineteenth-century liberal view that the benefits of a free market economy were universal—which is to say that, like many other abolitionists, he initially disapproved of slavery because he believed that freedom and prosperity simply went hand in hand—and freedom meant, in part, having willing workers and customers as opposed to unwilling ones. Thoreau, on the other hand, frequently portrayed abolitionist ideals as belonging strictly to a transcendental realm of moral choice, and here supported a second view of the campaign against slavery that few historians today stand ready to defend. Thoreau often said bluntly that abolition ran directly counter to the North's economic interests, and that the continuing acceptance of slavery was an expression of how deeply the nation had been corrupted by its economic wealth. In this context, putting an end to slavery was a matter of opting for justice whatever it might cost in economic terms. In contrast to Emerson, then, Thoreau apparently believed that acting on principle required his contemporaries to choose between their freedom and their prosperity.

Yet while these perspectives are at odds with what modern specialists have revealed about the tangled economic dimensions of slavery, there are other sentences that suggest that Emerson's and Thoreau's true sentiments regarding the relationship between abolition and the market are too complex to be set aside simply as dated or one-dimensional. Emerson did be-

---

8. Howard Temperley, "Capitalism, Slavery, and Ideology," *Past and Present* 75 (1977): 94–118; "Anti-Slavery as a Form of Cultural Imperialism," in *Anti-Slavery, Religion, and Reform: Essays in Memory of Roger Anstey*, ed. Christine Bolt and Seymour Drescher (Hamden, Conn., 1980), 335–50; "The Ideology of Antislavery," in *The Abolition of the Atlantic Slave Trade: Origins and Effects in Europe, Africa, and the Americas*, ed. David Ellis and James Walvin (Madison, 1981), 21–36.

lieve that slavery was an economic anachronism, but he never saw it as an accident or a "peculiar institution" standing outside of the mainstream of Western economic development. From the earliest times, he once observed, it was black slaves who had been the chief "producers of comfort and luxury in the civilized world."[9] (If Emerson retained his faith in the ideal of progress, it was by no means a blind faith.) Moreover, while Thoreau saw economic self-interest as one of the chief hurdles to effective opposition to slavery in the North, this would not prevent him from sometimes appealing to Northerners' concern about their property to stir opposition to slavery. Taking a close look at what Emerson and Thoreau had to say about the relationship between abolition and the workings of a market economy also shows that their opposition to slavery never turned solely on abstract appeals to conscience. Like other abolitionists, they sometimes fused economic and moral judgments so tightly that there is no point in drawing a line between them.

It is not my purpose to suggest here, however, that the intellectual foundations of their opposition to slavery were therefore more profound than modern historians have chosen to recognize. Neither Emerson nor Thoreau provided original or systematic accounts of the links between abolition and the market, and making better sense of their ambivalence and inconsistencies on this question will occupy some of my attention in the chapters that follow. There also is good reason for approaching their antislavery writings as something other than tight discursive essays. With the partial exception of Thoreau's "Resistance to Civil Government," their thinking about slavery first took shape in the form of public lectures and speeches.[10] Like other opponents of slavery, then, they spoke out chiefly to provoke and inspire. In this regard, a close reading of their texts also suggests that a large number of themes were being sounded at the same time—hence, it would be wrong to say that understanding the ways in which abolitionism was linked to the market was the most important of their themes.

Keeping these considerations in mind, then, the chapters in part 2 do not propose that Emerson and Thoreau offer us a neglected *interpretation*

9. Emerson, "Emancipation in the British West Indies," in *The Selected Writings of Ralph Waldo Emerson*, ed. Brooks Atkinson (New York, 1940), 832.

10. At times reprinted under the title "Civil Disobedience," Thoreau's essay originally appeared in print in May 1849, in the first and only volume of *Aesthetic Papers*, edited by Elizabeth Peabody. But the essay also had its origins in a lecture first delivered before the Concord Lyceum on January 26, 1848.

of the parallel development of abolitionist sentiment and America's market economy. They aim rather to establish two other points. The first is that both Emerson and Thoreau, although in somewhat different ways, can be approached as partial critics of American abolitionism itself—partial in the sense that their criticism was more a matter of complicating than challenging the existing values and strategies of that movement. The second (and perhaps more significant) point is that we ought to view their comments on the ties between abolitionism and the market chiefly against the background of a need they shared with other abolitionists: to understand the forces that impeded the success of abolition in America. During the two decades before the Civil War, like other opponents of slavery, both Emerson and Thoreau came to see the demand for abolition in America as an increasingly vain endeavor. All the events they referred to in their writings—from their Concord friend Samuel Hoar's futile effort, in 1844, to negotiate an end to seizures of black Massachusetts sailors in Southern ports to the hasty indictment, trial, and execution of John Brown fifteen years later—seemed to show that the abolitionist movement had yet to become an effective force in American life and that slavery remained a largely invulnerable ruling interest. In what follows, I want to show that keeping in mind the fact that Emerson and Thoreau viewed the historical predicament of American abolitionism in this way opens up a more nuanced appreciation of the themes they chose to sound in opposing slavery. Instead of taking them to task for not attempting to determine new policy, my approach rests on the assumption that Emerson and Thoreau—again like other abolitionists—had every reason *not* to keep faith with political and social institutions that consistently refused to present any significant opposition to slavery.[11]

In another respect, this approach is also meant to reverse what is currently thought to be the proper historical order of things in exploring the question of how abolitionist sentiment in general ought to be linked with the early development of market societies. Despite significant disagreements in attempts to explain how economic interest played a role in the spread of abolitionism, historians at the moment seem prepared to accept

---

11. See Kraditor, *Means and Ends in American Abolitionism*, 3–39. American abolitionists might also be approached as practitioners of crisis thinking, in the sense that, unlike their British counterparts in the first half of the nineteenth century, they were by circumstances forced to spend as much time considering what impeded their cause as what might serve to make it more attractive.

without much question that rapid social and economic changes in Britain and America in the first half of the nineteenth century supported equally striking changes in moral consciousness and social policy that marked that period. Restricting our attention to abolitionism (usually taken as the clearest expression of the latter changes), I do not doubt that we can speak of the first three decades of nineteenth-century British history as, in Martin Wiener's words, "years in which abolition was marching from victory to victory."[12] But the same narrative hardly applies to antebellum America. Until the Civil War, the American abolitionist movement by contrast was shaped by powerful feelings of defeat and the sense of a looming crisis that might permanently divide the nation. Most American opponents of slavery may have believed in moral and economic progress, but they also often spoke in anger and despair about the ascendancy of "Slave Power" and the refusal of Northern political leaders and judges to resist it. For those who fought for or defended abolition in America, then, there had yet to be enough in the way of widespread change either in moral consciousness or social policy when it came to slavery.[13] Most of the historical milestones in the American struggle over slavery, after all, turned out to be the work of opponents of the antislavery movement.

As a result, the relationship between efforts to end slavery and the larger social and economic changes taking place in antebellum America remained unclear; yet at the same time it came to dictate a strategy that alternated between criticism and accommodation. While abolitionists sometimes condemned trade and profit-seeking as concerns that served to rationalize the North's continuing complicity with the injustice of slavery, at other times they condemned slavery as an economic anachronism and believed that the demand for abolition could in fact be rooted in market values. Given the way in which they conceived of the historical predicament of American abolitionism, it would be unfair to stress the inconsistency of this approach at the expense of understanding its relationship to

12. Martin Wiener, "Market Cultures and 'Penal Cultures' in Britain, 1815–1900," unpublished paper presented at a conference on "The Culture of the Market," Murphy Institute of Political Economy, Tulane University, March 9–11, 1990.

13. There were important and long-standing connections between the British and American abolitionist movements. See Betty Fladeland, *Men and Brothers: Anglo-American Antislavery Cooperatives* (Urbana, 1971), and Howard Temperley, *British Antislavery, 1833–70* (Columbia, S.C., 1972), ch. 10. For a more detailed account of events that rendered optimism based on the British precedence increasingly irrelevant to American opponents of slavery, see David Turley, *The Culture of English Antislavery, 1780–1860* (London, 1991), ch. 7.

the overriding practical concern of the abolitionist movement, which clearly was to alter public opinion in the interest of a still unaccomplished transformation in moral sensibility. Those who had long since accommodated themselves to the injustice of slavery—the vast majority of Northern judges, ministers, politicians, and wealthy merchants—perhaps were beyond moral redemption. But the self-understanding of ordinary people in the Northern states was not. Hence, while Emerson, Thoreau, and other abolitionists criticized the passivity of their contemporaries, they also struggled not to alienate themselves from their popular audience. In practical terms, this meant that their calls to end slavery were not extended to demanding the creation of an entirely new moral sensibility, but instead to insisting that Northern men and women recognize that values they already embraced demanded repudiation of slavery.

A fully detailed demonstration of the prominence of this theme in the speeches and writings of American opponents of slavery other than Emerson and Thoreau would extend well beyond the boundaries of this book. But one particularly clear and significant statement of what might be described as the pragmatic side of American abolitionism is worth noting here. It appeared in a speech given by Wendell Phillips on January 27, 1853, in Boston before the Massachusetts Anti-Slavery Society:

> Our aim is to alter public opinion. Did we live in a market, our talk should be of dollars and cents, and we would seek to prove only that slavery was an unprofitable investment. Were the nation one great, pure church, we would sit down and reason of "righteousness, temperance, and judgment to come." Had slavery fortified itself in a college, we would load our cannons with cold facts, and wing our arrows with arguments. But we happen to live in the world—the world made up of thought and impulse, of self-conceit and self-interest, of weak men and wicked. To conquer, we must reach all. Our object is not to make every man a Christian or a philosopher, but to induce everyone to aid in the abolition of slavery. We expect to accomplish our object long before the nation is made over into saints or elevated into philosophers. To change public opinion, we use the very tools by which it was formed.[14]

We saw at the outset of this chapter that Phillips was an abolitionist whose views Emerson and Thoreau knew quite well. We shall see presently how their own efforts to alter opinions also attempted to "reach all."

---

14. Quoted in Louis Filler, *Wendell Phillips on Civil Rights and Freedom* (New York, 1965), 38.

4

"Emancipation in the British West Indies" and "The Fugitive Slave Law"

"EMANCIPATION IN THE British West Indies," delivered initially as a public address in the Concord Court House on August 1, 1844, was Emerson's first published statement of opposition to slavery. It appeared relatively late in his career, when he was forty-one, and more than a decade after antislavery sentiment had become a forceful presence in Concord and many other Northern communities. The speech was widely noticed and especially well received by the abolitionist movement, which long had been eager to have Emerson's endorsement of their cause. The original Concord address was carefully reported in Horace Greeley's *New York Tribune* and William Lloyd Garrison's *Liberator*. Privately, Emerson also received letters of thanks and appreciation from several of Massachusetts's leading abolitionists.[1] By mid-October, pamphlet editions of the Concord address had been published in both Boston and London.

---

1. Emerson's 1844 address also turned out to be the only one among many subsequent antislavery speeches that would be reprinted in pamphlet form. Thoreau served as the agent for the Women's Anti-Slavery Society of Concord (which had invited Emerson to deliver the address) and negotiated successfully for publication with James Munroe and Co. See Walter Harding, *The Days of Henry Thoreau: A Biography* (New York, 1962), 175. For Emer-

The reluctance with which Emerson approached the subject of slavery, however, is well known, and remains visible in his opening remarks when he noted candidly that he spoke "without the smallest claim to be a special laborer in this work of humanity" (83). A variety of attitudes explain his refusal to speak publicly against slavery before 1844. While Emerson thought the institution of slavery was a moral outrage, he had yet to reject the belief that blacks were innately inferior to whites. That belief was widespread, even within the abolitionist movement itself, and left open the possibility that blacks could never redeem themselves and so would have to endure slavery as their inevitable condition or be returned to Africa. Emerson also resented having to think about slavery. ("I do not wish to expiate," he proclaimed in "Self-Reliance," "but to live.") He felt most of what had to be said against it had already been said countless times, and loathed the controversy that surrounded its public discussion. Emerson also never considered himself an effective stump orator, admitting that he had neither the skills nor the passion of a committed social reformer.[2]

The significance of Emerson's public silence before 1844, however, can be overplayed. Thanks to the recent painstaking research of Len Gougeon, we know that he had not remained entirely offstage during the 1830s and early 1840s.[3] In his private actions, Emerson certainly had done more than the vast majority of his contemporaries, and it is mostly by the unusually activist standards in Concord (then already known as a haven for runaway slaves) that he seems timid. Still, it was not until he accepted the invitation of the Women's Anti-Slavery Society of Concord to speak at their celebration of the tenth anniversary of the British emancipation

---

son's attitudes toward slavery before the 1844 Concord address, see the thoughtful discussion in Linck C. Johnson, "Reforming the Reformers: Emerson, Thoreau, and the Sunday Lectures at Armory Hall, Boston," *Emerson Society Quarterly* 37 (1991): 235–89.

2. "Emancipation in the British West Indies," in *The Selected Writings of Ralph Waldo Emerson*, ed. Brooks Atkinson (New York, 1940). Page numbers included in the text refer to this edition. "Self-Reliance," in *Essays: First Series*, vol. 2, *The Collected Works of Ralph Waldo Emerson*, ed. Joseph Slater, Alfred R. Ferguson, and Jean Ferguson Carr (Cambridge, Mass., 1979), 31.

3. Len Gougeon, *Virtue's Hero: Emerson, Antislavery, and Reform* (Athens, Ga., 1990), chs. 2 and 3. Drawing on a vast array of primary documents—ranging from contemporary newspaper accounts to Emerson's own extensive correspondence and unpublished antislavery lectures—Gougeon has largely succeeded in revising the Elkinsian account of Emerson as a contemplative dreamer who stood aloof from the antislavery reform activity that swirled around him. While indebted to Gougeon's important study, I think he fails to show (for reasons discussed later in this chapter) that Emerson was in fact "a committed social reformer" (337).

that Emerson first gave sustained attention to the question of American slavery, and the result was a statement that focused squarely on a set of interrelated questions that preoccupied most serious opponents of slavery in his day. To begin with, what was it, in the late eighteenth and early nineteenth centuries, that had compelled some men and women to turn against an institution which, in one form or another, had been a common social practice in all earlier centuries? Why had slavery been attacked first and with such admirable success in Great Britain? What had been the social and economic impact of abolition in Great Britain and its colonies? And, finally, why had the attack on slavery made so little headway in the United States during the first half of the nineteenth century?

For answers to the first three of these questions, Emerson turned chiefly to two sources. The first, and most important, was *The History of the Rise, Progress and Accomplishment of the Abolition of the African Slave Trade by the British Parliament*, written by Thomas Clarkson, one of Britain's most famous abolitionists, and published in 1808. Clarkson's *History* provided Emerson with a detailed account of the horrors of the slave trade. It also offered him what historians have come to recognize as the first comprehensive account of the historical origins of the antislavery movement, and by 1844 it was Clarkson's account that served as the starting place for all careful study of that subject.[4] Emerson's second source was *Emancipation in the West Indies: A Six Month's Tour in Antigua, Barbadoes, and Jamaica, in the Year 1837*, co-authored by James A. Thome and J. Horace Kimball, two observers the American Anti-Slavery Society had sent to the British West Indies to report on the early results of the British experiment. From this work, which had quickly become a best-seller in the Northern states, Emerson learned more about the physical suffering of slaves. Yet he also

---

4. My account of Clarkson draws from Joseph Slater, "Two Sources for Emerson's First Address on West Indian Emancipation," *Emerson Society Quarterly* 44 (1966): 97–100; David Brion Davis, *The Problem of Slavery in the Age of Revolution* (Ithaca, 1975), 446–49, 538–41; and *Slavery and Human Progress* (New York, 1984), 117–29, 139, 140; and Howard Temperley, "Anti-Slavery as a Form of Cultural Imperialism," in *Anti-Slavery, Religion, and Reform: Essays in Memory of Roger Anstey*, ed. Christine Bolt and Seymour Drescher (Hamden, Conn., 1980), 335–50; and "The Ideology of Anti-Slavery," in *The Abolition of the Atlantic Slave Trade: Origins and Effects in Europe, Africa, and the Americas*, ed. David Ellis and James Walvin (Madison, 1981), 21–36. Emerson's knowledge of Clarkson appears to have antedated the summer of 1844 by several years. See "Self-Reliance," 35–36, where he cites Clarkson's central role in the abolitionist movement as an example of the ways in which "an institution is the lengthened shadow of one man."

found what he and many other American opponents of slavery seized on as evidence proving that the British experiment in emancipation had already proven to be something of an economic success. Among the findings Thome and Kimball reported was that Emancipation Day in fact had passed off uneventfully in the West Indies. Britain's scheme initially had allowed only for a program of gradual emancipation, in which ex-slaves were now employed as 'apprentices' and required to buy their freedom by forfeiting three-fourths of the profits to their former masters over a four-to six-year period. And yet, while "apprenticeship" was viewed by most abolitionists simply as slavery by another name, and at first met with considerable resistance on the island of Jamaica, Thome and Kimball also reported that the mass of freed black West Indians had continued to labor, glad and grateful for even a limited opportunity to work and earn money in a new system in which the physical guarantees of their enslavement had not yet been entirely removed.[5]

What emerged after several weeks of intensive reading in these volumes was a statement that both adapted and complicated what Emerson found there. Reading Clarkson's *History* clearly made an immediate and powerful impact on his understanding of slavery. Emerson praised Clarkson by name, and copied out long passages from his *History* illustrating the hideousness of the slave trade. More important, Clarkson's *History* also persuaded him to abandon the opinion—which he had defended only a few months earlier in "New England Reformers"—that abolitionists, like reformers with other causes, exaggerated the significance of their objectives.[6] Emerson now saw slavery as an evil unlike any other and, as a result,

---

5. My account of Thome and Kimball draws from Slater, "Two Sources for Emerson's First Address on West Indian Emancipation"; Gougeon, *Virtue's Hero*, 74–75; and Howard Temperley, *British Antislavery, 1833–70* (Columbia, S.C., 1972), 91 n. 83, 113–14. For the history of British slave emancipation in the West Indies more generally, see Robin Blackburn, *The Overthrow of Colonial Slavery, 1776–1848* (London, 1988), chs. 7–11.

6. See "New England Reformers," in *Selected Writings*, 449–51. Emerson initially spurned the characteristic method of reform—building organizations that concentrate numbers and resources to achieve a single purpose—as no different from the techniques of a commercial enterprise or political party. On this account, reform appears as one of the characteristic by-products of a market society, and hence a cause Emerson was unlikely to endorse. In the case of the abolitionist movement, however, there can be no question that Emerson's attitudes underwent fundamental modification as he prepared for his Concord Address. (Included in *Essays: Second Series* [1844], "New England Reformers" was first given in New York on March 3, 1844, as a public lecture read in Armory Hall. See Johnson, "Reforming the Reformers," for a full account of that lecture's immediate cultural setting.)

adopted Clarkson's view that the emergence of an international anti-slavery movement represented a monumental turning point in the evolution of man's moral perception. To some degree, he also came to share Clarkson's confidence that the work of emancipation would continue, despite the widespread resistance it still encountered in America.

There can be no question that, during the months in which he prepared his Concord address, Emerson came to absorb much of the ideology of liberal Christian abolitionism as Clarkson had so influentially defined it. Beyond this general identification, however, matters become difficult. It would be misleading to say that Emerson found in Clarkson all he needed to know about slavery and the early history of the abolitionist movement. What do we make, for example, of his refusal to reiterate one of Clarkson's central themes: the idea that abolitionism was essentially a religious struggle? Historians tell us that, following Clarkson's lead, American speakers who commemorated British abolitionist triumphs typically presented them as accomplishments that had served to revitalize Christianity and to atone for national guilt. Yet Emerson sounded neither of those familiar themes. Puzzling, too, is the fact that, while he repudiated immediate abolition, he expressed, at the conclusion of his remarks, passionate and eloquent sympathy for the revolutionary political struggles of West Indian slaves—thereby raising the question of whether he was a "moderate" or a "radical" abolitionist. Finally, while Emerson followed Clarkson in stressing the role of conscience in giving rise to what he called the "moral revolution" (850) of abolitionism, he plainly was aware that new economic considerations had helped support British emancipation and to define its purposes and effects. Or, put another way, Emerson recognized that British abolitionism was the distinctive product of what was then the world's most advanced commercial society, and this recognition invited an explanation of the way in which abolitionist sentiment had impressed itself on the economic interests of a nation in which (in Emerson's wording) it had once "seemed the dictate of trade, to keep the negro down" (844).

How, then, should we describe the general standpoint from which "Emancipation in the British West Indies" was composed? It is worth emphasizing that Emerson claimed some measure of objectivity in his approach, if only because he saw himself as attempting to meet American opponents of abolition on their own ground by discussing the question of slavery's economic viability. Indeed, at the outset, he stressed that he was intent on persuading "any man who thinks the ruin of a race of men a small matter, compared with the last decorations and completions of his own comfort—who would not so much part with his ice-cream, to save them from rapine and manacles." Emerson's opening argument against slavery was not a moral one in his view, but based instead on an appeal to enlightened self-interest, and thereby designed to show even the most coldly self-interested of his contemporaries that "their cream and vanilla are safer and cheaper by placing the negro nation on a fair footing than by robbing them" (832).

In place of Clarkson's theologically based account of the origins of abolition, Emerson went on to provide what he took to be a more balanced causal explanation in which material and moral motives had run parallel and proved to be mutually reinforcing. In his view, the "moral revolution" that gave rise to British emancipation had no single source, no primary motive. To be sure, individual appeals to moral conscience had been important, but so had appeals to national pride and economic self-interest. Unlike other opponents of slavery, who assumed they represented the cause of right-thinking over prejudice and error, Emerson recognized that while the morality of slavery had often been questioned, one of the main reasons it had not been successfully attacked before the end of the eighteenth century was that slavery long had been deeply embedded in the economic life of Western nations. For centuries, he observed, slavery had been accepted as a "dictate of trade," an economic necessity required to keep blacks working for whites, because it was assumed that "by the aid of a little whipping, we could get their work for nothing but their board and the cost of whips" (844). Emerson also was quite clear in saying that only at the moment when both morality and self-interest began to join in opposing slavery had the work of abolition actually been able to get underway.

I

We have explored enough of "Emancipation in the British West Indies"—even though this discussion has taken us only roughly one-third of the way through the 1844 address—to see that Emerson designed it with an intricate framework. The complexity of his purposes, however, seems yet to have registered in modern scholarly appreciation of his thinking. The typical approach today is to judge his efforts by contemporary standards, and the results are usually found to be unimpressive. David Brion Davis, for instance, has presented Emerson as a figure who, while a "rebel in theology," otherwise walked in step with nineteenth-century liberal Protestants in taking for granted that slavery "was in every way detrimental to both virtue and progress." Howard Temperley has gone further in citing Emerson's 1844 address as an example of American abolitionists' readiness "to invent evidence" proving that British emancipation, only ten years after its proclamation, was already a clear economic success.[7]

It is true that Emerson came to share many of the assumptions of other opponents of slavery in his day, and that specialists in the history of slavery now tell us that much of what nineteenth-century abolitionists believed has proved to be either false or naïve. As an economic system, slavery was not—as Emerson and most other abolitionists assumed—in decline in the first half of the nineteenth century. Modern historical research has made it clear that, during the heyday of abolitionism, slavery was both economically competitive and compatible with nonslave counterparts throughout the world—even though it was being hobbled or eliminated in one locale after another. Nineteenth-century defenders of slavery, then, also appear to have been correct to reject the abolitionist claim that their institution was doomed and destined to be replaced by a free-labor system that would serve them much better. But to describe Emerson's view of British emancipation simply as a case of "inventing evidence" is stretching the point. Based on figures Temperley himself cites, it is arguable that in its initial phase, emancipation in the British West Indies turned out to be a mixed economic blessing. By 1846 sugar production had dropped by 50 percent in Jamaica, but that drop did not occur immediately, and during the four years immediately following emancipation—precisely the period of time Thome and Kimball considered in their influential book—Jamaican sugar production had declined by only 10 percent. Moreover, on some of the smaller islands, such as Barbadoes and Antigua, production actually increased during the late 1830s and early 1840s. And all of this suggests that it would be more accurate to say, then, that Thome and Kimball, and those who trusted their account of the economic impact of British eman-

---

7. Davis, *Slavery and Human Progress*, 124; Howard Temperley, "Capitalism, Slavery, and Ideology," *Past and Present* 75 (1977): 110 n. 45. See also Gougeon, *Virtue's Hero*, 75–85, 87–90, which offers a more admiring account of Emerson's 1844 address, yet tends to underestimate the variety of its concerns by approaching it as a statement of Emerson's "pure American idealism" (348).

cipation, exaggerated prospects for continuation of what, in the early 1840s, still appeared to be a partial success.[8]

Putting aside the question of Emerson's religious views for a moment, there also remains room for disagreement about the extent to which he was simply repeating what could have been said by various other liberal idealists in his day. The habit of seeing Emerson as an idealist pure and simple obscures what we have just established in a close examination of the opening of the 1844 address—namely, that his understanding of the origins of the abolitionist movement, at one important level, does resemble that of more skeptical late twentieth-century historians, since he recognized that in accounting for the success of British abolition what needed to be explained was why an institution that long had seemed to serve the national interest was destroyed, in part, as a result of changed perceptions of what that interest entailed. My point here, however, is not to acclaim Emerson's objectivity or to recast him as a modern historian of slavery before his time. Emerson's recognition that those who promoted British emancipation were motivated by far more than an unselfish desire to help the downtrodden is, after all, just the starting point for a now very complex debate involving ethical and epistemological questions that plainly never occurred to him.[9] Seen against the background of that debate, it may also be fair to say that what "Emancipation in the British West Indies" offered as an explanation of the economic underpinnings of British emancipation does not turn out to be particularly original or persuasive. In Britain, economic interests built up its slave system; now the application of more enlightened principles had served to dismantle it. "The laws of Nature are in harmony with each other," Emerson proclaimed. "That which the head and heart demand is found to be, in the long run, for what the grossest calculator calls his advantage. The moral sense is always supported by the permanent interests of the parties. Else, I know not how, in our world, any good would ever get done" (845). These sentences did

---

8. Temperley, "Capitalism, Slavery, and Ideology," 103; Robin Blackburn, *The Overthrow of Colonial Slavery, 1776–1848* (London, 1988), 459–64, points out that plantation output in 1834–36 was comparable with that of previous years, and that while annual sugar production dropped sharply in the early 1840s, the material condition of freed men probably improved during the same period, with wages and the growth of small landowning among former slaves leading in most colonies to more stable family life based on production for local use, rather than for international markets.

9. See Thomas Bender's Introduction to *The Anti-Slavery Debate: Capitalism as a Problem in Historical Interpretation* (Berkeley, 1992), 1–13, for a general overview.

repeat the dogma of liberal abolitionism. But if Emerson really believed the same thing was in the long run also bound to "get done" in America, it seems unlikely he would have gone on to compose the rest of his address as he did. In fact, once he had finished his account of British emancipation, Emerson immediately remarked that while studying Clarkson's *History*, he had been unable to read a page of it without "the most painful comparisons" (847) to what had been taking place in his own country. In America, he continued, there were in fact no "patriots and senators who heard the slave's cause," because the majority of its free states, as any reader of congressional debates could readily see, were now "schooled and ridden" by a minority of slave owners (850). Or, put more sharply, Emerson sensed that, while British emancipation continued to serve many American abolitionists as an example of the unfolding of an immanent and progressive historical design, it was not at all clear how America would come to enter into that design.

So why had America—next in line on the list of the world's most powerful "trading nations"—failed to follow Britain's example? Emerson's attempt to answer that question had sent him to the U.S. Congressional Record, and his account of what he found there led to an abrupt reversal in the generally confident mood of his 1844 address. More significant, it also forced him to consider the very different political context within which the problem of slavery was being addressed in America. In his handling of this new theme, Emerson quickly revealed himself to be a thinker ready to embrace much of the sectional political rhetoric that had first emerged as part of the abolitionist movement in the 1830s and, as we shall see, came to dominate political debate in the 1850s.[10] By contrast to Britain's success in engaging in a decorous national debate and "reaching out the benefit of the law to the most helpless citizens in her world-wide realm," Emerson offered a picture of America as a nation in which slavery was making a mockery of its legal principles and institutions. Especially galling in his view was the refusal of the political leaders of his own state to protect free black seamen, some of whom were at the time being seized and jailed when Massachusetts ships put into Southern ports. He condemned the seizures as a "damnable outrage" (848), and denounced his

---

10. On the significance of sectionalist rhetoric in the antebellum period, see Eric Foner, *Politics and Ideology in the Age of the Civil War* (New York, 1980), chs. 2 and 3; and Ronald G. Walters, *The Anti-Slavery Appeal: American Abolitionism after 1830* (Baltimore, 1976), ch. 7.

state for continuing to trust the safety of its own free inhabitants to the federal government.

Yet if Massachusetts was in no position to "defend its own people in its own shipping" (since it had no jurisdiction in South Carolina or Louisiana, the two worst offenders in this regard), what goals ought congressmen chosen to speak for "a million freemen" now to set for themselves? Their first aim, Emerson answered, had to be obtaining the release of all black citizens of Massachusetts held in prison without criminal charges, a goal that required "the strictest inquisition" to discover the location of free blacks brought into slavery by local Southern laws. Then "let order be taken," he continued, "to indemnify all such citizens of Massachusetts." As for the dangers to the Union in pursuing such an ideal, Emerson made his sectional loyalties quite clear: "The Union is already at an end," he replied, when citizens of Massachusetts could be seized in Southern ports: "I thought the deck of a Massachusetts ship was as much the territory of Massachusetts as the floor on which we stand. It should be as sacred as the temple of God" (848).

Such impassioned sectionalist rhetoric figured prominently in "Emancipation in the British West Indies," but other aspects of the address make it difficult to say exactly how much weight Emerson himself may have assigned to it. He plainly had little confidence that the political leaders of his state would ever pursue, let alone attain, the aims he had endorsed. The depressing accounts of "tameness and silence" he found in the Congressional Record suggested that Massachusetts's current senators and representatives would never stand up to the Southern states or pursue the cause of abolition. Still, for all the anger and dismay that colored his view of American politics in 1844, there was as yet no sense of crisis in Emerson's thinking about slavery, and he refused to endorse disunion as a necessary solution to America's deepening sectional conflict about slavery. While he now saw slavery as an evil unlike any other, Emerson was not yet ready to say explicitly that it demanded more active and widespread popular opposition in the Northern states. (This would come only in the aftermath of the new Fugitive Slave Law of 1850.) Moreover, for all his political pessimism, Emerson clearly also knew what was expected as a conclusion to speeches that marked the anniversary of the British emancipation. The 1st of August, in the end, was not a day set aside chiefly for condemning the evils of slavery and the cowardice of Northern politicians or for debating strategy. It was rather a day of promise on which all American opponents of slavery met to celebrate what Britain had done and to call for a closing of ranks—an occasion when abolitionists gathered, in words Emerson himself used at the outset of his address, to "exchange congratulations" (831). It also is worth noting again that the 1st of August had come to be a day on which British emancipation typically was hailed as a harbinger of Christ's final salvation of mankind. Emerson chose to bring his remarks to a close, however, with a strikingly different and more secular vision of what lay ahead for America once slavery had been abolished.

"The First of August marks the entrance of a new element in modern politics," he proclaimed, "namely, the civilization of the negro" (853). Not satisfied with a history of abolition that told only of "the concession of the whites" (854), the conclusion of "Emancipation in the British West Indies" underlined what Emerson called the "earning of the blacks" in resisting their masters:

> the arrival in the world of such men as Toussaint, and the Haytian heroes, or of the leaders of their race in Barbadoes and Jamaica, outweighs in good omen all the English and American humanity. The anti-slavery of the whole world is dust in the balance before this—is a poor squeamishness and nervousness. . . . I esteem the occasion of this jubilee to be the proud discovery that the black race can contend with the white. (855)

If his earlier refusal to celebrate the religious significance of the British emancipation left most of his original Concord audience uncomfortable, these words very likely stunned those who were listening closely. In the mid-1840s, when even the most radical abolitionists still wanted to believe the end of slavery would come about in a peaceful and orderly fashion, and that emancipation precluded or would prevent the kind of racial warfare and revolutionary violence that had occurred in Haiti in 1804, Emerson's praise for Toussaint and other unnamed "anti-slaves" arguably represented the most startling of all the views he expressed in his Concord address.

Yet to what end? It is clear that in voicing his admiration for struggles West Indian slaves had earlier undertaken on their own behalf, Emerson was refusing to portray black slaves simply as victims. Perhaps more important, however, he was also assigning a political meaning to the prospect of emancipation that few contemporary abolitionists would have been ready to endorse. For if, in Emerson's view, it was the Caribbean slave revolts that seemed to provide the clearest proof of the slaves' desire and ability to overthrow their needless subordination to their white masters, it followed that it was not just the whites' economic way of life that would be imitated once all· slaves were freed; their democratic political achievements would be copied as well. In place of the prospect of Christian salvation, then, Emerson's final thrust in "Emancipation in the British West Indies" was a forceful declaration of political equality on behalf of American blacks. "Man is one," he insisted near the end, and "you cannot injure any member, without a sympathetic injury to all the members. America is not civil, whilst Africa is barbarous" (856). In making that declaration, Emerson also left behind his earlier assumption that blacks were inferior by nature. He now demanded the admission of American blacks to political and economic institutions that whites had reserved for themselves, and presented what he took to be evidence suggesting they were already fully qualified for admission.[11]

A final question remains, however. Viewed historically, how ought we to assess the merits of the hopeful vision of assimilation set out in "Emancipation in the British West Indies"? Some modern commentators find the message unsatisfying. David Brion Davis, for example, has suggested that liberal abolitionists like Emerson might have retained some conception of freed black West Indians as "a corporate group, entitled by race or a common ill-fortune to their own way of life."[12] There is some justice in this view. In considering the situation of the slaves, Emerson did immodestly assume that their primary demand was to have the same political and economic rights exclusively reserved for their white masters. It is also the case that this assumption invited premature judgments about the actual fruits of victory, once the first steps to end exclusion were being taken. Emerson did not closely consider what new economic roles were actually available to former British slaves during the 1840s. Slaves had simply been excluded from activities in which their masters freely engaged, and that, in the final analysis, appears to be the chief injury that their masters had done to them. For that matter, Emerson never considered the possibility that the

---

11. It is fair to ask: What evidence is there that Emerson's 1844 address was actually read by his contemporaries along the lines I've pursued here? This is not the place for a detailed answer, but it is worth noting that Wendell Phillips kept copies of Emerson's pamphlet on hand for distribution at the time of his speeches, and that during the 1850s Phillips would come to tell the story of Toussaint's insurrection, as Emerson had earlier, as proving beyond all question the capacity of the black race for self-government. (See James B. Stewart, *Wendell Phillips: Liberty's Hero* [Baton Rouge, 1986] 105–6, and 97–116, for Phillips's egalitarian racial views more generally.)

12. Davis, *Slavery and Human Progress*, 122.

injury could be overcome, and nothing else be changed. It was important only to win equal opportunity for blacks, not to worry about what the opportunity was for. Hence, Davis's charge that Emerson's understanding of what freedom entailed for black West Indians—and by implication for still enslaved black Americans—was incomplete and one-sided.

Yet something more can be said briefly in sympathetic explanation of Emerson's liberal assimilationist position. First of all, consider the view that freed black slaves would simply want to be free side by side with their former masters. The difficulties Davis sees in "Emancipation in the British West Indies" derive from this crucial assumption. But so, too, did its remarkably antiracist egalitarian force—which suggests that we ought to interpret the assumption at once as a sign of Emerson's generosity as well as his cultural arrogance. Moreover, those two qualities taken together surely are what made opposition to slavery possible at the time Emerson wrote, when there was of course little or no knowledge of how incomplete contemporary ideals of freedom were so long as slaves had no opportunity to pursue them.

As for Emerson's account of how successful some former Western slaves had been in actually imitating free white men, it may be correct to say the story Emerson told about British emancipation in 1844 was misleadingly happy in some respects. But it is unfair simply to stop there, as Davis apparently wants to, since Emerson did not draw attention *only* to action that had given ex-slaves opportunity to exercise the same economic freedoms as whites. As we have seen, he also celebrated the fact that some slaves had fought to gain their political freedoms as well. Here the point to stress again is that emancipation as Emerson conceived it can hardly be described as a passive transformation of the victims of slavery. Indeed, what Emerson apparently wanted to draw attention to in his 1844 address was the black slaves' two-sided imitation of the conduct of their white masters, since that imitation not only provided him the main outlines of a historical narrative; it contained critical standards of conduct as well. The concrete expression of freedom for ex-slaves would be full participation in both a democratic state and a competitive economic marketplace, and there is no question that the two were inseparable in Emerson's mind. As he sketched his vision of an American emancipation still to come, however, Emerson was not blindly celebrating the economic and political institutions of his nation. In addressing his own contemporaries, there can be little question that Emerson was criticizing a society whose accomplishments were still deeply compromised by the injustice of slavery. He was at the same time, however, appealing to them as a connected critic, urging them to see that they had no reason to continue to exclude blacks from political and economic institutions they mistakenly had thought to make only for themselves.[13]

2

Emerson was jarred out of his qualified optimism in the early 1850s by the Fugitive Slave Law. The new bill, which went into effect on September 18, 1850, authorized federal commissioners, rather than state judges, to process fugitive cases in the North. It also obliged all Northern citizens to assist federal marshals in the recapture of escapees. Severe new penalties were prescribed for persons who abetted escaped slaves, and fugitives themselves were deprived of trial by jury or opportunity to testify. Emerson's initial response to the passage of the bill was muted; he believed that the law would simply be ignored by local authorities in Northern states, and hence required no open opposition. But efforts to enforce the Fugitive Slave Law in fact were quick and widespread. Over the course of the early 1850s, the law also became the primary target of abolitionist resistance, with Boston three times serving as the setting for some of the most visible cases involving attempts to rescue fugitive slaves. The first came on February 18, 1851, when members of Boston's local vigilance committee forcibly freed Frederick Wilkins (locally known as "Shadrach") from jail and arranged for his transport to Canada. Shadrach's escape raised a national furor, and Boston then became one of the main objects of elaborate and costly government efforts to prevent the success of any future rescue efforts. In April 1851 a second escaped slave, Thomas Sims, was seized in Boston. This time more extensive precautions were taken, and after legal appeals were exhausted, Sims was returned to Savannah. Finally, three years later, in May 1854, Anthony Burns was arrested and charged with being a fugitive slave. While Burns's case was being heard by federal commissioners, a small group of abolitionists stormed the Boston courthouse in an attempt to free him. But the

---

13. My account of "Emancipation in the British West Indies" is indebted to Michael Walzer, *The Company of Critics: Social Criticism in the Twentieth Century* (New York, 1988), ch. 9, which explores and defends Simone de Beauvoir's argument for "the assimilated woman" in ways I have made extensive use of here.

the attack was turned away by federal marshals, and Burns was removed from Boston under heavy guard and returned to his owner in Virginia.[14]

In the face of all this, it perhaps is no surprise to find that Emerson's earlier hopeful vision of assimilation gave way to anger and fear. "Now at last we are disenchanted," he announced in March 1854, "and shall have no more false hopes" (875).[15] During the early 1850s Emerson came to share a general recognition within the American abolitionist community that their cause had suffered a shock so profound as to call into question all possibilities of peaceful institutional reform. He saw passage of the bill as conclusive evidence that the ultimate intentions of the Southern states were to spread slavery into the North and thereby to destroy the civil liberties of free states. The new Fugitive Slave Law, he proclaimed, disclosed "the secret of the new times, that Slavery is no longer mendicant, but was become aggressive and dangerous" (867).

Just as ominously, the new law also disclosed, in Emerson's view, that acceptance of slavery was still the general rule in the North, despite more than two decades of abolitionist effort. He observed that it was not merely Daniel Webster and other Northern politicians who had "decided for Slavery" (866). In Boston, "the tameness is indeed complete" (180), Emerson said in his first address on the Fugitive Slave Law, given in Concord on May 3, 1851. After the rescue of Shadrach in February, he dejectedly commented, "the only haste . . . was, who should first put his name on the list of volunteers in aid of the marshal" (180–81). Boston's local vigilance committee offered and encouraged some popular resistance, but support for the new bill in fact turned out to be widespread, and Emerson was stunned at the "passive obedience" with which the city's population greeted efforts at enforcement. The affluence of Boston, he observed, was partly to blame. It had blunted the sense of injustice among the city's residents. Consent to the new law showed that "our prosperity had hurt us, and that we could not be shocked by crime" and that "our bellies had run away with our brains" (867). Equally disturbing in Emerson's view was the fact that Boston's intellectual and cultural elite had acquiesced as well. There had also

---

14. My account of the Fugitive Slave Law follows James McPherson, *The Battle Cry of Freedom: The Civil War Era* (New York, 1988), 78–87, and Gougeon, *Virtue's Hero*, ch. 5.

15. "The Fugitive Slave Law," in *Selected Writings*, 859–76. Atkinson's collection reprints only the second of two different addresses that Emerson gave regarding the Fugitive Slave Law, that read in New York City on March 7, 1854. An earlier address was given in Concord on May 3, 1851, and can be found in *Miscellanies*, vol. 11, *The Complete Works of Ralph*

been a "disastrous defection (on the miserable cry of Union) of men of letters, of the colleges, of educated men, nay of some preachers of religion," he concluded, and that, too, had helped bring about "the darkest passage" in America's history (867).

Gay Wilson Allen, one of Emerson's modern biographers, has said that in the course of the 1850s his view of the new law became so bitter that he veered toward anarchism.[16] But this isn't quite right. Emerson certainly was outraged that his countrymen had embraced what he called an "immoral" and "quadruped" law (866), and now dismissed the possibility that the federal government would ever act decisively to end slavery. These new attitudes, however, did not preclude attempts to consider or engage in alternative plans of political action. In fact, if one thinks of democratic "politics" in some of its usual senses—supporting candidates for political office and attempting to influence elections—Emerson himself at first chose to express his opposition to slavery in a conventional way. During May 1851, the month after Thomas Sims had been removed from Boston, Emerson became directly involved in the congressional campaign of John Gorham Palfrey (1766–1881), the Middlesex County candidate of the recently formed Free Soil Party. And at Palfrey's request, Emerson agreed to repeat his first Fugitive Slave Law address on several occasions throughout the county.[17]

Emerson's involvement in conventional politics, however, turned out to be short-lived. Palfrey lost a closely fought election, and Emerson would not speak out against the law again until March 1854. There also is room for disagreement here, for reasons I'll discuss at the end of this chapter, about the historical significance of Emerson's public activity in response to the Fugitive Slave Law. A close reading of what he had to say about the law, however, leaves little reason to doubt that his understanding of slavery was now marked by a greater political realism, especially by his recognition that the chief problem of abolition now lay in the question of how North-

---

Waldo Emerson, ed. Edward W. Emerson (Boston, 1903–4), 177–214. Page numbers in the text refer to these editions.

16. Gay Wilson Allen, *Waldo Emerson: A Biography* (New York, 1981), 556.

17. Gougeon, *Virtue's Hero*, chs. 5–9, now provides the most detailed and comprehensive account of Emerson's many ties to the antislavery movement during the 1850s. Still useful is the more personal account in James Elliot Cabot, *A Memoir of Ralph Waldo Emerson*, 2 vols. (Boston, 1893), 2:574–612; see esp. 585–86, where Cabot recounts an episode in which a speech for Palfrey Emerson gave at Harvard was greeted with hisses and catcalls that made it impossible for him to continue.

ern complicity might be overcome. Emerson had touched on this issue in "Emancipation in the British West Indies," but his account there had been ambivalent—at first speaking doubtfully about the ability of Northern political leaders to "defend the weak and the poor," yet in the end postponing any final reckoning with the question of how much proponents of abolition in America could rely on their "political agents" (850). His two addresses on the Fugitive Slave Law, however, made it plain that Emerson now believed abolitionists ought no longer look to Northern political leaders to aid their cause.

Not unlike other opponents of slavery, Emerson thought Webster's support for the Fugitive Slave Law had made this lesson painfully obvious. But that was not the only lesson he drew from Webster's unexpected failure to bring his country to its senses. What appalled Emerson about Webster's putting his "personal and official authority" (865) behind the Fugitive Slave Law was not simply that morally Webster had chosen to stand on the wrong side. Rather, it was that on the question of slavery Webster, like the vast majority of his countrymen, had displayed no moral sensibility whatsoever. He had approached slavery strictly as a question of defining and enforcing workable legal statutes, thereby hoping to place slavery outside the realm of a continuing national debate. Yet the resolution Webster had in mind, Emerson went on to observe, was not simply amoral in its spirit; it had turned out to be politically unworkable as well. Before passage of the new law in 1850, the blatant inconsistencies in state and federal court decisions regarding slavery had shown that appeals to the rule of law could not eliminate the underlying moral question. After 1850 the "final measure" (198) Webster thought he had orchestrated with new legislation in fact turned out to have settled nothing. Whatever one's view of the new bill, Emerson observed, Webster's "final settlement" clearly had "dislocated the foundations" (199), since slavery was now the "one sole subject for conversation and painful thought throughout the continent" (199). From this it followed, too, that it was Webster himself who had failed to grasp the magnitude of the political problem posed by slavery, precisely because he failed to see that in America appeals to the rule of law were no longer of any practical use in resolving disputes about its future. Moreover, while those who followed Webster had wanted to believe that the new law would serve to remove slavery as the cause of sectional conflict, in practice reliance on the new law was aiding the steady expansion of slavery at the same time as it provoked more angry opposition from the abolitionist movement.

For Emerson, the practical upshot of Webster's political failure was plain enough: the time had come for true abolitionists to withdraw "all foolish trust in others." The passage and early enforcement of the Fugitive Slave Law demonstrated that too much of abolitionism had been based on false assumptions about the moral superiority of Northern institutions. "These things show," he wrote, "that no forms, neither constitutions, nor laws, nor covenants, nor churches, nor bibles, are of any use in themselves. The Devil nestles comfortably into them all" (870). Or, put more sharply, the leaders of economic, political, and religious institutions in Northern states had never had any intention of acting to end slavery. Their talk of disunion had proved to be a hollow threat, and now their acceptance of the new bill had brought a cultural crisis in Northern states that appeared to leave individuals opposed to slavery no choice but to dissolve the union between themselves and their states.

It is worth stressing here that after passage of the Fugitive Slave Law, Emerson was quite open in his endorsement of civil disobedience as an appropriate way of resisting the Fugitive Slave Law. In his second public address against the law in New York City on March 7, 1854 (the fourth anniversary of Webster's congressional speech in favor of the bill), Emerson commented: "no man has a right to hope that the laws of New York will defend him from the contamination of slaves another day until he has made up his mind that he will not owe his protection to the laws of New York, but to his own sense and spirit. Then he protects New York. He only who is able to stand alone is qualified for society" (870–71). This is one example of what prompted Allen's speculation about Emerson veering toward anarchism. Yet it isn't fair to stop here, because Emerson did not go on to present civil disobedience as the only possible response. While abolitionists may have had no choice but to "draw off from foolish trust in others," they also had no choice but to continue with the work of criticizing Northern complicity. Emerson's endorsements of civil disobedience, in other words, were hedged by considerations of other possibilities for action. The law had to be disobeyed, but a way also had to be found to have it "abrogated and wiped out of the statute-book" (212). Repeal of the Fugitive Slave Law would again confine slavery to Southern states, and that in turn might provide new ground on which to reconsider the possibility of ending slavery altogether. Indeed, Emerson still held out the possibility that free Northern states might choose to use their wealth to redeem themselves and their country as a whole:

Why not end this dangerous dispute on some ground of fair compensation on one side, and satisfaction on the other to the conscience of free states? It is really the great task fit for this country to accomplish, to buy that property of the planters, as the British nation bought the West Indian slaves. I say buy,—never conceding the right of the planter to own, but that we may acknowledge the calamity of his position, and bear a countryman's share in relieving him; and because it is the only practicable course and is innocent. Here is a right social or public function, which one man cannot do, which all men must do. (208)

Did Emerson, at such a late date, really believe that America was prepared to follow Britain's example? It is clear that he knew the cost of such a settlement would be huge—"two thousand millions of dollars" (209) was his announced estimate—and that in the North "the heart of financiers, accustomed to practical figures" (210), would shrink at the prospect of even discussing such a plan. The broader point to note here, however, is that, even in his most pessimistic moods, Emerson resisted the thought that there were no peaceful "practicable" solutions to the problem of American slavery. He clearly did recognize that there was something deeply wrong with Northern institutions, but he would not accept the conclusion that they were past saving. "Nothing is impractical to this nation," Emerson insisted, "which it shall set itself to do" (209). It was not until Brown's raid on Harper's Ferry, as we shall see in chapter 6, that he acknowledged that his nation as a whole would never set itself to end slavery.

In the end, both of Emerson's Fugitive Slave Law addresses, as he himself stressed, were centrally concerned with the question, "What shall we do?" (206). The concluding paragraphs of the 1854 address suggest that by the mid-1850s Emerson had come to believe that the work of abolishing slavery in America now required a new sort of politics, one perhaps best described as a cultural struggle in which now politically disillusioned Northern intellectuals like Emerson openly joined forces with the organized advocates of abolition. This is what Emerson said near the end of his March 4, 1854, address on the Fugitive Slave Law and The Tabernacle in New York City:

Let the aid of virtue, intelligence and education be cast where they rightfully belong. They are organically ours. Let them be loyal to their own. I wish to see the instructed class here know their own flag, and not fire on their comrades. We should not forgive the clergy for taking on every issue the immoral side; nor the Bench, if it put itself on the side of the culprit; nor the Government, if it sustain the mob against the law.

It is a potent support and ally to a brave man standing single, or with a few, for the right, and out-voted and ostracized, to know that better men in other parts of the country appreciate the service and will rightly report him to his own and the next age. Without this assurance, he will sooner sink. (874)

Emerson perhaps owed his audience more about the practical details of the cultural alliance he envisions here. In fact, given the "defection of men of letters" that he had decried at the outset of his address, hope for a new alliance between abolitionists and "the instructed class" seems like something of a non sequitur. Still, the broad outlines of what Emerson wanted seem clear enough: not the abandonment of political struggle against slavery, but the end of its one-sidedness. And it was precisely to that end that he insisted the time had come for Northern intellectuals to play a more active public role in both defending and defining the cause of abolition. In private correspondence, he described his address in New York as "a plea for freedom addressed to *my set*," and at the close of his 1854 address he would end by telling fellow members of "the instructed class" where they ought to stand and how they should conduct themselves. Their first task, he concluded, was simply to tell the truth: there had always been powerful bastions of support for slavery in the North as well as in the South, and they ought to be condemned as such. "We should not forgive the clergy for taking on every issue the immoral side," Emerson insisted, "nor the Bench, if it put itself on the side of the culprit; nor the Government, if it sustain the mob against the law" (874). The second was to acknowledge that the abolitionist movement had been right from the start. It was the abolitionists who had played the role of Cassandra in telling a story their countrymen had not wanted to hear namely, that the South would never agree to end slavery—and they alone had made honest efforts to measure the enormous cost of setting things right.

3

More will be said in chapter 6 about the ways in which the themes we have explored in this chapter were replayed in Emerson's response to the news of John Brown's raid at Harper's Ferry in October 1859. Two points bear emphasizing by way of an interim summary here. The first concerns the familiar image of Emerson in American historiography discussed in chapter 3; the second concerns Emerson's relationship to the American abolitionist movement. Perhaps no opinion about Emerson remains so widespread among American historians as Stanley Elkins's view that he was an "anti-institutionalist," that when it came to slavery his political imagination simply went blank.[18] In closely examining Emerson's antislavery speeches and writings, this chapter has underlined some of the ways in which his understanding of slavery was in fact focused on institutions, on what he often referred to as the "forms" of the American life. The general drift of his thinking here can be summarized as an uneasy movement back and forth between fears and hopes. In looking back, the fears now surely appear more plausible than the hopes. By the mid-1850s Emerson believed that, as a result of their failure to end slavery, most of the cultural and political institutions that held American society together had broken down to such an extent that they had forfeited all popular trust. Yet there were carefully detailed hopes as well: for all his criticism of American institutions, Emerson believed they could be provided with new foundations, and felt that he and other opponents of slavery had an important role to play in that work. Now I should stress at once that, in trying to show that Emerson wrestled with the dilemma of slavery as an American institution, I do not mean to suggest that he ever resolved that dilemma for himself or for his contemporaries. Whatever one makes of his views, however, it surely is the height of historical hubris to fault him for not keeping some kind of more simple faith with political and social institutions that consistently refused to oppose slavery.

My second point concerns two different ways in which we can understand the complex role Emerson came to play in antislavery politics. First, there is the matter of his ties to the abolitionist movement. Here it is correct to say that, while Emerson was never a recruit to that movement, he did come to play an important role in giving abolitionists cultural legitimacy in Northern states. He was also a source of inspiration for some of

---

18. See Anne C. Rose, *Transcendentalism as a Social Movement, 1830–1850* (New Haven, 1981), 219, who echoes Elkins and Frederickson in saying that Emerson was largely disengaged from the abolition crusade, and in concluding that there "was an abstraction in his approach to slavery" that rendered his "occasional musings on agencies of abolition . . . comparatively desultory." I have tried to show here that Emerson's antislavery writings and speeches were hardly desultory musings.

them, even though he was always guarded in his personal associations.[19] For Emerson himself, the chief practical dilemma he faced as an opponent of slavery was to find ways of overcoming the passivity of the North's cultural elite without having "his set" become simply a mouthpiece for the abolitionist movement. The widespread acceptance of the Fugitive Slave Law in Northern states made the urgency of this task clear to him. Looking back, however, it is arguable, too, that the efforts Emerson actually made to forge "the instructed classes" into a cultural counterpart of the abolitionists turned out to be quite modest in scope. There were, as Gougeon has carefully documented, many public lectures against slavery in the 1850s, as well as private letters traded with Oliver Wendell Holmes and Horatio Greenough in which Emerson condemned their open racism. But there would be no new journal, no fully detailed manifesto defining a role for intellectuals in helping regenerate Northern culture, no acts of civil disobedience. It also is puzzling that all but one of Emerson's several antislavery lectures and speeches in the 1840s and 1850s would remain unpublished during those decades.[20] Until his controversial public defense of Brown, Emerson never quite put his way of living on the line when it came to slavery.[21]

---

19. The historical significance of the pamphlet edition of Emerson's 1844 address on "Emancipation in the British West Indies" has generally been underestimated by historians. Its continuing significance in lending cultural legitimacy to the cause of abolition is suggested by the presence of excerpts from the pamphlet in Hinton Rowan Helper's *The Impending Crisis of the South* (Baltimore, 1857). Rowan's volume, which appeared in several editions, was the most elaborate contemporary exposition of the economic case against slavery. Used extensively by the Republican Party as campaign propaganda, one hundred thousand copies of *The Impending Crisis* were distributed by a group of Republican congressmen in 1859. (The brief introduction to the excerpts from the 1844 address describes Emerson as "the most practical and profound metaphysician in America" [150].) Admiration for Emerson in the North was matched by increasing scorn in the South. In April 1861 a review of *Conduct of Life* in *The Southern Literary Messenger* concluded by suggesting that Emerson "ought to be abated by Act of Congress, and his works suppressed" (327).

20. Between 1854 and 1857 Emerson also compiled a sizable notebook devoted to American slavery and abolition. "Notebook WO Liberty," in *The Journals and Miscellaneous Notebooks of Ralph Waldo Emerson*, ed. William H. Filman et al. (Cambridge, Mass., 1960–), 14: 373–430, contains the text of several speeches Emerson delivered during his lecture series on "American Slavery" in the winter of 1854–55. Its contents suggest that Emerson was giving serious thought to writing a book on the history of American slavery, but this project was never completed.

21. Gougeon's *Virtue's Hero* exaggerates the extent to which Emerson's public opposition to slavery rendered him a fully committed social reformer. Closer to the mark was the brief but nuanced characterization Wendell Phillips offered in a speech before the Massachusetts

Having earlier faulted Elkins and other American historians for unfairly taking Emerson to task in not saying or doing more to fight slavery, I hasten to add that my point here is not a roundabout restatement of their long-standing complaint. I acknowledge the limits of Emerson's efforts, yet I want to understand them with greater sympathy than modern historians have been able to muster. My alternative interpretation of his efforts can be summarized as follows. Emerson's conduct and thinking regarding American slavery reflected an essential ambivalence about the way in which he, struggling to remain a connected critic of his society, chose to conceive his opposition. From 1844 to 1861 Emerson saw the struggle to end American slavery as, above all, an effort to end the continuing moral degradation of his fellow citizens in free Northern states. To accomplish that goal, he had to draw attention to the North's own open complicity with slavery and condemn it as the outcome of the political and moral cowardice of Northern leaders. Yet at the same time he had to champion certain values and achievements that he saw as setting North and South apart.[22] That alone, after all, is what allowed him to hold on to the belief that Northern states—especially his beloved Massachusetts—would somehow regain their true moral and political bearings and act to end slavery. Before the coming of civil war, Emerson was, then, both highly critical of Northern states and intensely loyal to them. Pulled so powerfully in opposite directions, it does him no discredit to conclude that, at its deepest levels, his position in opposing slavery reflected an ambivalent attachment to the North's way of life. Under the circumstances, it is difficult to imagine what other position he might have taken.

Anti-Slavery Society in Boston on January 27, 1853: "[Emerson's] services to the most radical antislavery movement have been generous and marked. He has never shrunk from any odium which lending his name and voice to it would incur. Making fair allowance for his peculiar taste, habits, and genius, he has given a generous amount of aid to the antislavery movement, and never let its friends want his cordial 'Godspeed.'" See *Wendell Phillips on Civil Rights and Freedom,* ed. Louis Filler (New York, 1965), 33–34.

22. It is worth noting here that when, in his 1844 address, Emerson turned from discussing the course of British emancipation to consider political developments in his own country, "the painful comparisons" he documents speak to the conduct of New England, rather than America. See "Emancipation in the British West Indies," 847, where Emerson said of his feelings while reading Clarkson's *History:* "Whilst I have read of England, I thought of New England."

5

"Resistance to Civil Government" and "Slavery in Massachusetts"

THOREAU SAW American slavery as a national disgrace, a moral and social evil worse than any other, and he hated it and those who defended it without qualification. That hatred was conveyed in the angriest sentences he ever wrote. One of the repeated themes of Thoreau's antislavery writings was the pernicious influence of Northern newspapers on popular understanding of what was at stake in the struggle to end slavery. He condemned several proslavery Boston newspapers by name in "Slavery in Massachusetts," asking rhetorically: "Could slavery suggest a more complete servility than some of these journals exhibit? Is there any dust which their conduct does not lick, and make fouler still with its slime?" The worst of them was the *Boston Herald*: "When I have taken up this paper with my cuffs turned up," Thoreau wrote, "I have heard the gurgling of the sewer through every column" (101).[1]

Viewed historically, however, there was nothing unusual about Thoreau's anger. He echoed the feelings of many other opponents of Amer-

---

1. "Slavery in Massachusetts," in *The Writings of Henry David Thoreau, Reform Papers*, ed. Wendell Glick (Princeton, 1973). Page numbers included in the text refer to this edition.

ican slavery, and was by no means alone in saying that slavery could never be humanized or gradually reformed. The central puzzles of Thoreau's opposition to American slavery instead lie in what I will speak of as his inconsistencies and his silences. The inconsistencies are more conspicuous than the silences. One emerges from a careful reading of his antislavery essays: while Thoreau often pointed to economic self-interest as one of the chief hurdles to popular support for abolition in the Northern states, he also at times appealed to self-interest in trying to stir popular opposition to slavery. Another can be seen in juxtaposing his essay on "Slavery in Massachusetts" and a passage at the outset of *Walden*. Delivered initially as an address before some three thousand people gathered at an antislavery celebration organized by William Lloyd Garrison in Framingham on July 4, 1854, then quickly printed in the *Liberator* and the *New York Tribune*, the essay was in part a fierce condemnation of both the political leaders and the ordinary citizens of Thoreau's home state for failing to resist federal enforcement of the Fugitive Slave Law. And yet less than three weeks later the first edition of *Walden* was published, and there he would observe that, given various other injustices in American society, the priority given to slavery bordered on being "frivolous."[2]

I

Thoreau's inconsistencies can be explained, even if they cannot be logically resolved. The anger he felt about slavery ultimately was detachable from his criticisms of the general course of American economic development. Moreover, while Thoreau saw little reason to celebrate the continuing development of America's market economy, he recognized, as we shall see, that at least one of the ruling ideas of the market—property understood, in part, as the right to self-ownership—could be rendered something more than a rationalization of economic self-interest. (He didn't mean that abolitionists were frivolous in any absolute sense, but rather that it was "frivolous" to allow the problem of "foreign" [Southern] slavery

---

2. *Walden*, ed. J. Lyndon Shanley (Princeton, 1971), 7: "I sometimes wonder that we can be so frivolous, I may almost say, as to attend to the gross but somewhat foreign form of servitude called Negro Slavery, there are so many keen and subtle masters that enslave both North and South. It is hard to have a Southern overseer; it is worse to have a Northern one; but worst of all when you are the slave-driver of yourself."

to distract his contemporaries from slavery [understood as lack of self-ownership] in Northern states.) Finally, as for the American abolitionist movement itself, Thoreau's antipathy to slavery never kept him from finding fault with the organized opponents of slavery.

What I have called Thoreau's silences, however, are somewhat harder to sort out, and yet arguably more important in grasping what was distinctive about his opposition to slavery. Concerning one of those silences—he took no interest in considering what the example of Britain's emancipation of its West Indian slaves in 1834 meant for American opponents of slavery—there is perhaps no great mystery. Because Thoreau was for immediate and unconditional abolition, it is reasonable to assume that, unlike advocates of more gradual reform, he thought there was nothing to be learned from Britain's earlier politically drawn-out and economically costly efforts to end slavery.[3] Two other silences are more enigmatic. For all his hatred of the injustice of slavery, Thoreau never cast himself in two roles that we know were regularly assumed by other opponents of slavery: redeemer of corrupt white Southern society and liberator of suffering black Americans. While there are some strains of evangelical rhetoric in his anti-slavery writings, Thoreau never employed the notion of a "Slave Power" conspiracy—even when he defended John Brown—to express his opposition. He also never publicly hinted at what he thought America might become once slavery was eliminated. Nor did he ever make any public comment on the question of race.

Thoreau could hardly have been unaware of the central importance of these issues in the American abolitionist campaign. Several years before he spoke out against slavery, Garrison and his followers had recognized that the North's failure to take decisive action to end slavery had to be explained, in part, as a consequence of their own region's racial prejudices. Hence, many of those who campaigned for the end of slavery in antebellum America came to condemn and try to remove limits on the freedom of Northern blacks. Thoreau, however, remained entirely silent about the question of Northern racial attitudes and practices, and never openly speculated about what would become of Southern slaves once they were free.

---

3. See ibid., where in the same paragraph that Thoreau described the priority given to slavery as "frivolous," he wrote: "What a man thinks of himself, that it is which determines, or rather indicates, his fate. Self-emancipation even in the West Indian provinces of the fancy and imagination—what Wilberforce is there to bring that about?" Thoreau's point here can be interpreted in different ways, but it strikes me as consistent with what I attempt

A *"Vexed and Disorganizing Question"*

These silences have been almost entirely ignored in modern interpretations of Thoreau's antislavery writings. What do they mean? At the very
least, I think they suggest that while Thoreau believed much of what the
organized opponents of American slavery had been saying since 1830, he
did so without what he took to be certain illusions that continued to sustain their visions of a restored or reborn America. Thoreau, as I interpret
his views in this chapter, thought that in the face of national resistance
abolitionists displayed too much confidence in predicting both the course
and the endpoint of their struggle. I also think his skepticism here means
that his silences have to be understood, in part, by contrasting them to
what might be called the false universalism of other Northern abolitionists, one prominent example of which Thoreau doubtless knew by way of
Emerson's 1844 address on "Emancipation in the British West Indies."[4]
More conventional Northern opponents and critics of slavery like Emerson viewed it as an affront to progressive national ideals, thereby condemning it as an institution that had prevented America from forging a single
national identity rooted in universal liberal values. This in turn explains
why American abolitionists, however deeply they may have divided over
the question of tactics, typically presented their struggle against slavery as
one that would end when the slaveholding Southern states finally came to
adopt the norms and achievements of the North. In Thoreau's view, however, this view of what was at stake in the abolitionist crusade was false
because it had prevented Northern opponents of slavery from adequately
acknowledging the practical significance of the resistance to abolition
they encountered close to home. As a result, in denouncing American slavery, Thoreau never wrote of a potential triumph of light over darkness.
Indeed, his opposition to slavery in the end was haunted by a deep pessimism that had less to do with the power of Southern slaveholders, or the
suffering of Southern slaves, than with what he called "the time-serving
irresolution" (108) of the vast majority of his white Northern contempo-

---

to show in this chapter is one of the neglected central claims of his antislavery writing—
namely, the fight against American slavery had to begin with a transformation of Northern
culture and moral sensibility.

4. It was Thoreau who acted as Emerson's agent in arranging with James Munroe and
Company for publication of his address as a pamphlet. See also Thoreau, "Ktaadn," in *The
Maine Woods*, ed. Joseph J. Moldenhauer (Princeton, 1972), 34, where he recounted his discovery of a copy of the pamphlet "half buried by leaves" at a loggers' campsite, noting that
it "had made two converts to the Liberty party here."

raries. In 1854, almost twenty-five years after abolitionism had become a conspicuous presence in American life, Thoreau observed that while much had been said about American slavery during his lifetime, "I think that we do not even yet realize what slavery is"—and there can be no question that it was the North's passivity and indifference he had in mind when he made that remark (96).

Yet even as he underlined and lamented the North's irresolution and self-deception, it is clear that Thoreau wanted them to end. Hence, while refusing to embrace the hopeful visions that sustained the abolitionist movement in the face of resistance, he joined it in the effort to define ways of ending Northern complicity. Tossed between fear and hope in his understanding of American slavery, Thoreau was determined to pursue hope. Even while his hope was considerably more circumscribed than that which inspired organized opponents of slavery, he too spoke and wrote against slavery chiefly to inspire opposition. What follows here, then, is an attempt to retrace the complex path Thoreau followed as he tried both to keep his distance from the abolitionist movement and to define the fight against American slavery as a project that had to focus chiefly on a transformation of Northern culture. Until that was accomplished, Thoreau believed, any effort to tell the South what to do about slavery would remain transparently hypocritical.

2

While my main concern here can be seen as an examination of the ways in which Thoreau argued for a shift in some of the priorities of the abolitionist movement, it would be misleading to imply at the start that his attempt to define a more effective plan of action represented a wholly new departure. We know, for example, that the bitter protest that Thoreau voiced over the annexation of Texas and the war with Mexico at the outset of "Resistance to Civil Government" was already widespread in Northern states by the mid-1840s. So, too, was talk of disunion and civil disobedience as practical steps to opposing the further expansion of slavery. (In 1845 both the Massachusetts and the Ohio legislatures had threatened to refuse compliance with the federal statutes enabling Texas statehood.) As I attempt to make better sense of the complexity of Thoreau's own response to slavery, then, the first point that I want to explore is the extent to which he continued to draw on attitudes and values that other opponents of American slavery in his day had already articulated before him.[5]

One largely unnoticed parallel between Thoreau and organized opponents of slavery lay in their shared belief that the abolitionists' basic task was to create a deeper awareness among their contemporaries of what slavery required to be done in their name. In practice, this usually involved forsaking conventional politics to pursue various projects in "moral suasion" meant to translate popular antislavery feelings into concrete acts of personal resistance. Voicing opposition to slavery in print was one of the central means of resistance: scores of newspapers, books, magazines, and pamphlets whose titles already numbered into the thousands by the time Thoreau made his widely noticed contributions.[6] So too were petition campaigns, and countless speeches and sermons delivered week in and week out at "antislavery celebrations" that took place throughout the Northern states. There were also individual efforts to break ties with established institutions that tolerated or defended slavery. First in religion, and later in politics, acts of "coming out"—of individuals separating themselves from proslavery institutions—were justified as a means of quarantining both Southern slaveholders and those who defended or protected them. Withdrawal from existing churches, for example, was advocated as a necessary response when they resisted serious antislavery commitments. Somewhat more controversial were calls for political "disunion"—withdrawal of

---

5. The literature on the attitudes, strategies, and values of American abolitionism is voluminous. My account draws from Aileen S. Kraditor, *Means and Ends in American Abolitionism: Garrison and his Critics on Strategy and Tactics, 1834–1850* (New York, 1970); James B. Stewart, *Holy Warriors: The Abolitionists and American Slavery* (New York, 1976); Ronald G. Walters, *The Antislavery Appeal: American Abolitionism after 1830* (Baltimore, 1976); Eric Foner, *Politics and Ideology in the Age of Civil War* (New York, 1980); and Robert William Fogel, *Without Consent or Contract: The Rise and Fall of American Slavery* (New York, 1989), 201–387.

6. It is striking that such a familiar point should remain so inadequately explored and understood. While the American antislavery movement is of course a road well-trodden by historians, we do not as yet have a detailed account of the central role printing and publishing played in that movement. The spread of "print" undoubtedly served to expand conventional limits of causal perception and moral responsibility along lines suggested by Thomas L. Haskell in "Capitalism and the Origins of the Humanitarian Sensibility, Part 1," *American Historical Review* 90 (April 1985): 339–61; "Capitalism and the Origins of the Humanitarian Sensibility, Part 2," *American Historical Review* 90 (June 1985): 547–66. (Emerson was aware of the importance of the newspaper in spreading abolitionist sentiment in America. See "The Fugitive Slave Law," in *The Selected Writings of Ralph Waldo Emerson*, ed. Brooks Atkinson (New York, 1940), 861–62.)

support from the American Constitution, a document radical abolition-ists condemned as an evil compact conceived to preserve and perpetuate slavery. As a strategy to express one's personal commitment to end slavery, Garrison and his followers also justified disunion as a temporary 'moral secession,' defending it as a reasonable interim strategy for a true abolition-ist to pursue while seeking the end to slavery elsewhere. Critics of this approach, however, a group that had included Emerson before passage of the Fugitive Slave Law in 1850 changed his view, thought the threat of disunion only served to make abolitionists appear menacingly unpatriotic. And that appearance seemed confirmed by sometimes flamboyantly de-fiant gestures, the most notorious of which was Garrison's public burning of a copy of the United States Constitution at the 1854 4th of July anti-slavery rally in Framingham where Thoreau first delivered "Slavery in Mas-sachusetts" as a public address.

While Thoreau never gave his unqualified support to the organized opponents of American slavery, there seems little reason to doubt that he admired and, to some degree, shared their determination to create a deeper national consciousness about slavery. The three essays he pub-lished in defense of John Brown remain perhaps obvious instances of "moral suasion." And, as we shall see, it was Brown's eloquence in speaking out against slavery at his trial—not the violence of his Harper's Ferry raid—which Thoreau wanted to emphasize in those pieces. But a desire to stir public opinion no less clearly defined certain passages in his earlier writ-ings. At the outset of "Resistance to Civil Government," he insisted that on the question of slavery ordinary citizens of the free Northern states remained agents of their own mastery, even in the face of the long-standing complicity of their cultural and political institutions. "Let every man make known what kind of government would command his respect," Thoreau urged, "and that will be one step toward obtaining it" (64). More pointedly, near the end of "Slavery in Massachusetts," he announced: "It is not an era of repose. We have used up all our inherited freedom. If we would save our lives, we must fight for them" (108).

Both essays also went on to conceive strategy for a popular fight against slavery in terms already endorsed by other abolitionists. In fact, viewed from one angle, "Resistance to Civil Government" can be seen as both a recounting and a justification of Thoreau's own political "coming out." The detailed description of his night in the Concord jail—highlighted in the form of a bracketed section in the final third of the essay—beckoned readers to see exactly what refusing one's allegiance to an unjust government might entail. Moreover, in defending his refusal to pay the Massachusetts poll tax, Thoreau was careful to explain what he presented as a close logical relationship between the strategies of disunion and civil disobedience, and he thereby also gave greater precision to a plan of action that Garrison had been the first to advocate but then left quite vague. Writing in 1845 to explain how disunion would come about, Garrison had seemed to hold out the possibility that a single individual, not just his state, might secede from the Union to express opposition to slavery. In "Resistance to Civil Government," Thoreau would explain more clearly that for opponents of American slavery disunion actually entailed a sequence of two linked choices—the first being a matter of state politics; the second, of individual moral choice.[7] He certainly believed that the glaring injustice of slavery justified free Northern states in acting to dissolve the Union, and never quite foreclosed the possibility of such action taking place. But he also went on to stress that as long as the Northern states refused to do their duty, individual opponents of slavery had little choice but to dissolve their ties with their home states. Or, as he put it more succinctly five years later in "Slavery in Massachusetts," "Let each inhabitant of the State dissolve his union with her, as long as she delays to do her duty" (104).

Disunionist assumptions have sometimes made Thoreau and other abolitionists appear indifferent to the historical fate of their nation. It is worth noting, however, that their calls for individual expressions of conscience were in fact often accompanied by patriotic appeals to the past of local communities, especially by the frequent reminder that all the New England states had a collective identity as free political communities. If slavery jeopardized the Union, it could not be allowed to undermine the freedom of the Northern states, and so those who preached abolition fashioned a Northern sectional ideology in which they often cast themselves as redeemers of their native states. This was a side of abolitionism that Thoreau recognized and affirmed in his earliest antislavery writing: an April 1844 *Dial* review of Nathaniel P. Rogers's antislavery weekly, *Herald of Freedom*.[8] It also appears frequently in the rhetoric of both "Resis-

---

7. On Garrison and disunion, see Kraditor, *Means and Ends in American Abolitionism*, 198–203, 206–8; Walters, *Antislavery Appeal*, 130–33.

8. See "Herald of Freedom," in *Reform Papers*, 50. Thoreau said of Rogers's weekly: "No other paper that we know keeps pace so well with the forward move of the restless public sen-

tance to Civil Government" and "Slavery in Massachusetts," where Thoreau repeatedly made it clear that one of his chief concerns was "the destiny" (91) of Massachusetts and its citizens.

For Thoreau, as for other contemporary abolitionists, appeals to local patriotism were thus joined to the commands of individual conscience in justifying the belief that the continuing expansion of slavery had made secession by Northern states inevitable. Additional support for disunion came from their analysis of the ways in which the American Constitution had institutionalized the slave system, thereby obligating the federal government to maintain injustice. In the view of abolitionists, advocacy of disunion and civil disobedience was not simply a matter of protecting the moral and political integrity of the Northern states. It also involved an explanation of why they felt that they had no choice but to cut the legal and political threads that held America together. Here abolitionists emphasized that while America's Declaration of Independence initially had promised all its citizens a birthright of liberty, the makers of the Constitution had subverted that promise by compromising with slave interests. Far from venerating the Constitution, then, most abolitionists also came to insist that the legal and political structures it had created were defective from the outset, and concluded that the effort to rectify its defects required a momentous moral transformation.[9]

The belief that the Constitution was a proslavery compact no less clearly informed Thoreau's opposition to slavery. In "Resistance to Civil Government," he insisted that pushing for action at the federal level — whether by way of petitions or electoral campaigns — was pointless, for the

---

timent and thought of New England." He also included excerpts from Rogers's writings that illustrated the way in which he raised "the anti-slavery 'war-hoop'" on the occasion of the 1843 New England Anti-Slavery Convention in Boston. Rogers's strategy was to appeal to each state in New England in a name-by-name litany that began with Massachusetts.

9. There is now a large literature on this complex subject; my account draws from Walters, *Antislavery Appeal*, 8, 42, 131–32, 136–37; and Fogel, *Without Consent or Contract*, 329–38. There was also a strain of "antislavery constitutionalism" among abolitionists. Perhaps the best known instance can be found in the views of Frederick Douglass, who reversed his earlier stance that the Constitution was simply a proslavery instrument that he could neither respect nor support. The reversal was perhaps not surprising when one considers that most antebellum black Americans probably recognized the harsh view of the Constitution voiced by Garrison and Thoreau as too despairing. On Douglass, see Sanford Levinson, *Constitutional Faith* (Princeton, 1988), 74–80, 216 n. 79.

nation's legal system had never been designed to make all Americans free. Like other radical abolitionists, Thoreau believed that there was no practical remedy for the evil of slavery to be found in the workings of America's government precisely because its founding Constitution itself "was the evil." From this it followed that, again like other radical abolitionists, Thoreau had little respect for his nation's founding fathers. He spoke dismissively of Jefferson and Adams as figures who had allowed guarantees of slavery to be written into the Constitution and in the process forged "an agreement to serve the devil" (103). In Thoreau's own time, Daniel Webster was of course the devil's chief servant when it came to American slavery. In "Resistance to Civil Government," Thoreau acknowledged with grudging respect that Webster's often eloquent defense of the Constitution had served to make him America's most respected politician. Yet he also underlined the extent to which that defense required Webster to remain blind to the larger truth that America's Constitution had created a nation in which justice "may consist with wrong-doing."

Finally, while abolitionists fashioned a sectional ideology to show Northerners how slavery represented a rejection of and threat to their most cherished values, they eventually came to see that their calls to action were being dismissed or ignored by the vast majority of their contemporaries. Popular rejection of abolition in Northern states in turn suggested that positive appeals to local patriotism alone would not suffice. As a result, the sectional ideology of abolitionists—unlike that of the defenders of slavery—often became fiercely self-critical and pessimistic. Accusations of cowardice brought against Northern religious and political leaders were broadened to become more sweeping indictments of the corruption of Northern institutions. This course initially led some abolitionist clergy to form new churches and new denominations based on antislavery principles. Later it led Garrison and his followers into an uncompromising struggle for equal civil rights for free Northern blacks. It led, as well, to a recognition that slavery was inextricably involved in the economic and political structures of the entire nation, thereby allowing slave owners and their defenders to wield tremendous influence in the Northern states. In this context, the North's refusal to take decisive action against slavery came to be explained—and angrily denounced—as the outcome of the region's increasingly commercial and materialistic culture. (It was difficult "to plant the self-sacrifice of Anti-Slavery," Wendell Phillips once complained, in the midst of a "money-loving country, intensely devoted to gain."[10]) Abolitionists argued that the North had suffered morally from its economic good fortune, and so the struggle to end the suffering of Southern slaves became a struggle against their region's own self-degradation. In practical terms, this meant abolitionists also came to challenge all social and economic institutions that required or justified the North's continuing complicity with slavery, among which they included churches, courts, newspapers, and universities.

Once again we find Thoreau repeating much of this analysis of the forces opposing abolition in the North and of the strategy needed to meet and overcome them. In "Slavery in Massachusetts," he proclaimed that the majority of Americans clearly were not "men of principle" (102). And while the essay began with a biting condemnation of the Massachusetts governor's readiness to support enforcement of the Fugitive Slave Law in his state, Thoreau concluded that the worst that could be said against him was "that he proved no better than the majority of his constituents would be likely to prove." He also insisted at the outset of "Resistance to Civil Government" that the chief opponents to abolition in Massachusetts were not distant Southern politicians, "but a hundred thousand merchants and farmers here, who are more interested in commerce and agriculture than they are in humanity." He then went on to say that as an opponent of slavery his quarrel was not with "far off foes, but with those who near at home, co-operate with, and do the bidding of those far away, and without whom the latter would be harmless" (68). Like other abolitionists in his state, Thoreau obviously believed that the affluence of Massachusetts was partly to blame for its passivity and indifference. "The more money, the less virtue," he declared, since the wealth of rich men inevitably put to rest moral questions that otherwise they would be taxed to answer. Even more disturbing to Thoreau, as we have seen already, were the proslavery editors and writers of the Northern popular press. He saw them as the current masters of popular opinion, and hence the most important targets of abolitionist efforts in the North. The practical upshot of that view was an explicit and angry appeal to "free men of New England" to boycott the Boston *Herald*, *Post*, *Mail*, *Journal*, *Advertiser*, *Courier*, and *Times*. Those who continued to read these

---

10. Phillips, as quoted in Walters, *Anti-Slavery Appeal*, 113.

proslavery newspapers, Thoreau wrote, were "in the condition of the dog that returns to his vomit" (100).[11]

3

So far I have concentrated on the ways in which "Resistance to Civil Government" and "Slavery in Massachusetts" embodied values and practical concerns characteristic of the abolitionist movement as a whole. This approach makes it possible, first of all, to identify a still widespread misunderstanding of the relationship between Thoreau's views and the more conventional commitments of American abolitionists in the 1840s and 1850s. It has often been said that, while Thoreau insisted upon the immediate necessity of ending slavery, his stance as a conscientious objector never aimed at actual political reform, but was instead inward-oriented and concerned mainly to avoid complicity with evil. Bertram Wyatt-Brown has even gone so far as to say that Thoreau never "took an active part with the radicals in the great cause of the day" and had little influence upon the immediatists they knew.[12] It should be clear by now, however, that the format and many of the main arguments and presuppositions of Thoreau's essays served to align him closely with other radical abolitionists of his day. He accepted that the chief work of an abolitionist was to educate Northern public opinion and thereby to effect a profound change in the ideology of the Northern states. He also shared the widespread view that the struggle over slavery in America had resulted in an irreconcilable conflict between Northern and Southern states. While re-

---

11. The feeling of contempt was mutual; see, e.g., the June 19, 1849 *Boston Courier* review of *Aesthetic Papers* (1849), the volume in which Thoreau's "Resistance to Civil Government" first appeared. "We must dismiss Mr. Thoreau," the *Courier* commented, "with an earnest prayer that he may become a better subject in time, or else take a trip to France, and preach his doctrine . . . to the red republicans."

12. Bertram Wyatt-Brown, *Yankee Saints and Southern Sinners* (Baton Rouge, 1985), 26–31. Wyatt-Brown apparently has overlooked Thoreau's widely noticed appearance at Garrison's controversial antislavery celebration in Framingham on July 4, 1854. It was Horace Greeley's reprinting of Thoreau's address in the *New York Daily Tribune* of August 2, 1854, which assured his participation received national attention. See, e.g., the notice of *Walden* that appeared in the *New Orleans Daily Picayune* of August 24, 1854; this brief announcement mentions that an earlier "specimen of Mr. Thoreau's quality" could be found "in the 4th [of] July oration he delivered at the Abolitionists' traitor-celebration, where Garrison signalized the occasion by burning a copy of the [C]onstitution."

jecting the notion of a "Slave Power conspiracy" to describe the intentions of the Southern states, Thoreau clearly was something of a Northern sectional ideologist. He shared with Emerson and many others the assumption that in America the need to uphold freedom and justice had devolved upon the leaders and ordinary citizens of free Northern states. While this side of Thoreau's opposition to slavery has hardly registered in modern scholarship, all of his writings against slavery suggest that in the end his deepest feelings about the question were engaged with his fellow citizens of Massachusetts, where his home state is alternatively described as "base and servile" yet still potentially "the champion of liberty" (106). Those feelings were reflected too in his criticisms of Northern abolitionists' obsession with the conduct of Southern states, an obsession he saw as serving to deflect attention away from the North's own continuing complicity.[13]

A second reason for stressing Thoreau's ties to the mainstream abolitionist movement is that this approach puts us in a position to see more clearly how far Thoreau went in modifying or challenging some of the other values and strategies that were characteristic of the movement. There can be little question that Thoreau wanted his name and his writings to be of use to those actively committed to ending slavery. We know, too, that despite his refusal to attach religious meaning their struggle, Garrison and his followers certainly welcomed his support and thought that, at some level, it made a difference. But Thoreau made it clear his views of slavery were never entirely interchangeable with those of other abolitionists.[14]

---

13. See, e.g., Thoreau's thinly veiled allusion to Samuel Hoar's controversial mission to Charleston in November 1844, in "Resistance to Civil Government," 75–76. Concord's leading lawyer and former congressman, Hoar had been sent to investigate charges that free black sailors from Massachusetts had been seized while in port. The mission was regarded as an insult in South Carolina, and Hoar was forced to leave without a reply. The refusal of South Carolina's governor to answer Hoar's questions also quickly came to be seen in Northern states as an insult to one of the most prominent citizens of Massachusetts. Thoreau's view, however, was that the episode represented another example of the way in which his state was "anxious to foist the sin of slavery upon her sister" (75). On the Hoar mission, and Emerson's view, see Gay Wilson Allen, *Waldo Emerson: A Biography* (New York, 1981), 427–30.

14. The point was underlined with particular emphasis at the outset of his most popular lecture, "Life Without Principle," in *Reform Papers*, 155: "A man once came a considerable distance to ask me to lecture on Slavery; but on conversing with him, I found that he and his clique expected seven-eighths of the lecture to be theirs, and only one-eighth mine; so I declined."

So the question remains: Where exactly did he depart from the prevailing assumptions of other abolitionists?

Thoreau's departure is evident in at least three areas, I would suggest. Perhaps the most obvious of these was his reluctance to find personal meaning and direction in his opposition to slavery. In "Resistance to Civil Government," Thoreau said plainly that he had not been arrested to expiate any personal sense of guilt. While sharing the shame of American slavery, he clearly resented that sharing. He also admitted with exceptional candor that he never considered himself a useful guide to social reform. "I came into this world, not chiefly to make this a good place to live in," he wrote, " but to live in it, be it good or bad" (74).[15] Historians today frequently argue that the extraordinary moral stamina of the vast majority of American opponents of slavery flowed, in great part, from their conviction that they were soldiers arrayed under the generalship of God to fight a sin whose presence in American society represented a barrier to both personal and national salvation.[16] But Thoreau certainly was no "holy warrior." He never spoke of American slavery as a sin, and found Christianity Janus-faced on the matter of slavery; in his view, the Bible spoke the language of political passivity as readily as the language of civil resistance.[17]

Thoreau's refusal to partake of the missionary zeal that characterized mainstream abolitionism may also help account for his unwillingness to see abolitionism as part of a broader campaign to create a better American society. Here it is important, however, to consider carefully what Thoreau meant when he said that his opposition to slavery was something that pertained chiefly to the question of what each individual must do in the face of a legally sanctioned injustice. Two brief passages, in particular, deserve close scrutiny:

---

15. Thoreau's sentiments here echoed those voiced earlier by Emerson in "Self-Reliance," *Essays: First Series*, vol. 2, *The Collected Works of Ralph Waldo Emerson*, ed. Joseph Slater, Alfred R. Ferguson, and Jean Ferguson Carr (Cambridge, Mass., 1979), 31: "I do not wish to expiate, but to live. My life is for itself and not for a spectacle."

16. Donald M. Scott, "Abolitionism as a Sacred Vocation," in *Antislavery Reconsidered: New Perspectives on the Abolitionists*, ed. Lewis Perry and Michael Fellman (Baton Rouge, 1979), 51–74; Stewart, *Holy Warriors*.

17. See "Resistance to Civil Government," 77–78, where Thoreau commented that the familiar biblical injunction—"Render therefore to Caesar that which is Caesar's, and to God those things which are God's"—typically left Christian believers "no wiser than before as to which was which; for they did not wish to know."

Unjust laws exist: shall we be content to obey them, or shall we endeavor to amend them, and obey them until we have succeeded, or shall we transgress them at once? (72–73)

I wish my countrymen to consider, that whatever the human law may be, neither an individual nor a nation can ever commit the least act of injustice against the obscurest individual, without having to pay the penalty for it. (96)

It is fair to say that by posing the problem of slavery in such terms, Thoreau seemed to suggest, as many commentators have observed, that abolition was irrelevant to the collective accomplishment of any larger religious or political goals. Or, put another way, in these passages, acting to end the injustice of slavery appears to be chiefly a matter of individuals separately choosing to disobey those laws that happened to support slavery, and aiming to do no more than avoid lending themselves to a gross injustice they condemned.

Yet there may be some reasons for exercising caution in pursuing this familiar line of analysis. Nancy Rosenblum has suggested recently, for example, that while Thoreau's opposition to slavery originated in fear of his own complicity in the evil of slavery, it would culminate in a broader "assault on every government and all laws."[18] But this probably overestimates the practical significance of his well-known conviction that all social and political institutions, at some level, were coercive and unjust. It certainly would be a mistake to overlook the fact that Thoreau recognized a special moral urgency in efforts aimed at the elimination of slavery. In "Resistance to Civil Government," he said plainly he was refusing his allegiance to a proslavery government, not government per se. He also insisted that the injustice of slavery was unlike any other, precisely because its legal protections required Americans to be the active agents of injustice to others. Moreover, it is not accurate to assume that Thoreau's call for civil disobedience aimed at complete individual detachment, not concrete political reform. Thoreau plainly had no desire to plunge into the political arena, and he shared the radicals' doubt that projecting the abolitionist program into a struggle for political office would ever lead to a breakthrough. Yet the "peaceable revolution" he explicitly called for in

---

18. Nancy L. Rosenblum, *Another Liberalism: Romanticism and the Reconstruction of Liberal Thought* (Cambridge, 1987), 108–9.

"Resistance to Civil Government" was hardly a summons to political retreat. His immediate purpose was clear enough: to define a strategy that would stop the machinery of government in individual Northern states so long as those states allowed the federal government to continue to enforce the Southern slave owner's right to his human property. And the practical means to that end were equally clear: on the one hand, private citizens must refuse to pay their state poll tax bills; on the other, local political officials must resign their offices. In short, it is apparent that Thoreau recognized that individual acts of civil disobedience by themselves would not suffice. It was only when action was taken on both of these fronts—"civil resistance" to government from within as well as from without—that the "peaceable revolution" he envisioned as a means to end American slavery might be accomplished.[19]

There can be no question, however, that Thoreau's plan of action here never pointed to anything beyond the elimination of Northern complicity with slavery, and I would argue that it is precisely here that we find the heart of Thoreau's differences with other American abolitionists. Despite often deep disagreements about strategy, the two primary subgroups of the American abolitionist movement, most American historians now seem to agree, saw their cause as part of a crusade to create a freer and more just nation. To be sure, radical abolitionists like Garrison and his mainly New England followers believed that American society, in the North as well as in the South, was immoral, with slavery only the worst of its many sins. Yet at the same time they looked forward to accomplishing a thoroughgoing change in America's institutional structure. Moderate abolitionists, on the other hand, who viewed the Garrisonians as impractical fanatics, considered Northern society fundamentally sound and so believed that abolition of slavery would eliminate a deviation from the nation's essential goodness, thereby preserving and strengthening its just arrangements. Whatever their differences in analyzing America's condition, however, both radical and moderate abolitionists anticipated hopeful outcomes to their

---

19. Richard E. Flathman, *Toward a Liberalism* (Ithaca, 1989), 163–64, has argued that "The familiar criticism that civil disobedients either do not understand authority or aim to destroy it (that they are in fact revolutionaries or anarchists) is belied by the details of their thought and action," and that there are in fact various ways in which the theory and practice of civil disobedience can be said to accommodate authority and law. Flathman doesn't discuss "Resistance to Civil Government," but this line of analysis could be applied usefully to Thoreau's famous essay.

struggle that Thoreau plainly never came to endorse. Where the Garrison-ians believed that abolition would lead to the creation of a new America, and moderates argued it would remove an unnecessary flaw, Thoreau saw irreparable damage and division. Or, put more sharply, the political strug-gle over American slavery, as we find it presented in his writings, had sig-naled an inescapable disintegration of national patriotism. At the outset of "Resistance to Civil Government," for example, he observed that the American war with Mexico over the annexation of Texas suggested the struggle to end slavery might very well cost Americans "their existence as a people" (68). Later, attempting to make sense of the failure of the "free men of New England" to resist enforcement of the Fugitive Slave Law, he described his first response as "having suffered a vast and indefinite loss," a loss that he could not explain until it occurred to him that "what I had lost was a country" (106). Where other opponents of slavery thought that threads cut for the sake of abolition could be resewn, Thoreau saw them to be permanently rended.

This side of Thoreau's antislavery thinking can be described as a rejec-tion of what Howard Zinn once described as an "hypothesis of common interest" that underlay all strategies to end slavery.[20] It is arguable that in the years before Brown's raid on Harper's Ferry, Thoreau stood alone in pub-licly expressing his glum belief that the struggle over slavery had already resulted in the political suicide of his nation—a prospect that even the most radical abolitionists of his day would have disavowed. I would sug-gest, too, that this attitude throws some light on the puzzles of Thoreau's silence about the racial dimensions of slavery and of his refusal to embrace the rhetoric of "Slave Power." For if Thoreau assumed that there were actu-ally two nations in antebellum America, only one of which could still hope to be free, it would seem to follow that his writings were addressed exclusively to shaping the opinions of the potentially free half of a now parted nation. Moreover, if Thoreau saw his chief responsibility in speak-ing out against slavery to be unmasking "the cowardice and want of prin-ciple in Northern men," it might follow, too, that he thought Southern slaves and slave owners would be left to fend for themselves, once the ties between North and South were fully broken.[21]

---

20. Howard Zinn, "Abolitionists, Freedom-Riders and the Tactics of Agitation," in *The Antislavery Vanguard: New Essays on the Abolitionists* (Princeton, 1965), 435.

21. Michael Meyer, "Thoreau and Black Emigration," *American Literature* 53 (November 1981): 380–96, pursues an oblique reference in Thoreau's journal to suggest that, in the after-

4

The exact character of the alternative position Thoreau wanted to defend here, however, evades any simple summary. Sometimes it appears that his chief purpose in speaking out against slavery was to underline the fact that both the political and cultural leadership and the ordinary citizens of Northern states together were agents of the horrible injustice of slavery. Sometimes he also seems fixed on a criticism of the abolitionist movement itself frequently made by modern American historians—namely, that the movement was based on self-flattering assumptions about the supposed moral superiority of Northern states. (No one could accuse Thoreau of directing his moral outrage against the oppression of slavery in the South while ignoring what some have come to insist was a similar oppression then coming to life in the industrializing factories of the North.[22]) Yet if Thoreau was a critic of other abolitionists, he always remained, like Emerson, a partial or connected critic—a figure intent on complicating rather than rejecting most of what they had already said before him. Moreover, if we see Thoreau as a partial critic of both "radical" and "moderate" abolitionism, he then becomes an unlikely advocate of *one* correct abolitionist doctrine. He certainly did not come to see civil disobedience or individual acts of violent resistance as the only promising means of opposing slavery; in fact, he usually presented them as choices that few individuals would ever make. Nor did he ever quite close off all hope for existing abolitionist strategies. In fact, in "Slavery in Massachusetts" he appears to have reversed his earlier view that all institutional efforts to combat slavery were pointless. The failure of state and federal courts to overturn slavery, he now argued, left little choice but to "trust to the sentiment of the people." "In their vote," he wrote, "you would get something of some value, at least, however small" (97).

For all its complexity, then, Thoreau's central message in speaking out

---

math of John Brown's failed raid, he entertained the idea that black emigration to Haiti could be a practical solution. But all the evidence here, as Meyer himself concedes, is circumstantial. It should be said, too, that even had Thoreau actually found colonization sensible, it would not necessarily follow that he also believed (as Meyer asserts) blacks "to be inherently docile and vulnerable to white dominance" (396).

22. See *Walden*, 7. It is worth noting here, however, that while Thoreau thought it did make some sense to compare Southern slaves and Northern wage-laborers, he ultimately saw no reason to lump the two together as variations on the single theme of labor exploitation.

against slavery remained that the complicity of free Northern states such as Massachusetts had to be recognized and overcome. And the effort to convey this message meant, in turn, that he—like other radical abolitionist thinkers—had to find ways of sustaining ties to the political and economic order of a region whose institutions he saw as deeply implicated in an abominable injustice. In brief, Thoreau at times may sound like he wanted to stand alone in his opposition to slavery, but he also wanted to be heard, to be effective, and in pursuit of his larger practical goal, he recognized that sometimes he had to speak with the language and the values of those he criticized.

Thoreau's endorsement of many of the main assumptions of the sectional ideology of mainstream abolitionism, which we have already considered above, provides the most obvious example of this self-understanding. There was an ideological foundation for Thoreau's abolitionism, in other words, and it was one shaped out of his loyalty to what he took to be the established moral and political values of free Northern states, as well as to the commands of his conscience. It is arguable, too, that Thoreau's determination to remain a connected critic of the "free men of New England" provides a plausible explanation for what I spoke of at the outset of this chapter as the apparent inconsistency of his attitudes toward their economic values. There were, as we have seen, harsh sentences in both "Resistance to Civil Government" and "Slavery in Massachusetts" where Thoreau seemed to say that the North would have to choose between its new wealth and traditional moral and political values. In this context, Thoreau presented the triumph of market principles and institutions in antebellum America not as a measure of the South's failure, but of the North's. He noted, too, that the economic supports of slavery in the North were even more formidable than its political ones, and condemned "free trade" as a slogan that had served to rationalize the continuation of complicity with the injustice of slavery. There are other sentences, however, that make Thoreau's true sentiments harder to read, for they suggest that he sometimes saw that opposition to slavery could in fact be based on market values. Near the end of "Slavery in Massachusetts," for example, commenting on the passive response of his contemporaries to the enforcement of the Fugitive Slave Law, he observed:

> I am surprised to see men going about their business as if nothing had happened. I say to myself—Unfortunates! they have not heard the news. I am

surprised that the man whom I just met on horseback should be so earnest to overtake his newly-bought cows running away—since all property is insecure—and if they do not run away again, they may be taken away from him when he gets them. Fool! does he not know that his seed-corn is worth less this year—that all beneficent harvests fail as you approach the empire of hell? No prudent man will build a stone house under these circumstances, or engage in any peaceful enterprises it takes a long time to accomplish. (107)

The call for opposition to slavery in this passage, at first glance, appears to have little to do with either moral conscience or economic sacrifice. Thoreau suggests quite plainly that the Fugitive Slave Law—one of whose provisions empowered United States marshals to deputize citizens of Northern states on the spot to aid in seizing fugitive slaves (and to impose stiff criminal penalties on anyone who harbored a fugitive or obstructed his capture)—represented an unrecognized menace to ordinary economic activity in the North. While Thoreau never doubted that eliminating slavery would cost Northerners a great deal, here he held out the possibility that enforcement of the new Fugitive Slave Law might cost them even more.

In saying that the 1850 Fugitive Slave Law had made all property insecure, however, Thoreau can be said to be making a moral as well as a prudential point. For if federal pursuit of fugitive slaves threatened to interfere with Northern men going about daily "peaceful enterprise it takes a long time to accomplish," continuing legal recognition of the right of the individual to own another person at the same time represented a rejection of a central moral assumption that served as the foundation of all forms of private property: the right of self-ownership. Now this view was hardly peculiar to Thoreau; here again he echoed the sentiments of other abolitionists who also equated self-ownership with freedom, and so fused economic and moral beliefs so tightly there is little point in drawing a line between them. But the ideological implications of this equation remain open to interpretation. Most contemporary American historians tend to approach the abolitionists' appeal to the right of self-ownership chiefly as a matter of establishing, in Ronald Walters's view, a "propaganda advantage." Often accused of undermining the slave owners' legally recognized right to property, abolitionists are sometimes said to have simply reversed the indictment (as Thoreau did in the passage above) and cast the slaveholder and his supporters in the role of economic menace. While this certainly describes part of the abolitionists' purpose in appealing to the sanctity of property, it would be an oversimplification, in Thoreau's case at least, to go on to suggest that when he said "all property was insecure" he remained, as Walters puts it, "within ancient, ultimately conservative, assumptions about the rights of individuals to possess the goods accumulated by their labor" and thereby unwittingly advanced the interests of the Northern bourgeois class.[23] This approach is inadequate in dealing with Thoreau, in part, because it serves to obscure what should be seen as a genuine ambivalence that informed his understanding of the relationship between abolitionism and Northern economic institutions. As we have already seen, Thoreau was never hesitant to condemn the unconcerned wealthy elite of his own state, and it would be absurd to suggest that he ever dreamed of a new "Yankee South" as one of the outcomes of abolition. Yet a second and perhaps more significant point to note here is that in trying to stir up opposition to slavery it also proved impossible for him to see all of Massachusetts as somehow in the wrong. Thoreau obviously wanted to make its citizens uncomfortable about the absence or inadequacy of their efforts to end slavery. But he never said with certainty that they had to make themselves over completely to eliminate its specific injustice. On the question of what bearing Northern economic institutions and beliefs had in the struggle to end American slavery, then, Thoreau can be said to have criticized market values from within as well as from without, appealing to certain values he never fully embraced as his own, yet recognizing too that those values could be enlisted in the cause of abolition.

Another example of Thoreau's mixing of criticism and accommodation can be seen in his contrasting appeals to property in "Resistance to Civil Government." There he began by saying that concern for property compromised a commitment to justice, since property owners "cannot spare the protection of existing government, and they dread the consequences of disobedience to it to their property and families" (78). Yet in the essay's last paragraph, Thoreau argued, in effect, that the property owner's "dread"

---

23. Walters, *Antislavery Appeal*, 122. While Thoreau does not mention these details explicitly, it is worth noting that the new law required expenses of capturing and returning Southern slaves to be borne by the federal treasury, and fined U.S. marshals and deputies who refused to help slaveowners capture their property. The provisions of the 1850 law are summarized in Stanley W. Campbell, *The Slave Catchers: Enforcement of the Fugitive Slave Law* (Chapel Hill, 1970), 23–25.

was misconceived. Fear of losing the "protection" of government here gave way to the recognition that the "authority" of even "a strictly just" form of government—that which has "the sanction and consent" of the individuals governed—remains an "impure one," and hence open to individual acts of disobedience. No government "can have a pure right over any person and property but what I concede to it" (89), Thoreau wrote, thereby recasting property ownership as a ground for resistance rather than compromise.

Two final points need to be noted briefly. My account of Thoreau's stance in opposing American slavery clearly cannot be squared with the familiar picture of him as one of a group of Northern intellectuals who welcomed a looming national catastrophe. The catastrophe had already occurred in Thoreau's view when legal protections for slavery had been written into the U.S. Constitution. The question of moment with him, then, was whether or not "free men" in the Northern states would act to repair the damage slavery had inflicted on their own communities. "Slavery in Massachusetts" showed that in 1854, almost a quarter-century after the American abolitionist campaign had begun, Thoreau believed that the movement as yet had accomplished little of significance. Yet it showed, too, that he was not ready to despair or to give up his anger. In that essay's two concluding paragraphs, he appears to have been saying that his anger remained tied to some sort of hope, for at least he could still find solace in a natural world "still young and full of vigor" (108) for the continuing irresolution of his contemporaries. The evocative language of the concluding paragraphs, however, also reflects the views of someone who remained unclear about exactly what action such solace might inspire. It comes as no surprise, then, to discover that for five years after the summer of 1854 Thoreau chose not to speak again in public against slavery. The Dred Scott decision in 1857 passed without any comment in his diary, private letters, or later published writings. Only the unexpected news of John Brown's raid on Harper's Ferry moved him to think once more about how to take an effective stand for abolition.

6

John Brown and
the Crisis of the Union

THE FIRST REPORTS of John Brown's raid at Harper's Ferry on October
17, 1859, were not welcomed by Northern abolitionists, all of whom were
initially shocked by the violence of the raid and immediately condemned
it. But Brown's action thrilled Thoreau, and quickly brought him out of
five years of silence that had followed publication of "Slavery in Massachusetts." "John Brown's career for the last six weeks of his life was meteor-
like," he later recalled, "flashing through the darkness in which we live. I
know of nothing so miraculous in our history."[1] Those same six weeks were
also a time during which defending Brown became Thoreau's consuming
purpose. Against the strong opposition of Concord's Republican Town
Committee, he delivered his "Plea for Captain John Brown" as a public
address in the Concord Town Hall on October 30, twelve days after Brown
had been captured by the United States militia. ("I do not send for your

---

1. "The Last Days of John Brown," in the *Writings of Henry David Thoreau, Reform Papers*,
ed. Wendell Glick (Princeton, 1973), 145. The text of this essay was prepared for delivery
at a John Brown "celebration" on July 4, 1860, in North Elba, New York, where Brown was
buried on the farm he had owned. It first appeared in print in the July 27, 1860 issue of the
Liberator.

advice," he replied to the committee, "but to announce that I am to speak.") Three days later he repeated the address before a larger audience at the Tremont Temple in Boston, then again in Worcester on November 3. Thoreau's "Plea" was reported or summarized in several Boston and New York newspapers, which as a group condemned his statement as a misconceived defense of a fanatic. The widespread attention Thoreau's speech received, however, also suggests that his was perhaps the first important defense of Brown at a time when the news of Harper's Ferry had met almost universal condemnation in North and South alike. When Brown was hanged in Virginia on December 2, Thoreau took the lead in organizing a simultaneous commemorative service in Concord. Here he shared the stage with Emerson and others in reading elegiac selections from Marvell, Sir Walter Raleigh, and Tacitus. Speakers had agreed to read selections from the writings of others, one participant later reported, because they feared that, in voicing their own sympathetic views of Brown, they risked being viewed as advocates of treason.[2]

Emerson's initial response to the news of Brown's raid was, by comparison, more cautious and uncertain. At first, he speculated privately that Brown was a heroic man who had temporarily lost his sanity, and began to draft a letter to the governor of Virginia, Henry Wise, pleading for Brown's life on grounds of insanity. The letter was never completed, however, and Emerson's subsequent public statements in defense of Brown showed few of his private reservations. Easily the most controversial of those statements occurred on November 8. While in the midst of delivering a lecture on courage to the Parker Fraternity at the Music Hall in Boston, Emerson interpolated into his prepared text a spontaneous description of Brown, which the next day the *New York Daily Tribune* reported as follows: "The Saint, whose fate yet hangs in suspense, but whose martyrdom, if it shall be perfected, will make the gallows as glorious as the cross." The comment made for a nationwide controversy that continued into the early months

---

2. Thoreau, as quoted in Len Gougeon, *Virtue's Hero: Emerson, Antislavery, and Reform* (Athens, Ga., 1990), 240. The details of my narrative account of Thoreau's initial involvement with Brown are drawn from Michael Meyer, "Thoreau's Rescue of John Brown from History," in *Studies in the American Renaissance*, ed. Joel Myerson (Boston, 1980), 301–16; and Gougeon, *Virtue's Hero*, chs. 7 and 8. Accounts of the initial lecture version of Thoreau's "Plea" appeared in the *Boston Atlas and Daily Bee*, the *Boston Daily Advertiser*, the *Boston Post*, Garrison's *Liberator*, and the *New York Tribune*. The most severe criticism came in the November 3, 1859 *Springfield Republican*, which observed: "This Thoreau seems to be a thorough fanatic—why don't he imitate Brown and do good by rushing to the gallows."

of 1860, and served to link Emerson with Thoreau in his willingness to risk public disapproval and scandal in rallying to Brown's defense. In Boston, Emerson also joined a committee created at the beginning of November to raise contributions to aid in the legal defense of Brown and his companions. Ten days after the Parker Fraternity address, he attended a meeting at Tremont Temple in Boston "For Relief of the Family of John Brown," and there made a short speech in which he described the Harper's Ferry raid as a "commanding event" that eclipsed "all others which have occurred for a long time in our history." Emerson also praised Brown as a "patriot" and "the rarest of heroes, a pure idealist, with no by-ends of his own," and publicly proclaimed himself part of "the family of John Brown."[3]

After John Brown's execution, when James Mason of Virginia was appointed chair of a Senate committee to investigate the activities of the "Secret Six" who had backed the Harper's Ferry raid, both Emerson and Thoreau figured prominently in events that grew out of the Mason committee's efforts to capture one of its prominent members, Franklin Sanborn. Then head of the Concord Academy and locally known as one of Emerson's protégés, Sanborn had received a summons to appear before the committee in January 1860, but fearing for his personal safety refused to do so, and twice fled to Canada. After returning from his second flight, Sanborn mistakenly had become convinced that the Mason committee had lost interest in his case, but agents of the committee presented themselves in Concord with an arrest warrant on the evening of April 3. Sanborn resisted, and his confrontation with the agents quickly drew an angry crowd of Concord supporters that included Emerson. While Emerson joined a group that openly challenged the legal authority of the agents, Sanborn's lawyer managed to secure a writ of habeas corpus. The following day in Boston, Chief Justice Lemuel Shaw voided the Mason committee's arrest warrant on a technicality, and Sanborn returned to Concord in triumph. That evening, at a town meeting called in his honor, he shared the stage with Emerson and Thoreau. To all those present, the practical lesson of the attempted capture of Sanborn was obvious enough: not even Concord was now safe from the aggressive power of Southern slaveholders.

---

3. "John Brown," in *The Selected Writings of Ralph Waldo Emerson*, ed. Brooks Atkinson (New York, 1940), 879–80. The details of my account of Emerson's initial involvement with Brown are drawn from John McAleer, *Ralph Waldo Emerson: Days of Encounter* (Boston, 1984), 532–33; John J. McDonald, "Emerson and John Brown," *New England Quarterly* 44 (September 1971): 377–96; and Gougeon, *Virtue's Hero*, chs. 7 and 8.

The meeting concluded with the group, including Emerson and Thoreau, endorsing resolutions that stated the "fame of old Concord" had been served "by the chivalrous rescue of one of our most honored citizens," and that "the doctrine of the Revolution, that 'resistance to tyrants is obedience to God,' is our doctrine."[4]

I

In the final decades of the nineteenth century, one frequently cited reason for including Emerson and Thoreau in the American canon of required learning was the exceptional courage they supposedly had shown in speaking out at once for John Brown when the vast majority of their contemporaries initially condemned the raid on Harper's Ferry as the work of a dangerous fanatic. (It is worth noting here that it would be Franklin Sanborn, as much as anyone, who labored to arrange for the posthumous canonizations of Emerson and Thoreau—and not surprisingly, the controversy surrounding John Brown figured prominently in his admiring accounts of their careers.[5]) In recent decades, however, commentators have displayed little interest in considering any of the risks Emerson and Thoreau took in defending Brown and have focused instead on the question of how much they knew about the twisted life of a man they supported before his capture and then sought to canonize after his trial and execution. The standard reply has been that Emerson and Thoreau either knew little of, or simply chose to ignore, Brown's violent misdeeds—especially his leading role in the brutal murders of five unarmed proslavery men at Pottawatomie Creek, Kansas, in May 1856—for the sake of making him a transcendental hero. And the practical upshot of their naïve idealization is said to have laid the groundwork on which others quickly came to construct the Brown legend.[6]

---

4. For a more detailed discussion of Emerson, Thoreau, and the "Secret Six," see Jeffrey Rossbach, *Ambivalent Conspirators: John Brown, the Secret Six, and a Theory of Slave Violence* (Philadelphia, 1982); and Gougeon, *Virtue's Hero*, ch. 8.

5. See, e.g., Sanborn, *Personality of Emerson* (Boston, 1902), 86–89; *Henry D. Thoreau* (Boston, 1917), 285–89, 383, 478, 481, 484, 486, 487; *Table Talk*, ed. Kenneth Walter Cameron (Hartford, 1981), 65, 161, 250.

6. On the roles Emerson and Thoreau played in giving life to the Brown legend, see James C. Malin, *John Brown and the Legend of Fifty Six* (Philadelphia, 1942), ch. 11. The key figure in the story is James Redpath, whom Malin describes as "the first man to qualify as Brown's biographer." Redpath's *Public Life of Captain John Brown* appeared on January 10,

There are, however, at least two problems with the current approach. One is the anachronistic assumption that Emerson and Thoreau, writing in the heat of events, somehow could have managed to be more objective guides in helping others understand a figure whose career to this day remains one of the great challenges in American historiography.[7] The second, which interests me more given the concerns of the second part of this book, is a curiously persistent refusal to investigate fully what Emerson and Thoreau themselves hoped to accomplish in defending Brown. There can be no question that their descriptions of Brown's character and activities were incomplete and misleading in some respects. He was by no means the "quiet and gentle child" Emerson spoke of in a second speech about John Brown at Salem on January 6, 1860, nor the "Angel of Light" Thoreau tried to evoke in his "Plea." But taken in their entirety, the accounts of Brown we find in Emerson and Thoreau were by no means blank endorsements. To dismiss them as whitewashes is to ignore the fact that neither Emerson nor Thoreau ever said that Brown's raid had charted a path that other opponents of slavery were now obliged to follow. It also is to mitigate their unmistakable contention that Brown's chief legacy did not lie in bloodshed, but in what they extolled as the moral eloquence of the self-defense he presented after his arrest. Emerson said quite plainly it was not the raid on Harper's Ferry so much as Brown's "speeches to the court" that had interested the nation in him. "Everything that is said of [John Brown] leaves people a little dissatisfied," he observed at the outset of his Salem speech, "but as soon as they read his own speeches and letters, they are heartily contented,—such is the singleness of purpose which justifies him to the head and the heart of all." Thoreau echoed this view when he com-

---

1860, and was dedicated to Wendell Phillips, Emerson, and Thoreau, whom Redpath referred to as the "highest talent in the nation" and praised as those "who, when the mob shouted, 'madman,' said 'Saint!'" This volume was quickly followed by *Echoes of Harpers Ferry* (1860), in which Redpath gathered "the best speeches, sermons, letters, poems and other utterances of leading minds in Europe and America, called forth by John Brown's invasion of Virginia." This collection included Thoreau's "Plea for Captain John Brown," Emerson's two speeches on Brown, as well as the readings each had given at the Concord memorial service on December 2.

7. Meyer, "Thoreau's Rescue of John Brown from History," 302–7, forcefully questions the view that Thoreau knew little of Brown's violent activity in Kansas by reconstructing contemporary newspaper accounts of Brown's past that appeared shortly after the Harper's Ferry raid. Given the deep contempt with which Thoreau viewed Northern newspapers, however, it can hardly be surprising that he would have disregarded accounts that documented Brown's involvement with the massacre at Pottawatomie Creek.

mented that Brown "could afford to lose his Sharps' rifles, while he retained his faculty of speech, a Sharps' rifle of infinitely surer and longer range." Brown's raid, Thoreau recognized immediately, meant that abolitionists now had little choice but to contemplate the likelihood of more violence if they ever hoped to settle the question of slavery. Yet it also put Thoreau himself back in the camp of "moral suasion" as a remedy for American slavery. One of the great blunders of those who captured and tried Brown, he would later observe, was that they "did not hang him at once, but reserved him to preach to them."[8] It was the eloquence of Brown's "preaching," more than anything else, that Thoreau saw as the ground on which to judge his actions.

2

This is not the place, however, for an extended exploration of the many issues involved in understanding how Emerson and Thoreau responded to Brown or how their responses helped give rise to the Brown legend. What follows focuses primarily on certain attitudes and themes that grew directly out of their earlier antislavery writings. I proceed mostly by furnishing several largely ignored or misunderstood passages with some brief commentary. The commentary itself does not aim to refute the verdict that Emerson and Thoreau were selective in their accounts of Brown, but rather to draw attention to some of the neglected complexity of those selective accounts, and thereby reinforce the general line of analysis pursued in chapters 5 and 6.

(a) There can be little question that the immediate historical purpose Thoreau and Emerson shared in defending Brown and his followers was to counter the almost universal condemnation with which the news of the Harper's Ferry raid was greeted in Northern states.[9] "I read all the newspapers I could get within a week after this event," Thoreau observed near the outset of his "Plea," "and I do not remember a single expression of sympathy for these men." We have seen already that Thoreau long had viewed

---

8. Emerson, "John Brown," in *Miscellanies* (Boston, 1878), 279, 276; Thoreau, "A Plea for Captain John Brown," 127.

9. On the response in Massachusetts, see Betty L. Mitchell, "Massachusetts Reacts to John Brown's Raid," *Civil War History* 19 (March 1973): 65–79. On the national repercussions of Harper's Ferry, see James McPherson, *The Battle Cry of Freedom: The Civil War Era*

with contempt the North's largely proslavery press, so the harsh treatment of Brown in Northern newspapers could hardly have come as a surprise to him. Nonetheless, it is clear that he was outraged by what he read, and stressed that his chief motive in speaking out was to provide a sympathetic alternative to what he saw as a slanderous campaign against Brown being waged by the Northern popular press. "I would fain do my part to correct the tone and the statements of the newspapers, and of my countrymen generally respecting his character and actions," he proclaimed. "It costs nothing to be just. We can at least express our sympathy with, and admiration of, him and his companions, and that is what I now propose to do."[10]

Emerson apparently took little notice of the popular press's very negative accounts of Brown. Yet he used the occasion of Brown's raid to condemn other Northern institutions. In his speech at the Tremont Temple in Boston, Emerson angrily contrasted Brown's "courage and integrity" with the cowardice of most Northern judges, who were willing to do "substantial injustice" because they feared "a collision between their two allegiances." In saying that Brown's idealism was based on his ability to see "how deceptive the forms are," Emerson clearly had not forgotten how federal courts, complying with the new Fugitive Slave Law of 1850, had handled the cases of Sims, Shadrach, and Anthony Burns. He also found it ironic that the only public figure ready to speak with any measure of sympathy for Brown had been Virginia's Henry Wise, governor of the state in which Brown was tried and executed. "It is the *reductio ad absurdum* of Slavery," he observed, "when the governor of Virginia is forced to hang a man whom he declares to be a man of the most integrity, truthfulness and courage he has ever met." Thoreau saw the same lesson in Wise's stance, but gave it a harsher twist when he went on to describe Brown and his followers as "almost the first Northern men whom the slaveholder has learned to respect."[11]

(b) Neither Emerson nor Thoreau appears to have been deeply concerned with justifying what Brown had done at Harper's Ferry. It is true that Thoreau wrote that he would "not be forward to think him mistaken

---

(New York, 1988), 202–13; also see the vivid account of the alarm Brown's raid caused in one Southern state in Clarence L. Mohr, *On the Threshold of Freedom: Masters and Slaves in Civil War Georgia* (Athens, Ga., 1986), ch. 1.

10. "Plea," 122, 111.

11. "John Brown," in *Selected Writings*, 880–81; "Plea," 128.

in his method who quickest succeeds to liberate the slave," and that he was troubled by the failure of Garrison and other Northern abolitionists to rally at once to Brown's defense. Like Emerson, however, he made it clear that expressions of sympathy for Brown did not require approval of his method or his principles. "What though he did not belong to your clique!" Thoreau insisted, "recognize his magnanimity. Would you not like to claim kindredship with him in that, though in no other thing he is like, or likely, to you?" In fact, both Thoreau and Emerson had remarkably little to say about the raid itself. They of course knew that it had failed, yet also commented that they knew little about its actual purposes. "We do not know the facts about it," Thoreau remarked, and there is no sign that either he or Emerson ever came to understand that Brown himself had planned the raid to spark a possible slave uprising that would spread throughout the South.[12]

What formed the basis for most of the attention Emerson and Thoreau gave to Brown was instead the persona he himself attempted to create in letters and speeches made public during the time of his trial and execution.[13] Hence, they followed his lead in downplaying violence and bloodshed and stressing instead his larger spiritual mission—a mission that consisted primarily of speaking the truth about slavery. The John Brown Emerson and Thoreau sought to memorialize had never meant to spark an abolitionist-led slave rebellion in Southern states; he was instead a figure who had acted alone, giving his life to "the cause of the oppressed," with the more limited purpose of running off "five hundred or a thousand slaves." Moreover, after his arrest and during his trial, he had, by way of letters and speeches, brought new hope to opponents of slavery, who still relied chiefly on moral suasion, believing that slavery would end when Northerners were convinced of its sinfulness and injustice. "In teaching us how to die," Thoreau wrote, Brown and his followers had "at the same time taught us how to live," and in his view the chief measure of the success of

---

12. "Plea," 133, 123-24, 138.

13. McDonald, "Emerson and John Brown," 391-93, has shown, for example, that both the facts and the phrasing of Emerson's January 6, 1860 Salem speech were drawn from a long autobiographical letter Brown had written on July 15, 1857. The letter, written to the son of George L. Stearns, was made available to Emerson in December 1859, and later reprinted in Redpath's *Public Life of Captain John Brown* and in F. B. Sanborn, *Memoirs of John Brown* (Concord, 1878), 7-11. Contemporary newspaper accounts of Brown's testimony in his own behalf were available in the *New York Herald*.

the Harper's Ferry raid would be whether it served to create and sustain a revival of abolitionist sentiment in the North.[14]

(c) For Emerson and Thoreau, then, Brown was less a national hero than a partisan one. As with their earlier antislavery writings, they defended Brown, in large part, in a shared effort to touch the consciences of the ordinary citizens of free Northern states. To this end, it is clear that they wanted their contemporaries to see that Brown was, in certain respects, one of them. In trying to counter the press's charges that Brown was crazy, Emerson and Thoreau argued that he in fact embodied the traits of self-control, common sense, civic responsibility, and devotion to family that they took to be among the characteristic moral values of free Northern men. Emerson called Brown a "representative of the American Republic," but the synopsis of Brown's life that he provided stressed the "the perfect Puritan faith" of his New England ancestors and Brown's own "far-seeing conduct and skill" as a man who had once made his living as a shepherd and herdsman. What was known of Brown's past, Emerson observed, told of a figure who had secured "one year with another, an honest reward, first to the farmer, and afterwards to the dealer." Seen from this angle, Brown became "a merchant prince, not in the amount of wealth, but in the protection of the interests confided to him." Thoreau made the same point somewhat more concisely in his "Plea," when he wrote that Brown "was by descent and birth a New England farmer, a man of great common sense, deliberate, and practical as that class is, and tenfold more so."[15]

(d) As with the broader question of slavery, it seems fair to say Emerson's and Thoreau's deepest feelings about Brown were engaged with what they took to be the inadequate response of their own contemporaries in Northern states. For Emerson, Brown's act only served to stir memories of how the honor of Massachusetts had been "trailed in the dust" when its courts had failed to protect the freedom of runaway slaves. In the final portion of his November 18 speech, Emerson also remarked, in a thinly veiled allu-

---

14. Thoreau, "Plea," 125, 134. In his Salem speech, despite an opening promise to "cling" to the history of Brown's life, Emerson in fact barely alluded to events at Harper's Ferry. See "John Brown," in Emerson, *Miscellanies*, 275–81.

15. Emerson, "John Brown," in *Selected Writings*, 879; Thoreau, "Plea," 112–13. Lewis Perry, *Radical Abolitionism: Anarchy and the Government of God in Antislavery Thought* (Ithaca, 1973), 256, argues that the martyrdom of Brown "fed Thoreau's hatred of the respectable, commercial world." But this view must ignore Thoreau's desire to show that Brown himself had come from that same world.

sion to the precarious status of Northern supporters of Brown's scheme, that the citizens of his state now had to prepare to act when federal courts would likely fail again. It would be foolish to believe, Emerson observed, that when the United States Court in Virginia had finished with "its present reign of terror," and then "sends to Connecticut, or New York, for a witness," it would want him to participate in an impartial hearing. "No it wants him for a party; and it wants him for meat to slaughter and eat." Confronted with the power of the federal courts, a local writ of habeas corpus would offer little protection, and Emerson concluded with the clear suggestion that popular civil disobedience now had become the only practical alternative to a legal system fully committed to the preservation of slavery.[16]

There remains something of a puzzle, however, in understanding why Emerson and Thoreau chose to be among the first to speak out for John Brown. The grounds on which they had opposed slavery, after all, were in important ways different from Brown's—and each of them in fact would note some of those differences even as they defended him. Unlike Brown, before October 17, 1859, neither Emerson nor Thoreau had seen the elimination of slavery in America as central to the missions of their lives. They had never previously spoken of slavery as a "sin" to be opposed because it violated the Christian Golden Rule. Nor had they endorsed what they clearly took to be Brown's optimistic interpretation of the Constitution or his belief that the campaign to end slavery was a struggle to preserve the Union of the States. As we saw in the previous two chapters, by the mid-1850s both Emerson and Thoreau, like other radical abolitionists, had come to believe both that the Constitution had been designed and interpreted to provide legal guarantees for slavery, and that those who sought abolition had little choice to press for the dissolution of the unjust federal system the Constitution had established.

Although it is difficult to measure the extent to which Brown caused Emerson and Thoreau to reevaluate these views, it is certainly misleading to say that Brown ever possessed, even for a short time, a hypnotic hold over them. Too much can be made of Thoreau's initial view that Brown's action had raised the question of whether abolitionists were ready to kill or be killed in the struggle to end American slavery. For he at the same time described Brown's "respect for the Constitution, and his faith in the

---

16. "John Brown," in *Selected Writings*, 881–82.

permanence of this Union" as "old-fashioned," and given Thoreau's own views of the Constitution, the adjective cannot have been meant as a compliment. Also, as we shall see, Brown's example would not cause him to abandon his despairing view of the politics of American slavery.[17]

Emerson, too, recognized that Brown condemned slavery as both a sin and "an obstruction to the Union," and he saw that it was here Brown had found moral and political justification for violence as means to end slavery. It is hard to read the brief passage in which Emerson underlined these points, however, as an unqualified endorsement of Brown's views and conduct:

> He believes in two articles—two instruments, shall I say?—the Golden Rule and the Declaration of Independence; and he used this expression in conversation here concerning them, "Better that a whole generation of men, women and children should pass away by a violent death than that one word of either should be violated in this country." There is a Unionist— there is a strict constructionist for you. He believes in the Union of the States, and he conceives that the only obstruction to the Union is Slavery, and for that reason, as a patriot, he works for its abolition.

The tone of these remarks is somewhat puzzling. There surely is admiration for Brown here, but it comes in company with a gentle mocking of his naïve view of what the struggle against slavery entailed. While Brown's courage and patriotism were beyond question in Emerson's view, his intelligence apparently was not, since Brown's justification of violence seems to be portrayed in this passage as the outcome of a simple-minded reasoning that Emerson made no effort to disguise. Indeed, at the conclusion of his November 18 speech in Boston, he distanced himself from Brown's brand of violent abolitionist patriotism by concluding that the best way for opponents of slavery to honor Brown's memory was to secure "freedom and independence in Massachusetts," a more circumscribed project in which Brown surely would have taken little interest.[18]

---

17. "Plea," 112.

18. "John Brown," in *Selected Writings*, 880, 882. Additional evidence that Emerson's speeches on Brown's behalf were not seen as unqualified defenses of his character can be found in a letter Emerson received from Franklin Sanborn shortly after his Salem speech. Not surprisingly, Sanborn had high praise for Emerson's synopsis of Brown's life, but also noted that "your criticism of the *man* is an apt answer to such censures as that in the last Atlantic that I would fain see it soon printed." The "censures" alluded to here refer to a sharply critical review of James Redpath's *Public Life of Captain John Brown* that had just

(e) While both Emerson and Thoreau admired Brown because they thought he might shame the North into action, they were not wholly of one mind in explaining what new practical initiatives might be taken. Emerson attempted to fit Brown into the framework of the disunionist assumptions of Northern sectional ideology that Thoreau never quite fully accepted. In his view, Brown's trial and conviction by a United States Court provided new evidence of the unabated strength of "Slave Power," and the practical lesson of the failed effort at Harper's Ferry was not more violence but the need to renew Northern efforts to dissolve the Union of the States. Thoreau's judgment of Brown, on the other hand, was characteristically tied to a much harsher judgment of the Northern states. He was considerably more troubled than Emerson by the North's refusal to acknowledge Brown as one of its own, less convinced that Brown was the epitome of Northern values than a virtuous aberration whose significance others would never grasp. "He was too fair a specimen of a man to represent the like of us," Thoreau concluded, and it is arguable that one of the main reasons why Thoreau immediately sided with Brown was because his act served as an unmistakable reminder of a point Thoreau himself frequently made—namely, that the abolitionist movement had accomplished astonishingly little in their efforts to end American slavery. "It was no abolition lecturer that converted him," Thoreau noted in the first speech he gave in defense of Brown.[19]

(f) While Emerson's and Thoreau's absorption with Brown was intense, it also turned out to be short-lived, and did little to draw either of them more deeply into the abolitionist movement. Each refused offers to write Brown's biography. After composing "The Last Days of John Brown" early in the summer of 1860, Thoreau, in declining health, took no further interest in the public controversy that continued to surround Brown. Emerson remained peripherally involved in fundraising efforts for Brown's widow and children, but his Salem speech would be his last contribution of any length to the literature and mythology of John Brown. And when his lecture on "Courage" was later published in *Society and Solitude* (1870), his earlier controversial comments on Brown were omitted.

---

appeared in the *Atlantic Monthly*, March 1860, 378–81. It was Sanborn who subsequently arranged for the inclusion of Emerson's Salem speech in Redpath's *Echoes of Harper's Ferry*, 119–22. See *The Letters of Ralph Waldo Emerson*, ed. Ralph Rusk, 6 vols. (New York, 1939), 5:188, n. 5.

19. "Plea," 127, 113.

3

There is of course much more to say about Emerson's and Thoreau's views of Brown and about their place in giving rise to his legend.[20] For my purposes, however, enough evidence has been explored here to suggest that in speaking out for Brown Emerson and Thoreau remained what they had been before the Harper's Ferry raid: opponents of slavery who found themselves standing at some distance from the organized opponents of slavery; thinkers who despaired of conventional political and legal solutions but remained ready to help in the work of inspiring popular opposition to slavery; and more often critics of the North's compromising stance than of the South's injustice.

There also is added reason here for discounting the claim that Emerson and Thoreau formed part of a group of Northern intelligentsia who naïvely welcomed the looming catastrophe of violent civil war. Thoreau lived to see the coming of that war, but it did little to change his long-standing gloomy assessment of the political stakes involved in the struggle to end American slavery. His view remained that the North would be better off without the South, and before his death in May 1862, his private correspondence suggests that he welcomed military confrontation only because he anticipated it might allow Southern states to secede from a political union that for some time he had believed was not worth preserving. In a letter written in the early spring of 1861, shortly after Lincoln's election and just before the South's assault on Fort Sumter, Thoreau commented that secession was bound to be accomplished in some manner by the southern states, and added: "If the people of the North thus come to see clearly that there can be no *Union* between freemen and slave-holders, & note & act accordingly, I shall think that we have purchased that progress cheaply by this revolution. A nation with 20 million freemen will be far more respectable & powerful, than if 10 millions of slaves & slave-holders were added to them."[21] What Lincoln would later call a house divided, in Thoreau's view deserved to remain divided.

Before the Confederate attack on Fort Sumter, Emerson felt much the same, although with a different end in mind. He, too, thought the Union

---

20. The most recent account focusing on the latter issue is Richard O. Boyer, *The Legend of John Brown: A Biography and a History* (New York, 1973), chs. 1 and 2.
21. Letter reprinted in *Concord Saunterer* 12, no. 3 (Fall 1977): 20–21.

had ceased to exist some time before the actual secession of the new Confederate states in February 1861. (The price paid for the nation's compromise with slavery, he told the Massachusetts Anti-Slavery Society in Boston on January 24, 1861, was "the South actually separating . . . in sympathy, in thought, and in character from the people of the North.") Rather than leading to permanent disunion, however, secession was for Emerson (as for Garrison and most other abolitionists at the time) a hopeful development that promised to isolate the now Confederate states, thereby turning the corrupting influence of slavery inward and bringing about its inevitable destruction, and the eventual return of the South to the Union. Given that view of the likely result of secession, it also is not surprising that, unlike Thoreau, Emerson welcomed the outbreak of war in April as an unanticipated opportunity to accomplish quickly both emancipation and the cultural and political redemption of the South.[22]

Those hopes of course were quickly proved false by the unexpected defeat of the Union army at the first battle of Bull Run in July 1861. Yet Emerson did not waver in his belief that the North's involvement in the war turned largely on the question of emancipation, and that the war ought not end until slavery had been dealt a death blow. In an address delivered at the Smithsonian Institution on January 31, 1862, he declared that emancipation was "the demand of civilization," and thus the moral imperative that defined and justified the North's purpose in going to war. Yet he stressed, too, that the difficult course of the war had now rendered emancipation a political and military necessity. Above all, Emerson feared that if the measure was not adopted soon, the North "impatient of defeats, or impatient of taxes" would "go with a rush for peace; and what kind of peace shall at that moment be easiest attained." The probable outcome would be concessions that allowed for the continuation of slavery, and then the horrible prospect that "the whole torment of the past half-century will come back to be endured anew." Emerson went on to say that emancipation had also become a potentially useful military measure. In his Smithsonian speech, he speculated that a declaration of emancipation might serve to create a pro-Union army of slaves "in the rear of the Enemy." In August 1862 he later noted in his journal that a second

---

22. Emerson, "American Civilization," as quoted in Gougeon, *Virtue's Hero*, 265. My account of Emerson's response to the Civil War draws largely from Gougeon's richly detailed ch. 8, although I also want to show that he has overlooked some of the self-imposed limits of Emerson's efforts to promote the cause of emancipation and Union.

consideration—the possibility of the South itself declaring unilateral emancipation in order to gain European support—added weight to the view that the North had to adopt the measure as soon as possible.[23]

When Lincoln finally issued the Emancipation Proclamation on September 22, 1862, Emerson carefully commended him as a figure who "has been permitted to do more for America than any other American man," explaining his guarded praise by saying that events in fact had left the president with no other choice. Emancipation had come about as the inevitable response to the political fact that, even had the North agreed to a peaceable secession of the Southern states, "the divided sentiment of the border states made peaceable secession impossible, the insatiable temper of the South made it impossible, and the slaves on the border, wherever the border might be, were an incessant fuel to re-kindle the fire." Emerson recognized that the war "was and is an immense mischief," yet he stressed that it also had brought with it belated recognition of a point abolitionists had been making for decades—namely, that the ultimate intention of the Southern states was to spread slavery to the North. Hence, in Emerson's view, it was primarily political self-preservation that compelled Lincoln to announce that the aim of the war was "to break up the false combination of Southern society, to destroy the piratic feature in it which makes it our enemy only as it is the enemy of the human race, and so allow its reconstruction on a just and healthful basis."[24]

Emerson was committed to emancipation and the restoration of the Union no matter what the cost, and confident that the war would bring the North's advanced cultural norms to the South. Yet his views of the Civil War have left many modern historians dissatisfied. In the final analysis, Emerson's response was, according to Daniel Aaron, typical of most other Northern intelligentsia who also saw the war "as a celestial railroad to authentic nationhood, or as a testing ground for the martial spirit."[25] Yet a careful examination of all that Emerson said and did surely uncovers

---

23. Emerson, "American Civilization," as quoted in Gougeon, *Virtue's Hero*, 280.

24. Emerson, "The Emancipation Proclamation," in *Selected Writings*, 886, 889–90.

25. Daniel Aaron, *The Unwritten War: American Writers and the Civil War* (Cambridge, 1973), 34–38. Aaron's somewhat patronizing judgment of Emerson turns mostly on a selective reading of his 1862 Smithsonian lecture on "American Civilization." Also see Lewis E. Simpson, *Mind and the American Civil War: A Meditation on Lost Causes* (Baton Rouge, 1989), 61–69, who follows Aaron in arguing that Emerson approached the Civil War with the blinders of "a New England and, principally, a Massachusetts man." Simpson's portrait of Emerson as a naïve sectional ideologist is also very selective, ignoring his outrage about

a more complicated and interesting response. While by no means blind to the huge costs of fighting the war, there can be no question that Emerson was fully committed to the North's effort to win the war. Yet there also can be no question that he usually honored that commitment largely on his own terms, and continued to keep his distance from the organized opponents of slavery who immediately became the most vocal supporters of the war. Shouted down by a mob that disrupted the conclusion of his January 1861 speech to the Massachusetts Anti-Slavery Society, the following year Emerson declined Wendell Phillips's offer to return to finish his remarks. Similarly, in September 1861, when Phillips joined William Lloyd Garrison, Franklin Sanborn, and George Stearns to form the Emancipation League, Emerson doubtless was invited to join, but apparently declined. Three years later, his response to Stearns's request that he speak to a public meeting of the league in Boston, contains a partial explanation for why he chose to stand apart: "Much experience has taught me to be very cautious in making speeches in behalf of any cause to which I have a good will. If the hours of your Emancipation League admit of my being in town, I will try to attend it, but not speak to it, as I hope for its success."[26] There is no evidence that Emerson ever attended the meeting, and he perhaps owed Stearns something more in the way of a candid acknowledgment of his own long-standing reluctance to speak in public about the "causes" he favored. Yet the comment that he was "very cautious in making speeches" seems candid enough as a description of the way Emerson had sought to serve the causes of emancipation and Union since the war began. Apart from brief speaking engagements at the Smithsonian and (in November 1864) at a teachers' convention in Pennsylvania, Emerson confined himself to addressing polite and sympathetic audiences gathered at fundraisers and public lectures in Concord and Boston. (He delivered his formal address on the Emancipation Proclamation, for example, at the Music Hall in Boston, on Sunday morning, October 12, speaking with others, yet at a time and a place that were characteristically "cautious.") During the war, Emerson also briefly entertained the idea of collecting his now many antislavery speeches, beginning with "Emancipation in the British West Indies," for publication in a single volume. Yet that project never got

the conduct of New England during the 1850s and overlooking the fact that Emerson believed that only if Union forces fought for emancipation, as well as for Union, would their cause be just.

26. *Letters of Ralph Waldo Emerson*, 5:375.

underway, and the volume, eventually entitled *Miscellanies*, would await posthumous publication by other hands.[27]

Emerson's Smithsonian lecture and his address on the Emancipation Proclamation, however, did quickly find their way into print in the *Atlantic Monthly*.[28] Yet here too it seems fair to say that they were directed at an audience already familiar with his name and writings, and thus prepared to accept Emerson on his own terms. Instrumental in founding the Boston magazine, and having already contributed several poems and literary essays since the appearance of its first number in November 1857, the Emerson of the *Atlantic Monthly* was less a man who occasionally served "causes" of others than a major cultural presence in his own right. And it is this more formidable and free-standing figure we now move on to consider.

---

27. *Journals and Miscellaneous Notebooks of Ralph Waldo Emerson*, 15:167, 362–63; Gougeon, *Virtue's Hero*, 293–94.

28. Emerson, "American Civilization," *Atlantic Monthly*, April 1862, 502–11, and "The President's Proclamation," *Atlantic Monthly*, November 1862, 239–49. James C. Austin, *Fields of the Atlantic Monthly* (San Marino, Calif., 1953), 301–2, comments that Emerson's work "was always sought and always welcome when it arrived, and he received the top rate of pay." Perhaps more significant is the fact that, as of 1860, the *Atlantic* and Emerson shared the same publisher, Ticknor and Fields. In Fields's hands, one function of the *Atlantic*, not surprisingly, was to print his authors and keep proclaiming them unparalleled. (See Richard Broadhead, *The School of Hawthorne* [New York, 1986], 54–55.)

3

"Scribbling Gentry": Emerson and Thoreau in the Literary Marketplace

In looking at the library of the Present Age we are first struck with the fact of the immense miscellany. It can hardly be characterized by any species of book, for every opinion old and new, every hope and fear, every whim and folly has an organ.

— Emerson, "Thoughts on Modern Literature"

We are a race of tit-men, and soar but little higher in our intellectual flights, than the columns of the daily paper.

—Thoreau, *Walden*

7

"A Vast Cultural Bazaar":
The Antebellum Literary Marketplace

THE FINAL PART of this book examines how Emerson and Thoreau experienced changes that the emergence of America's market economy brought to the production, circulation, and status of writing during their own time. In doing so, these chapters address questions originally designed to test and add texture to the portraits of Emerson and Thoreau as connected critics that I drew in parts 1 and 2. How did they understand the changes the market brought to American culture? What were their expectations in publishing? Who were their first readers? How did those readers initially come across their writings, and what happened to them during those encounters? Did they manage to grasp the complex mix of criticism and hope that Emerson and Thoreau put before them? As I gathered and worked through the material that answers these questions, it was hardly a surprise to discover that Emerson and Thoreau had views of antebellum culture altogether as complex and divided as their views of the economic forces that were in the process of transforming it. Nor was an elaborate act of historical reconstruction required to see that knowledge of their work reached the American reading public in a variety of ways, and that their publications figured more prominently in antebellum culture than standard accounts allow.[1] It did become clear early on, however, that the range of responses both writers evoked among their contemporaries was too broad and diverse to be gathered neatly within the interpretive framework I've employed thus far; hence, I will make more limited use of it in the last part of this book. (Emerson and Thoreau are not exceptions to the rule that a writer cannot dictate her reception.) Many of their contemporaries, as we shall see, certainly did respond to the particular aspects of their thinking and writing to which I have drawn attention with the label "connected critic." A few even offered general interpretations that anticipate much of what I attempted to show in part 1 in arguing that Emerson and Thoreau should be approached as loyal critics of their society, writers intent on showing their contemporaries that they were falling short of their own announced ideals.[2] Yet a disparate variety of other things were said about Emerson and Thoreau when their writings first appeared, and nothing resembling a consensus or an official interpretation of their work was in place by the time the Civil War began.

For these reasons, the final part of this book presents accounts of Emerson and Thoreau that will be more institutional than textual and biographical; that is, it will be less concerned with how each of them viewed changes the market brought to antebellum culture, than with the various meanings their writings initially took on within that culture.[3] This chapter thus traces the most important ways in which market forces trans-

---

1. Comprehensive annotated bibliographies now exist for both Emerson and Thoreau; see Joel Myerson, *Ralph Waldo Emerson: A Descriptive Bibliography* (Pittsburgh, 1982); Robert E. Burkholder and Joel Myerson, *Emerson: An Annotated Secondary Bibliography* (Pittsburgh, 1985); Raymond R. Borst, *Henry David Thoreau: A Descriptive Bibliography* (Pittsburgh, 1982); and *Henry David Thoreau: A Reference Guide, 1835–99* (Boston, 1987).

2. In Emerson's case, among the most striking was Harriet Martineau's early portrait in *Retrospect of Western Travel*, 3 vols. (London, 1838), 3:228–40. Martineau's Emerson was the author of "The American Scholar," an essay in which he showed that, "While apart from the passions of all controversies, he is ever present with their principles, declaring himself and taking his stand, while appearing to be incapable of contempt of persons, however uncompromising may be his indignation against whatever is dishonest and harsh" (230). In Thoreau's case, as we shall see in ch. 9, characterizations of him as a Diogenes-like figure were not uncommon.

3. My approach to the question of how the writings of Emerson and Thoreau were received by their contemporaries derives, in part, from the recent work of reader-response literary critics. (For useful surveys of this field, see S. R. Suleiman and I. Crossman, eds., *The Reader in the Text: Essays on Audience and Interpretation* (Princeton, 1980), and Elizabeth Freund, *The Return of the Reader: Reader-Response Criticism* (London, 1987). For cultural and intellectual historians, the chief insight of this school of textual interpretation is perhaps its

formed the institutional arrangements of the culture into which Emerson and Thoreau launched their publications. It also is intended to provide an account of the American literary marketplace considerably more variegated than most current students of Emerson and Thoreau have chosen to employ. Chapters 8 and 9 recount the initial publishing and reception histories of those works we have come to regard as the classic writings of Emerson and Thoreau, and examine the various processes by which they first became visible and gained authority and meaning. The high status we assign to those writings of course has had causes that have changed and multiplied over time. What I want to propose in these final chapters is that one of its original (and largely overlooked) causes lay in the workings of the antebellum literary marketplace itself.

I

Emerson and Thoreau wrote and published during decades when a new kind of culture was forming in America. For simplicity's sake, we now usually speak of the outcome of this transformation as the creation of America's literary marketplace—a gradual yet sweeping change that saw the printed matter of books, magazines, and newspapers displace local networks of oral communication to become the essential means of mass communication and increasingly dominant source of cultural activity.[4] Such a culture, to be sure, had begun to take shape in the final decades of the eighteenth century; as Cathy Davidson and others have demonstrated, in the

---

forceful and sophisticated reminder that texts assume historical significance only when they are actually read, and largely in terms of *how* individuals or groups of readers happen to come across and respond to texts at hand. Seen in this light, the recovery of a text's historical meaning becomes less a matter of uncovering a single overarching meaning in the text itself, than of revealing particular historical conditions that bring about its various possible effects. See W. Iser, *The Act of Reading: A Theory of Aesthetic Response* (Baltimore, 1979), 18.

4. There is as yet no comprehensive history of the development of the antebellum literary marketplace, despite the existence of a great many specialized works on different aspects of authorship and publishing during the period. The cornerstones for study of the subject, however, remain William Charvat, *Literary Publishing in America, 1790–1860* (Philadelphia, 1959), and *The Profession of Authorship in America, 1800–1870: The Papers of William Charvat*, ed. Matthew J. Bruccoli (Columbus, 1968). Also see Russell Nye, *Society and Culture in America, 1830–60* (New York, 1974), and Lewis Perry, *Boats Against the Current: American Culture Between Revolution and Modernity, 1820–1860* (New York, 1993), which appeared when this book was in production.

aftermath of America's Revolutionary War, there were dramatic increases not just in levels of popular literacy and education, but also in the sheer number of books available for circulation.[5] Yet books and more widespread popular literacy were a necessary, not a sufficient cause, for the development of the antebellum American literary marketplace as I intend to consider it here. Equally important were technological innovations such as the cylinder rotary press, stereotyping, and electrotyping, which did not appear until the first half of the nineteenth century. These innovations, which led to a more sweeping cultural reorientation, speeded up the printing process by mechanizing operations that previously had been performed by hand, thereby allowing for the production of books in larger editions and at lower prices than ever before. In 1855 one prominent American publisher estimated that an average of 52 books had been published annually in the United States between 1830 and 1842; by contrast, in 1853, the year before *Walden* appeared, 733 works had been printed—an increase of 800 percent in less than 20 years. The growth in numbers printed in first editions of mid-nineteenth-century books was greater still: initial press runs of 10,000 were not uncommon by the midcentury, and some first editions even went as high as 100,000 copies.

Together with this dramatic increase in the overall supply of books, publishers began to market a variety of new kinds of books. Some designed volumes intended to add prestige to the mere possession of a book. The antebellum period was the heyday of richly bound ornamental books known as "literary annuals" (compendiums of excerpts taken from already published books of poetry and prose) and "gift books" (collections of various kinds of articles, fictional forms, and poetry). Other publishers began the practice of printing individual books in series formats that were designed to popularize the latest literary products and scientific discoveries of the day. Among the most successful of these was the "Family Library" produced from 1830 on by J. J. Harper, with titles that included biographies, histories, natural science, and travel literature. The New York publishing house of Wiley and Putnam also made use of the series format in its effort to promote an indigenous "high" literary culture. Under the editorship of Evert Duyckinck in 1845, it launched "The Library of American

---

5. On the initial impact of print in America, see Cathy N. Davidson, *Revolution and the Word: The Rise of the Novel in America* (New York, 1986), 3–37; and William L. Joyce, David D. Hall, Richard D. Brown, and John B. Hatch, eds., *Printing and Society in Early America* (Worcester, 1983).

Books," which was brought out in parallel with "The Library of Choice Reading," an already successful series of well-established English classics. It would be Ticknor and Fields, however, that during the 1850s brought Duyckinck's project to fruition, and in the process became the first great publisher-patron of American authors. Under the leadership of James T. Fields, the Boston publisher not only built a stronger list than Wiley and Putnam—by 1860 its writers included Emerson (brought to the house in 1859), Hawthorne, Holmes, Longfellow, Lowell, Stowe, and Thoreau—it also pioneered new ways of marketing American literature. During the 1850s it was Fields who began the practice of advertising beyond local markets. He used a nationwide network of friendly ties with editors of newspapers and magazines in which he advertised his books to prompt favorable reviews, in some cases including reviews he had written himself.[6]

The historical emergence of the American literary marketplace during the antebellum period can also be traced by examining the data on the growth of magazines and newspapers. The periodical press came into its own during the 1840s and 1850s: in 1825 there had been fewer than 125 American magazines; by 1860 there were about 600. Most of these new periodicals appealed to local or special interests. The early years of the antebellum period were especially prolific in the founding of religious periodicals and weekly newspapers, and as late as 1850 religious periodicals still outnumbered the new genre of popular literary magazines. None of them, however, ever attained the national circulation and influence of their secular counterparts, which came to fashion an eclectic literary genre with contents that included fiction and verse, biographical and historical essays, as well as travel sketches and illustrations. By the end of the 1850s, leading monthlies such as *Godey's Lady's Book* (1830–98), *Peterson's Ladies' National Magazine* (1842–98), and *Harper's New Monthly Magazine* (1850–) all claimed to have more than one hundred thousand paid subscribers. The circulation of other more short-lived ventures such as *Graham's Magazine* (1841–58), *Putnam's Monthly Magazine* (1853–57), *The United States Magazine and Democratic Review* (1837–59), and *Sartain's Union Magazine* (1847–52) was also substantial, ranging from twenty thousand to seventy thousand. It is important to note as well that, by the end

---

6. See John Tebbell, *A History of Book Publishing in the United States*, vol. 1, *The Creation of an Industry, 1630–1865* (New York, 1972), pt. 4, for a more detailed account of the antebellum period. My accounts of Duyckinck and Fields draw from Richard H. Broadhead, *The School of Hawthorne* (New York, 1986), 53–55.

of the antebellum period, the commercial success of these new American literary magazines gradually had served to increase substantially the rates that well-known writers received for their articles. During the 1840s *Graham's* and *Godey's* were the leaders in advancing prices for magazine writing, with payment ranging from $4.00 to $12.00 a page for prose, and $10.00 to $50.00 dollars a poem, with higher rates to more famous contributors. *Putnam's* "normal price" of $3.00 per page was probably the average among other general literary periodicals. Rates did not rise dramatically during the 1850s, yet by the end of that decade, Mott has pointed out, the standard set by the *Atlantic Monthly*—$6.00 a page—compared favorably to that of leading British literary magazines.[7]

Perhaps most important and spectacular of all the developments that signaled the emergence of the literary marketplace, however, was the proliferation of daily and weekly newspapers, which quickly came to be seen as a uniquely powerful American cultural institution—the nation's "second breakfast," as Emerson once approvingly described it. During the antebellum period, the number of American papers almost tripled—from 1,200 to 3,000—and came to exist in far greater numbers and variety than in any European country at the time. With newspaper postage fixed by law at one cent per copy up to one hundred miles, and after 1845 free up to thirty miles, newspapers came to make up 90 percent of the mail during the antebellum period while providing only one-ninth of postal revenues. Almost every American town of moderate size had a daily paper; most large cities had several, and even remote frontier settlements issued their own weeklies. The majority of dailies had circulations of a few thousand, and the great mass of weeklies only a few hundred. During the 1840s, however, a new generation of "penny press" newspapers based in Northern cities acquired dramatic increases in circulation, which in turn gave them increasingly prominent roles in shaping cultural and political attitudes in their local communities. The best-known of these remains Horace Greeley's *New York Tribune*, which thanks to the success of a weekly edition designed for national circulation, also established itself as America's largest and most influential newspaper. Yet the daily edition of Greeley's newspaper, which had a circulation of 77,000 at the end of 1860, had several powerful rivals in its ability to influence local opinion. In 1860, in

7. Frank Luther Mott, *A History of American Magazines, 1741–1850* (New York, 1930), 504–12, and *A History of American Magazines, 1850–65* (New York, 1938), 20–21.

New York, the *Herald* also claimed 77,000, and the *Sun* 59,000; and both the *Boston Herald* and the *Philadelphia Inquirer* averaged 65,000 in 1862.[8] While such numbers hardly signaled that antebellum newspapers came to be seen as reliable agents of public information, they do describe the most palpable change in the reading matter of ordinary Americans as the nation moved gradually from an era of scarcity to that of abundance.

As with books, the dramatic increase in the overall supply of magazines and newspapers brought with it a rich and diverse bill of fare that added to the glut of printed information. Some periodicals were themselves little more than books in disguise, providing anthologies of various kinds of articles and fiction. The absence of an international copyright law also allowed for the pirated reprinting of articles from leading British and French magazines, and periodicals such as *Littell's Living Age* (1844–96) and *The Eclectic Magazine* (1844–98) for several decades earned their livelihood from this practice. Notices and reviews of books were ubiquitous, and the steady growth in the size of magazines was attributable, in part, to efforts their editors made to keep track of what many perceived as an ongoing bibliographical deluge.[9]

While the vast majority of antebellum newspapers were the mouthpieces of political parties, when the electioneering season ended, they still provided an extraordinary variety of information. Together with reports on local, national, and sometimes international news, newspapers printed compilations of agricultural and commercial data, and reports on recent developments in science. Their pages also included advertisements for new products and new business opportunities, and at the same time provided the publicity that oiled the new national lecture system of the 1840s and 1850s. As Donald Scott has shown, it was newspapers in fact that helped make lectures significant cultural events by printing advertisements about who was lecturing where and when, as well as stories about particular lectures, and editorials proclaiming the importance of the lecture as a new cultural institution. Some key metropolitan newspapers, especially the *New York Tribune* and the *Boston Herald*, also played central

---

8. The figures cited come from Frank Luther Mott, *American Journalism: A History, 1690–1960* (New York, 1962), 403. Emerson, "The Fugitive Slave Law," in *The Selected Writings of Ralph Waldo Emerson*, ed. Brooks Atkinson (New York, 1940), 861–62, credited newspapers, for all the "chaff" they contained, with supplying ordinary Americans with "fact, thought, and wisdom in the crude mass, from all regions of the world."

9. Mott, *History of American Magazines, 1741–1850*, 306–9, 747–49.

roles in nationalizing the reputations of leading figures in the popular lecture circuit—a group that of course included Emerson and, from time to
time, Thoreau.[10]

2

So much is now well known to specialists when they consider changes
in the literary culture of antebellum America. Yet the question of how this
unprecedented abundance of print altered the workings of that culture has
been posed and approached in different ways. From literary historians we
usually hear that the most striking development within antebellum culture was an unprecedented growth in the production and consumption of
novels; and on the face of it, the numbers supporting this view are quite
striking. During the 1820s 128 American novels were published, almost
forty more than had been published in the previous 50 years, and five times
the number published during the previous decade—and yet more than
double that number appeared in the 1830s; and the total more than dou-
bled again in the 1840s, to nearly eight hundred. In 1826 James Fenimore
Cooper's *The Last of the Mohicans* qualified as a best-seller with 5,750
copies in circulation; in contrast, between 1845 and 1851 George Lippard's *The Quaker City* sold some 210,000 copies, making it the country's
best-selling novel before the appearance of Harriet Beecher Stowe's *Uncle
Tom's Cabin* in 1852. In that year alone, the sales of Stowe's antislavery saga
outdid Lippard's earlier aggregate figure, and estimates of total copies
purchased before the Civil War range as high as five million. While no
other antebellum novel even approached these figures, there were several
others that enjoyed remarkable commercial success during the 1850s—
particularly Fanny Fern's *Ruth Hall* (1855), logging sales of 55,000, and
Maria Cummins's *The Lamplighter* (1854), surpassing 40,000 within eight
weeks.[11]

This is not the place to consider the ongoing and complicated discussion of whether antebellum America gained or suffered from this unprec-

---

10. Robert A. Gross, "Printing, Politics, and the People," *Proceedings of the American Antiquarian Society*, vol. 99, pt. 2, 1989, 386; Donald J. Scott, "Print and the Public Lecture System," in *Printing and Society in Early America*, 278–99.

11. The figures cited here are drawn from Michael Gilmore, "The Book Marketplace I,"
in *The Columbia History of the American Novel*, ed. Emory Elliott (New York, 1991), 54.

edented growth of popular interest in fiction.[12] For my purposes, however, it is important to observe that most scholars who concentrate their efforts on interpreting antebellum fiction appear to be guided by two closely related assumptions regarding the institutional organization of American culture during the three decades prior to the Civil War. The first is that the entire antebellum period can be approached as a time when a dramatic increase in the productive power of American publishing served to make book-publishing into a major industry that catered to the demands of a new mass reading public. The other is that in this new setting, where the preferences of a mass readership supposedly came to govern the workings of the literary marketplace, all writers of poetry and prose were compelled to come to terms with an altogether new culture in which "literature" had been reduced to the status of a commodity, and where success for writers now meant appealing to an anonymous, distant, and unknown audience—or the "partial and noisy readers of the hour," as Emerson once described them. Taken together, both assumptions also have served to support the now widely accepted view that the antebellum period therefore must be approached as the time when the emergence of the market served to open the split between "mass" and "high" culture that remains so familiar today.[13]

Contemporary scholars are still adding chapters to this story of antebellum culture as a time when America's shift from oral to print culture was fully accomplished, and when novels commanded a new nationally oriented mass culture that displaced local and predominantly oral cultures. But recently a number of American cultural historians have called this approach into question for various reasons, and thereby laid the ground-

---

12. There is now a large literature on this subject; for a recent survey, see the references cited in Mary Kelley, *Private Woman, Public Stage: Literary Domesticity in Nineteenth-Century America* (Oxford, 1984), Preface.

13. Emerson, "Spiritual Laws," in *Essays: First Series*, vol. 2, *The Collected Works of Ralph Waldo Emerson*, ed. Joseph Slater, Alfred R. Ferguson, and Jean Ferguson Carr (Cambridge, Mass., 1979), 89. The most influential study tracing the beginnings of modern mass culture back to the antebellum period remains Ann Douglas, *The Feminization of American Culture* (New York, 1977). But also see, among others, Michael T. Gilmore, *American Romanticism and the Marketplace* (Chicago, 1985), 1–17, and Stephen Railton, *Authorship and Audience: Literary Performance in the American Renaissance* (Princeton, 1991), 3–22, who claims that American writers at midcentury stood "alone on the stage of literary performance. Writers did not necessarily have to tremble, but it was directly before the public that they had to perform. For almost any validation of his or her identity as an American artist, the writer was directly dependent on their response" (19). Railton never provides any details concerning the actual audiences of nineteenth-century American writers.

work for somewhat different approaches. One group, led by Donald Scott, retains the view that print did indeed become the central force for change in antebellum culture, but argues that the dynamics of America's emerging literary marketplace cannot be understood in isolation from forms of oral communication that continued to characterize the culture of both elite and ordinary Americans. Scott in particular has shown that the spread of the popular lecture system during the 1840s and 1850s was one of the most important by-products of the new world of print, since many of its prominent figures included editors, journalists, and writers. Not surprisingly, the most frequent topics of discussion within lyceums—biography, history, natural science, and travel—mirrored those found in antebellum books, magazines, and newspapers. But the national lecture system was at the same time an institution that helped sort out and assimilate the huge supply of facts and opinions created by a new culture of abundant print. And in this respect, Scott has argued persuasively, the lecture system itself, during its heyday, may have been America's first truly national cultural market.[14]

Other historians have followed Scott in stressing that oratory was as ubiquitous as print in the antebellum period, although they speak of its practical implications in slightly different terms. Lawrence Levine has argued, for instance, that the frequent and prominent staging of Shakespeare's plays throughout antebellum America helps reveal the existence of a "shared public culture" in which the spoken word remained a central part of American life, and in which Shakespeare thus had no difficulty finding a central place. Equally important, the integration of Shakespeare's drama in antebellum culture also brings into question the practice of seeing that culture on a vertical plane neatly divided into a hierarchy of inclusive adjectival categories such as 'high,' 'low,' 'pop,' 'mass,' 'folk' and the like. The continuing use of such terms, Levine insists, only serves to obscure the dynamic complexity of American culture in the first half of the nineteenth century.[15]

---

14. Scott, "Print and the Public Lecture System," and "The Popular Lecture and the Creation of a Public in Mid-Nineteenth-Century America," *Journal of American History* 66 (March 1980): 791–809. Lectures had been an important part of American culture since the late eighteenth and early nineteenth centuries. Carl Bode, *The American Lyceum: Town Meeting of the Mind* (New York, 1956), remains the standard account of how earlier lectures and lyceums developed into a national lecture circuit.

15. Lawrence W. Levine, *Highbrow/Lowbrow: The Emergence of Cultural Hierarchy in America* (Cambridge, 1988), ch. 1. Also see David S. Reynolds, *Beneath the American Renaissance: The Subversive Imagination in the Age of Emerson and Melville* (New York, 1988).

Richard Brown, too, has recently shown that the cultural interests of antebellum America were large and diverse in ways that our standard literary histories have tended to underestimate. Yet where Levine sees the continuing existence of a "shared popular culture," Brown argues that in a society where both print and public speech were ubiquitous, a comprehensive culture in fact became ever more remote, and eventually even no longer an ideal. By the end of the antebellum period, he observes, America had gone from being "a society where public information had been scarce, and chiefly under the control of the learned and wealthy few," to one in which a new abundance of public information found its way to a diverse variety of consumers by way of "specialized printing and public speech, perhaps also specialized information." Or, put somewhat differently, patterns of information diffusion that before the antebellum period had reinforced cultural cohesion now became the foundation of cultural fragmentation and diversity.[16]

Perhaps most significant of all, for my purposes, it now also appears that the familiar view that improvements in the technology of antebellum American publishing quickly served to put books within the physical and financial reach of ordinary people is not holding up under close empirical investigation. There of course can be no question that the long-term trend was a steady increase in the number of book titles, and especially of novels. Yet the numbers themselves, while suggesting that writing books for publication became increasingly common, do not support the view that, before the mid-1850s at the earliest, the reading habits of antebellum America's extraordinarily literate public ought to be understood primarily in terms of the books they bought. At the outset, the dramatic increase in the number of books available was not accompanied by a comparable increase in the velocity and extent of their circulation. While libraries and reading societies grew in numbers, most Americans could not as yet afford to join them. Books also remained very difficult to distribute for sale before 1850, when railroads first began to link up different regions of the country and provide Northern publishing houses with access to the American interior. (Before midcentury, only the Bible—not surprisingly, the first book printed

---

Reynolds attempts to show that all the great writers of the American Renaissance were profoundly affected by the popular culture of their time; chs. 8 and 9 of this study are concerned with the traffic in the other direction.

16. Richard D. Brown, *Knowledge Is Power: The Diffusion of Information in Early America, 1700–1865* (Oxford, 1989), 286. Brown also goes on to argue that "Choices, the multiplicity

with stereotyped plates in America—was nationally distributed, thanks to the efforts of the American Bible Society's traveling agents and local auxiliaries.) Robert Gross also recently has reminded us that the problems involved in creating a national marketplace for books were political as well as economic and geographic. While the Postal Act of 1790 had allowed American newspapers to circulate throughout the country at cheap rates (with editors exchanging papers for free), it at the same time had banned books from mailbags. It is true that, beginning in July 1839, books did for a time move through the mail in great quantities, when enterprising papers such as *Brother Jonathan* (1839–43) and *New World* (1840–44) seized upon a loophole in the postal laws to issue pirated reprintings of popular British novels in huge "story-paper" formats. But America's first "paperback revolution" not only turned out to be relatively short-lived—in April 1843 the Post Office changed its policy and began charging book postage on cheap reprints—it also did considerable economic damage to both American book publishers and writers at the time it occurred. The Post Office's new ruling in time served to kill off the leading serial reprinters, but not before a widespread competition in cheap reprints had led to price-cutting that glutted the market and severely reduced revenues of regular publishers who also had brought out cheap reprints of their own. In 1843 retail prices of books were driven so low, according to John Tebbel, it became extremely difficult for publishers to make money off the sales of new books by American authors, and it was not until the late 1840s that prices again rose to levels where some profits were possible.[17]

Dealing in books remained risky for yet another reason. We know that something of an Anglo-American market for books came into existence in the antebellum period, with many leading American publishers now establishing their own agents in London. Yet distribution costs were often discouragingly expensive. Mail service was not only costly, but notoriously

---

of groups and individuals generating information, the widespread diversity of religious and political opinion that circulated through commercially developed regions—these realities made pluralism a central feature of American society" (p. 294).

17. Charvat, *Literary Publishing in America*, 40–41; Charles Sellers, *The Market Revolution: Jacksonian America, 1815–46* (New York, 1991), 369–70; Gross, "Printing, Politics, and the People," 388–90; Tebbel, *History of Book Publishing*, 1:240–51. Also see Nathan O. Hatch, *The Democratization of American Christianity* (New Haven, 1989), ch. 5, for a more detailed account of the ways in which an explosion of popular printed material in the first half of the nineteenth century brought about a shift from a relatively coherent Christian culture to a fragmented and competitive one.

slow and unreliable. High exchange rates meant that imported British books sometimes became too expensive for the American market, and freight and duty charges only compounded that problem by adding further to the cost of books. Perhaps most damaging of all, however, was the absence of an international copyright law. This not only made it difficult for publishers and writers to benefit financially from even modestly success-ful ventures; it made the practice of literary piracy commonplace on both sides of the Atlantic until the passage of the International Copyright Law in 1891.[18]

Finally, Ronald Zboray has pieced together a somewhat different pat-tern of evidence to argue against the notion that books—with only a few well-known exceptions—ever became the object of mass consumption before the Civil War. Despite the glowing accounts of growth in produc-tion and readership provided by antebellum American publishers, the ear-liest innovations in nineteenth-century print technology served to create new markets for books whose lavish illustrations and elaborate bindings made them luxury items well beyond the reach of most Americans. During the antebellum period, technological innovations and the expansion of the book market did cut the average price of hardcover books to between $0.75 and $1.25—which was roughly half the cost of books in the late eigh-teenth century. (The first editions of both sets of Emerson's *Essays* and of *Walden* were priced at $1.00.) However, as Zboray has pointed out, in an economic setting where skilled white male workers made only about $1.00 a dollar a day, and white female workers usually only a quarter of that, the $1.00 price of most antebellum books represented a full one-sixth of a man's weekly wages and well over half of the woman's wages—equivalent today to anywhere between $50.00 and $100.00. In this regard, it is worth noting that most of the story-papers of the early 1840s also appear to have stood out of the reach of ordinary Americans. Only a handful of these papers sold for as low as 12 1/2¢; the most common price was 50¢. More-over, while it may be reasonable to consider these supplements as mass-

18. For a more careful discussion of the emerging Anglo-American literary marketplace, see Clarence Gohdes, *American Literature in Nineteenth-Century England* (New York, 1944). The absence of an international copyright law also calls into question the assumption that the emergence of the literary marketplace entailed the reduction of literature to the status of a commodity. In the international marketplace, a writer's published work clearly was less his private property than an object in the public domain. For a more detailed discussion of international copyright, see Tebbel, *History of Book Publishing*, 1:558–61.

market items in their own time, publishers could make a profit on a sale of five thousand copies, and even the most successful issues of the story-papers rarely sold more than thirty thousand. Finally, and perhaps most significant, those few books that could be bought cheaply by Americans during the 1840s and 1850s typically were novels by French and British authors, whose writings were as yet unprotected by an international copyright law, and whose popularity revealed America's continuing cultural dependency. By contrast, few American novels appeared in very inexpensive editions before the mid-1850s, and the continuing high prices for American-authored books, Zboray concludes, suggests that antebellum technological innovations in printing hardly brought American literature in book form to the masses.[19]

3

All this recent scholarship has enriched our understanding of the dynamics of antebellum American culture. But what precisely does it have to do with Emerson and Thoreau? First of all, and perhaps obviously by now, it has made it difficult to find one straightforward historical generalization that would encapsulate all the diverse and sometimes contradictory developments that characterized the culture into which they launched their publications. In this regard, it may be somewhat misleading to speak, as I have up to this point, of *the* American literary marketplace, for what recent scholarship tells us about is clearly not the appearance of a single literary marketplace, in which professional writers for the first time came to confront a new mass audience of readers, but rather of the emergence of an open and pluralistic culture in which the new forms of print remained closely bound up with other more traditional forms of cultural activity, and sought to gain the attention of diverse audiences of individuals who clearly still wanted to look and hear, as well as to read. Here it should be kept in mind as well that other cultural entrepreneurs, operating out of the same urban centers where editors and publishers presided over

---

19. Ronald J. Zboray, "Antebellum Reading and the Ironies of Technological Innovation," in *Reading in America: Literature and Social History*, ed. Cathy N. Davidson (Baltimore, 1989), 180–200; and *A Fictive People: Antebellum Economic Development and the American Reading Public* (Oxford, 1992).

the world of print, also took advantage of new technologies and the general rise of personal wealth during the antebellum period to expand the production and consumption of the fine arts, music, and theater. Joined with the huge amount and variety of fact and opinion available in print, this babble of voices that competed to instruct and entertain antebellum Americans served to create what Scott has described aptly as "a vast cultural bazaar."[20]

To say all this is not to ignore the fact that the evidence still points toward a fundamental transformation from an oral to a print culture. What we confront, however, must at the same time be described as a historical change still in the early stages of development at the time when Emerson and Thoreau wrote and published, and in which the creation of what we have come to call "mass culture" remained only one among many possible outcomes. Viewed from this angle, it also appears that while the assertion that antebellum America was "a nation of novel readers" may correctly express the aspirations of novelists and their publishers, it hardly serves as an accurate description of the dominant cultural activity of the antebellum period. There was no one dominant activity. Indeed, when Emerson himself, in 1840, examined "the library of the present age," he described it as an "immense miscellany," underlining the fact that the new abundance of books and other printed material had given rise to a literary culture that as yet could not be "set in very exact order." There was no one species of book that characterized his age, Emerson insisted, "for every opinion old and new, every hope and fear, every whim and folly has an organ."[21] Similarly, while Thoreau was often harshly critical of what he saw as the bland and trivial concerns of America's "modern cheap and fertile press," his criticisms of popular reading tastes in his own day do not neatly register an emerging split between "elite" and "mass" culture. Thoreau, too, recognized the heterogeneity of antebellum culture, even though in unflattering terms. His age was presided over by various "cliques," he observed in his journal, most of which were "of a sectarian or party character." Newspapers, magazines, colleges, and all forms of government and

---

20. Scott, "Print and the Public Lecture System," 292. Richard Brown chooses to speak of the growth of a "competitive information marketplace" in *Knowledge Is Power*, 268–96. That phrase may provide a more historically accurate generalization about changes that took place, but I suspect it is unlikely to take hold.
21. Emerson, "Thoughts on Modern Literature," *Dial* (October 1840): 137.

religion "expressed the superficial activity of a few," he continued, and when confronted with that activity, the mass of ordinary Americans were "either conforming" or simply "not attending."[22]

A comprehensive discussion of all these difficulties of classification obviously would carry us well beyond the boundaries of the last part of this book. I draw attention to them briefly here, however, to suggest some of the reasons why in the final two chapters of this book I attempt to avoid certain well-established positions regarding the early literary careers of Emerson and Thoreau. First of all, I want to resist the current practice of immediately approaching them as professional writers whose economic livelihood and cultural status depended primarily upon their ability to appeal to a new mass reading audience. This approach requires us to ignore the fact that, while a growing number of the contemporaries of Emerson and Thoreau certainly did attempt to become self-supporting writers, each of them was protected (although in somewhat different ways) by money and social position from the full force of the marketplace to shape their lives and determine how they would represent themselves in their work. (This surely is part of what Thoreau meant when, two years after the publication of *Walden*, he described himself as a member of the "scribbling gentry.") Certainly neither of them was drawn to writing primarily by a lack of personal resources. At the start of his career as a publishing author, Emerson was already a wealthy man by contemporary standards. His first wife had bequeathed him an estate with an annual income of $1,200, and that money not only provided him with financial freedom; it also allowed him to pay the printing and composition costs of *Nature*, *Essays* [First Series], and *Essays: Second Series*, and *Representative Men*.[23] (It also is worth

---

22. *The Journal of Henry Thoreau*, ed. Bradford Torrey and Francis H. Allen, 14 vols. (Boston, 1906), 11:86–87. For an insightful recent discussion of Thoreau's views of the popular literary culture of his day, see Robert A. Gross, "Much Instruction from Little Reading: Books and Libraries in Thoreau's Concord," *Proceedings of the American Antiquarian Society*, vol. 97, pt. 1, 1987, 129–88. Gross is careful to point out that, while Thoreau undoubtedly felt unsympathetic toward what passed for popular literary culture, his hostility came less from the aristocratic conviction that popular reading tastes had corrupted an inherently superior elite culture than from his belief—expressed plainly in the journal entry cited here—that the new literary culture of the masses was a wholly synthetic concoction imposed on them from above.

23. *The Correspondence of Henry David Thoreau*, ed. Walter Harding and Carl Bode (New York, 1958) 441–42. On Emerson's income from his first wife's estate, see John McAleer, *Ralph Waldo Emerson: Days of Encounter* (New York, 1984), 108. For details on Emerson's publishing contracts with James Munroe and Company, see Joel Myerson, *Ralph*

noting here that Emerson was remarkably generous to other writers in need of money—especially to Thomas Carlyle, for whom Emerson borrowed money at his own risk to pay the production costs of the first American editions of Carlyle's writings.) Thoreau was by no means as wealthy as Emerson, yet getting a living was never a serious practical problem for him either. He could (and often did) work at the Thoreau family pencil and graphite business, which prospered despite the economic hard times of the late 1830s and early 1840s, and found ready employment as a land surveyor in Concord during the 1850s.[24] It seems clear, too, that neither Emerson nor Thoreau began writing out of a desire for popular acclaim. Emerson's literary debut as the anonymous author of *Nature*—a book first issued in a small press run of volumes bound in fifteen varieties of cloth and color types, with five different stamp designs for its cover—hardly signaled the arrival of a professional writer. (Indeed, given its ornate design and high price, it surely makes more sense to think of *Nature* as a gift book than a work produced for widespread sale.[25]) By contrast, while Thoreau published under his own name, he chose to write only two books during his lifetime, and never actively pursued what arguably could have been a very successful (and well-paying) career as a "magazinist." Moreover, it is unlikely that a figure who emphasized that writing was an adjunct to a variety of other occupations ever thought of his publications as objects designed for mass consumption or personal profit. (In Thoreau's most frequently delivered lecture, "Life Without Principle," he introduced himself to his audiences as a surveyor; and when he died in 1862, the Concord town clerk recorded his occupation simply as natural historian.[26])

Second, while it is true that few antebellum Americans were wealthy

Waldo Emerson: A Descriptive Bibliography (Pittsburgh, 1982), 14–15, 43, 111, 210–11; and *Emerson's 'Nature'—Origin, Growth, and Meaning*, ed. Merton M. Seals and Alfred R. Ferguson (New York, 1969), 65–68.

24. See Henry Petroski, "H. D. Thoreau, Engineer," *South Atlantic Quarterly* 90 (Winter 1991): 39–60, for a more detailed account of John Thoreau and Company. There is little doubt, Petroski observes, that before Henry David Thoreau became a literary celebrity the best pencils he and his father made were already without peer in this country.

25. There apparently is no surviving record of what James Munroe and Company charged for individual copies of its elegant first editions of *Nature*. We do know, however, that Emerson's share of sales was fixed at 33 1/3¢ per copy; and given prevailing royalty rates of 10 percent to 15 percent per copy, $3.00 seems a conservative estimate of its price.

26. "Life Without Principle," in *The Writings of Henry David Thoreau, Reform Papers*, ed. Wendell Glick (Princeton, 1973), 155. Thoreau doubtless meant he was a surveyor in more than just the professional sense, but there is no question that surveying was his part-time pro-

enough to purchase copies of the first editions of the books Emerson and Thoreau published, there are good reasons to reconsider the now dominant view of their books as commercial failures. It is unlikely that so many authorities can have been completely mistaken in adopting this view, and I will make no effort to refute it altogether here. Emerson and Thoreau can hardly be called authors of immediate best-sellers, even when measured by what now seem the modest standards of the antebellum period. No more than 496 copies of the first American edition of *Nature* were sold between 1836 and 1849. Thoreau fared somewhat better with *Walden*, with two thousand copies of the first edition selling out in eight years and a second small printing appearing in 1862. The mistake in this familiar story, however, lies in the belief that such apparently unimpressive numbers can be taken as a clear measure of the cultural status of these publications at the time they first appeared. As we shall see, Emerson first became a well-known figure in American culture, in part, because his contemporaries took notice of the unexpected success that *Nature* and several other early essays enjoyed in Britain, where his lionization was based on several thousand inexpensive pirated editions of his writings that appeared during the early 1840s. It is now well known that Thoreau's first book, *A Week on the Concord and Merrimack Rivers* (1849), sold very poorly and left him in considerable personal debt. Yet if the extent to which a book is reviewed reflects the extent to which editors and reviewers think it important, *A Week* was hardly an unknown failure in its time. Not all of the leading antebellum literary periodicals reviewed it, but most did, and usually in laudatory terms. Moreover, as we shall see, Thoreau himself came to understand that the inadequacies of his first publisher—James Munroe and Company—had much to do with the meager sales *A Week* enjoyed; and his decision to publish *Walden* with Ticknor and Fields resulted both in brisk sales and nationwide acclaim when it first appeared.[27]

Finally, it should be said that, whatever approach one takes in exploring

---

fession during the 1850s. This aspect of Thoreau's career is discussed more fully in Leo Stoller, *After Walden: Thoreau's Changing Views of Economic Man* (Stanford, 1957), ch. 2.

27. Borst, *Henry David Thoreau: A Reference Guide, 1835–99*, 7–11, lists some sixteen reviews and notices of *A Week* that appeared during the year following its publication, among the more remarkable of which was a review (with numerous excerpts) that appeared on the front page of the June 13, 1849 *New York Daily Tribune*. Given the widespread critical notice *A Week* received, one could argue that the central cultural puzzle of Thoreau's first book was why it proved to be a commercial failure. I explore that puzzle in more detail in ch. 9.

the literary careers of Emerson and Thoreau, they remain complex in ways we are still only beginning to understand, and in the final part of this book I pretend to do more than explore some of the less well-known processes by which their writings first attracted popular audiences and gained cultural authority. To carry my story beyond the antebellum period, I would need to shift ground to consider why the openness and pluralism of the literary marketplace before the Civil War later gave way to a culture more clearly divided into "high" and "low" spheres. Here the rise of fiction designed for a mass reading audience would become more directly relevant to understanding their places within American culture, yet so too would the decline of the national lecture system. It also seems likely that during the period on which I concentrate—years marked out roughly by the appearance of *Nature* in 1836 at one end, and Thoreau's death in 1862 at the other—very few of the contemporaries of Emerson and Thoreau came to their writings as countless have since the late nineteenth century: sitting alone in silence, holding individual books containing their work, and struggling to interpret the pages they read. In fact, when we consider the writings of Emerson and Thoreau as they first appeared within American culture, it may be better to think of them as two distinct sets of texts, an ensemble of what might be called first-and second-hand publications: the first-hand being actual books and pamphlets that in their original full editions were purchased by a relatively small, affluent elite; the second-hand being excerpts from, and reprints of, those same writings that were made accessible to countless other readers by way of anthologies, magazines, and newspapers. There are of course great difficulties in deciding what to make of this fact. Did the tens of thousands of readers who found passages from Emerson and Thoreau in the pages of Greeley's *New York Tribune* during the 1840s and early 1850s, for example, simply skim through them as entertaining filler, or read them carefully for instruction and edification?[28] And what do we make of the several brief and glib notices of the sort that Emerson and Thoreau received in widely circulated antebellum periodicals such as *Godey's Lady's Book* or *Peterson's Magazine*? Did these serve to dilute the significance of their writings or somehow integrate them into popular

---

28. Brown, *Knowledge Is Power*, 273–74, notes that the eighteenth-century practice of collecting newspapers and binding them for reference faded out as newspapers became items of ephemeral mass consumption. But at the same time there were "no clear boundaries between accumulation and consumption, since the information one person chose to accumulate another might merely consume."

culture? It is easy to gather evidence showing that nineteenth-century Americans could find excerpts from and reviews of their work in a wide variety of sources; it is quite another matter to attempt to read over the shoulders of those who encountered Emerson and Thoreau second-hand. For the moment, however, I think it may be enough to say that acknowledging the existence of such problems at least opens up the possibility of an analysis that will begin to attend more carefully to the complex substance of their early literary careers rather than to issues that usually seem to reflect the concerns of different epochs in our cultural history.

The general point of view that informs the final chapters of this book, therefore, is one that recognizes that the antebellum literary marketplace was a locale of diverse and sometimes competing concerns. This point of view also provides us with the best approach to understanding how Emerson and Thoreau first appeared and gained compelling force in American culture. It would be too much to say that their writings, like Shakespeare's drama or *Uncle Tom's Cabin*, became integral parts of antebellum culture at all its various levels. Yet neither were they simply ignored or set aside as an elite supplement to more popular reading fare. As we shall see, there was scarcely any aspect of antebellum America's heterogeneous literary culture in which the writings of Emerson and Thoreau were not introduced, excerpted, and discussed, and the list here includes religious periodicals, newspapers, national literary magazines, and abolitionist publications, as well as gift books and literary anthologies. Or, put more strongly, Emerson and Thoreau became prominent figures within the culture of their own day, because in various ways both of them contributed to and helped constitute America's emerging literary marketplace. And the question that requires thoughtful study here is not so much whether their writings were correctly understood, but how and why they first came to attract widespread attention.[29]

---

29. In focusing primarily on the contemporary reception of Emerson and Thoreau to answer this question, I do not mean to underplay the significance of the fact that both figures knew quite well that the antebellum literary marketplace embraced diverse audiences. Their writings attest to a desire to reach a wide variety of readers, from classically trained educated gentlemen who caught their Greek and Latin puns, to ordinary readers who followed the penny press. This side of their cultural identities, however, has received extensive and thoughtful treatment in recent scholarship. See, e.g., Reynolds, *Beneath the American Renaissance*, 92–103, 484–506; and Robert Sattelmeyer, *Thoreau's Reading: A Study in Intellectual History with Bibliographical Catalogue* (Princeton, 1988).

8

"The Emerson Mania":
The Publication and Reception of
Emerson's Writings, 1836–1850

THE STORY OF how Emerson made it difficult for his contemporaries to judge the importance of what we now consider his "classic" texts is familiar. The received account, which has its origins in William Charvat's pioneering studies of the antebellum book trade, runs like this: at a time when American writers who wanted a national hearing brought their work to publishers in New York and Philadelphia, Emerson chose instead to take his writing to James Munroe and Company, a distinguished Boston publishing house at the time, yet also one that had neither the interest nor the resources to promote his books outside of New England. Scarce and expensive, Munroe's first editions of *Nature* (1836), *Essays* (1841), and *Essays: Second Series* (1844) found their way into the hands of remarkably few of Emerson's contemporaries, and it was not until *Representative Men* appeared in 1850 that Emerson, at the age of forty-seven, actually managed to author a book that gained a broad national hearing and yielded him substantial royalty payments. The comprehensive bibliography recently compiled by Joel Myerson offers no interpretive account of the contemporary reception of Emerson's early publications, but his data on

Munroe's high prices and small press runs appear to supplement and reinforce Charvat's story about delayed national recognition.[1]

I

While Charvat's account of Emerson's lackluster debut remains the cornerstone for current study of the reception of Emerson's writings between 1836 and 1850, I want to set a more eventful narrative against it in this chapter.[2] To do that, I begin far from modern commentaries, with an account of the immediate impact of Emerson's early writings that first appeared in *The English Review* in September 1849. Its author remains unknown, but the magazine in which it appeared is now remembered as the first English literary review to include American books regularly in its offerings. We know as well that this largely forgotten account of Emerson quickly found its way to American audiences by way of reprintings that appeared in *Littell's Living Age* and the *Eclectic Magazine*, two antebellum

---

1. William Charvat, *Literary Publishing in America, 1790–1850* (Philadelphia, 1959), 23, 29, 30, 50, 86 n. 25; *The Profession of Authorship in America, 1800–1870: The Papers of William Charvat*, ed. Matthew J. Bruccoli (Columbus, 1968), 74, 286–87, 297. Joel Myerson, *Ralph Waldo Emerson: A Descriptive Bibliography* (Pittsburgh, 1982), 9–202. We do not know exactly how many copies were printed in the first edition of *Nature*, published in Boston on September 9, 1836. The surviving record of Emerson's account with Munroe, however, suggests quite plainly that there was never any great popular demand for the book. Munroe bound only 496 copies between the end of March 1837 and the close of 1842. No sales were reported after 1844, and another five years would pass before a second edition of 250 copies again appeared with Munroe's imprint. Emerson's subsequent publications fared somewhat better, yet here too Munroe's sales figures suggest that his early work at best had limited popular appeal. Munroe printed two pamphlet editions of the Phi Beta Kappa Address (first in September 1837, then again in January 1838), but 190 of the 1,015 copies that comprised these early editions were still in stock as late as January 1844. The first edition of 1,000 copies of Emerson's Harvard Divinity College Address was almost sold out by the end of 1839, yet it then remained out of print in America until reappearing ten years later as one of the pieces in *Nature, Addresses, and Lectures*. Finally, while only three years separated Munroe's original editions of Emerson's two series of *Essays*, it took more than ten years to sell 1,048 copies of the first series; and although the 2,000 copies of the first edition of the second series sold out in a year, a second edition would not appear until 1850.

2. It should be noted that Charvat never pretended to offer a thorough account of Emerson's early literary career. But the assumption that, in publishing with Munroe, Emerson somehow had confined the audience for his early writings almost entirely to New England is now well established. See, among others, Lawrence Buell, *New England Literary Culture: From Revolution through Renaissance* (Cambridge, 1986), 35–36.

magazines whose commercial success derived, in large part, from reprinting articles clipped from prestigious British periodicals. The most striking passage in the *English Review*'s closely printed thirteen-page article—which carried "The Emerson Mania" for its title—is its first paragraph:

> The reputation enjoyed by that "transatlantic thinker," whose name we have set forth in the head to these remarks, suggests matter for grave reflection. When we find an essayist of this description, who seems to be "a setter forth of new gods," belauded alike by Tory and Radical organs, by "Blackwood" and "the Westminster," by the friends of order and disorder—when we find his works reproduced in every possible form, and at the most tempting prices, proving the wide circulation they must enjoy among the English public generally—we feel that we too should not leave them disregarded, that we should bestow something more than the mere incidental notice on them which we have hitherto found occasion to indite. We are credibly informed that these essays find many readers and admirers amongst the youth of our universities. Here is a more special "moving cause" for our examination into this theme,—the "rationale" of what we may call the Emerson mania. We shall discuss a few of the leading tenets of the Emersonian philosophy, as calmly and dispassionately as we may; and if we give offence to the idolaters of this "transatlantic star," we can only say that truth is too serious a matter to be trifled with, and that we hold ourselves bound, in this instance, to speak out plainly.

Given the tone of this introduction, it is not surprising that what followed was less a calm and dispassionate discussion of Emerson's writings, than an agitated and hostile indictment in which he was labeled a "mighty phrasemonger" and "narrow fanatic," and then condemned for "inculcating self-idolatry" and failing to "recognise and adore his God." Yet, while *The English Review* found no cause to celebrate the "wide circulation" Emerson's writings had achieved in early Victorian Britain, more remarkable for my purposes here is the fact that its view of Emerson as an extraordinary American writer who had become a "transatlantic star" during the 1840s obviously bears no resemblance to that provincial figure we encounter in the received account, and it might well be asked why.[3]

The first thing to be said by way of an answer is that knowledge of Emerson's writings within British culture at the end of the 1840s was wide-

---

3. Anon., "The Emerson Mania," *English Review* 12 (September 1849): 139-52. Walter Graham, *English Literary Periodicals* (New York, 1930), 218-19, provides a more detailed

spread because it was based, in part, on editions of his writings that Charvat and subsequent American literary historians have either overlooked or downplayed without explanation.[4] The immediate occasion of *The English Review*'s effort to halt the spread of "the Emerson mania" was its belated reckoning with two books: an authorized British edition of Emerson's second series of *Essays*, published by John Chapman in 1844; and a pirated edition of *Nature* published during the same year in a volume that included "The American Scholar," "The Divinity School Address," "Literary Ethics," and "Man the Reformer."[5] But the opening remarks in *The English Review* also mention a variety of other British publications by or about Emerson whose identities are easy enough to determine. Myerson's bibliography shows that, while Munroe's elegant and expensive edition of *Nature* sold very slowly in America, by 1849 in Britain it had appeared in seven pirated editions, four of which were inexpensive pamphlets that contained reprintings of "The American Scholar," "The Divinity School Address," "Man the Reformer," and several other essays Emerson published during the 1840s. (By August 1844, according to a bookseller's report passed on to Emerson in a letter from Theodore Parker, sales of the various British pirated editions approached between five thousand and six thousand copies—and it was a pity, added Parker, that "this could not be made to give you money.") Emerson mania itself, however, probably had its starting point somewhat earlier in Harriet Martineau's widely noticed *Retrospect of Western Travel* (1838), where in describing the themes of "The American Scholar," she had proclaimed Emerson "a remarkable man . . . without knowing whom it is not too much to say that the United States

---

account of the *English Review*. The Emerson article was reprinted in full in *Littell's Living Age* 23 (November 24, 1849): 344–50, and excerpted in the *Eclectic Magazine* 23 (December 1849): 546.

4. Mary Kupiec Cayton, "The Making of an American Prophet: Emerson, His Audiences, and the Rise of the Culture Industry in Nineteenth-Century America," *American Historical Review* 92 (June 1987): 602, has noted that a "transatlantic connection" contributed to the furthering of Emerson's reputation during the 1840s. The pirating of Emerson's writings was considerably more widespread, however, than she chooses to suggest. There is no mention of this side of Emerson's career in Buell, *New England Literary Culture*.

5. Chapman probably printed eight hundred to one thousand copies of his edition of the *Essays*, which sold well enough to call forth three additional printings during 1845. The pirated edition attacked by *The English Review* appears to be *Nature: An Essay. And Orations* published by William Smith in London in 1844. Myerson estimates that 2,500 copies of this book were printed in forty-seven pages in double columns. Chapman's edition sold for 3s. 6d.; Smith's, for 1s. 6d.

cannot be fully known." By 1850 there was scarcely a major aspect of early Victorian literary culture in which Emerson's name and ideas had not been introduced and discussed. Other American writers of course also gained attention in Britain at the same time. Yet it was Emerson, as William J. Sowder has shown in an important but generally overlooked study, whom British commentators of remarkably diverse interests and opinions regarded as the outstanding American writer of his generation, and he was in turn the one who received the greatest number of reviews and notices. (In this regard, it might also be worth noting that the first publication that yielded Emerson a substantial royalty check was not *Representative Men*, but the English edition of Emerson's first collection of essays, which Thomas Carlyle had helped produce in 1841.[6])

We know too, chiefly by way of his extensive correspondence with Carlyle at the time, that Emerson was well aware of the widespread interest his writings had attracted in Britain. Carlyle kept him informed, to some extent, of both the British reviews and the pirated editions of his work. At first, Emerson was surprised and uneasy in the face of acclaim he had neither anticipated nor wanted to encourage. Referring to Harriet Martineau's lavish praise for "The American Scholar," he remarked in a May 10, 1838, letter to Carlyle: "Meaning to do me a signal kindness (& a kindness quite out of all measure of justice) she does me a great annoyance—to take away from me my privacy & thrust me before my time (if ever there be a time) into the arena of the gladiators, to be stared at."[7] But by 1844

---

6. Harriet Martineau, *Retrospect of Western Travel*, 3 vols. (London, 1838) 3:228. Also see Joel Myerson, *Ralph Waldo Emerson: A Descriptive Bibliography* (Pittsburgh, 1982), 46–48, 97–108, 117–20, 149, 151–54, 569–70, for dozens of other British editions of Emerson's writings published during the late 1830s and 1840s. Among the more remarkable are *Nature: An Essay and Lectures on the Times*, published by H. G. Clarke and Company in 1844 in an edition of three thousand copies selling for 1s.; and the two 1842 English editions of "Man the Reformer" printed as pamphlets that sold for 3d. William J. Sowder, *Emerson's Impact on the British Isles and Canada* (Charlottesville, 1966), esp. 1–28. In January 1844 Emerson received $121.02 for sale of some five hundred copies of *Essays* reprinted by James Fraser.

7. *The Correspondence of Emerson and Carlyle*, ed. Joseph Slater (New York, 1964), 185. Both as it bears on the personal trials and triumphs of the two writers between whom the letters passed, and upon the many changes the market brought to the world of letters during the middle decades of the nineteenth century, this correspondence remains a historical document of inestimable and still inadequately explored importance. Charvat took no notice of earlier editions of the letters, and scholars who more recently have studied Emerson's ties to the literary marketplace continue to ignore them. Slater provides a useful introduction, but sets aside as "tedious" Emerson's and Carlyle's many discussions of the hurdles they faced in publishing their writings.

Emerson clearly had decided his time in fact had come, for such protests had given way to concerted efforts to circumvent the pirates and orchestrate his own appearances in the British literary arena. In September of that year, he sent a set of the American proofs of *Essays: Second Series* to John Chapman in an effort to arrange for a simultaneous publication of the book in Britain. This arrangement, designed to give Chapman the British copyright on Emerson's new collection, did little to slow the pirating of Emerson's other writing during the 1840s. Yet it served as the first step in establishing Chapman as Emerson's British publisher for the balance of the decade, and thereby allowed him to reap at least some economic reward from the considerable demand for his work in Britain.[8]

2

Emerson the "transatlantic star" who emerges from the pages of *The English Review* in 1849 surely has as much claim to be considered an actual historical figure as his almost mirror opposite, that provincial figure who first came to life in Charvat's account of antebellum literary publishing. Regardless of how one might choose to describe Emerson's place in American culture before 1850, there can be no question that by midcentury in Britain his publications had served to make him the best-known and most widely quoted American writer of his generation. The full story of his reception in early Victorian Britain shows too that he was by no means a one-dimensional cultural celebrity. Not only was his standing a matter of partisan dispute; understanding the nature and sources of his popular appeal formed an important dimension of such disputes. Yet I also think the contrast between the accounts of Emerson to be found in *The English Review* and in Charvat's scholarship is significant in pointing to a number of neglected issues involved in considering the reception of Emerson's writings and the accompanying development of his reputation within Ameri-

---

8. Chapman also served as the English agent for the *Dial* during the early 1840s, and Emerson would subsequently send him a set of the proofs of *Poems* (1847) and *Representative Men* (1850) for use in setting English editions. While Chapman's editions sold well, the practice of pirating Emerson's publications remained widespread during the 1840s, usually at prices well below those asked by Emerson's appointed publisher. (See Myerson, *Ralph Waldo Emerson*, 116–19, 151–54, 215–23, 569–70.) George Routledge and Company became Emerson's English publisher after 1850.

can literary culture before 1850. This chapter does not pretend to offer a comprehensively revised history of the American reception of Emerson writings during that period, still less a survey of his "influence" upon or personal ties to other contemporary American and British writers. Rather, it focuses primarily on the ways in which Emerson's American contemporaries, like those in Britain, had opportunities to come to terms with his writings in settings other than the scarce and expensive volumes published by James Munroe and Company; on, that is, an Emerson whose identity as a writer was initially established and mediated in America by religious periodicals, literary magazines, and newspapers. My interest in this largely neglected side of Emerson's early literary career also takes for granted that we cannot reconstruct the relationship Emerson had with his first American readers by assuming that he must have been a figure who presented the same face to all of his contemporaries. I do want to suggest that, by 1850, despite modest sales of Munroe's editions of his books, Emerson's reputation as a writer had become a formidable one. Yet it was at the same time no more monolithic in antebellum America than it was in early Victorian Britain. Emerson was integrated into the loosely organized literary culture of his own country for much the same reason he was attended to in Britain: because, first and foremost, many voices, speaking from different places within American culture, and with different concerns, singled him out as a figure whose views ought not to be disregarded.

Even if restricted to the period before 1850, however, a step-by-step recounting of every facet of Emerson's reception during these years would extend well beyond the boundaries of a single chapter. My narrative, then, will be fairly selective, and attempt to explore what I consider the most prominent institutional settings within which Emerson's early writings were initially presented and understood. I will touch only in passing on his career as poet, literary critic, and lecturer. By the end of this period (one marked, as we have seen in the previous chapter, by the development of a variety of competing and overlapping literary markets), Emerson had acquired the status of an inescapable presence in American culture. He was more than simply another American writer, having achieved a mystique of originality then typically associated with important writers, but he had not yet become an authoritative voice. At the same time, however, he had moved from being regarded as a false and dangerous prophet, stigmatized by his most severe critics as a thinker who threatened to "rob us of our religious faith," to occupying a secure place as the preeminent American literary figure of his generation—an author who, as Theodore Parker put it in another largely forgotten contemporary assessment of his early literary career, had "won by his writings a more desirable reputation, than any other man of letters in America has yet attained."[9]

Some aspects of Emerson's reputation explored in this chapter may not be news to scholars who have consulted the comprehensive secondary bibliography of writings about Emerson that Myerson and Robert Burkholder have recently compiled. It is now perhaps easy enough, with some digging guided by that invaluable volume, to establish that popular knowledge of and interest in Emerson's writings before 1850 was not confined to a small New England coterie wealthy enough to purchase Munroe's original editions of his work. It remains difficult to explain what this discovery means, however, because what little close study has been given to the early reception of Emerson's writings lately not only largely ignores the vast body of writings that first greeted his publications, but typically seems less interested in understanding the popularity of his work than in explaining it away. The dominant view at the moment appears to be that if we want to think of Emerson as a "popular" writer in his own time we must understand his fame and success as developments that had little to do with any widespread understanding of his cultural ideals and social criticism. Mary Kupiec Cayton, for instance, has asked us to believe that Emerson's average admirers were incapable of grasping his broad designs as a thinker, but instead selectively misread his ideas, using them simply as "the basis for a secular faith that focused on materially defined progress, unlimited wealth, and conspicuous social achievement." R. Jackson Wilson, on the other hand, has maintained that Emerson's nineteenth-century admirers actually took him at his word, embracing him as a serious writer and seeker after truth. Yet Emerson's popular triumph, Wilson goes on to argue, thereby had his contemporaries buying into what amounted to a bill of goods, for while the figure Emerson fashioned of himself in his writings was that of an idealist poet-philosopher, the "real" Emerson was a writer engaged in activity he felt compelled to disguise—namely, producing for "the literary marketplace" and hoping to profit from his success. Where Cayton sees Emerson's popularity to be based on a widespread misreading

---

9. [J. W. Alexander, Albert Dod, and Charles Hodge.] Review of *An Address Delivered Before the Senior Class in Divinity College, Cambridge, Sunday Evening, 15 July, 1838*, in *Biblical Repertory and Princeton Review* 11 (January 1839): 100; [Theodore Parker.] "The Writings of Ralph Waldo Emerson," in *Massachusetts Quarterly Review* 3 (March 1850): 205.

of his intentions, Wilson says that his admirers naively took him at his word. Either way, however, Emerson is rendered a writer whose true identity lay well beyond the grasp of his nineteenth-century audience.[10]

It is not my purpose to deny that the relationship between Emerson and his contemporary readers was a complex one. But the historical problem of reconstructing that relationship can hardly be solved if we fail to keep continuously in mind that the public image of Emerson was manifold before 1850. It follows, too, that if Emerson's significance was as unsettled in his own time as it has again become in ours, any effort to reconstruct the original cultural phenomenon that was Emerson requires us to make sense of the full mix of admiration and criticism that first greeted his work or, more precisely, to conceptualize him in a manner that attempts to remain as true to the actual variety of his identities as possible, rather than searching simply to find some single figure underlying them all.

3

In proceeding now to reconstruct the initial American reception of Emerson's writings along these lines, it may be useful to distinguish, briefly and schematically, three stages that corresponded to changes in the relationship that his early publications had with various institutions that competed to define the place of serious writing during the antebellum period. Viewed chronologically, there can be no question that these stages ran closely parallel—at times so closely they seem indistinguishable. For example, Martineau's flattering characterization of Emerson as a figure "without knowing whom it is not too much to say that the United States cannot be

---

10. Cayton, "Making of an American Prophet," 619; R. Jackson Wilson, *Figures of Speech: American Writers and the Literary Marketplace, from Benjamin Franklin to Emily Dickinson* (New York, 1989), 3–19, 161–218. Wilson acknowledges "a particularly large debt" to Charvat in his preface (xiii), but then proceeds with a study that ignores Charvat's early efforts to explore the ways in which publishers and booksellers, journals and reviews, joined to mediate the relationships between antebellum writers and their various audiences. Moreover, Wilson's view that "since the middle of the eighteenth century, probably the most commonly expressed view of the market among writers on both sides of the Atlantic was that it was a foul thing, holding out nothing to the true artist but a temptation to compromise the promptings of genius in order to win the favor of the 'multitudes'" is at best a large oversimplification. For a more nuanced approach to this issue, see Alvin Kernan, *Printing Technology, Letters & Samuel Johnson* (Princeton, 1987), chs. 3–6.

fully known" appeared during the same year his Divinity School Address made him known to most of his contemporaries in New England as the leader of an extreme and largely unintelligible literary sect.[11] Nonetheless, while the three stages of Emerson's literary career between 1836 and 1850 do overlap, keeping them analytically distinct will be helpful in developing a more detailed understanding of the various ways in which his writings initially came to find public attention and acclaim.

During the first stage his ideas and writings were discussed chiefly in the pages of Northern religious periodicals, approached primarily as contributions to a still active and widespread discussion regarding the proper relationship among literature, philosophy, and religious belief. It is in this setting that it still makes historical sense to approach Emerson as Francis Bowen did in "Transcendentalism" in the January 1837 *Christian Examiner*, in an article that remains perhaps the single most widely quoted of several early appraisals of *Nature*. Like most other names for cultural and literary movements, the term "Transcendentalism" has a tendency to dissolve when an unambiguous definition is called for, and it should be remembered that Emerson himself (for reasons we explored in chapter 1) complained of being fastened with that label by some of his contemporaries.[12] Still, if we take the simple core nineteenth-century meaning of "Transcendentalism" to lie in Bowen's warning that Emerson's writings threatened to inspire not simply a break with existing Protestant literary and philosophical traditions, but a break more drastic than one that might have occurred in a continuous process of growth and development, the term remains a useful guide in tracking precisely what was at issue in the heated controversies that at first surrounded Emerson's writings within the world of antebellum Protestant letters.

---

11. It is worth noting that when Andrews Norton indicted the Harvard students who invited Emerson to speak at Divinity Hall, his criticism began with an attack on Martineau, whom he described as a "foolish woman" who had "stimulated the vanity of her flatterers by loading them in return with the copper coin of her praise, which they easily believed was as good as gold." See Norton, "The New School in Literature and Religion," in the *Boston Daily Advertiser*, August 27, 1838, p. 2, col. 2, rpt. in *Critical Essays on Ralph Waldo Emerson*, ed. Robert E. Burkholder and Joel Myerson (Boston, 1973), 31–32.

12. Michael Lopez, "De-Transcendentalizing Emerson," *Emerson Society Quarterly* 34 (Nos. 1 and 2; 1988): 80, 89, reminds us that, while during the antebellum period "Transcendentalism" was generally synonymous with "incomprehensibility and impracticality," from the standpoint of literary history what was most influential in Emerson's own essay on "The Transcendentalist" was its vividly suggestive critique of the excessive idealism of his generation of New England intellectuals.

During the second stage Americans were invited to consider other characterizations of Emerson's purpose and significance based on a steadily growing supply of excerpts, notices, and reviews available in newspapers and literary magazines. While Bowen's review certainly played an important role in defining Emerson's early reputation—especially as it came to be repeated and expanded in the wake of the Divinity School Address—it was by no means authoritative. Beginning as early as February 1838, when Elizabeth Peabody answered Bowen's criticism in a flattering review of *Nature* that appeared in the first volume of the *United States Magazine and Democratic Review*, Emerson found reviewers who seemed largely indifferent to the theological controversy that surrounded his early writings, and stressed instead other aspects of his writing—spontaneity, originality, and inspiration—which were seen to be characteristic of his literary "genius." Emerson was by no means everywhere treated with reverence by those who considered themselves the new arbiters of American literary culture. Complaints about the unintelligibility of his ideas were commonplace, as were related protests at the obscurity of his language. (In April 1841 *Arcturus* published an early general introduction to Emerson that described his characteristic method of composition to be "transposition, involution, and a consciousness approaching obscurity."[13]) By the mid-1840s, however, such complaints were offset by another general rule when it came to Emerson: despite his well-known obscurities, he now had to be considered, for a variety of reasons, perhaps the most original literary figure American culture had produced.

The third and final stage, which began roughly in the mid-1840s and thus overlapped with the second, is that in which Emerson came to be a cultural figure in his own right; or, more precisely, in which it now became commonplace to identify him either as the founder or as one of the essential figures of a recently emerged American literary and intellectual tradition. Perhaps equally important, during the second half of the 1840s, the growing popularity of his writings also becomes apparent, as both his poetry and his prose became more readily available in a broad range of lit-

---

13. W. A. Jones, "Ralph Waldo Emerson," *Arcturus* 1 (April 1841): 278–84. Founded by Cornelius Matthews and Evert Duyckinck, the short-lived *Arcturus* (1840–42) might be considered one of America's first "high" culture periodicals. Its contributors included Hawthorne, Longfellow, and Lowell; and Jones was one of the leading literary critics of the 1840s. Duyckinck would later found and edit the more successful and influential *Literary World* (1847–53), the first important American weekly devoted primarily to the discussion

erary settings. While Munroe's editions of his books and pamphlets remained hard to come by, Emerson's writings found their way to ordinary Americans by way of a steadily growing number of excerpts and partial reprintings that appeared in anthologies, gift books, literary magazines, and newspapers.[14]

It may be axiomatic that the historical reception of most writers who become and remain prominent in their own culture proceeds through stages that reflect accompanying changes in public understanding of their work.[15] What strikes me as not yet fully appreciated or understood in Emerson's case, however, is the remarkable speed with which he arrived at stage 3, where in effect it became mandatory, despite the modest sales of the first American editions of his books, for educated Americans to establish where they stood in relation to his ideas and writings. In taking the full measure of that accomplishment, however, I think it especially important at the outset that we not let the even more dramatically successful development of his reputation after 1850 obscure the fact that the very mixed reception Emerson initially received—mostly because of his close identification with "Transcendentalism"—suggests that popular interest in his views was likely to fade after the late 1830s. In this regard, it also is interesting to speculate about how much we would have to alter our understanding of his early career had Emerson restricted himself to lecturing in the early 1840s, as his correspondence with Carlyle suggests he was tempted to do.[16] It is arguable that his place in the history of American culture

---

of books. See Frank Luther Mott, *History of American Magazines, 1741–1850* (New York, 1938), 711–12, 766–68. I discuss Duyckinck in greater detail in ch. 9.

14. There is some evidence suggesting that pirated British editions of Emerson's writings also found their way to America. In 1841 Rev. D. G. Goyder, a Swedenborgian minister in Glasgow, reprinted *Nature* in its entirety in his miscellany *The Biblical Assistant, and Book of Practical Piety*. Editions of Goyder's book were printed for sale in Boston, as well as in Glasgow, London, Manchester, and Liverpool. It also seems likely that other pirated editions found their way to the American literary marketplace.

15. See, e.g., Stefan Collini, "From Dangerous Partisan to National Possession: John Stuart Mill in English Culture, 1873–1933," in *Public Moralists: Political Thought and Intellectual Life in Britain, 1850–1930* (Oxford, 1991), 311–41. My approach to Emerson in this chapter is much indebted to Collini's thoughtful account of Mill's posthumous career.

16. *Correspondence of Emerson and Carlyle*, 143. Emerson reported to Carlyle in 1836 that he had earned $350 in lecture fees; two years later the sum was $800. Emerson in fact had remarkably little to say about his own writing in early correspondence with Carlyle, and at first seems reluctant to even think of himself as "a writer." Part of the explanation of this, as Emerson would put in a letter of October 30, 1841, was that he was "haunted with brave dreams of what might be accomplished in the lecture room" (308).

would have been significantly diminished, and he would now have to be seen as a figure who never allowed his ideas to gain close study during his lifetime, and whose reputation therefore derived almost entirely from the persona he projected as a speaker—a fate that suggests a much simpler relationship with his contemporaries than the one I have set out to reconstruct here. In my view, then, what initially set Emerson apart from other literary figures of his generation, and as a result gave him extraordinary public standing, was not his well-known success as a lecturer—the development of his national reputation in this realm in fact occurred during the 1850s—but rather a unique relationship he came to establish, by way of his early writings, with the editors, readers, and reviewers of several of the most important Northern religious periodicals that shaped (and attempted to police) American literary opinion when his career began. Over the course of the 1840s Emerson became, as Francis Bowen would put it in a later and generally overlooked account of his early career, "a chartered libertine" within the world of American Protestant letters.[17] To understand how Emerson managed to gain his cultural "charter," however, we have to begin by returning for a close look at the various assessments of Emerson's writings that were offered by religious periodicals at the time of their first appearance.

4

Antebellum religious periodicals as a group were a noticeably hybrid literary genre. Theological concerns and controversies were of course their raison d'être, and the abundance of religious periodicals both reflected and sustained the heterogeneity of Christian belief. Yet many religious periodicals, especially those published in Northern states, had various interests in addition to theology, with some giving space to literature, natural history, philosophy, and contemporary social and political problems, that it is easy to forget, as Frank Luther Mott observed in his multivolume history of American magazines, their essentially religious origins and purpose. While belief and convention dictated that theology always be treated with

---

17. [Francis Bowen] "Nine New Poets," *North American Review* 64 (April 1847): 406. Bowen served as editor of the *North American Review* from 1843 to 1854, and his was the first review of any of Emerson's writings to appear in what had long been recognized as one of the nation's leading literary periodicals.

the utmost respect, this rule did not preclude concerted efforts to observe high literary and intellectual standards. In this regard, it is important to remember that the Harvard Unitarian community from which Emerson emerged regarded study of literature, philosophy, and the fine arts as invaluable aids to personality development as well as an important means of social control, and its two leading periodicals—the bimonthly *Christian Examiner* (1824–69) and the weekly *Christian Register* (1821–)—devoted a large proportion of their space to conscientious discussions of belles lettres. But Unitarian publications were by no means alone in looking upon literature and philosophy as means to help form the taste, refine the sentiments, and determine the manners of individual Christians. That belief also informed the editorial practices of the leading Presbyterian periodical of the antebellum period, *The Biblical Repertory and Princeton Review* (1837–71). While now remembered chiefly as a fortress of Old School Presbyterianism and a purely theological review, the pages of a typical issue during the late 1830s and 1840s included notices and occasional long reviews of new publications in philosophy, natural history, and travel literature. And the same was true of its counterpart in New Haven, the *Quarterly Christian Spectator* (1819–38). The assumption that literature and philosophy, when properly understood, could serve as a wholesome stimulant to belief also openly informed the titles some Unitarians chose to give their periodicals—for example, the *Monthly Miscellany of Religion and Letters* (1839–43), a short-lived Boston publication incorporated into the *Christian Examiner*, and the more well-known *Western Messenger: Devoted to Religion and Literature* (1835–41), founded in Cincinnati as an organ of Unitarian religion. Members of other Protestant denominations, however, appear to have taken that assumption to be so deep-seated it needed no highlighting. The Methodist Church in New York for a time produced its own literary monthly, the *National Magazine* (1852–58), an eclectic publication with departments of both religious and literary news, as well as woodcut illustrations. And Caleb S. Henry, an Episcopalian priest with particular interests in older English writers and contemporary German literature, founded and edited a well-respected literary quarterly he named the *New York Review*.[18]

---

18. The standard account of the impact that the "literary humanism" of Harvard Unitarianism had on American letters is Daniel Walker Howe, *The Unitarian Conscience: Harvard Moral Philosophy, 1805–61* (Cambridge, Mass., 1970), esp. ch. 7. Also see Mott, *History of American Magazines, 1741–1850*, 131–39, 529–35, 669–71.

This rich mixture of cultural concerns was evident in the ways in which several Northern religious periodicals received Emerson's earliest writings. Those who condemned him for having exceeded what the *Biblical Repertory and Princeton Review* described as "the limits of liberal Protestantism" grudgingly conceded that his unacceptable ideas had been conveyed in writing of sometimes enthralling beauty. Others who registered milder dissents attempted to distinguish between Emerson's ideas and his person, arguing that he at least had to be admired for the intellectual honesty and independence he displayed in voicing his unorthodox views. Still others tried to cast Emerson as both a literary genius and an inspirational Christian reformer. Answering Andrews Norton's charge that the Divinity School Address smacked of atheism in its questioning of historical Christian doctrine, the *Western Messenger* (one of the most enthusiastic early champions and publicists of Emerson's writings) commented: "If Mr. Emerson disbelieves in all our present historical Christianity, how happens it that instead of opposing it, he opposes its defects?"[19]

The differences among these interpretations may begin to suggest something of the divergent range of responses Emerson's early writings evoked in Northern antebellum religious periodicals. What is more significant for my purposes here, however, is that while Emerson's early writings undoubtedly had more critics than admirers among those who edited and wrote for religious periodicals, it cannot be said that their criticisms, in most cases, were based on willfully misleading presentations of his views; in fact, in numerous instances they also included substantial excerpts from Emerson's texts themselves. Bowen's lengthy appraisal of *Nature* in the *Christian Examiner*, for example, can be seen as typical of the way in which commentators for American religious periodicals provided what might be called unintended assistance to the spread of what they perceived as Emerson's extreme views. Bowen's overall evaluation was, to be sure, disparaging enough, beginning with his complaint that the effort required to read *Nature* was "often painful, the thoughts excited are frequently bewildering, and the results to which they lead us, uncertain and obscure." Yet for all his discomfort, Bowen

---

19. Anon., "The School of Hegel," *Biblical Repertory and Princeton Review* 12 (January 1840): 31–32; [Chandler Robbins], Editorial Response, *Christian Register* 17 (September 29, 1838): 154–55; [James Freeman Clarke], "R. W. Emerson and the New School," *Western Messenger* 6 (November 1838): 38. For a more detailed account of the *Western Messenger*, see Robert D. Habich, *Transcendentalism and the Western Messenger: A History of the Magazine and Its Contributors, 1835–41* (Rutherford, N.J., 1985).

did go on to give Emerson space to speak for himself, providing readers of *The Christian Examiner* with several direct quotations from *Nature*, including among them an only slightly garbled version of what later became its two most famous sentences. (Bowen's version read: "Standing on the bare ground, my head bathed by the blithe air,—and uplifted into infinite space—all egotism vanishes. I became a transparent eyeball." This leaves out the adjective "mean" before "egotism"; "became" is "become" in Emerson's text.) Perhaps more important, Bowen's appraisal contained evidence, in the form of two long summary paragraphs immediately following the quotations, which showed he also had made the effort to read *Nature* and apparently meant to provide a fair account of Emerson's major themes before exposing the inadequacies of his views. This was Bowen's précis:

> The purpose of the book, so far as it may be said to have a purpose, is, to invite us to the observation of nature, and to point out manifestations of spirit in material existences and external events. The uses to which the outward world is subservient are divided into four classes,—Commodity, Beauty, Language, and Discipline. These ends the writer considers as the final cause of every thing that exists, except the soul. To the consideration of each he allots a chapter, and displays, often with eloquence and a copious fund of illustration, the importance of the end, and the aptitude of the means provided for its attainment. In the latter part of the work, he seems disposed to neutralize the effect of the former, by adopting the Berkeleyan system, and denying the outward and real existence of that Nature, which he had just declared to be so subservient to man's spiritual wants. Of the chapters on "Spirit" and "Prospects," with which the work concludes, we prefer not to attempt giving an account, until we can understand their meaning.

> From this sketch of the author's plan, it would seem, that he had hardly aimed at originality. What novelty there is in the work, arises not from the choice or distribution of the subject, but from the manner of treatment. The author is not satisfied with that cautious philosophy which traces the indirect influences of outward phenomena and physical laws on the individual mind, and contemplates the benevolence of the Deity in particular instances of the adaptation and subserviency of matter to spirit. He contemplates the Universe from a higher point of view. Where others see only an analogy, he discerns a final cause. The fall of waters, the germination of seeds, the alternate growth and decay of organized forms, were not originally designed to answer the wants of our physical constitution, but to

acquaint us with the laws of mind, and to serve our intellectual and moral advancement. The powers of Nature have been forced into the service of man. The pressure of the atmosphere, the expansive force of steam, the gravity of falling bodies, are our ministers, and do our bidding in levelling the earth, in changing a wilderness into a habitable city, and in fashioning raw materials into products available for the gratification of sense and the protection of body. Yet these ends are only of secondary importance to the great purpose for which these forces were created and made subject to human power. Spiritual laws are typified in these natural facts, and are made evident in the whole material constitution of things. Man must study matter, that he may become acquainted with his own soul.

This of course is not a substitute for careful and sympathetic discussion of the many issues that Bowen himself, despite his subsequent questioning of Emerson's purpose and "originality," saw to be at stake in a full evaluation of *Nature*. Yet as a reasonably accurate summary of those issues, the opening of Bowen's uneasy review, it seems fair to say, represents an important early service rendered Emerson by one of the most highly respected of antebellum America's religious periodicals.[20]

Over the course of the late 1830s and 1840s, dozens of writers for other Northern religious periodicals amplified and repeated Bowen's warning that readers of Emerson risked being exposed to a view of the world that amounted to "a disturbed dream." Yet most of them followed him in working through writings that left them disturbed and then providing broadly correct accounts of what they found. This is perhaps most true in the case of the first pamphlet edition of the Divinity School Address. Much has been written about the cultural crisis Emerson's address immediately provoked within the community of New England Protestants, and his sally into theological disputes that had already split that community of course at once lent added credibility to Bowen's suggestion that he was at the head of a "Transcendentalist" conspiracy.[21] Yet this familiar account has tended to obscure the fact that the family quarrel that ensued immediately

---

20. F[rancis] B[owen], "Transcendentalism," *Christian Examiner* 21 (January 1837): 372–74, as rpt. in *Emerson's 'Nature'—Origin, Growth, Meaning*, ed. Merton M. Sealts Jr. and Alfred R. Ferguson (New York, 1969), 82.

21. For more detailed recent accounts of the crisis, see Anne C. Rose, *Transcendentalism as a Social Movement, 1830–1850* (New Haven, 1981), ch. 3; and Mary Kupiec Cayton, *Emerson's Emergence: Self and Society in the Transformation of New England* (Chapel Hill, 1989), ch. 7.

after the address was given at Harvard in late August 1838 also grew to be a two-year controversy of printed words that not only catapulted Emerson from relative obscurity to a highly visible place in American Protestant literary culture, but also allowed for more considerably widespread knowledge of the printed text of the address than Munroe's modest sales figures alone might suggest. While much of the attention the pamphlet edition of the Divinity School Address first received came from the Protestant literary community in and around Boston, it was never limited to that. The final months of 1838, and the whole of 1839 and 1840, saw a steady stream of periodical reviews and newspaper articles both in America and in Britain. Many of these, predictably enough, faulted Emerson for not having the expected unity of religious and literary values, but that criticism again did not mean Emerson was not given a fair hearing or allowed to speak for himself. The controversy over the Divinity School Address began to spread outside of Boston as early as September 1838, when a full reprinting of Andrews Norton's first attack of Emerson (his polemic against "The New School of Literature and Religion" in the August 27, 1838, *Boston Daily Advocate*) appeared in *The Christian Watchman*, a New York Baptist newspaper, which in the following month would also publish its own hostile review of the pamphlet. By January 1839 substantial reviews had appeared in the *Western Messenger* and the *Quarterly Christian Spectator* (an orthodox Presbyterian monthly published in New Haven), and *The Biblical Repertory and Princeton Review*, all of which contained substantial excerpts from Emerson's text. Perhaps the most intriguing of the several early reviews of the address, however, was that in the *Southern Rose*, a Charleston-based literary journal. It predicted a quick collapse for Emerson's reputation as "a new comet or rather meteor . . . shooting athwart the literary sky of old Massachusetts," yet then proceeded to quote at considerable length from both the Divinity School Address and Munroe's more recent pamphlet edition of Emerson's 1838 "Oration" at Dartmouth College.[22]

The publication of Norton's *Discourse on the Latest Form of Infidelity* in

---

22. "New School in Literature and Religion," *Christian Watchman* 19 (September 7, 1838): 142; anon., review of *An Address . . .* , *Christian Watchman*, ca. mid-October 1838; [James Freeman Clarke] "R. W. Emerson, and the New School," *Western Messenger* 6 (November 1838): 37–47; [J. W. Alexander, Albert Dod, and Charles Hodges], review of *An Address . . .* , *Biblical Repertory and Princeton Review* 11 (January 1839): 95–99; [Samuel Gilman], "Ralph Waldo Emerson," *Southern Rose* 7 (November 24, 1838): 100. The *Southern*

July 1839 marked the onset of the second phase of a controversy that now became Anglo-American in scope, with participants coming to include writers for British literary periodicals. In September 1839 John Heraud, the editor of the *Monthly Magazine*, joined Harriet Martineau as a second early champion of Emerson in Britain by responding to criticisms of the address that had been made by Orestes Brownson in his *Boston Quarterly Review*. More significant still was a twenty-seven-page, double-column article on "American Philosophy—Emerson's Work" that appeared in the March 1840 *London and Westminster Review*. Written by Richard Monckton Milnes (who later helped orchestrate Emerson's successful lecture tour in Britain in the winter of 1847–48), this piece in retrospect can be seen as the first overall assessment of prose writings Emerson had published in the late 1830s. While troubled by his criticisms of historical Christianity, and noting that he had borrowed many of his ideas from Carlyle, Milnes nonetheless declared that because Emerson's views had been "arrayed in language so freshly vigorous, so eloquently true," he had managed to give birth to a distinctively "American philosophy" in which "the poetry of daily life and the dignity of labor" were the central themes. As he presented Emerson to his readers in these terms, Milnes also allowed them to encounter more directly the "vigor" and "eloquence" of his language by way of several lengthy excerpts drawn from *Nature* and the addresses Emerson had given at Harvard and Dartmouth. It is worth noting here that Milnes' long and generally admiring article takes on added historical significance in thinking about Emerson's early literary career if we recall that the *London and Westminster Review* was also published in an American edition in New York.[23]

Following the controversy generated by the Divinity School Address,

---

Rose was one of several changing titles given to a weekly magazine published in Charleston during 1832–39. It was edited by Caroline Howell Gilman, the wife of Unitarian minister Samuel Gilman, who had been educated at Harvard and came to Charleston from Gloucester, Massachusetts. For a more detailed history, see Sam G. Riley, *Magazines of the American South* (New York, 1986), 191–94.

23. [John Heraud] "A Response from America," *Monthly Magazine*, 3rd ser. (September 1939): 344–52. In "Mr. Emerson's Address," *Boston Quarterly Review* 1 (October 1838): 500–514, Brownson had praised the beauty of Emerson's language, but also protested his narrow "egotism." Heraud replied that Brownson had greatly exaggerated the extent to which Emerson meant to emphasize the individual over the public good. R[ichard] M[ockton] M[ilnes], "American Philosophy—Emerson's Works," *London and Westminster Review* 33 (March 1840): 345–72. (In the American edition, Milnes' article appeared in vol. 33 [October 1839–March 1840], 186–201.)

the publication of Emerson's first collection of *Essays* in January 1841 provided another chance for an overall assessment of his writings and ideas.
Several religious periodicals again launched by now predictable attempts
to discredit or marginalize Emerson by representing him as outside or at
odds with the mainstream of American Protestant culture. *The New York
Review* described the *Essays* as a "godless book" that advocated views that
were "essentially false and mischievous." *The Christian Examiner* similarly
classified the *Essays* as a volume that "cannot be said to contain any system
of religion, morals, or philosophy." Most disturbing of all in its view was
the irreverence Emerson had shown in frequently coupling the name of
Jesus "with that of other great philosophers and thinkers, as if he had been
on a level with them, and no more; a mere teacher, philanthropist, or
system-maker." The *Monthly Miscellany of Religion and Letters* likewise saw
the *Essays* as only providing further evidence that Emerson "preaches not
a Gospel, a Saviour, a God, that satisfies" true Protestant devotion and
belief. The most hostile review of all came from the *Biblical Repertory and
Princeton Review,* which dismissed the *Essays* as a book "constructed with
a view of hoaxing the public" and in which Emerson's lack of philosophical depth had been disguised by his obscure language. Harsh as their estimates were, however, most of those who reviewed the *Essays* for religious
periodicals were also inclined to follow earlier critics in providing a reasonably accurate summary of Emerson's more prominent concerns, as well as
in offering citations from his new volume. The description of the "philosophical aspects" of the *Essays* in the *New York Review,* for example,
singled out the radical individualism that it saw as informing Emerson's
vision of American culture, offering a summary description of "Self-Reliance" that pointed out that Emerson "represents every man as superior
to all other men; every man as utterly independent of other men," and
then quoted what has since become one of its more famous sentences—
"No law can be sacred to me but that of my own nature." Almost one-third
of a nine-page review that appeared in the May 1841 *Christian Examiner*
was given over to extracts taken from "History," "Compensation," and
"Spiritual Laws," and this piece quickly found its way to readers in New
York by way of a full reprinting that appeared in the June 1841 *Knickerbocker.* Even the *Biblical Repertory and Princeton Review,* after charging
Emerson with authoring a book that was little more than a hoax, allowed
its readers to decide the issue for themselves by devoting the bulk of the
first four pages of its closely printed review to several long excerpts taken

from "Self-Reliance," "Heroism," "The Over-Soul," and "Circles."[24]

And so it went on. The story I have been telling about the responses that Emerson's early writings evoked in Northern religious periodicals more or less repeated itself with each of Emerson's successive publications during the 1840s, with the only noticeable changes involving a steady increase in the number of individuals and publications involved, and the plot continuing to thicken by becoming both more "transatlantic" and Southern in its setting. Yet the early assistance that Northern religious periodicals provided in building Emerson's reputation went beyond simply drawing attention to his views. It bears emphasizing here that, even at the height of the Divinity School Address controversy, Emerson's estrangement from the cultural norms of liberal Protestantism was not everywhere perceived as complete. Outspoken critics such as Andrews Norton were minority voices; in fact, his condemnation of Emerson was so sneeringly hostile that others, who were then also critical of Emerson's unorthodox views, were moved to defend him and treat his views seriously. More important, the question of the practical significance of Emerson's ideas also remained open to dispute. Some argued that the obscurity of Emerson's language had already served to make him something of a menacing spellbinder. The *Quarterly Christian Spectator* labeled the Divinity School Address a "labyrinth of dark words," and *Monthly Miscellany of Religious Letters* warned that Emerson's *Essays* were dangerous to undiscriminating admirers. Others echoed Bowen, however, in saying that Emerson's obscurity would render his unorthodox views harmless. Commenting on Emerson's new-found fame as lecturer in Boston, an anonymous writer in the July 1840 *Christian Examiner* observed that "it is by no means a safe conclusion, the Reviewers must understand, that because Mr. Emerson was admired . . . he was therefore received as a master or authority in either philosophy or religion; for we suppose it true that not an individual out of his crowd of hearers at the close of his lectures could have stated with any confidence what his religious or philosophical system was; whether he himself was theist, pantheist, or atheist."[25] Brownson too underlined Emerson's

---

24. Anon. review of *Essays*, *New York Review* 8 (April 1841): 510–11; C. C. F[elton], "Emerson's Essays," *Christian Examiner* 30 (May 1841): 254; B.B.M., "Emerson's Essays," *Monthly Miscellany of Religion and Letters* 5 (August 1841): 91; [J. W. Alexander], "Pantheism," *Biblical Repertory and Princeton Review* 13 (October 1841): 539.

25. Anon. review of *An Address* . . . , *Quarterly Christian Spectator* 10 (November 1838): 670; "Emerson's Essays," *Monthly Miscellany* 5 (August 1841): 90–97; Anonymous review of

lack of a clear "system" in his review of the *Essays*, although interpreting its absence in considerably more flattering terms. Emerson ought not be approached as a philosopher, Brownson observed, because he had not set out to solve any intellectual problems or offer any practical instruction. It then followed, according to Brownson, that Emerson ought not be censured as a dangerous thinker either, since he proposed nothing in the way of "practical instruction." Instead, he had to be taken as "a seer, who rises into the regions of the Transcendental, and reports what he sees, and in the order in which he sees it."[26]

Also open to continuing debate over the course of the 1840s was what proved to be the more significant question of how to come to terms with the remarkable beauty of Emerson's writing. Although primarily intent on exposing the errors and inadequacies of his theological views, almost all the early reviews of Emerson in religious periodicals—again beginning with Bowen's article in the January 1837 *Christian Examiner*—included testimonies to his considerable talents as a writer. The very first observation Bowen made, in fact, was that he had found "beautiful writing" in *Nature*, and dozens of subsequent commentators followed with more effusive and elaborately divided praise. The unnamed reviewer of Emerson's first collection of *Essays* in the August 1841 *Monthly Miscellany of Religion and Letters* observed: "We have seldom read a book in so many moods of mind; now delighted by its poetical images, now bewildered by its philosophy; at one time excited by its virtuous aspirations, and then suddenly chilled through by its religious abstractions. Its author's imagination is a perfect kaleidoscope of brilliantly mingling pictures, his philosophy a proteus of ever shifting forms, his religion obedience to the suggestions of his nature—changing with the hour." A similar mixture of admiration and regret was voiced in the January 1842 *New York Review* appraisal of "Method of Nature": "We know of few things of the kind more beautiful in American literature; we know as few more false and dangerous. It is painful for us to speak of anything so exceedingly beautiful, and still more painful to believe it."[27]

Two Articles from the Princeton Review, ed. Andrews Norton, *Christian Examiner* 28 (July 1840): 388.

26. [Orestes A. Brownson], "Emerson's Essays," *Boston Quarterly Review* 4 (July 1841): 292.

27. "Transcendentalism," *Christian Examiner* 21 (January 1837): 91; "Emerson's Essays," *Monthly Miscellany*, 91; anon. review of "Method of Nature," *New York Review* 10 (January 1842): 219.

There is no need for extensive citation here, however, except to illustrate briefly how the practice of distinguishing between the realms of literature and theology in judging Emerson both allowed for, and over time surely served to encourage, a transformation in public understanding of his cultural identity that allowed him to gain his formidable reputation as a writer, even in the face of continuing efforts by religious periodicals to expose fundamental errors and inadequacies in his views. A particularly instructive example in this regard would be the general appraisal of Emerson that appeared in the March 1847 *Christian Examiner* in a review of his *Poems* written by Cyrus Bartol. This review can be read, in part, as an elaborate restatement of the characteristic ambivalence with which most Northern religious periodicals approached Emerson between 1836 and 1850. Bartol began with two long paragraphs extolling the "genius" of Emerson's poetry and prose: "We know of nothing in the whole range of modern writers," he declared, "superior in original merit to his productions." He then drew back, however, with a by now familiar inventory of the inadequacies of Emerson's religious views; for all the beauty in his writing, there was "no recognition in his pages of the Christian faith, according to any, however, catholic, idea of it which we are able to form." Yet, while Bartol was unmistakably divided in his views of Emerson, what makes his effort to walk a thin line between praise and condemnation particularly instructive is his recognition, openly expressed in the last paragraph of the review, that protests concerning Emerson's undermining of religious sentiment now seemed altogether beside the point. By 1847 it appears that the spell cast by Emerson simply had become too powerful to be broken by once again rehearsing the fundamental shortcomings of his religious views. Indeed, it is Bartol himself who provides eloquent testimony to the power of that spell not only in the opening paragraphs of his review, but again in its penultimate sentence, where he expressed his wish that Emerson continue to enjoy "the largest success in all that he has done to refine and elevate the community" even though he was "obliged by a sense of duty to put in a protest against the soundness of much that is implied in his various publications." What we see in Bartol's appraisal of Emerson, in short, is an illustration of the way in which the early grudging acknowledgment of the beauty and "genius" of Emerson's work by writers for religious periodicals over time had become the basis for a resigned recognition that Emerson had succeeded in establishing a new model of literary excellence that could no longer be judged primarily by means of the assumptions of those who believed that literature, at some level, must remain an agent of Christian belief.[28]

There is of course much more to tell in a story that continued well past 1850, in now perhaps countless pages of American religious periodicals. For the student of Emerson's early reception, however, the chief interest of all this clearly is that this is where the story must begin. Emerson's literary career in the late 1830s and early 1840s unfolded in a culture in which the spiritual and literary activity overlapped, and there can be little question that it was at this intersection that Emerson at first wanted to make his mark. The contributors, editors, and subscribers of the Northern religious periodicals that initially judged Emerson's work formed a central part of antebellum America's literary elite, and everything Emerson published early in his career was written, in part, to gain their attention and influence their behavior.[29] It would be misleading to conclude (for reasons we will consider in the following section) that editors and reviewers in religious periodicals were also the primary source of public information about Emerson's ideas and writings before 1850. While the American debate over the religious implications of Emerson's thinking would continue until his death, it was most intensely heated during the late 1830s and early 1840s, and may properly be said to have spent itself—outside of Southern states at least—by 1845.[30] Even so, it is reasonable to suppose that in the

---

28. C[yrus] A. B[artol], "Poetry and Imagination," *Christian Examiner* 42 (March 1847): 250–70, as rpt. in *Critical Essays on Ralph Waldo Emerson*, ed. Robert E. Brukholder and Joel Myerson (Boston, 1983), 117, 118, 122. An 1835 graduate of the Harvard Divinity School, Bartol was also a long-time acquaintance of Emerson, who had hosted an early meeting of the Transcendentalist Club.

29. However inadequate James Munroe and Company may have been in promoting his publications, Emerson's choice to continue his ties with this publisher until 1850 shows that he continued to identify himself with the world of Protestant letters in New England. Munroe, it is worth noting, was also publisher of the *Christian Examiner* and *Christian Register*, and the *North American Review*, all periodicals that served as the cultural platforms of liberal New England Protestantism.

30. The contemporary reception of Emerson's writings in Southern periodicals and newspapers awaits a full-length study. Entries in *Emerson: An Annotated Bibliography*, show that the *Southern Quarterly Review* (1842–57) and the *Southern Literary Messenger* (1834–64) combined to provide educated Southerners with a slow but steady flow of reviews and notices. By 1860 Emerson's role in bringing cultural legitimacy to the abolitionist movement also appears to have been well known, and had rendered his name and writings anathema to Southern commentators. See, e.g., E. Boyden, "The Epidemic of the Nineteenth Century," *Southern Literary Messenger* 31 (November 1860): 365–74; and [George William

absence of the attention of Northern religious periodicals, the cultural presence that was Emerson before 1845 would have been less visible, the need to reckon with his early writings less pressing and limited to a much smaller regional constituency, and generally subject to less notice from educated Americans. Finally, it was also crucial to the subsequent development of Emerson's reputation that so much of the discussion of his work in the religious periodicals should have been focused squarely on the question of whether his extraordinary powers as a writer were such that he be allowed to stand fully outside of the cultural assumptions that guided the thinking of those who taught and believed that serious literary writing ought to remain the servant of traditional religious belief. During the late 1830s and early 1840s, as we have seen, this question could be handled in various ways. Some simply said "no"; others counseled him to temper his approach. By the mid-1840s, however, when the interest and acclaim of other literary institutions in antebellum America had allowed Emerson to emerge as a cultural figure in his own right, it would be handled with steadily increasing deference to his growing reputation.

5

In considering the second stage in the reception of Emerson's writings, and attempting to explain more fully why disapproving labels that religious periodicals applied to his publications never came to dictate public understanding, our starting point has to be the increasingly dominant position taken by new literary institutions in New York and Philadelphia in shaping national understanding of the cultural significance of American writers. We have come to see the late 1830s and 1840s, precisely the historical moment when Emerson was first publishing his "classic" works, as a time of sharp transition in American literary culture. In the early decades of the nineteenth century (as we saw in the previous chapter), the number of books published in America grew significantly, yet the institutional organization of publishing remained almost entirely decentralized. Most publishers marketed their products in the communities where they

---

Bagby] review of *The Conduct of Life*, *Southern Literary Messenger* 32 (April 1861), which urged Congress to suppress Emerson's works.

happened to live, and the reputation of a successful author was thus typically local in scope. Charvat showed, however, that while the process of centralization in the antebellum book trade proceeded very slowly, it did have its clear beginning in New York and Philadelphia—two cities which, close together and connected by abundant ocean, river, and road transportation, came to form what he called "the publishing axis" of antebellum America. After 1830 literary traffic and writers moved between the two cities in steadily growing numbers, with some publishers having offices in both places, and almost all of them establishing agents. This new market situation in time served to foster what might be called the cultural ascendancy of New York and Philadelphia, where during the 1840s and 1850s printing and publishing became major industries, and where men like Evert Duyckinck, Horace Greeley, George Graham, Rufus Griswold, and George Palmer Putnam were eager to find and promote native literary talent by way of general literary periodicals and newspapers that gained unprecedented national circulation and gave their editors central roles in shaping popular reading tastes and cultural attitudes.[31]

The columns and pages of various magazines and newspapers published in New York and Philadelphia provided the most important setting for alternative evaluations of Emerson's writings during the decade of the 1840s. Not only did the question of the religious implications of his writing come to lose its significance here—in December 1844 *Graham's Magazine* announced that the religious controversies surrounding Emerson were now only of historical interest[32]—but, of even greater consequence for the placing of Emerson within antebellum culture, editors and reviewers in New York and Philadelphia clearly found something about Emerson that marked him as different from other writers of his day, and in turn took seriously the possibility that he had succeeded in establishing an altogether new position in American culture. The upshot was that Emerson's public image split into what might be considered two continuously updated versions of the divergent appraisals first provided by Francis Bowen (in the Boston-based *Christian Examiner*) and Elizabeth Peabody (in the

---

31. Charvat, *Literary Publishing in America, 1790–1850*, ch. 1. The standard account of antebellum literary life in New York remains Perry Miller, *The Raven and the Whale: The War of Words and Wits in the Era of Poe and Melville* (New York, 1956); but also see Thomas Bender, *New York Intellect: A History of Intellectual Life in New York City from 1750 to the Beginnings of Our Own Time* (Baltimore, 1987), chs. 4 and 5.

32. Anon. review of *Essays: Second Series*, *Graham's Magazine* 25 (December 1844): 293.

New York-based *United States Magazine and Democratic Review*).[33] On the one hand, Emerson came to gain qualified acceptance as what Bowen later correctly described as "a chartered libertine" within the world of Anglo-American Protestant letters. On the other, for readers of newspapers and literary magazines in New York and Philadelphia, Emerson came forward as the poet-philosopher who had staked his claim to being America's first true literary genius.

The significance of this split for the subsequent development of Emerson's reputation as spokesman for American cultural ideals should be fairly obvious. (Viewed more broadly, it also of course signaled the diminishing power of religious periodicals in defining and enforcing literary standards within American culture.) In essence, Emerson's own steady and diverse stream of publications over the course of the 1840s, accompanied by widely circulated reviews and notices his work attracted in New York and Philadelphia, served to shift public attention away from the religious controversies that had originally surrounded his views in Northern religious periodicals, and focus it instead largely on the "literary" and "philosophical" sides of his achievements. This shift—quickly reinforced and sustained by the unexpected attention Emerson's writings gained in British periodicals—then made it increasingly acceptable to approach Emerson not as an errant Christian thinker, but rather as a preeminent American man-of-letters, a professional writer and lecturer who appealed to the highest artistic and intellectual aspirations of his countrymen, and whose efforts to spur Americans to attend to the distinctive concerns of their emerging national culture deserved both close attention and respect.

While this identification of Emerson as an exemplar of American culture was first publicly made by British writers in 1838 and 1839, during the early 1840s it also became a familiar way for New York and Philadelphia magazines and newspapers to assign him his historical place. The earliest instance came in a review of *Essays* that appeared in the April 1841 *New Yorker* (1836–41), a general weekly founded by Horace Greeley, where an anonymous writer proclaimed that "the opinion is fast becoming general and ripening into a conviction, that [Emerson] is one of the profoundest thinkers and loftiest spirits in the land." In looking back, this claim seems

---

33. [Elizabeth Palmer Peabody], "Nature—A Prose Poem," *United States Magazine and Democratic Review* 1 (February 1838): 319–21, rpt. in *Emerson's 'Nature'—Origin, Growth, and Meaning*, 90–97.

only slightly premature in its timing. Three years later, the Philadelphia-based *Graham's Magazine*, then the most widely circulated general literary periodical in America, would observe that Emerson's "claim to be considered one of the most original and individual thinkers that the country has produced is now beginning to be generally acknowledged." In 1846 the *Knickerbocker* magazine likewise would describe Emerson as perhaps "the most distinguished of contemporary American philosophical writers."[34]

Given my concerns here, however, it again is important not to allow the powerful hold that such familiar characterizations would come to have on many educated Americans after 1850 obscure the fact that, during the first half of the 1840s, Emerson was by no means an object of unqualified praise among those who were prepared to look past the theological controversy his early writings had produced. In fact, at its inception, Emerson's alternative identity as America's preeminent poet-philosopher also came subdivided between (1) flattering accounts of him as the most important and original mind of his generation (with Horace Greeley remaining the most vocal and influential representative of this approach), and (2) various more skeptical (and at times very disparaging) appraisals that measured Emerson's message in social and political terms and found it impractical or obscure. The cultural fault-line between those who proclaimed Emerson an inspirational genius and those who faulted him as an impractical dreamer, not surprisingly, also served as a rough indicator of attitudes regarding a second issue that figures centrally in any effort to reconstruct views of his cultural significance during the early 1840s: the question of how much effort Emerson's contemporaries thought ought to be given to reading works that admirers and critics alike agreed made extraordinary demands on their audience. In the early 1840s nothing was more apparent about Emerson to his reviewers than the difficulty of his prose. Not only were his texts seen as having departed from certain basic assumptions guiding Protestant literary culture; they did so in ways that made it difficult—even for largely uncritical admirers such as Greeley—to sum up neatly the alternative ideals he endorsed, as one might sum up this or that more conventional contribution to contemporary American literature or theology. Above all else, it was the difficulty of Emerson's literary style that became

---

34. Anon. review of *Essays*, *New Yorker* 11 (April 3, 1841): 45; anon. review of *Essays: Second Series*, *Graham's Magazine* 25 (December 1844): 293; J. F. Jackson, "American Scholarship," *Knickerbocker* 28 (July 1846): 4.

the chief target of his critics in the secular press, with complaints about the unintelligibility of his ideas usually justified by pointing to the obscurity of his language. "The prevailing defect" of Emerson's *Essays*, complained W. A. Jones in his review for *Arcturus* in April 1841, was a want of continuity: they "were not one and the same throughout, but made up of centoes, full of scattered, heterogeneous thoughts and fancies." In its review of "Method of Nature," the December 1841 *Knickerbocker* repeated this complaint by describing Emerson as "one who thinks much, often deeply, but who writes muddily," with ideas that were "covered with a grotesque garb of motley language." Others simply threw up their hands and announced that Emerson had not justified the demands he made on his readers. Edgar Allan Poe's well-known dismissal of his writing as "twaddle" in the January 1842 *Graham's Magazine* would be echoed and amplified a year later in *Brother Jonathan*, where Emerson was grouped with Carlyle as two among a new breed of nineteenth-century writers who "do not know there is any such language as English."[35]

Even among those who refused to see Emerson's language as an unmanageable challenge to ordinary intelligence there remained considerable uncertainty in defining the relationship between his sometimes startling literary style and the practical ideals that informed his new vision of American culture. In an otherwise admiring early review of *Nature*, the *Western Messenger* found it necessary to concede that, while some of its readers would welcome the book as "the effusion of a prophet-like mind," others would consider it "mere moonshine." Later, responding to the negative review of the *Essays* in *Arcturus* in the pages of the April 3, 1841, *New Yorker*, Greeley too conceded that there were many incapable of understanding his views—and, as we shall see, Greeley himself was often noticeably elusive in explaining exactly what he understood Emerson's message to be.[36]

Obviously, not all encounters with Emerson's language during the early

---

35. [W. A. Jones], "Ralph Waldo Emerson," *Arcturus* 1 (April 1841): 278–84; anon. review of "The Method of Nature," *Knickerbocker* 18 (December 1841): 559; E. A. Poe, "An Appendix on Autographs," *Graham's Magazine* 23 (January 1842): 44–49 (Poe here also described Emerson as one of the "mystics for mysticism's sake"); anon. review of Carlyle, *Past and Present*, *Brother Jonathan* (May 27, 1843): 109–10.

36. [Samuel Osgood], "Nature," *Western Messenger* 2 (January 1837): 385; anon. review of *Essays*, *New Yorker* 11 (April 3, 1841)—while the reviewer is unnamed, I see little cause to doubt Greeley was the author.

1840s turned out to be quite this negative or uncertain. Early admirers insisted that Emerson was a literary genius precisely because of the way in which his writing resisted easy paraphrasing and translation. In answering Bowen's charge that the account of the relationship between mind and matter in *Nature* was obscure and inconclusive, Peabody argued that Emerson's purpose had not been to give his own solution to that enigma, but to do what was next best: "he tells us the condition of solving it ourselves." Approached in these terms, the confusion and sense of mystery produced by reading Emerson could be accepted as deliberate by-products of the high demands he made on his audience. Greeley once observed that Emerson was often "eccentric in expression . . . sometimes to the point of perspicuity," yet then asked rhetorically, should "new thoughts be clothed in perfectly plain and trite expression?" It also did not seem to concern Emerson's admirers, for that matter, that other writers had given voice to visions and ideals like his, since their discoveries clearly had not seeped through in ways that rivaled Emerson's extraordinary prose or made it appear less novel.[37]

It bears emphasizing again, however, that even among Emerson's growing number of admirers in the early 1840s, there was as yet no consensus when it came to defining his significance for American culture at large. The discovery of the enthralling power of Emerson's writing became something of a stock episode in his reception history over the course of the 1840s, but it also supported disparate accounts of how the increasingly prominent position of his work ought to be understood. While admirers observed that Emerson's place in American culture had come to involve a great deal more than the scandal of "Transcendentalism," the positive images that his name and writings invoked remained heterogeneous. Some followed Brownson in casting Emerson in the role of the "seer," whose purpose was not so much to persuade his audience to abandon false belief, as to display the inadequacies of the view of American culture on which those beliefs were grounded. And here was another way Emerson's difficult and idiosyncratic vocabulary could be accounted for, since it could be said to form a necessary part of his effort to disclose aspects of human experience that more familiar ways of writing and talking inevitably distorted or denied. In this regard, Emerson's identity as an American sage also

---

37. Peabody, "Nature—A Prose Poem," 94; also see Milnes, "American Philosophy— Emerson's Works," 186–87.

stemmed from frequent comparisons to Carlyle—an approach that took hold, in part, because Andrews Norton's attack on the Divinity School Address had pointed to Carlyle as the "hyper-Germanized Englishman" who had been among the chief sources of Emerson's new and dangerous views. Yet it also stemmed, as we shall see later in this chapter, from Emerson's work as advocate, editor, financial supporter, and distributor of the several American editions of Carlyle's writings that were produced between 1836 and 1847.[38]

Others argued, however, that labeling Emerson a sage or (in Norton's less flattering term) "speculatist" was misleadingly one-dimensional in defining what had come to be the broad scope of his concerns. With the appearance, in the early 1840s, of Emerson's reviews and literary essays in the *Dial*, for example, a new image of him as a literary critic developed alongside that of the sage. Some observers who earlier had found his writings difficult and obscure now discovered and commended a figure they described as writing more immediately accessible prose and providing important insights for those attempting to make sense of what Emerson himself called the the "immense miscellany" of American literary culture. Despite its sometimes harsh criticism of his *Essays*, *Arcturus* provided several early notices of Emerson's writings in the *Dial*, one of which proclaimed that he had joined the ranks of "the best critics in the country." Similarly, Greeley's *New Yorker*, in the course of one of several favorable notices of the *Dial*, singled out Emerson's "Thoughts on Modern Literature" for special praise. By 1844 it was hardly surprising that the biographical sketch of Emerson in Rufus Griswold's anthology *Poets and Poetry in America* identified him as a writer who had "great merit" as a poet, but who was best known at the time for his "critical and philosophical writings." Finally, in this regard, there was again Greeley, who typically seemed content to provide excerpts from Emerson's writings, while briefly proclaiming Emerson a cultural phenomenon that needed no detailed explanation beyond his characterization as "one of the most gifted, original, and bounteous spirits of the age." It apparently did not matter greatly, so far as he was concerned, what Emerson himself saw his main concerns to be,

---

38. Norton, "New School in Literature and Religion," 32–33; Emerson's address was also said to offer a cheap imitation of "the vice of [Carlyle's] mannerism" in "Transcendentalism," *Biblical Repertory*, 95. See Slater's introduction to *Correspondence of Emerson and Carlyle*, 17–29, and sec. 5 of this chapter, for a more detailed account of Emerson's activity as "Carlyle's editor" in America.

since it was his primarily mythic qualities as America's first true literary genius that Greeley most wanted to play up.[39]

Three especially significant early appraisals of *Essays: Second Series*— two that appeared in New York, and the other in Philadelphia—exemplified and gave expression to the continuing uncertainty regarding Emerson's increasingly prominent cultural standing in the mid-1840s: Margaret Fuller's review on the front page of the December 7, 1844 *New York Daily Tribune*, and those of two unnamed writers that appeared at roughly the same time in *Graham's Magazine* and the *United States Magazine and Democratic Review*. Yet when closely examined these three reviews also help us to understand how the perceived difficulty and obscurity of Emerson's language ultimately came to be resolved in his favor. There is of course no reason why Emerson's contemporary reviewers should have agreed in defining exactly what demands he was making on his readers. But their disagreements, as we shall see, did not prevent them from marveling at the creative brilliance of his language or from affirming that his writings challenged readers in ways that required their utmost attention and respect.

Fuller's review began with a brief defense of Emerson against continuing attacks on his views in religious periodicals. She praised him as a writer who promised to arouse the "nobler energy" of the American public by providing the invaluable service of championing "the claims of individual culture in a nation which tends to lay such stress on artificial organization and external results." And for this, Fuller predicted, "History will inscribe his name as a father of the country, for he is one who pleads her cause against herself." Yet in trying to account for what she understood to be the actual reception of Emerson's writings to date, Fuller felt obliged to sketch a rather different story. She plainly knew something of the unexpected popularity his work was then enjoying in Britain, yet chose to contrast it to what she perceived as considerably more limited interest at home. "Copies of Mr. Emerson's first published little volume 'Nature,'" Fuller wrote, "have there been sold by thousands in short time, while one edition has needed seven years to get circulated here. Several of his Orations and Essays from 'The Dial' have also been republished there, and met with a reverent and earnest response." Fuller interpreted this contrast, in part, as evidence of two cultures at

---

39. Anon., "Criticism in America," *Arcturus* 3 (May 1842): 400–406; anon. review of the October 1840 *Dial, New-Yorker* 9 (October 1840): 78; Rufus Wilmont Griswold, *The Poets and Poetry of America* (Philadelphia, 1842), 237–38; anon., "Mr. Emerson's Cration [sic]," *New York Weekly Tribune*, October 30, 1841, 5, cols. 1–2.

sharply different stages of development. In the early 1840s it was clear that more Englishmen had the "leisure" to hear Emerson's voice, she observed, and as a result "a far larger number have set foot in the speculative region and have ears refined to appreciate these melodious accents." Americans, by contrast, were still in the first stages of "bringing out the material resources of the land," and so not generally prepared as yet for "the enjoyment of books that require attention and reflection."[40]

Fuller went on to make it clear, however, that the relative neglect of Emerson within American culture was not simply a matter of his countrymen temporarily ignoring the spiritual for the material. She conceded that several now familiar charges leveled against him—in her words, "obscurity," "excess of fancy in proportion to imagination, and an inclination, at times, to subtlety at the expense of strength"—had some color of truth in them. She also commented that, while the prose of Emerson's second collection of essays was noticeably more accessible than that of the first, he had yet to write "one good work, if such a work be one where the whole commands more attention than the parts." In no one essay in the second collection, Fuller continued, were Emerson's main concerns so obvious as to help readers focus attention on the broad outlines of his arguments. The result was that "single passages and sentences engage our attention too much in proportion," and the experience of reading the essays ultimately serves to "tire like a string of mosaics or a house built of medals."

Even so, Fuller went on to conclude that Emerson's claim on the attention of his contemporaries could be vindicated on two other counts. The first was his "sincerity"—by which she apparently meant to suggest that Emerson was a literary artist whose writings ought to be approached as works of art that offered genuine and uncompromising expression of his own inner life. The other was, for all its difficulty, Emerson's language—the animating force of "which, if sometimes obstructed and chilled by the critical intellect, is yet the prevalent and the main source of his powers."[41]

Although considerably more concise than Fuller's, the review of *Essays: Second Series* in the December 1844 *Graham's Magazine* was no less significant an attempt to define public understanding of Emerson, appearing as it did in what was then antebellum America's most widely circulated general

40. [Margaret Fuller], "Emerson's Essays," in *New-York Daily Tribune*, December 7, 1844, 1, cols. 1–3, and in *New-York Weekly Tribune*, December 14, 1844, 2, cols. 1–3, rpt. in *Critical Essays on Ralph Waldo Emerson*, 91–96.

41. Ibid., 95–96.

literary periodical. Its unnamed author began, as Fuller had done, by pondering the general cultural significance of a writer who sometimes "flies above our comprehension or apprehension." The Emerson who emerges from this appraisal, however, was hardly the neglected figure she had invoked, but instead a writer whose

> reputation has now passed from notoriety into fame. It was the fashion once to class him among the wildest class of those mystics whom much transcendentalism had made mad; but his claim to be considered one of the most original and most individual thinkers the country has produced, is now beginning to be generally acknowledged. The number of his readers is constantly increasing; and men seem willing to like him for what he is, instead of hating him for what he is not.

The claim that religion no longer remained an important ground on which to judge Emerson perhaps would have surprised Fuller, but *Graham's* admiring review shared at least one important premise in common with her appraisal: Emerson's reputation in America as yet had little to do with a popular understanding of "the truth or error of his genius." Those who liked him were mostly taken in by the "charm" of his writings, which in turn could be accounted for in terms of the various licenses Emerson was entitled to take in his capacity as a literary genius: "His wit, his fancy, his sharp insight, his terse expression, the extreme subtlety of his conception of beauty, the oddity of many of his illustrations, the quiet fearlessness of his defiance of conventionalism, and the individuality which pervades all, give an interest to his compositions, apart from the questionable notions of theology, or metaphysics, society or government, which they appear to convey."[42] Reading Emerson, in other words, was chiefly a matter of taking in an extraordinary linguistic show, without worrying about what it all added up to, or even whether it added up to anything at all.

A similar sense that Emerson ought to be approached as a difficult yet powerfully entertaining intelligence was also evident in the review of *Essays: Second Series* that appeared in the June 1845 *United States Magazine and Democratic Review.* Placing Emerson in a tradition of great philosophers and poets who understood the spirit of their times, a self-proclaimed "disciple" here observed that such understanding by definition meant that Emerson had transcended "the existing order of things," and thereby come

---

42. Anon. review of *Essays: Second Series, Graham's Magazine* 25 (December 1844): 293.

to overlook it "from a point of view above the level of his contemporaries, and attainable as a common standpoint, only to succeeding generations." He also hastened to add, however, that this did not mean Emerson's "large faith and intuitive reason" as yet had had no influence on his contemporaries. "Few persons could so command the rapt attention of a popular audience," the reviewer continued, "to thoughts so abstruse, expressed in language so delphic and poetic." Or put more simply, Emerson commanded the attention of his audience and invited their sympathy "by a power which they cannot analyze, by a spell that transcends their knowledge."[43]

Taken together, these three reviews of *Essays: Second Series* bear detailed examination not because they were particularly novel or perceptive. As we saw earlier in this chapter, the view that Emerson commanded attention less for what he wrote or said than for the extraordinary ways in which he wrote and spoke in fact had been a central theme in his reception beginning in the late 1830s. It also is worth noting again that these reviews disagreed among themselves regarding the question of how widely known Emerson's writing had become during the early 1840s. Even so, it seems reasonable to conclude that these prominent appraisals, taken as a group, contributed to the building of a mystique of originality that had come to surround Emerson's name and writings by 1845. Or, put another way, what we see here, and in the efforts of numerous other editors and reviewers in New York and Philadelphia during the mid-1840s, is the cloud of theological controversy that had hung over Emerson in the late 1830s not only lifting, but lifting in a way that allowed him to gain the authority of a uniquely gifted American spell-binder, whose writings were now said to be continuously engaging even while providing no easily accessible wisdom for readers to carry away.

6

Perhaps needless to say, the increasingly widespread discussion of Emerson's writings that took place in the newspapers and literary magazines of New York and Philadelphia during the 1840s did not preclude the possibility that contemporaries who followed it, yet never recorded their re-

---

43. "A Disciple," "Emerson's Essays," *United States Magazine and Democratic Review* 16 (June 1845): 589–602, rpt. in *Critical Essays on Ralph Waldo Emerson*, 96–116.

sponses, arrived at judgments altogether different from those we have explored thus far. Here it bears emphasizing that, as with the controversy surrounding Emerson in religious periodicals, the parallel discussions that took place in the secular press of New York and Philadelphia frequently included extensive excerpts from his writings. In her early effort to shift the main ground of judgment on Emerson's writing from theology to literature, Peabody's flattering appraisal in the *Democratic Review* included several long selections from *Nature* and "The American Scholar"—and shows as well that, in the late 1830s, knowledge of that writing was hardly limited to the elite circle of New England Unitarianism. (Roughly one-third of Peabody's review consisted of passages drawn directly from Emerson's texts.) During the 1840s several other literary periodicals in New York and Philadelphia would come to join the *Democratic Review* in affording Emerson's writings significant coverage. Initially, few would be quite so positive in their evaluations of Emerson's thinking as Peabody had been, or as generous in including excerpts from his writings. Yet here too it was common practice to give him at least some space to speak for himself, and it is not surprising that such space became more plentiful as editors and reviewers came to acknowledge that Emerson had gained a formidable reputation. Between 1840 and 1850, for example, the *Knickerbocker* magazine would publish six notices and five reviews, culminating in March 1850, with a flattering retrospective appraisal of his literary career during the previous decade. In a long review that generously excerpted from both sets of *Essays* and the recently published *Nature: Addresses and Lectures,* Emerson was presented as a national prophet whose "'dreams' . . . may be becoming realities through the mind of the nation." Similarly in Philadelphia, during this time *Graham's Magazine* would run ten notices and three reviews, the last of which praised *Representative Men* as "one of the most fascinating books ever written." It also is worth noting that Rufus Griswold, literary editor at *Graham's* in 1842 and 1843, would be the first figure to make selections of Emerson's writings available in anthologies: first in *Poets and Poetry of America* (1842), and then in *Prose Writers of America* (1847), each of which was published in several editions by the Philadelphia publisher Carey and Hunt and sold in the thousands.[44]

---

44. Anon. review of *Essays: Second Series* and *Nature: Addresses and Lectures*, *Knickerbocker* 35 (March 1850): 255; anon. review of *Representative Men*, *Graham's Magazine* 35

Greeley's early efforts on Emerson's behalf also merit a brief comment here. It is well known that reviews and notices of Emerson's writings, as well as notices about his activities as a lecturer, were regular features of Greeley's newspapers. Yet it seems likely too that before 1845 at least, it was Greeley who served as the single most important source of popular knowledge of Emerson's name and ideas. We know that at a time when popular demand for the sorts of reviews and books in which Emerson's writings could be found remained very small, Greeley saw one of his duties as a "newspaperman" to include the promotion of a new generation of American writers. And the Emerson of the early 1840s clearly was one of the chief beneficiaries of Greeley's labors as the nation's cultural watchdog. Greeley-edited publications, beginning with the *New Yorker* and continuing with the daily and weekly editions of the *Tribune*, provided a steady stream of reviews and notices that in effect served to nationalize Emerson's reputation well before any of his publications had gained any significant commercial success—and in the case of his contributions to the *Dial*, despite the fact the magazine failed to gain an adequate list of subscribers. Or, put in his own language, Greeley made his notices of Emerson's early publications and lectures part of "the information daily required by all those who aim to keep 'posted' on every important occurrence." And while Greeley was of course in no position to dictate any sort of national consensus regarding Emerson, he did gain and hold institutional power that he used to provide what at that time was arguably a more important service: the continuing publicity needed to make and keep Emerson's name and writings visible in American culture at large.[45]

But it will not do to leave the matter here, with the suggestion that over

---

(March 1850): 221; Griswold, *Poets and Poetry of America*, 237–38, and *Prose Writers of America* (Philadelphia, 1847), 440–446. During the 1840s in New York, *Arcturus* and its successor *The Literary World* (arguably two of America's first "high"-cultural journals) also combined to publish five reviews and almost three dozen notices. The author of the important anonymous review in the *Knickerbocker* of 1850 was Charles Loring Brace (1826–90); see Thomas Bender, *Toward an Urban Vision: Ideas and Institutions in Nineteenth Century America* (Baltimore, 1975), 138.

45. Horace Greeley, *Recollections of a Busy Life* (New York, 1868), 142. Emerson's ties to Horace Greeley have never received extended study. But see Joel Myerson, *The New England Transcendentalists and the 'Dial': A History of the Magazine and Its Contributors* (Rutherford, N.J., 1980), chs. 2–4; and Ann Douglas, *The Feminization of American Culture* (New York, 1977), 331–38. I discuss Greeley, and his equally important ties to Thoreau, in greater detail in ch. 9.

the course of the 1840s Emerson's writings made him a central figure in antebellum culture primarily because they borrowed strength from the attention they received from new literary institutions in New York and Philadelphia. Certainly Emerson did owe much of his early success to his arriving at precisely the moment when one mode of literary and intellectual discourse was yielding in authority and importance to another—when a once presupposed interdependence of literature, philosophy, and theology that informed the judgments initially passed on his writings by leading Northern religious periodicals was being displaced by a new belief, voiced with steadily growing influence by the editors, publishers, and reviewers in New York and Philadelphia, that literature and philosophy represented distinct ways of knowing that no longer required the legitimation of theology. It cannot be said, however, that the cultural phenomenon that was "Emerson" during the 1840s was thus simply the invention of the new literary culture of New York and Philadelphia. Cultural phenomena tend to have biographical explanations, as well as institutional ones, and in the case of Emerson no elaborate act of historical investigation is needed to see that a second and perhaps equally important reason why interest in him became national in scope by 1850 was that by then he had come to write on an extraordinarily wide range of topics, and had seen his work reviewed, excerpted, and republished in a diverse array of literary settings. Many of Emerson's early admirers, to be sure, felt that defending his name and writings was in general tantamount to defending the right of "literature" to have an autonomous identity within American culture. But that is not the same thing as saying that there was a single set of terms and judgments used in approaching the writings Emerson produced during the 1840s. Rather, the breadth of his literary output was such that it served to place and keep him at the center of a network of different and sometimes competing cultural representations.

We can get a clearer sense of the diverse sides of Emerson's cultural identity by taking a somewhat closer look at the publications that appear to gain him the greatest popular attention during the 1840s. Here there can be little question that any informed contemporary observer looking back on Emerson's career between 1836 and 1850 would have recognized that he initially secured a prominent position in antebellum literary culture, in large part, as the result of the acclaim his poetry received. Munroe's first edition of his *Poems*, published in October 1846, quickly became the most widely reviewed and celebrated of his early books. The 1,500 copies in the initial printing sold out early in 1847, and was followed that year by three additional printings.[46] Yet Emerson's reputation during the 1840s was hardly restricted to his poetry. At the time his *Poems* first appeared, he had already become an important and visible figure in the American antislavery movement. As we saw in chapter 4, his speech at the 1844 Concord jubilee of the British emancipation in fact had served to make him something of a hero to that movement, with the address gaining immediate notice and praise from William Lloyd Garrison in *The Liberator* and Nathaniel Rogers in the *Herald of Freedom*, and pamphlet editions of the speech appearing in both Britain and America. One abolitionist would later recall that Wendell Phillips kept copies of this pamphlet on hand for distribution at the time of his speeches, suggesting that Emerson probably let Phillips and the Massachusetts Anti-Slavery Society have the text of his address. Len Gougeon also has showed that such respect was sustained and increased by Emerson's continuing and well-publicized identification with the cause of abolition in the second half of the 1840s. It seems fair to add here, however, that for Emerson's audience in the antislavery movement, neither the complexity of the views he put forward, nor his own equivocations regarding strategies for abolishing American slavery, ever appear to have been a cause of great concern or interest. It apparently was enough to be able to say that "Emerson" had in some manner taken the side of abolition.[47]

A second way in which to monitor the increasing diversity of Emerson's reputation during this period is to consider the complex variety of settings within which the question of his reputation could be explored. Some of Emerson's earliest critics complained, as we have seen, that his writings would be of little or no use to a society preoccupied with trade and money-

---

46. The *Dial* published the majority of Emerson's early poems. Apart from Griswold's selections in *Poets and Poetry of America*, however, the chief source of early popular knowledge of his poetry undoubtedly was the "gift book." During the 1840s Emerson contributed poems to *The Gift*, *The Diadem*, and *The Token*, each a very successful series of annual publications. For a more detailed account, see the references to Emerson in Ralph Thompson, *American Literary Annuals and Gift Books, 1825–1865* (New York, 1936), *passim*.

47. The line between Emerson's identity as a poet and his increasingly prominent role in the antislavery movement was not always clear-cut. In 1850 he would contribute five poems to the antislavery annual, *The Liberty Bell*. See Len Gougeon, *Virtue's Hero: Emerson, Antislavery, and Reform* (Athens, Ga., 1990), 144–45. Abolitionists themselves frequently wrote poems to express their outrage against slavery. See, for example, John Pierpont, *Antislavery Poems* (Boston, 1843), and William Lloyd Garrison, *Sonnets and Other Poems* (Boston, 1843), both briefly reviewed by Emerson in the *Dial* 4 (July 1843): 134.

making. (Emerson's books, observed the reviewer of *Essays* in the May 8, 1841 *Boston Daily Times*, were either neglected or dismissed as unintelligible by "the real bone and muscle of the community," which in turn left him with an interested audience made up only of "young men with fine coats, and young women with fine curls.") In looking back, however, it is clear that both Emerson's publications and the continuing disagreements they came to provoke did have economic value to several classes of people attempting to make their livelihood in the new American literary marketplace. Here it is worth noting again the controversy and acclaim that Emerson provoked in Britain during the 1840s did not escape the notice of the editors of the *Eclectic Magazine* and *Littell's Living Age*, two antebellum periodicals that offered selections and full reprinting of articles drawn from contemporary British literary periodicals. During the late 1840s and early 1850s most of the important British reviews of Emerson's writings were excerpted or reprinted in one or the other of these popular magazines.[48]

In this regard, it also is worth stressing that there is no evidence suggesting that Emerson's contemporaries found it odd that, while he spoke of purposes that appeared to transcend the marketplace, he was at the same time producing for a new literary marketplace made up of individuals who were paying to read what he had to say. In fact, while it is a mistake to think of Emerson as a writer-for-hire during the stages of his career we are examining in this chapter, he did spend a remarkable amount of his time in the late 1830s and early 1840s in helping produce and publicize American edi-

---

48. Anon. review of *Essays, Boston Daily Times*, May 8, 1841. [William Henry Smith], "Emerson," *Eclectic Magazine* 13 (February 1848): 145–58, rpt. from December 1847 *Blackwood's Edinburgh Magazine*; anon., "The Emerson Mania," *Eclectic Magazine* 23 (December 1849): 546, rpt. from September 1849 *English Review*; anon. review of *Representative Men, Eclectic Magazine* 20 (May 1850): 143, which noted that nearly all the leading British journals had noticed the book and reprinted passages from reviews in January 19, 1850 *Athenaeum* and ca. April 1850 *Britannia*; [James A. Froude], review of *Representative Men, Eclectic Magazine* 26 (July 1852): 360–68, rpt. from May 1852 *Eclectic Review*; anon. "Ralph Waldo Emerson," *Littell's Living Age* 1 (May 1844): 41, rpt. from January 1844 *Foreign Quarterly*; anon., "Essays: Second Series," *Littell's Living Age* (January 18, 1845): 139, rpt. from November 24, 1844 *Spectator*; anon. review *Essays: Second Series, Littell's Living Age* (January 25, 1845): 244, rpt. from November 30, 1844 *Examiner*; George Gilfillan, "Ralph Waldo Emerson; or The 'Coming Man,'" *Littell's Living Age* 4 (April 15, 1848): 97–103, rpt. from January 1848 *Tait's Edinburgh Magazine*; anon., "The Emerson Mania," *Littell's Living Age* 23 (November 24, 1849): 344–50, rpt. from September 1849 *English Review*; anon., "Representative Men," *Littell's Living Age* 25 (April 6, 1850): 37–38, rpt. from January 12, 1850 *Spectator*; anon. review of *Representative Men, Littell's Living Age* 26 (July 6, 1850): 1–16, rpt. from May 1850 *British Quarterly Review*.

tions of Thomas Carlyle's writings, and this activity—in addition to allowing him to become fully acquainted with the many practical difficulties involved in Anglo-American literary commerce[49]—served to link him very closely and visibly with the cause of a writer who was entirely dependent upon the sales of his writings for his livelihood.

The Emerson–Carlyle connection during the late 1830s and 1840s had a rich variety of private and public dimensions that have yet to be fully understood. Given my concerns here, however, we need look briefly at only three of them. The first is simply the skill and generosity Emerson displayed in helping build Carlyle's reputation in America. While the bulk of Carlyle's most acclaimed books—*Sartor Resartus* (1833), *The French Revolution* (1837), *Chartism* (1839), *Heroes and Hero Worship* (1841), and *Past and Present* (1843)—were written during the time of his closest involvement with Emerson, he was hardly a prominent figure when Emerson first took up the work of arranging for American editions of his work. In borrowing to pay the production costs of those editions, then, Emerson put himself in the position of risking a sizable portion of his personal wealth on Carlyle's behalf. The remarkable success of his undertakings—"You yourself opened this American silvermine to me," Carlyle would later write in gratitude—of course meant that Emerson eventually recovered his investments, but royalties (nearly $3,000 over an eleven-year period) went entirely to Carlyle, thereby saving him from the poverty and emotional breakdown that loomed when Emerson first took up his cause as a professional writer.[50]

---

49. The Emerson–Carlyle *Correspondence* in the late 1830s and 1840s shows that both figures recognized that writing for a "transatlantic" literary marketplace for books involved considerable economic burdens for authors as well as publishers. Apart from the high cost of publishing books and the threat of literary piracy, these risks included expensive and unreliable mail service, customs charges that added to the cost of distributing books, and differences in exchange rates that made the sale of English editions of Carlyle's works in America prohibitively expensive. Carlyle commented in a letter of June 24, 1839, that the "notable finance-expedient, of printing in the one country what is to be sold in the other" had helped lower the cost of distributing his writings in America, but it had not taken "vandalic custom houses into view." See *Correspondence*, 238.

50. *Correspondence of Emerson and Carlyle*, 235. Carlyle's letters to Emerson in the late 1830s show he was both angry and extremely depressed with the reception his work had been accorded in Britain. The commercial side of their friendship began with Emerson's arranging for James Munroe and Company to print an American edition of *Sartor Resartus* in April 1836. The book sold quite well—a total of 1,166 by mid-September—but no arrangements had been made to pay royalties to Carlyle. Carlyle received generous royalties from all subsequent editions of his work that Emerson helped produce, and welcomed payment with delight and gratitude that was openly expressed in his letters to Emerson. "There never came

Two aspects of the public side of Emerson's mastery of his role as "Carlyle's editor," however, are more directly relevant to my discussion here. The steady stream of Emerson's editions of Carlyle's publications (beginning with *Sartor Resartus* in 1836, and continuing on to a second collection of *Critical and Miscellaneous Essays* in 1847) served not only to make a formidable reputation for Carlyle in America, but also, as we have seen already, to define Emerson's standing as well. "Carlyle's editor" was at the same time "the American Carlyle," with comparisons made between them commonplace, and reinforcing the views of those who praised him as the Concord Sage as well as those who dismissed him as a dangerous and unintelligible dreamer. Yet this side of the Emerson–Carlyle connection had a second dimension that has been largely overlooked by scholars concerned with explaining early Emerson's standing in antebellum literary culture. The commercial success of Carlyle's writings in America inevitably put the process of literary pirating in motion. While Emerson made various efforts to circumvent the pirates, he met with only mixed results. In October 1843, for example, just as his edition of *Past and Present* had appeared, he reported angrily to Carlyle that a pirated story-paper edition of the book had also been issued in New York for 12 1/2¢, adding that "of this wretched copy several thousand were sold, whilst our 75 cent edition went off slower." Yet when viewed from another angle, Emerson's labors in attempting to counter the pirating of Carlyle's work at the same time served to give him a highly visible role in drawing public attention to current economic practices in the international literary marketplace. Two examples of this labor, among several, can serve to illustrate the point.[51] The first was the brief preface he wrote to the American editor of *Past and Present*, published by Little and Brown in Boston in 1843. Entitled "American Editor's Notice," and signed "R. W. Emerson, Concord, Mass., May 1, 1843," the preface announced: "This book is printed from a private copy in manuscript, sent by the author to his friends in this country, and is pub-

---

money into my hands I was so proud of," he wrote on February 8, 1839, after a letter from Emerson arrived in Chelsea with a bill of exchange for 100 pounds and the news that Little and Brown's edition of *The French Revolution* had been sold out before the first year. See *Correspondence*, 211.

51. Both can be found in *Correspondence of Emerson and Carlyle*, 346, n. 2, 378, n. 2. Emerson's services to Carlyle are also noteworthy in warning against simply conflating the verdict of Emerson's reviewers with the verdict of the literary marketplace. Emerson's place in his own time, in other words, cannot be established simply by way of a close reading of contemporary reviews, even though this of course remains essential to the task.

lished for his benefit. I hope this notice that the profits of the sale of this edition are secured to Mr. Carlyle will persuade every well disposed publisher to respect his property in his own book." Two years later, in a letter printed as the "Advertisement" to Carlyle's *Critical and Miscellaneous Essays* published by Carey and Hart in Philadelphia in 1845, Emerson drew attention to the fact Carlyle had negotiated generous terms for his royalty payment:

Messrs. Carey & Hart,

Gentlemen:—I have to signify to his American readers, Mr Carlyle's concurrence in this new edition of his Essays, and his expressed satisfaction in the author's share of pecuniary benefit which your justice and liberality have secured to him in anticipation of the sale. With every hope for the success of your enterprise,

I am your obedient servant,
R.W. Emerson
Concord, June, 1845

For anyone interested in assessing the historical truth of the claim that, at the outset of his career, the figure of himself Emerson tried to create was that of a literary artist "moved by purposes much more elevated than profit," there can hardly be more clear-cut evidence suggesting that his economic motives should be defined in more complex, and perhaps altogether different, terms. Clearly, part of the plight of the writer as Emerson knew it, both by way of his work as Carlyle's editor and his own extensive experience with British literary pirates, was that in the international marketplace publications of a successful author were in fact there for the taking—not his private property to be traded freely for personal profit, but rather objects in the public domain that could be (and were) reprinted by publishers overseas without punishment or legal recourse. Seen against that background, however, the passages above also suggest that Emerson had little reason to doubt that his contemporaries would pay to read an author who was quite explicit about his right to be paid. Indeed, the premise of his pleas on behalf of authorized editions of Carlyle's work appears to be that insisting openly on that right might encourage sales of only those publications that showed "respect" for an author's "property in his own book."[52]

---

52. Carlyle reciprocated, to some degree, with comparatively more limited efforts to arrange for publication of Emerson's work in Britain. He also thereby joined Emerson in fighting the pirating of Emerson's writing. See esp. Carlyle's preface to Chapman's 1844 edi-

Finally, it is not surprising that, with the increasing prominence of Emerson's name and writing in American culture at large, over the course of the 1840s he came to be subject to a diminishing number of attempts to dismiss his views simply by condemning the difficulty of his language and the supposed nebulousness of his ideas. His critics of course did not simply grow silent. During the late 1840s religious periodicals in Britain in particular continued to roll out the complaint that Emerson's views were subversive of mainstream Christian belief, and Americans were kept aware of this side of Emerson by way of reprintings in *The Eclectic Magazine* and *Littel's Living Age*. But by 1850 this familiar criticism was sounded more infrequently in American religious periodicals, and in some important cases comes across more as a pro forma lament than an outright condemnation. In the face of Emerson's increasingly secure reputation as America's preeminent man-of-letters, the formerly ambivalent protests of *The Christian Examiner* in particular were now neatly resolved in favor of Emerson. Cyrus Bartol's review of *Representative Men*, for example, commented that Emerson's unconventional religious views still prevented orthodox Christians from considering him a great teacher, but then went on to say that there was nonetheless "a height of manhood in him and his works which requires us to mingle reverence and affection even with the exception of our blame."[53] It was an awkward, but nonetheless accurate, summary of a view that many Americans living in Northern states doubtless had already taken in attempting to reconcile their Christian beliefs with the inescapable recognition that, by 1850, Emerson had earned himself a very high place in American culture.

7

The story of Emerson's early literary career traced in this chapter differs in several important respects from that usually told by modern interpreters. First of all, the "literary marketplace" as Emerson experienced was considerably more heterogeneous and non-hierarchical than is typically suggested.[54]

---

tion of *Essays: Second Series*, v–vi, in which he equated the work of British literary pirates with "theft" and assured the English public that Chapman's edition was authorized by Emerson, who in turn would receive pecuniary benefit from its sales.

53. C[yrus] A. B[artol], "Representative Men," *Christian Examiner* 48 (March 1850): 314.

54. As Jane Tompkins has shown in Nathaniel Hawthorne's case, the building of a literary reputation is, in part, a political matter that involves an author's personal connections.

The now familiar contrast in which Emerson is cast as a "market-oriented" writer contemplating an audience that is unknown, anonymous, and distinct is too extreme (if not entirely anachronistic) to take in all the details displayed in a full history of the publication and initial reception of his "classic" prose writings. Against the familiar narrative of delayed national recognition, I have set another that in fact bears close resemblance to one first sketched by Theodore Parker in a contemporary assessment of Emerson mentioned briefly at the outset of this chapter. As it appeared in the March 1850 *Massachusetts Quarterly Review*, Parker's assessment ran as follows:

> Mr. Emerson has won by his writings a more desirable reputation, than any other man of letters in America has yet attained. It is not the reputation which brings him money or academic honors, or membership of learned societies; nor does it appear conspicuously in literary Journals as yet. But he has a high place among thinking men, on both sides of the water; we think no man who writes the English tongue has now so much influence in forming the opinions and character of young men and women. His audience steadily increases, at home and abroad, more rapidly in England than America.[55]

This verdict is not precisely the one I've tried to support, but it comes close. The audience for Emerson's writings, as we have seen, did steadily increase both at home and abroad over the course of the 1840s, although the story told in this chapter suggests that it grew at least as rapidly in America as it did in England—and this thanks, in large part, to the widespread attention his writings did receive from "literary journals" as well as religious periodicals and newspapers. Yet Parker's broad opening claim seems accurate enough, if by "desirable reputation" he meant to draw attention to two other relatively straightforward points. First, despite the fact that sales of Emerson's writings had yet to bring him substantial economical and institutional rewards, there was scarcely any major aspect of American or British literary culture in which, by 1850, his name and ideas had

---

But the evidence in Emerson's case does not support the view that the high standing his writings had attained by 1850 can be explained simply as the result of a national literary establishment selecting "classics" that flattered their own values, interests, and claims to special discernment. The fact is there was no such establishment before 1850, and it was just beginning to form when the Civil War began. See Jane Tompkins, *Sensational Designs: The Cultural Work of American Fiction, 1790–1860* (New York, 1985), ch. 1.

55. Parker, "The Writings of Ralph Waldo Emerson," *Massachusetts Quarterly Review* 3 (March 1850): 205.

not been introduced and discussed.[56] And second, one simply could not say the same of any other American writer, either of Emerson's own generation or before.

Parker would go on, however, to speak of Emerson's "desirable reputation" in a third sense that the story told in this chapter calls into question. The primary purpose of Parker's subsequent account of Emerson's career up to 1850 was, in fact, to hold up Emerson as an irenic figure who embodied values and beliefs characteristic of antebellum American culture. To do that, however, Parker apparently found it necessary to suppress any mention of American slavery and of Emerson's then already well-established role in the abolitionist movement. Any figure elevated as quickly and as high as Emerson was between 1836 and 1850 undoubtedly represents something of a looking glass through which his culture ought to be viewed. Yet perhaps the most important point that emerges from the story of the reception of Emerson's writings as I have told it here is that, whatever their author's original intentions may have been, they never found a single audience of readers, but instead spanned various groups that split along religious, literary, political, and regional lines. In some of these settings, Emerson was decried as an atheist and a menacing fool, in others celebrated as a uniquely gifted writer and a democratic visionary. Beyond Parker's general identification of Emerson as a figure who had attained "a high place among thinking men," then, there was no widely shared agreement on how to categorize Emerson.[57] If not all things to all people, he was many things to many people living in a society undergoing both a profound transformation of its cultural and economic institutions and an increasingly bitter division over its political future.

---

56. It may also be the case that as Emerson realized he had become a cultural figure in his own right, he felt more compelled to address publicly the central political and cultural issues of his day—which may help explain his increasingly visible role in the abolitionist movement over the course of the 1850s, as well as the timing of his speaking out in defense of John Brown.

57. It is worth noting here that at the time Parker's fifty-five-page article appeared in the *Massachusetts Quarterly Review* he was a considerably more dedicated abolitionist than Emerson ever became. And if Parker had any criticism to offer in 1850, however, it would have been that Emerson was not involved enough in the antislavery movement. While the absence of such criticism remains puzzling, it also is worth noting that Parker did follow the practice of other contemporary reviewers in providing generous excerpts. Indeed, almost half of his article consisted of long selections taken from Emerson's extant publications—thereby providing readers with what amounted to perhaps the first small anthology of his work.

Finally, these conclusions are also significant in pointing to some unexplored questions concerning the more dramatic impact Emerson's writings would make on American audiences after 1850. We still know remarkably little about the processes by which Emerson's work came to be canonized. There can be no question that, by 1850, Emerson had become one of the best-known writers of his generation, and that his reputation was Anglo-American in scope. But this is not the same thing as saying he was the dominant or representative American cultural figure of the time—no one writer of his generation ever gained such titles. Perhaps more interestingly, it also is not the same thing as saying that his high cultural standing was dependent upon any one text or set of texts. There were, to be sure, some voices that proclaimed *Nature* and "The American Scholar" to be masterworks that would stand the test of time, but these were as yet few in number. Most of Emerson's contemporaries either avoided or were simply indifferent to the question of exactly which of his writings had served to establish and sustain his authority within American culture. Or, put somewhat differently, the story of Emerson's contemporary reception as I have told it suggests that the writings he published before 1850 exercised more authority over some people than others, and that authority was sustained in his readers by a considerable number of distinct concerns. What caused the complexity of Emerson's historical identity to diminish as his cultural authority increased remains a question in need of more careful study. To carry the story begun in this chapter beyond 1850, one of course would have to define and explore the terrain of a culture more clearly divided into "high" and "low" spheres. But one also would have to account for a narrowing in the very broad range of interests and qualities that had made Emerson's writings important to his first audience of readers.

9

"Peculiarly Suited to All Classes": The Publication and Reception of *Walden*, 1854–1862

THIS FINAL CHAPTER attempts to revive a Thoreau we no longer know, a historical figure largely lost from sight in our continuing contest to show how many demands his writings make on late twentieth-century readers. As with the chapter that preceded it, then, I start again some distance from current discussions, this time approaching Thoreau by way of a largely forgotten preface to a two-volume edition of *Walden* that was published in 1909 by the Bibliophile Society of Boston. Its author was Henry Hardy, then president of the society, who began by observing that Thoreau "needs no introduction to the literary world," and then explained why in the following terms: "Thoreau's writings are peculiarly suited to all classes," he wrote. "They are alike instructive and entertaining: to the poorer classes because he proves conclusively what comfort, and even happiness, may be enjoyed with the minimum of effort and expense; and to the opulent they satisfy an important desideratum in the form of the most wholesome entertainment."[1]

---

1. *Walden*, 2 vols. (Boston, 1909), 1:ix. This elegant and expensive book was the editorial handiwork of Franklin Sanborn, who selectively rearranged what is known as the Bixby manuscripts to make what he saw as a "complete edition." These manuscripts were parts of

I

Given what bibliographers tell us about the publication of Thoreau's writings during the fifteen years prior to 1909, Hardy seems at once both incomplete and perceptive in his appraisal. He did not go on to provide anything resembling an adequate account of the ways in which those writings had come to gain their "peculiar" appeal. Hardy simply ignored the question of why "the poorer classes" might have found it important (or reassuring) to hear Thoreau repeating the familiar call to make the best of misfortune. He also chose not to explain to the affluent membership of the Bibliophile Society—apart from offering a cryptic warning that Thoreau had "many peculiar and quixotic ideas"—how the "wholesome entertainment" Walden provided ought to be squared with its often scathing critique of the materialism of American life.[2] In another sense, however, Hardy was quite right simply in suggesting that Thoreau's writings had gained widespread appeal among his contemporaries. While the Bibliophile Society's edition of Walden was a collector's item assembled exclusively for the membership of an elite literary organization, it appeared at a time when Thoreau's works were in fact being packaged for every level of the American literary marketplace. Beginning in 1894 his books and essays would become a staple for middle-class home libraries in a new format Houghton Mifflin Company perfected to identify and bring to market America's standard authors: the Riverside Edition of the Complete Works. (Emerson's had appeared in 1883.) Two years later, when Walden first came into the public domain, that book also became available in numerous cheap cloth

---

the seven revisions that Thoreau made of Walden before publication, and Sanborn's edition contains some 12,000 words not in the volume Thoreau himself published in 1854. While the Bibliophile Society edition is dismissed as "preposterous" in the Historical Introduction to Walden, ed. J. Lyndon Shanley (Princeton, 1971), 372, its several striking engravings and photographs make this book something of a prototype for many subsequent illustrated (and comparably expensive) editions of Thoreau's writings. It also is interesting to speculate what Sanborn thought of Hardy's cheerful preface. Sanborn, himself once a controversial figure in the American abolitionist movement, doubtless knew that Walden had enjoyed high prestige among some opponents of American slavery, for whom the book conveyed a rather different lesson. In a review published in the December 16, 1854 National Anti-Slavery, for example, Lydia Maria Child observed that Walden taught "more impressively than any number of sermons could, that this Western activity of which we are so proud, these material improvements, this commercial enterprise, this rapid accumulation of wealth . . . are vastly overrated" (3).

2. Ibid., x.

and paperback editions, thereby spreading Thoreau even more widely throughout American culture.[3]

Although incomplete in some respects, then, Hardy's pronouncements regarding Thoreau's broad popular appeal are accurate enough. More important for my purposes here, they also stand as persuasive testimony to a view of his career that modern commentators have not taken seriously. To be sure, like Emerson, Thoreau has enjoyed a prominent role in most modern versions of the story of American culture. Yet where Emerson has often been cast in various central roles, Thoreau typically is made to play his recalcitrant and estranged child, and in turn is presented as a writer whose concerns and complaints we only recently have begun to take with the seriousness they deserve. ("The full significance of *Walden* has never been felt until today," Henry Canby proclaimed in 1939, only thirty years after Hardy observed that the book needed no introduction to American audiences.) The received account of Thoreau's career asserts with monotonous regularity that he cannot be included in the ranks of immediately successful American writers, and the supposed commercial failure of his publications is regularly held up as a sure sign of the exceptional complexity and depth of his writings. Moreover, modern biographers and literary historians frequently go on to assert that the practical upshot of Thoreau's publishing failures was to strengthen his native resolve not to pander to public tastes, which—it usually goes without saying—were then being corrupted by the magazines, newspapers, and novels that provided the shallow reading fare of most ordinary Americans in his day.[4] (A somewhat less dramatic addendum to this familiar story might note that Thoreau, like Emer-

---

3. In 1906 Houghton Mifflin also published the "Manuscript" and "Walden" editions of Thoreau's writings, each of which included all but small portions of his journals. Between 1896 and 1909 some sixteen different editions of *Walden* were printed by various British and American publishers. *Walden* was published in "The World's Classics" of Oxford University Press in 1906 (reprinted in 1910 and 1924), and in "Everyman's Library"—a joint undertaking of J. M. Dent in London and E. P. Dutton in New York—in 1908. See Raymond R. Borst, *Henry David Thoreau: A Descriptive Bibliography* (Pittsburgh, 1982), 25–29, for a more detailed inventory.

4. Canby, as quoted in Frank Luther Mott, *Golden Multitudes: The Story of Bestsellers in the United States* (New York, 1947), 154. Among many other more recent works that present Thoreau as a writer who never gained a proper (or popular) audience in his own time, see Ann Douglas, *Feminization of American Culture* (New York, 1977), 7; Michael T. Gilmore, *American Romanticism and the Marketplace* (Chicago, 1985), ch. 2; Lawrence Buell, *New England Literary Culture: From Revolution Through Renaissance* (Cambridge, 1986), 63; Denis Donoghue, *Reading America: Essays in American Literature* (New York, 1987), 43; and

son, initially also made it difficult for his contemporaries to assess the merits of his writings, because he too made popular access to his work difficult by choosing James Munroe and Company to launch his first book—*A Week on the Concord and Merrimack Rivers* [1849]—into American culture.)

This account of the initial publication and reception of Thoreau's writings seems inadequate on several counts. To begin with, it has underplayed or simply ignored Thoreau's modest yet clear success in establishing his name as a magazine writer. While he published comparatively few reviews and essays during his lifetime, most of them would appear in the prominent literary periodicals of his day, beginning in 1843 with two pieces in the *United States Magazine and Democratic Review*, and ending in 1862 with Thoreau, now terminally ill with tuberculosis, completing four articles (including "Walking" and "Life Without Principle") that the *Atlantic Monthly* would publish during the year following his death on May 6. In between, the appearance of at least four other articles—"Thomas Carlyle and His Works" in *Graham's Magazine* in 1847; "Ktaadn and the Maine Woods" in *The Union Magazine* in 1848; "Excursion to Canada" in *Putnam's Monthly Magazine* in 1853; and "Cape Cod" again in *Putnam's* in 1855—identify Thoreau as a writer who made his mark in the new world of antebellum literary journalism.[5]

Partly as a result of the slighting of Thoreau's accomplishments as a "magazinist," it also is only recently that we have begun to appreciate the extent to which popular reading preferences deeply informed both the themes and strategies of his writing. As Robert Sattelmeyer has pointed out, the bulk of what Thoreau wrote for publication during his lifetime was in fact either travel narrative or a closely related form of essay called the "excursion," all of which appeared at a time when the genre of travel literature enjoyed enormous appeal. It was also precisely against this background that James Russell Lowell—in his appraisal of *A Week* in the December 1849 *Massachusetts Quarterly Review*—presented the first care-

---

Stephen Railton, *Authorship and Audience: Literary Performance in the American Renaissance* (Princeton, 1991), 72–73. The most influential statement of the view that *Walden* only recently has met with "real comprehension" may be J. Lyndon Shanley's Historical Introduction in *Walden* (Princeton, 1971), 368–77.

5. It is worth noting here that in the process Thoreau also chose to test his skills in a cultural setting Emerson generally avoided. Apart from his contributions to the short-lived *Dial*, a magazine he of course helped found and edit, Emerson showed little interest in popularizing his writings by way of magazines before he began to publish poems and essays in the *Atlantic* in 1857—even though after 1845 he doubtless could have done so quite easily.

ful interpretation of Thoreau's cultural significance, in a review that can still be read as a perceptive introduction to his thinking. At a time when the net effect of travel literature, in Lowell's view, was that "more and more of the world gets disenchanted," Thoreau was "clearly the man we want" because the story of his travels was the work of a poet "who bears the charm of freshness in his eyes" and thereby conjures back "as much as may be of the old enchantment." The modern traveler who was typically a captive of modern science, and thus always approached nature as "a reluctant witness upon the stand" to be badgered "with geologist hammers and phials of acid," Thoreau had succeeded in restoring the "inheritance of the wonderful" by disentangling nature from "the various snarls of man."[6]

The received account of Thoreau's career has also assumed, again as in Emerson's case, that sales figures for the first editions of books can be taken as an incontrovertible measure of their popularity and cultural status. Here, too, we have failed to come to terms with the fact that substantial numbers of Thoreau's contemporaries had opportunities to consider his ideas and writings in settings other than the actual first editions of *A Week* and *Walden*. Thanks to the exertions of Horace Greeley, Thoreau's name and writings first became known in America in the early 1840s, several years before he published any of the books or articles for which he later became famous. And by the time of his death in 1862, there can be little question that the pages of Greeley's widely circulated *New York Tribune* had allowed tens of thousands of literate Americans of various backgrounds and interests to become acquainted with his name and work. Yet Greeley was by no means the only source of public information about Thoreau's activities and writings. In fact, as with Emerson, it appears that there was scarcely any aspect of antebellum American literary culture in which Thoreau's name and writings were not, at various times during the 1840s and 1850s, introduced and discussed. The reception of Thoreau's

6. Robert Sattelmeyer, *Thoreau's Reading: A Study in Intellectual History with Bibliographical Catalogue* (Princeton,1988), 47–49, 66. [James Russell Lowell], review of *A Week on the Concord and Merrimack Rivers*, in *Massachusetts Quarterly Review* (December 1849): 45, 43, 41, rpt. in *Thoreau Society Bulletin*, no. 35 (April 1951): 1–4. It is not clear how much this review, which included several long excerpts from *A Week*, did to promote public knowledge of Thoreau's first book. Walter Harding,, *The Days of Henry Thoreau: A Biography* (New York, 1962), 250, describes it as a "curiously mixed review," but quotes very selectively from Lowell's review. It is worth noting here, however, that the high praise Lowell had for *A Week* in the first several pages of his review—it was "the work of some bream Homer"—in effect retracted his earlier and much better-known portrait of Thoreau as only a poor shadow of

writings into American culture during his lifetime was not simply a matter of concern to those few among his contemporaries who could afford to buy the expensive first editions of his books. It also involved a substantial number of Americans across the country who found discussions of and excerpts from his writings in literary reviews, magazines, newspapers, and religious periodicals, as well as in gift books and literary anthologies.

A fully detailed survey of the various settings in which Thoreau's writings first became known to antebellum audiences, however, would extend well beyond the boundaries of a single chapter.[7] So here I again will be selective and attempt to provide mostly a careful survey of the ways in which Walden—whose publication in 1854 unmistakably prompted the most dramatic advance in public knowledge of his name and writings—first made contact with antebellum American culture. I shall largely ignore the history of the book's posthumous reputation, partly because most of the details of that story can be found elsewhere, partly because an extended account of exactly what Thoreau's own contemporaries had to say about Walden is missing from the vast scholarly literature on this book.[8] A close inspection of the earliest responses to Walden reveals that it was neither overlooked nor set aside as a too complex for the tastes of ordinary readers. I hope to show, in fact, that while it cannot be said that Thoreau's book came to form an integral part of popular literary culture in his day, it was for a variety of reasons important to that culture.

Finally, a full understanding of the reception of Walden requires a close look at Thoreau's own expectations and intentions in publishing the book, and at the ways in which these might help us make better sense of its initial reception. It is well known that Thoreau worked five years longer on Walden than he had originally intended. Expecting success with his first

Emerson in A Fable for Critics (New York, 1848), 32. (When Lowell later became the first editor of the Atlantic Monthly, he also quickly approached Thoreau to be a contributor.)

7. Scholars are still uncovering evidence that throws light on the question of how Thoreau's writings were received in antebellum magazines and newspapers. Although missing several important items, Raymond R. Borst, Henry David Thoreau: A Reference Guide, 1835–99 (Boston, 1987), 1–33, provides the most up-to-date general inventory.

8. There is a growing literature on the subject of Thoreau's posthumous reputation. John C. Broderick, "American Reviews of Thoreau's Posthumous Books, 1863–66: Check List and Analysis," Texas Studies in English 34 (1955): 125–39, remains a useful starting place. Also see Michael Meyer, Several More Lives to Live (Westport, 1977); and Lawrence Buell, "The Thoreauvian Pilgrimages: The Structure of an American Cult," American Literature 61 (May 1989): 175–99, and "Henry Thoreau Enters the American Canon," in New Essays on Walden, ed. Robert F. Sayre (New York, 1992), 23–52.

book, he apparently had planned to publish the second as early as 1849— in fact, an announcement that *Walden* would be published shortly was included in the first edition of *A Week*. Legend has it, however, that when it became clear that *A Week* was not selling, Thoreau's publisher refused to issue *Walden*, and as a result he would spend five additional years revising and refining it. By common consent, extensive revisions and additions served to make *Walden* a vastly better and more complex book. Yet Michael Gilmore has argued recently that the record of Thoreau's publishing difficulties also points to two deep ironies about the shape of his literary career before 1854. The first is that, if we choose to speak of *Walden* as a classic or masterpiece, it appears that the book achieved that status partly because of the workings of the literary marketplace in which it first reached print. *Walden's* "transcendence of history" as a work of literature, in other words, seems "rooted in the conditions of its production—its belated production—as a commodity to be marketed by publishers." Gilmore also goes on to underline the apparent added irony that, when viewed in this context, *Walden* unwittingly becomes "its own most effective reply to Thoreau's denigrations of commercial enterprise," since far from impairing the quality of the book, commercial considerations appear to have conspired to make it a much better one.[9]

The thought that the commercial failure of *A Week* served to make *Walden* a great book is dramatically appealing, but the full prehistory of *Walden* turns out to be complex in ways that this view apparently must choose not to recognize. Whether the first draft of Thoreau's second book was designed to be "inaccessible to the great majority of the public" remains open to question. (The opinion of many of its first reviewers, as we shall see, appears to be that it was not; and the complexity of the tale Thoreau told in *Walden* did not prevent the first edition of the book from becoming a modest commercial success.) It is a mistake to say, however, that Thoreau's publishers refused to print *Walden* when they saw that *A Week* was destined to be a commercial failure. At the time Thoreau's first book appeared, *Walden* was in fact already under contract with Ticknor and Fields, who also had agreed to publish at its own expense without even seeing a completed manuscript. In this regard, Thoreau's correspondence suggests that he later came to understand that one of the primary reasons for the unexpected commercial debacle of *A Week* was his own decision to

---

9. Gilmore, *American Romanticism and the Marketplace*, 49–51.

publish the book without the institutional backing of a strong publishing house.[10] By contrast, the power and prestige of Ticknor and Fields helped create new and considerably more favorable terms for the reception of his second book. A full history of the publication and reception of *Walden*, in fact, suggests that there was nothing ironic about the way in which the workings of the antebellum literary marketplace served to confer status on Thoreau. *Walden* was launched into American culture, as we shall see, by a publisher who specialized in identifying and promoting writers of high literary ambitions and skill.

2

The first edition of *Walden; or, Life in the Woods* was published by Ticknor and Fields in Boston on August 9, 1854. There were two thousand copies in octavo format in its first printing, each bound in dark chocolate cloth covers and priced at $1.00. The title and the publisher's name were goldstamped on the book's spine; both the front and back covers were blindstamped with a triple-rule border, and had small floral designs at each corner and a large ornamental design at the center. The title page of the first edition of *Walden* identified Thoreau as the author of "A Week on the Concord and Merrimack Rivers," and most copies included an eight-page Ticknor and Fields catalogue inserted at the back. In its overall physical appearance and design, *Walden* was entirely representative of the impressive productions that had served to identify Ticknor and Fields both as a publishing house committed to the publication of fine American literature and a model of good book-making. And if contemporary booksellers

---

10. Ticknor and Fields first accepted *Walden* in a letter written to Thoreau on February 8, 1849. See *The Cost Books of Ticknor and Fields and Their Predecessors, 1832–58*, ed. and intro. Warren S. Tryon and William Charvat (New York, 1949), 289. The publication of *Walden* prompted something of a revival of interest in *A Week*, with Thoreau receiving several letters asking where copies of his first book could be found. Replying to one inquiry about *A Week*, Thoreau would confide that his first book "had so poor a publisher that it is quite uncertain whether you will find it in any shop. I am not sure but authors must turn booksellers themselves"—which was precisely the position Thoreau was forced to assume after 1853, when Munroe returned seven hundred unsold copies of the book to him. In the summer of 1862 Ticknor and Fields reissued *A Week*, reprinting and possibly giving a new binding and title page to the copies that remained in Thoreau's possession at the time of his death. *The Correspondence of Henry David Thoreau*, ed. Walter Harding and Carl Bode (New York, 1958), 406.

shelved Thoreau's second book alongside other volumes that its prosperous and widely respected publisher had produced in the late 1840s and early 1850s, *Walden* undoubtedly would have stood on the shelves of the belles lettres department, alongside such already acclaimed works as Holmes's *Poems* (1848), Longfellow's *Evangeline* (1847) and *Poems* (1850), and Hawthorne's *The Scarlet Letter* (1850), *House of the Seven Gables* (1851), and *Blithedale Romance* (1852).[11]

There also seems to be little question that Ticknor and Fields expected *Walden* quickly to become a new addition to its growing list of commercial and critical successes. While Thoreau's publisher continued the common practice of publishing at the author's expense in the case of relatively unknown writers, Thoreau's publishing contract for *Walden* not only had the publisher bearing the full cost of production; it promised to pay him 15 percent royalties, 5 percent above its usual rate.[12] For reasons that remain unclear, however, Ticknor and Fields came to view *Walden* as something of a commercial disappointment—even though it doubtless knew that sales had far exceeded those of Thoreau's first book. There was an impressive initial flurry of orders: 566 copies of the book had been ordered by the end of the first week of publication, but then buying proceeded more slowly. At the end of the first year of publication, Ticknor and Fields would inform Thoreau in a note attached to a modest royalty check that some 256 copies of the first printing still remained unsold, and added: "We regret for your sake as well as ours that a larger number of Walden has not been sold." The first edition of *Walden* in fact did not sell out until 1859, and then remained out of print until March 1862, when Ticknor and Fields issued a small second printing of 280 copies. Between 1863 and 1890 *Walden* continued to be reprinted from plates made for the first edition, with perhaps some 7,300 additional copies being published during that period by Ticknor and Fields and then James R. Osgood, who had purchased all of Fields' stock and authors in 1871. When Osgood retired in 1880, his interest, including the sole printing rights on *Walden* and Thoreau's other writings, was bought by the new publishing house of Houghton, Mifflin and Company. And before coming into the public domain in

---

11. Raymond R. Borst, *Henry David Thoreau: A Descriptive Bibliography* (Pittsburgh, 1982), 17–18; see W. S. Tryon, *Parnassus Corner: A Life of James T. Fields* (Boston, 1963), 178–204, for a more detailed account of the publishing practices of Ticknor and Fields.

12. Even so, it is worth noting that the first edition of *Walden* cost Ticknor and Fields 43¢ a copy to produce. With the book priced at $1.00, this of course meant that, even with

1896, *Walden* would be published in 1,250 more copies from new plates produced for its now well-known "Riverside Edition."[13]

These modest sales figures surely tell us something about the cultural status of *Walden* during the second half of the nineteenth century, but the evidence here is not as unequivocal in its testimony as it might first appear. Whatever expectations Ticknor and Fields may have had regarding actual sales, it seems clear that the first edition of *Walden*, as with all of its other titles, was hardly a book produced for mass distribution. For example, while some copies of the book were sent directly to bookstores, the vast majority of initial sales appear to have come by way of individual orders mailed directly to the publisher. The records of Ticknor and Fields also show that first printings of its first editions rarely exceeded two thousand copies; and while *Walden*—unlike *Evangeline* or *The Scarlet Letter*—was no immediate sell-out, its production costs were almost fully covered by the 402 orders the firm had already received by August 9, the official day of publication. Perhaps more significant still, we know that, even with its modest sales figures, *Walden* turned out to be an immediate critical success, in large part because Ticknor and Fields had moved so decisively to draw attention to the book. During the weeks prior to its publication, several advance copies of *Walden* had been put in the hands of such well-placed Boston literary figures as John Sullivan Dwight, T. W. Higginson, and T. Starr King, each of whom returned very favorable notices of the book. (Dwight's appraisal was probably the most important of these, appearing as it did, on August 12, 1854, in *Dwight's Journal of Music*, then beginning to establish its reputation as one of the leading proponents of "high" culture in America.[14]) Yet it was not just the attention of Boston's cultural elite that Thoreau's

---

a 15 percent royalty rate and allowing for discounts to booksellers, the largest portion of the profit in sales of *Walden* went to Thoreau's publisher. See *Cost Books of Ticknor and Fields*, 289. There is no evidence suggesting this arrangement may have troubled Thoreau.

13. Borst, *Henry David Thoreau: A Descriptive Bibliography*, 19–21, 26. Because Borst does not list separately the number of copies produced after 1880 in the seventeenth through twenty-first printings of *Walden*, my figures are only a rough estimate based on Shanley's comment that an average of 460 copies a year were printed in 1881–88. (See Historical Introduction, in *Walden*, 371.) It also is worth noting here that editions of *Walden* first began to appear in Britain in 1884, when Houghton, Osgood sent sheets of its twenty-first printing to be bound in Scotland by David Douglass. On the reception and influence of Thoreau in late nineteenth-century Britain, see George Hendrick, "Henry S. Salt, the Late Victorian Socialists, and Thoreau," *New England Quarterly* 50 (September 1977), 409–22.

14. On Dwight, see Lawrence W. Levine, *Highbrow/Lowbrow: The Emergence of Cultural Hierarchy in America* (Cambridge, 1988), 119–22. During 1850 Dwight, Higginson, and

publisher initially sought out. Three weeks prior to the official publication date of *Walden*, Ticknor and Fields had also distributed advance sheets to the editors of several newspapers in Boston and New York. During late July and the first weeks of August, prepublication announcements appeared in the *Boston Transcript*, William Cullen Bryant's *New York Evening Post*, the *Boston Commonwealth*, the *Boston Daily Evening Traveller*, Greeley's *New York Tribune*, the *Norfolk Democrat*, the *Bunker-Hill Aurora and Boston Mirror*, and the *Boston Daily Bee*. Most of these notices also included selections taken from the advance sheets Ticknor and Fields had distributed, with the lengthiest excerpts appearing in the New York newspapers. Selections from "The Pond in Winter," "Former Inhabitants; and "Winter Visitors," and "Conclusion," totalling about 2,500 words, appeared on the front page of the July 24, 1854 *New York Evening Post*. Five days later Greeley was even more generous, filling five columns of the *New York Daily Tribune* with almost six thousand words taken from "Economy," "Sounds," and "Former Inhabitants; and Winter Visitors," and then reprinted this article in both the August 1 *New York Semi-Weekly Tribune* and the August 5 *New York Weekly Tribune*.

During the weeks that followed the official date of its publication, praise for *Walden* continued to spread, becoming national in its scope by the end of September. Thoreau's book would be positively noticed or reviewed by several prominent Northern literary magazines, including *Graham's*, the *North American Review*, *Godey's Magazine and Lady's Book*, *Peterson's*, and the *Knickerbocker*. *Walden* never came to receive the same widespread and intense scrutiny Emerson's writings had gained from Northern religious periodicals, but the book was neither overlooked nor dismissed out of hand. Certainly the longest, and arguably the most rigorous, contemporary review of the book appeared on September 2, 1854, in *The Churchman*, a weekly magazine published by the Protestant Episcopal Church in New York. Shorter notices of *Walden* also appeared in the *National Magazine*, the *Watchman and Reflector*, the *Puritan Recorder*, the *Christian Register*, and *The Christian Inquirer*. Other early admirers of *Walden* included Gamaliel Bailey, who reviewed it in his *National Era*, and

---

King had been members of the "Town and Country Club," forerunner of the later and more famous "select company of gentlemen," the Saturday Club, out of which grew the idea for the *Atlantic Monthly*. Thoreau was invited to join the Town and Country Club, attended its first meeting, but never showed up again; he later declined to take part in the Saturday Club. See Harding, *Days of Henry Thoreau*, 284; *Correspondence*, 235–40.

Lydia Maria Child, who reviewed both *A Week* and *Walden* for the American Antislavery Society's *National Antislavery Standard*.[15]

Finally, it is important to note that, even in its early stages, interest in *Walden* was not confined exclusively to the major population centers of the Northeastern states. Over the course of the two months following its publication, notices and reviews of the book appeared in the *Rochester Daily American*, the *Daily Ohio State Journal*, the *Cincinnati Daily Gazette*, the *Louisville Daily Courier*, the *Western Literary Messenger*, the *New Orleans Daily Picayune*, the *Richmond Enquirer*, and the *Southern Literary Messenger*. Knowledge of *Walden* even spread as far afield as California, when the September 25, 1854 *Daily Alta Californian* (then San Francisco's most important newspaper) included a description of the book's contents among its notices of new books, and two weeks later provided additional information about it by way of a second notice that appeared in Elizabeth Stoddard's column, "From Our Lady Correspondent."[16]

All this is an abbreviated account of where the first reviews and notices of *Walden* appeared, but there surely is enough here to discount the still familiar claim that *Walden* came into American culture generally unrecognized and unappreciated. In fact, what recent bibliographers have uncovered about the public response to Thoreau's book between the time of its publication and his death in May 1862 seems to invite a simple reversal of that claim. Bradley Dean's and Gary Scharnhost's valuable inventory of the reviews, excerpts, and notices of *Walden* that appeared during Tho-

---

15. Given Thoreau's comment, near the opening of *Walden*, that the primacy assigned to American slavery bordered on being "frivolous," it may seem surprising that committed abolitionists such as Bailey and Child took any interest in Thoreau's book. Yet each chose to ignore his early comment, and assimilated the author of *Walden* to their cause by presenting him as what modern historians speak of as a "sectional ideologist." In Bailey's case, Thoreau was presented as an exponent of "Yankee versatility"; in Child's, he was a New England moralist reminding local readers not to overrate the significance of their material improvements and rapid accumulation of wealth. [Gamaliel Bailey], review of *Walden*, *Natural Era* (September 28, 1854): 155; [Lydia Maria Child], review of *A Week on the Concord and Merrimack Rivers* and *Walden*, in *National Anti-Slavery Standard* (December 16, 1854): 3; both rpt. in *The Recognition of Henry David Thoreau*, ed. Wendell Glick (Ann Arbor, 1969), 8–12.

16. For a more detailed listing of early reviews, see Bradley P. Dean and Gary Scharnhorst, "The Contemporary Reception of *Walden*," in *Studies in American Renaissance*, ed. Joel Myerson (Charlottesville, 1990), 296–328. Stoddard had been signed in 1854 to send from New York City a series of bimonthly cultural newsletters that ran under the title "From Our Lady Correspondent." For a more detailed account, see James H. Matlack, "Early Reviews of *Walden* by the *Alta California* and Its 'Lady Correspondent,'" *Thoreau Society Bulletin* 128 (Spring 1975): 1–2.

reau's lifetime lists ninety-three items, some sixty-six of which had appeared by late November 1857, including among these forty-six that can be read as strongly favorable.[17] Several of the earliest reviewers in fact were so effusive with their praise that Ticknor and Fields selected blurbs it then ran in a second series of early newspaper advertisements in late August 1854. Emerson's private assessment of the initial reception of Thoreau's book—"All American kind are delighted with 'Walden' as far as they have dared to say. . . . We account Henry the undoubted King of all American lions."—at first glance hardly seems like an exaggeration.[18]

All this clearly represents widespread cultural recognition of some kind. Yet, as with the modest initial sales figures for *Walden*, the evidence bearing on America's "delight" and Thoreau's "lionization" is not as unequivocal as it might first appear. It is one thing to know that citations from, and notices and reviews of, Thoreau's book were plentiful, quite another to assign them more specific historical meaning, and there are several other aspects of the contemporary reception of *Walden* whose significance remains problematic. The most conspicuous may be that, while praise for Thoreau's book was effusive and widespread, detailed discussions of its contents were remarkably scarce. What little there was in the way of rigorous interpretation, as we shall see, came from a handful of reviewers who were sometimes sharply critical of the book. The common practice among the others was to provide reviews or notices that summarized the three opening chapters of *Walden*, and then offer excerpts taken largely from those chapters and the "Conclusion." The bulk of the prepublication notice of *Walden* that appeared in the *New York Daily Tribune*, for example, consisted of a partial reprinting of the Ticknor and Fields advance sheets, prefaced by a brief introduction that described *Walden* as a volume that promised to be "one of curious interest." It would seem fair to say, then, that one of the primary concerns of the bulk of the first reviews of *Walden* was simply to do the bidding of Ticknor and Fields in calling attention to one of its latest publications. There was room here for praise and criticism of *Walden*, but evaluations typically were very brief, and clearly

17. *Ibid.*, 293–95.
18. *The Letters of Ralph Waldo Emerson*, ed. Ralph Rusk (New York, 1989) 6 vols., 4: 459–60. For other enthusiastic private assessments, see letters to Thoreau from Daniel Ricketson and T. W. Higginson, *Correspondence of Henry David Thoreau*, 333, 336; and Harding, *Days of Henry Thoreau*, 338–41.

not intent—even in those few cases where reviews condemned the book—on creating deep controversy. As a result, despite the widespread notice *Walden* received during the late summer and fall of 1854, the first edition never provoked impassioned debates of the sort that had surrounded Emerson's early publications.

Dean and Scharnhorst have concluded that the overall effect of the contemporary reception of *Walden* was, in fact, merely to cement Thoreau's already established reputation as a "quaint" and "eccentric" American writer—labels that by their count appeared in thirty-four of sixty-six reviews. Closer inspection of many of those same reviews, however, shows that such labels were included in appraisals of *Walden* that also said there was "nothing in literature, that we know of, quite like this book" and that Thoreau's book was "a strikingly original, singular, and most interesting work" that would "attract as much attention as if it were a new book by Hawthorne or Emerson." While it is true that many of its first reviewers observed that *Walden* was the product of an "eccentric" sensibility, they also went on to say or suggest that its appearance undoubtedly had marked Thoreau's ascent into the ranks of acclaimed American writers. The *New York Evening Post's* early prediction that *Walden* would "take its place as one of the most unique and original accessions that have been made to American literature" was repeated in several subsequent reviews and notices. And even the small number of writers who condemned *Walden* as the work of a naysayer and misanthrope were prepared to concede, as the September 22, 1854 *New York Times* put it in the most abusive of the early appraisals, that Thoreau was "undoubtedly a man of genius" whose style would please "the literary man."[19]

Dean and Scharnhorst's conclusion is questionable on other grounds, since they fail to address the equally important question of what we should make of the abundance of excerpts from *Walden* in newspapers and mag-

---

19. "New Publications," *Salem Register*, August 10, 1854; *Boston Transcript*, July 21, 1854, 1; *New York Evening Post*, July 24, 1854, 1; "Notices of New Publications," *New York Times*, September 22, 1854, 3, col. 4. Among other laudatory reviews and notices acclaiming the originality and importance of *Walden*, see *Boston Daily Bee*, August 9, 1854, 2, col. 6; "Walden; or Life in the Woods," *Lowell Journal and Courier*, August 10, 1854, 2, col. 3; W., "New Publications," *Albany Argus*, August 15, 1854, 2, col. 7; "Recent Publications," *Cummings Evening Bulletin* [Philadelphia], August 19, 1854, 2, col. 2; *Philadelphia Sunday Dispatch*, August 20, 1854; "Book Notices," *Rochester Daily American*, September 16, 1854, 2, col. 5; and *Southern Literary Messenger* 20 (September 1854): 575.

azines. The story of the initial reception of Thoreau's book cannot be limited strictly to what its admirers and critics had to say about the book, for again as in the case of Emerson's publications, reviews and notices alike routinely allowed Thoreau to speak for himself and invited readers to assign their own meaning to *Walden*. The notice of *Walden* that appeared in the *Richmond Enquirer*, for example, consisted largely of thirteen different excerpts taken from "Economy," "Where I Live and What I Lived For," "Reading," and the "Conclusion"—all prefaced by an invitation for its readers to form their own judgments about Thoreau. The practice of generously citing from *Walden* was in fact so commonplace during the weeks immediately following its publication that one apparently knowledgeable reviewer, writing in the August 16, 1854 *Worcester Palladium*, found it worth stressing that even though many newspapers had already made much of the American public familiar with parts of *Walden*, "the whole of it is well worth being acquainted with," and named a local bookstore in which the volume was for sale.[20]

Yet what historical importance do we then assign to the fact that, while *Walden* immediately established itself as a literary work of exceptional significance and excerpts from the book were widely available, rigorous interpretations of its contents remained scarce? Do we say that most of *Walden*'s first reviewers (as well as the tens of thousands of other readers who knew nothing of the book apart from the excerpts provided by those reviewers) missed or overlooked the full force of the challenge that Thoreau had directed at them? Did the many newspapers and magazines that initially provided abridged access to *Walden* at the same time somehow impoverish popular understanding of its significance? There were some reviews, and not all of them harsh in their assessments, which seemed to confirm the *Boston Atlas*'s forecast that "Mr. Thoreau's volume will fall into the hands of few who can fully appreciate him or assimilate to him." The habit of reducing *Walden* to a book whose single overarching concern is said to be a sustained private encounter with the natural world dates back to the year of the book's publication: every chapter of Thoreau's book was "redolent of pine and hemlock," John Sullivan Dwight observed, thus perhaps inau-

---

20. "Literary," *Richmond Enquirer*, August 29, 1854, 2, col. 4; *Worcester Palladium*, August 16, 1854, 1, col. 4. Of the seventy-nine reviews and notices of *Walden* that appeared by the end of 1854, twenty-five included excerpts published as separate parts of the text, most drawn from its three opening chapters and its conclusion. See Scharnhorst and Dean, "Contemporary Reception of *Walden*," 296–321.

gurating the tradition of reading Thoreau's extensive cultural criticism out of *Walden*.[21]

And yet while *Walden* was by no means immune to drastic foreshortening and inadequate abridgement, a remarkable number of reviewers also did comment that Thoreau had written a book that addressed so many subjects they found it difficult to catalogue it in familiar terms. "There is nothing in literature, that we know of, exactly like this book," observed the August 10, 1854 *Salem Register* (in another of the early reviews that used the label "eccentric" in describing Thoreau). The August 19, 1854 *Saturday Evening Gazette* similarly described *Walden* as a book that had "thrown together . . . philosophy, politics, economy, mathematics, mechanics, with a dash of romance." (Exactly where the "romance" in *Walden* lies, however, is never explained.) Another notice described Thoreau's book as a collection of essays that he had composed while living at Walden Pond.[22] And finally, even reviewers chiefly concerned with the religious implications of *Walden* differed in their accounts of what they thought Thoreau was trying to say. Where *The Churchman* faulted him as an author who "frequently throws doubt over and suggests a spirit of disaffection to the sacred Scriptures," T. Starr King's appraisal in the *Christian Register* by contrast cast him approvingly as a sort of Old Testament moralist preaching to a people excessively concerned with material acquisition and comfort.[23]

What do these various broad characterizations of *Walden* add up to? It may be true that, at the time of its publication, Thoreau's book presented different faces to different readers. But that observation does not clear things up very much, since characterizations of the book in the end were not limitless in their numbers. What does seem clear, however, is that, even while degrees of specificity varied, most first reviewers recognized that *Walden* was a tale with a double plot—one about America's current cultural and economic practices, and the other about its author's encounter with the natural world. The *Boston Atlas*, for example, described

---

21. *Boston Atlas*, October 21, 1854, 1; [John Sullivan Dwight], "Editorial Correspondence," *Dwight's Journal of Music* 5 (August 12, 1854): 149–50. It remains hard to smell the "pine and hemlock" in the first three chapters of *Walden*.

22. "New Publications," *Salem Register*, August 10, 1854, 2, col. 3; *Saturday Evening Gazette* [Boston], August, 19, 1854, 2, col. 6; "Notices of Books," *Commercial Advertiser* [New York], August 29, 1854, 2, col. 4.

23. "Literature," *The Churchman* [New York], September 2, 1854, 4, cols. 1–4; [T. Starr King], "New Publications," *Christian Register* [Boston], August 26, 1854, 135, cols. 5–6.

Walden as a book in which Thoreau offered readers "a series of observations upon the pursuits of mankind, mingled with descriptions of natural objects. . . . His thinking is the indulging of those inexpressible mental sensations which visit all poetic natures in the midst of woodland solitudes. The rest, except the descriptive portion, is devoted to moralizing upon the emptiness of human aims and employments." And yet because many reviewers also recognized that Thoreau had made the two plots of *Walden* run parallel in a particularly complex way, it is hardly a surprise to find them also suggesting or stating plainly that a full understanding of *Walden* made demands on intellect and patience they had not taken or as yet had time to meet. After acclaiming Thoreau's "individuality of opinion, sentiment, and expression," and providing seven substantial excerpts from *Walden*, the reviewer for *Graham's Magazine* conceded that he had not done justice to the "attractiveness of this curious and original volume," and cautioned potential readers that considerable effort would be required to benefit from "the real wealth of individual thinking" that lay beneath the "somewhat presumptuous manner" in which Thoreau "dogmatizes." Similarly, the *Richmond Enquirer*—which described *Walden* as "a series of very able essays on architecture, philanthropy, reading, sounds, solitude, etc." held together in "graceful union" by Thoreau's story of his life while at Walden Pond—deferred summary judgment to its readers, giving over the bulk of its notice to excerpts it had selected from Thoreau's book. The *Worcester Palladium* was perhaps the most explicit of all in saying that *Walden* had at once distinguished itself from other literary "artificialities" of its day, and therefore was "a book to be read, and re-read, and read again, until another is written like it."[24]

Looking closely at the contemporary reception of *Walden*, I find no cause to dismiss the claim that praise for *Walden*, at some level, represented appropriate recognition of Thoreau's great and varied powers as a writer. The vividness of his writing about nature clearly recommended itself to many of *Walden's* readers. So too did his humor, for that matter, which several reviewers seem to have taken as a sign that Thoreau was a loyal critic of the society of his day. The opening pages of *Walden* "may seem a little caustic and cynical," T. Starr King observed in the *Christian*

24. *Boston Atlas*, October 21, 1854, 1, rpt. in *Critical Essays on Thoreau's 'Walden'*, 32–36; *Graham's Magazine* 45 (September 1854): 298–300; "Literary," *Richmond Enquirer*, August 29, 1854, 2, col. 4; *Worcester Palladium*, August 16, 1854, 3, rpt. in *Critical Essays*, 20–21.

Register, "but it mellows apace, and playful humor and sparkling thought appear on almost every page." The *Knickerbocker* grouped *Walden* with P. T. Barnum's recent autobiography in a review that cast the books as leading examples of what it called "Town and Rural Humbugs." The *Richmond Enquirer* likewise praised *Walden* as a book "written in a strain of bold but honest raillery." Finally, it also is worth noting here that several reviews approached *Walden* as a book in which Thoreau had delivered on the literary promise he had earlier shown in *A Week*—thereby suggesting that, despite the commercial failure of his first book, Thoreau's second book did not so much create as encounter an interested audience.[25]

Even so, we should be careful not to overlook the fact that the velocity and extent of the national hearing *Walden* gained during the months immediately following its publication were primarily a reflection of the power and standing of its publisher. Ticknor and Fields was not the largest publisher in America in the monetary sense, yet it had no rival as the self-proclaimed publisher-patron of "fine literature" written by native American authors, nor was it surpassed in the skill it displayed in promoting its books. In the case of *Walden*, the power of Ticknor and Fields was evident in at least two important aspects of the book's initial reception. The first was simply the remarkable geographical reach of its influence. It would be difficult to explain why, less than two months after its publication, *Walden* would have received reviews and notices in newspapers as far afield as Cincinnati, Richmond, New Orleans, and San Francisco, had Ticknor and Fields not, in the 1840s, begun the practice of advertising beyond local markets, and thereafter made nationwide advertising in newspapers into a central part of book production. (We have no figures on what was spent on marketing *Walden*, but if we include distribution copies and advance sheets, the sum surely was substantial. It also is possible that some of the contemporary notices were written by James T. Fields.) Conspicuous too was the frequency with which reviews mentioned that Thoreau's book was a new publication of Ticknor and Fields. One reviewer praised the elegant appearance of *Walden* as representative of the high "typographical taste

---

25. [T. Starr King], "New Publications," *Christian Register* (August 26, 1854): 135, cols. 5–6; "Town and Rural Humbugs," *Knickerbocker* 45 (March 1855): 235–41; "Literary," *Richmond Enquirer*, August 29, 1854, 2, col. 4. Mention of *A Week* was made in twelve contemporary notices and reviews of *Walden*. See, e.g., "Thoreau's Life in the Woods," *New York Evening Post*, July 24, 1854, 1, and "New Books," *Daily Ohio State Journal*, August 19, 1854, 3, col. 2.

and style" of its publisher. Another commended "the convenience of the light octavo form" that Ticknor and Fields had generally adopted for its publications. Given Thoreau's publisher's unrivaled skill in the practical arts of book promotion, it may seem curious at first glance that none of the several reviews that identified Ticknor and Fields as the publisher of *Walden* went on to say that special effort should be made to purchase the book. Seen from another angle, however, it seems fair to say that here we find an implicit recognition that the advertising campaigns Ticknor and Fields launched on behalf of its writers were not designed to sell its costly books to a mass reading audience, so much as to make national the fame of the writers it chose to sponsor. The niche within the antebellum literary marketplace conquered and controlled by Ticknor and Fields in the 1850s was one where success was defined more in terms of status than of sales. And mere mention of the name of *Walden*'s publisher, it appears, sufficed to locate the book immediately in this niche.[26]

3

Two final items among the first notices and reviews of *Walden* deserve additional comment here. To say that the power and prestige of Ticknor and Fields served to guarantee the general acclaim *Walden* initially received is not the same thing as saying it dictated all the details of contemporary evaluations the book elicited. *Walden* had its share of harsh and inadequate reviews. Within two months of its publication, there appeared two lengthy appraisals of Thoreau's book—the first an anonymous review of roughly six thousand words in the September 2, 1854 *Churchman*, the other one of roughly 4,700 words by Charles Frederick Briggs in the October 1854 *Putnam's Monthly Magazine*—which, because they stand out as the most extended efforts to come to terms with *Walden* in the year of its publication, bear close examination in any effort to put together a coherent account of the various bits and pieces of this story.

The Churchman's review made its way into *Walden* exactly as Ticknor and Fields would have hoped: by identifying Thoreau as a figure "known

---

26. Tryon, *Parnassus Corner*, 226–28. (As early as April 1849, Nathaniel Willis described Ticknor and Fields as the "announcing room" of "great" American literature.) "New Books," *Louisville Daily Courier*, October 4, 1854, 2, col. 2; "Recent Publications," *Newark Daily Advertiser*, August 21, 1854, 2, col. 2.

among literary circles by his association with the good company of EMER-SON and HAWTHORNE, and by his production of a book a few years since, 'A Week on the Concord and Merrimack Rivers.'" The book itself was then described as the work of both a "lover of nature" and a "humorist."[27] For *The Churchman*, however, Thoreau was hardly a comic writer, but rather a humorist in the archaic sense: an eccentric figure who had written the story of an odd and whimsical experiment in living, and a Diogenes-like thinker as well, who looked upon the characteristic cultural and economic activities of his contemporaries as "so many impediments to the free growth of the unfettered man."[28] Approached in these terms, Thoreau was then taken to task for pandering to the popular misconception that a philosopher must typically be an "impracticable" man who "rails at society and is disposed to submit to as few of its trammels as possible, and who has the credit of resources within himself that the majority of people do not possess, and, in fact, do not much care for." In this role, Thoreau was also described as a figure "at war with the political economy of the age," and who preached to his readers the doctrine that "the fewer wants man has the better, while in reality civilization is the spur of many wants."

After casting Thoreau in the role of cultural naysayer, *The Churchman* review of *Walden* then went on to provide a brief summary of the book's first two chapters, reprinting five long passages from "Economy" and "Where I Lived and What I Lived For"—all of which then were again said to illustrate an "excessive love of individuality" that could not bear the test of practical examination. Conceding that there was such a thing as a "neglect of a proper cultivation of a man's isolated individual life," *The Churchman*'s reviewer insisted that Thoreau's peculiar account of the ways in which "the soul needs restraint, sequestration, and repose" told of an experiment available only to an elite few. He complained as well that the

27. "Literature," *The Churchman* [New York], September 2, 1854, 4, cols. 1–4, rpt. in Dean and Schamhorst, "Contemporary Reception of *Walden*," 310–16. The one other contemporary review that compares in length to the two I discuss in this section is the mixed appraisal that appeared in the October 21, 1854 *Boston Atlas*, 1, rpt. in *Central Essays on 'Walden,'* 32–36. I do not explore it in detail here, however, since the others can be shown to have been far more significant in determining Thoreau's cultural reputation at the time.

28. Several other contemporary notices and reviews of *Walden* also referred to its author as a modern-day Diogenes. See, among several such references, "Walden; or Life in the Woods," *Lowell Journal and Courier*, August 10, 1854, 2, col. 3, which mentions that Thoreau was sometimes called the "Concord Diogenes"; "Review of New Books," *Peterson's Magazine* (October 1854): 254, where Thoreau is introduced as "a modern Diogenes."

depth and sincerity of Thoreau's "grudge against civilization" were called into question by having hastened back to society with a book that published his many complaints.

The Churchman's reviewer clearly was bothered by most of what he understood Walden to be saying. The worst of it, however, was that "MR. THOREAU so frequently throws doubt over and suggests a spirit of disaffection to the sacred Scriptures." There was not quite as much of this in Walden as there had been in Thoreau's first book, the reviewer conceded, but "a little of this nonsense is quite too much." For all its generally sharp criticism of Walden, however, The Churchman's review ended on a rather different note. Among its concluding remarks, there was an admission that the harsh opening characterizations of Thoreau were perhaps overdrawn. Despite his sarcasm and his denunciation of civilization, Thoreau may have been "only playing the part of an individual humorist," for he clearly knew "as much as any one how much he is indebted to civilization." It was also conceded that, when approached for this angle, parts of Walden in fact could be read with pleasure as a sometimes genial satire of its age. And two examples of the book's "philosophical humor" were illustrated by long excerpts taken from Thoreau's accounts of the habits of his Concord neighbors at the outset of "The Village," and his description of the Canadian wood-chopper and post-maker in "Visitors." Finally, The Churchman admitted that it had hardly done justice to Thoreau's chief forte as a writer, his "natural history observations," and its review concluded with a brief sentence of praise for his account of the battle of the ants in "Brute Neighbors."

I have recounted The Churchman's review of Walden at some length here not because it was particularly original or perceptive—although it would be a mistake simply to call it vapid or uninformative. Set alongside other notices and reviews, The Churchman's review was unusual both in its length and in the harshness of its criticism of Thoreau's cultural and religious views. In at least two important respects, however, it was also representative of the broader critical reaction to Walden at the time of its publication. First, as with other more positive notices and reviews, The Churchman clearly approached Thoreau primarily as a moralist, and in doing so its account of Walden adds evidence to support the conclusion that the initial popular appreciation and dissemination of Thoreau's book was closely, although by no means exclusively, bound up with the question of what he meant to teach his readers, and whether his lessons were practicable. *The Churchman's* extensive citations from *Walden* were also typical of the antebellum period's review style, which was, as we have seen, designed in part to make the contents of books more readily available at a time when the cost of most books still placed them beyond the reach of ordinary readers. Or, put another way, while *The Churchman's* uneasiness before *Walden*, both cultural and religious, seems obvious enough, so too does its willingness to follow other reviewers in allowing Thoreau to speak for himself. "We are not predisposed to throw any unnecessary obstacles in the way of this author," *The Churchman* claimed in guarded self-justification, noting that it would have been "reckless of its duty" if it had not questioned Thoreau's religious attitudes, yet suggesting too that it had fulfilled another "duty" by providing access to the actual contents of the book. And the claim was by no means disingenuous: of the roughly six thousand words in *The Churchman's* review, slightly more than half consisted of excerpts taken from *Walden* itself.

Why *The Churchman*, a never widely circulated and now largely forgotten antebellum religious periodical, should have taken such special interest in *Walden* is not apparent at first glance. But it certainly was no coincidence when *Putnam's Monthly Magazine*, a month later, came forward with its long and considerably more complimentary review of Thoreau's book. At the time of *Walden's* publication, Thoreau had both professional and personal ties to the recently established Philadelphia magazine. His "Excursion to Canada," serialized in four installments, had appeared in its opening numbers during the winter of 1853; and "Cape Cod," being readied for the printer during the summer of 1854, would appear in its pages during the following year. One of the editors of *Putnam's*, George William Curtis, was an old acquaintance, as well as a past resident of Concord (and Brook Farm "boarder") who in 1845 had helped Thoreau raise the timbers and roof of his cabin at Walden Pond.

Putnam's review was written by Charles Frederick Briggs, the magazine's original projector, who began by attempting to counter the charge that Thoreau was, as *The Churchman* had put it, a figure "at war with the political economy of the age." Briggs too, then, sought to focus attention primarily on the moral and cultural implications of *Walden*. While agreeing that it made sense to think of Thoreau as a modern Diogenes, he added the adjective "Yankee" to that characterization to stress that Thoreau was something more than a naysayer, and that his view of the reigning economic ethos of New England in fact had mixed emulation and respect with its criticisms. In Briggs's estimate, the author of *Walden* was a "genuine New Englander" in at least three respects. First of all, Thoreau had left no doubt that he had been "happy enough to get back among the good people of Concord" once his experiment had ended. In recounting the details of his stay at Walden Pond, he had also made it clear that he had not lost sight of "the advantages of living in what we call the world," never hiding the fact "that he occasionally went out to dine, and when the society of woodchucks and chipping-squirrels were insufficient for his amusement, he liked to go into Concord and listen to the village gossips in the stores and taverns." Finally, Briggs stressed that the primary lesson of *Walden* was modest and practicable—namely, "to show how cheaply a gentleman of refined tastes, lofty aspirations and cultivated intellect may live, even in these days of high prices." He also illustrated this side of the book by providing a careful and sympathetic summary of Thoreau's account of his first year at Walden Pond, with several excerpts from "Economy," including Thoreau's account of his income from farming during his first year at the pond. Briggs's view, in short, was that there was nothing cynical or mean-spirited in Thoreau's story of his experiment. "There are but few readers," he observed in closing, who would "fail to find profit and refreshment" in *Walden*.

While Briggs recommended, in very broad terms, that his contemporaries approach *Walden* with some of the attitudes that informed my discussion in chapter 2, again I have recounted his review here not because it was exceptionally perceptive or thorough in its appraisal. Indeed, as an account of Thoreau's purposes in writing *Walden*, it was in some respects a curious exercise. Casting Thoreau honorifically at the outset as a Yankee Diogenes, Briggs would later come back to speak of him somewhat condescendingly as a "philosophical vagabond." And apart from modest praise for *Walden* as a book that many "will find pleasure in reading," nothing was said about the book's significance as a contribution to American "literature." Even so, *Putnam's* review, in the end, can be said to have rendered *Walden* a major service simply by doing what most other contemporary reviews did—namely, providing a setting in which antebellum readers gained access to the book without having to purchase it. In fact, as with *The Churchman*, the bulk of Briggs's review was given over to text taken from Thoreau's book: of its roughly 4,700 printed words, more than three thousand came directly from *Walden* itself. And while we have no certain figures on the number of copies of *Putnam's* that sold in September 1854, a conservative estimate suggests that Briggs's review must have found its way into the hands of some 12,000 people.[29]

4

What I have presented so far in this chapter might be summarized simply as an attempt to show that *Walden* received a broad and well-informed public hearing during the weeks and months immediately following its publication. In looking back, there may be little in this initial hearing that a late twentieth-century literary critic might consider profound or original, but the public response to *Walden* was by no means as obtuse or vapid as some recent commentators have claimed.[30] On the contrary, excerpts from *Walden* were commonplace in magazines and newspapers across the country. And while the vast majority of contemporary reviewers registered their sense that Thoreau's book was an extraordinary literary achievement, their appraisals included a significant variety of opinions and points of view. Finally, it should be added that while *Walden* could hardly be considered an immediate best-seller, popular knowledge of the book continued to grow in various ways during the years before Thoreau's death in 1862. Thoreau himself would take a hand in popularizing *Walden* when he distilled the book's cultural criticism into what became, under a succession of titles, his most frequently delivered lecture. Possibly presented first in Philadelphia in late November 1854, under the title "Getting a Living," it would be repeated several times between 1854 and 1860. Although their importance is difficult to measure, two other vehicles for the popularization of Thoreau's name and writings included several passages from his writings collected in *Seed-Grain for Thought and Discussion*,

29. [Charles Frederick Briggs], "A Yankee Diogenes," *Putnam's Monthly* (October 4, 1854): 443–48. (Mott, *History of American Magazines*, 2:426 n. 25, notes that circulation figures for *Putnam's* varied from 12,000 to 20,000.) It may be worth noting that the earliest specific characterization of Thoreau as a Diogenes-like figure come to life in New England appears to come in a review of *A Week* (from an unidentified newspaper), rpt. in *Thoreau Society Bulletin* 130 (Winter 1975): 8.

30. See, e.g., the Introduction to *Critical Essays on Henry David Thoreau's 'Walden,'* ed. Joel Myerson (Boston, 1988), 1; and the preface to *The Recognition of Henry David Thoreau: Selected Criticism Since 1848*, ed. Wendell Glick (Ann Arbor, 1969), vii–viii. Despite its perhaps obvious dangers, the practice of praising the critical perceptions of one's own times at

a literary anthology compiled by Anna C. Lowell (sister-in-law of James Russell Lowell) and published by Ticknor and Fields in 1856, and a full reprinting of "Reading" that appeared in the January 1859 *Massachusetts Teacher*, a magazine published by the state's teachers' organization. Undoubtedly more immediately significant in keeping *Walden* visible within antebellum literary culture, however, were the substantial excerpts from the book that Evert Duyckinck included in his entry on Thoreau in his great *Cyclopaedia of American Literature* (1855). Duyckinck was by no means an uncritical admirer of *Walden*—as we shall see, he very probably had been the earlier unnamed reviewer of the book for *The Churchman*. Yet it seems very unlikely that interest in Thoreau's book was lessened by his strictures. Duyckinck's notice of *Walden* in the *Cyclopaedia*, at the very least, suggests that as early as 1855 one could not write about American literature without having at least some familiarity with Thoreau's book.[31]

Let me now address a central question that my revised account of the publication and first reviews of *Walden* has left out—namely, what did Thoreau himself make of the contemporary reception of *Walden*? Having spent several sometimes difficult years writing the book, one would guess that he must have been immensely satisfied to find his efforts rewarded with public acclaim and recognition. Yet there is scant evidence to suggest exactly what Thoreau thought the many complimentary notices and reviews of his book signified. Doubtless, he knew that his association with Ticknor and Fields had helped make *Walden* stand out and identify him as a writer of high literary ambition and skill. It is clear too that, unlike his publisher, Thoreau thought *Walden* had sold well enough. (Eighteen months after the book first appeared, replying to the question of how it had been received, he commented in private correspondence that "It has found an

---

the expense of past ones seems peculiarly widespread among modern literary historians and biographers who have studied Thoreau's career.

31. "Getting a Living" would be published as "Life Without Principle" in the October 1863 *Atlantic Monthly*; for a more detailed account of the history of the lecture, see the "Textual Introduction" to "Life Without Principle," in *The Writings of Henry David Thoreau, Reform Papers*, ed. Wendall Glick (Princeton, 1973), 369–73, and Walter Harding, "A Check List of Thoreau's Lectures," *Bulletin of the New York Public Library* 52 (February 1948): 84–87. Mrs. Anna C. Lowell, *Seed-Grain for Thought and Discussion* (Boston, 1856). "Reading," *Massachusetts Teacher* 12 (January 1859): 20–24; Evert A. and George L. Duyckinck, "Henry David Thoreau," *Cyclopaedia of American Literature*, 2 vols. (New York, 1855) 2: 653–56. Thoreau's ties to Duyckinck are discussed in more detail later in this section.

audience of excellent character, and quite numerous with some 2000 copies having been dispersed.") In the fall of 1855 Thoreau also made a brief entry in his journal—taking inventory of the various "faults" reviewers had found in his literary style—which suggests he had kept himself well-informed about what had been said about *Walden*. Apart from this, however, his letters and journals are strangely silent on the question of how he viewed the reception of *Walden*.[32] At the height of his literary fame in the autumn and early winter of 1854, Thoreau appears to have been largely indifferent to the success he had achieved. In looking back, it seems clear, too, that the appearance of *Walden* marked the end of his most productive period as a publishing writer. In the summer of 1855, *Putnam's* published three installments of "Cape Cod," and there would have been more had the serialization not been suspended after the magazine's editors apparently took umbrage at the content and tone of "The Wellfleet Oysterman," which would naturally have appeared next. It is true that, during the second half of the 1850s, Thoreau's lecturing became a somewhat more important part of his public life, and that in October 1859 he took a highly visible role in events that followed John Brown's raid on Harper's Ferry. But there seems little question that after the publication of *Walden*, his desire to see his name and writings in print was in abeyance, and rekindled only during the final year of his life, when he revised and rewrote the four essays published posthumously by the *Atlantic Magazine*.[33]

The question of Thoreau's own expectations in publishing *Walden* is

---

32. *Correspondence of Henry David Thoreau*, 407; for the journal entry, see Harding, *Days of Henry Thoreau*, 338. (It may be worth noting one other brief entry, in *The Journals of Henry Thoreau*, ed. Bradford Torrey and Francis H. Allen, 14 vols. (Boston, 1906), 8:103, where Thoreau recounts Emerson telling him that one of his acquaintances saw *Walden* simply as a satire.)

33. For a more detailed discussion of Putnam's decision to suspend publication, see the Historical Introduction to *Cape Cod*, ed. Joseph J. Moldenhauer (Princeton, 1988), 258–76; Sattelmeyer, *Thoreau's Reading*, 55–56. Sattelmeyer makes the familiar argument that as early as 1850 Thoreau had to accommodate himself to the "truth that no reliable public outlet for his work existed," and as a consequence turned increasingly to his journal as a mode of private expression (56). While Thoreau's journal undoubtedly provided his primary form of composition during the 1850s, it seems to me a mistake, for reasons we will consider below, to approach Emerson's literary career as the story of a figure who had set out to make a living primarily by way of his writing. The "truth" Sattelmeyer assumes in his account of Thoreau's career, then, is open to question, and suggests an alternative story of the sort I sketch in this section.

made even more complex if we approach it by way of his view of his literary career as a whole prior to the appearance of *Walden*. Here too there remains something elusive about his aspirations that frustrates an attempt to capture his purposes in a straightforward summary. Like Emerson, Thoreau had a long (and by now equally well-documented) struggle with the problem of a professional vocation.[34] Unlike Emerson, however, he never made a clear break to become a "professional" writer—if we want to use that term to describe the activities of someone who labored regularly to produce a steady flow of copy to meet the deadlines of printers and booksellers. Thoreau did of course spend much of his adult life writing, or preparing to write. Yet he always had and chose to pursue other means of support aside from publishing, and the volume of work he came to publish barely approached that of Emerson. During the first two decades of his career, Emerson authored seven books, numerous essays and reviews, and several dozen poems—and all only at the start of a publishing career that would remain productive until the early 1870s. By contrast, between 1843 and 1862 Thoreau wrote roughly the same number of poems, yet published only two books and a handful of articles. Moreover, where Emerson would live long enough to enjoy in full measure the cultural status bestowed on writers by the literary marketplace, Thoreau died before his publications became permanent landmarks in American culture, let alone major commercial successes. "The Writings of Henry David Thoreau" were the posthumous productions of other hands, beginning with the collection of his reviews and magazine articles Ticknor and Fields published in the years immediately after his death. By choice and temperament, Thoreau himself was a free-lancer who approached both publishing and lecturing as occasional activities. He not only prized his independence from the new cultural institutions that sought to embrace his generation of writers; he viewed them with ambivalence, suspicion, and occasional hostility. In Thoreau's view, one of the clearest signs of the blandness and timidity of

---

34. The most generally acclaimed recent study is a two-part psychobiography by Richard Lebeaux, *Young Man Thoreau* (Amherst, 1975), and *Thoreau's Seasons* (Amherst, 1984); also see Robert D. Richardson, *Henry Thoreau: A Life of the Mind* (Berkeley, 1986). Both authors see the significance of Thoreau's life to lie largely in its inner workings; hence the cultural setting within which Thoreau struggled to define his vocation is only thinly explored. Steven Fink, *Prophet in the Marketplace: Thoreau's Development as a Professional Writer* (Princeton, 1992), focuses on the cultural factors that shaped Thoreau's career between 1837 and 1849, yet begs the question of whether it makes historical sense to plot the story of his career as the emergence of a full-time "professional writer."

antebellum culture could be found in its choice of reading materials—and it was a choice that Thoreau usually found wanting.[35]

Yet it will not do to fall back on generalizations that say that he turned his back on the new forms of popular literary culture in his day and that he never came to think of himself as a professional writer. Thoreau at times maintained that his cultural importance lay in how he lived, not in what he wrote, but it was impossible for his contemporaries to separate one from the other. We know, for that matter, Thoreau was intensely proud of what he wrote. His private correspondence shows that, while he said that he never wrote for pay or to satisfy a wider reading public, he was a combative and impatient bargainer in negotiating his publishing contracts. Indeed, apart from his early contributions to the *Dial*, Thoreau usually insisted on being paid for whatever writing he did for magazines, was paid above the going rate, and was much offended when he was not paid promptly—which was usually the case.[36]

In sum, while Thoreau's hostility toward the antebellum literary marketplace was real enough, it does not consistently match up with the actual record of his career. Examined in its entirety, his conduct as a part-time man-of-letters was both varied and pragmatic. While hardly hammering out manuscript after manuscript, Thoreau experimented with his writings in different ways, beginning with the translations, reviews, and poems he contributed to the *Dial*, and ending with the *Atlantic Monthly* essays that included three examples of the "excursion" genre that enjoyed such popularity in his day. It also is worth noting again that Thoreau plainly had expected that the success of *Walden* would bring him the part-time employment as a lecturer he enjoyed during the late 1850s. Every year between 1855 and 1860, in fact, he offered his services on the national lecture sys-

---

35. Thoreau's frustrations with what he saw as the limitations of America's emerging literary marketplace have been masterfully explored by Robert A. Gross, "Much Instruction from Little Reading: Books and Libraries in Thoreau's Concord," *Proceedings of the American Antiquarian Society*, vol. 97, pt. 1, 1987, 129–88. In his reconstruction of the local historical context of the chapter on reading in *Walden*, Gross is careful (and correct) in pointing out that over the decade he spent writing and rewriting his second book, Thoreau had seen *both* "popular and official versions of Concord culture and found them wanting" (183).

36. See, for example, the more detailed account of the publication of Thoreau's articles in *Putnam's Monthly Magazine* in Historical Introduction, in *Cape Cod*, 260–83. The usual pay for early contributors to the magazine was $3.00 per page; Thoreau's rate of payment was $4.00. In 1847 he received $50.00 from *Graham's* for "Thomas Carlyle and his Works"; by 1862 the *Atlantic Monthly* would pay him $100.00 for each of his four posthumously published articles—a sum that exceeded the entire royalty for the first edition of *Walden*.

tem by way of notices featured in the *New York Daily Tribune*. Those notices apparently did not attract interest on a nationwide scale, but closer
to home Thoreau was more successful, delivering lectures in several different cities in New England, and as far south as Philadelphia.[37]

Can these disparate bits and pieces of an occasional literary career be
put together in a single coherent narrative? Or, more precisely, what bearing does Thoreau's career before the publication of *Walden* have for our
understanding of the contemporary reception of the book? Critics and biographers who have attempted to answer such questions usually construct
a narrative that begins by focusing on Thoreau's eight-month sojourn on
Staten Island in 1843, where he went in May to tutor the son of Emerson's
brother William, and at the same time supposedly launch his career as a
writer for New York literary magazines. The received account tells us that
Thoreau was an innocent hopeful who quickly discovered there was no
market for his work, became homesick and disoriented, and then wrote off
his efforts as an abject failure, returning to Concord in December to
resume work in the family pencil business.[38] But there are other threads in
the story of Thoreau's first visit to New York which, when pulled, require
us to construct a more complicated (and less unhappy) narrative. To begin
with, it is by no means clear that Thoreau planned his stay in New York
as an effort to become a self-supporting writer. The care with which he
negotiated the terms of his contract with William Emerson suggests that
he recognized the then perhaps obvious danger of finding himself dependent upon publishing for his income at a time when both book- and
magazine-publishing remained commercially risky ventures. (Emerson's
brother agreed to give him $100 a year, plus board, lodging, and a separate
room to study and write in; Thoreau in turn offered to assist his employer,
then County Judge of Richmond Court on Staten Island, with his clerical
duties in hopes of securing some additional income.) Thoreau's correspondence also shows that he was aware that he had arrived in New York as a
relatively unknown writer, with little money to contribute to his own
cause. In a candidly self-mocking account of his encounters with New

---

37. Harding, "Check List of Thoreau's Lectures," 84–87, provides a more detailed listing
of Thoreau's lectures after the publication of *Walden*. For the *Tribune* notices, see Borst,
Henry David Thoreau: A Reference Guide, 1835–99, 21, 23, 24, 28.

38. See, for example, the Historical Introduction to *A Week on the Concord and Merrimack Rivers*, ed. Carl F. Hovde (Princeton, 1980), 447–50; Richardson, *Henry Thoreau*, 131–
143; Lebeaux, *Thoreau's Seasons*, 36, 256; Fink, *Prophet in the Marketplace*, ch. 4.

York booksellers and publishers, he wrote to his mother: "I find that I talk with these poor men as if I were over head and ears in business and a few thousands were no consideration with me—I almost reproach myself for bothering them thus to no purpose—but it is very valuable experience—and the best introduction I could have."[39]

Yet if Thoreau knew he faced formidable hurdles in going to New York "to accomplish something in the literary way," it would then seem more plausible to see his practical intentions on this count simply as a matter of making himself better known to the leaders of the city's new publishing institutions. And if that alternative approach makes sense, it invites the telling of another and rather different story of the "beginning" of his literary career, one that would start by showing that he was successful at least to the extent of establishing professional contacts with two of New York's most important literary figures in the early 1840s—Evert Duyckinck and Horace Greeley—and then go on to consider the various ways in which he would continue to benefit from their ability to bring prestige and publicity to the work he published between 1843 and 1854, culminating with *Walden*.

Thoreau's relation to Duyckinck remains the much less carefully studied of the two, but in certain respects is an equally interesting and instructive case, chiefly because it helps us see that the commercial failure of Thoreau's first book was both a more complex and less damaging episode than we are usually taught to believe.[40] Duyckinck is now remembered as one of the first influential advocates of American literary nationalism during the 1840s, as well as a partially successful forerunner of James T. Fields in providing institutional supports for the development of an indigenous

---

39. Harding, *Days of Henry Thoreau*, 145–46; *Correspondence of Henry David Thoreau*, 135. Thoreau also quickly discovered that he had arrived in New York precisely at the time when the price wars that accompanied America's first short-lived "paperback revolution" had temporarily devastated established New York publishing houses. In a September 14, 1843 letter to Emerson, he wrote: "Literature comes to be a poor market here, and even the little that I write is more than will sell. I have tried the Democratic Review, the New Mirror, and Brother Jonathan [the two weeklies that had launched the first paperback revolution]. The last two, as well as the New World are overwhelmed with contributions which cost nothing, and are worth no more." (*Correspondence*, 139).

40. My account of Duyckinck, and of his dealings with Thoreau, draws from Perry Miller's still invaluable *The Raven and the Whale: The War of Words and Wits in the Era of Poe and Melville* (New York, 1956); Bender, *New York Intellect*, 141–43; Richard Broadhead, *The School of Hawthorne* (New York, 1986), 51, 53–54, 56; and the Historical Introduction to *A Week on the Concord and Merrimack Rivers*, 450–70. Also see Fink, *Prophet in the Marketplace*, ch. 5.

"high" American literary culture. An ambitious and practical man, Duyck-inck established and contributed to new kinds of American literary periodicals—*Arcturus, United States Magazine and Democratic Review,* and *Literary World* (the first important American weekly devoted chiefly to discussion of current books)—published in New York and designed in their standards to rival then more well-established British reviews. During the mid-1840s, as mentioned already, Duyckinck also served as an advisory editor to the New York publishing house of Wiley and Putnam, persuading its owners to publish native writers in a new "Library of American Books" series that was produced in tandem with its already popular "Library of Choice Reading," a set of American editions of well-established British and French classics. Wiley and Putnam's American library series commenced with a collection of Edgar Allan Poe's *Tales* and another of his poems in 1845, and later included Margaret Fuller's *Papers on Literature and Art* (1846), Hawthorne's *Mosses from Old Manse* (1846), and Melville's *Typee* (1846). We also know from Emerson's correspondence that Duyck-inck approached him unsuccessfully in August 1845 with a request for a contribution to the "Library of Choice Reading," and again two months later with another rejected offer to publish his poems in the American library series.[41]

There is no evidence that Thoreau actually met Duyckinck while he was in New York in 1843, but it would have been surprising if he had not. The two magazine pieces Thoreau sold while living in New York—a brief sketch called "The Landlord" and "Paradise (To Be) Regained," a long review of J. A. Etzer's utopian tract *The Paradise Within Reach of All Men*—both appeared in the newly established *United States Magazine and Democratic Review,* whose literary affairs Duyckinck largely managed during the early 1840s, and whose reputation as the most brilliant periodical of its time he was initially instrumental in establishing. Later, in March 1847, when Thoreau was nearing completion of the first draft of *A Week,* it

---

41. *Letters of Ralph Waldo Emerson,* 3:296–97, 301–2, 307–8. Emerson declined both offers, ruling out the possibility of a new compilation of his work in the "Library of Choice Reading" because Wiley and Putnam would have published such a work simultaneously in Britain, and that would have violated the terms of a "friendly understanding" with the London publisher John Chapman that assured him of title to any new British editions of Emerson's writings. Emerson refused the offer to publish his poems partly because his arrangements with Munroe and Company promised higher royalties, partly because he felt a large portion of the audience for his poetry "prefer in works of this kind a costlier style of book" (308).

would be Emerson who wrote to Duyckinck in an effort to have Thoreau's first book published as a new title in Wiley and Putnam's "Library of American Books." "Mr Henry D. Thoreau of this town has just completed a book of extraordinary merit," he wrote from Concord on March 12, 1847, in a letter informing Duyckinck that he had already told Thoreau his best course of action "would undoubtedly be, to send the book to you, to be printed by Wiley & Putnam, that it may have a good edition & wide publishing." Emerson also urged that Duyckinck propose Thoreau "good terms, & give his book the great advantages of being known which your circulation ensures."[42]

What actually transpired during the several months that followed, however, turned out to be an episode marred by bad luck and lost opportunities. Duyckinck replied immediately that he would be glad to read the manuscript. At the time, however, Thoreau was at work on a major addition to his first draft, and did not write to Duyckinck himself until he completed his revision near the end of May. The additional time he needed to finish his first draft, however, would prove very costly. It would be May 28 before Thoreau managed to mail his manuscript to Duyckinck, asking in an accompanying letter for a prompt decision, yet then again delaying the outcome when two weeks later he asked for it back again to make additional changes. Thoreau returned the manuscript on July 3, again expressing his impatience to have his book printed as soon as possible. What Thoreau apparently did not know as these events unfolded, however, was that the figure who in effect was acting as his literary agent in dealing with Wiley and Putnam had temporarily lost his influence there, having been fired in late April as editor of the *Literary World*, a magazine whose major source of financial support also happened to be Wiley and Putnam. For Thoreau, the upshot was that, while Duyckinck had a favorable opinion of his manuscript, his opinion failed to elicit the "good terms" Emerson had asked for, and Thoreau himself also appeared to have expected. Wiley and Putnam stalled at first, then did offer to print *A Week* in the "Library of American Books," but only if Thoreau bore the full cost of producing it.[43] He refused, although it is worth stressing here that it is by no means clear that he did so because he was unable or unwilling to publish at his own economic risk. In fact, in explaining his refusal of Wiley and Putnam's

---

42. Ibid., 384.
43. Miller, *Raven and the Whale*, 189, 199–20; Historical Introduction, *A Week*, 458–61.

offer to Emerson in a November 14, 1847 letter, Thoreau wrote that: "If I liked the book well enough I should not delay; but for the present I am indifferent. I believe this is, after all, the course you advised,—to let it lie."[44]

After another year spent in revising and expanding his original draft, Thoreau was again ready to approach publishers. Ticknor and Company (in which James T. Fields was still a junior partner at the time) offered to publish A Week, but again only if Thoreau provided a down payment of $450 to cover production costs. Thoreau declined, and next approached Emerson's long-time publisher, James Munroe and Company, who likewise proposed that he cover production costs, yet also offered to allow them to be recovered by way of the book's expected sales, so long as Thoreau guaranteed full reimbursement. Thoreau accepted, and on May 30, 1849, with none of the fanfare that would later accompany the publication of Walden, the first edition of A Week appeared in Boston. With little stake in the book's economic success, Munroe provided little in the way of advance publicity. Two brief notices appeared in the May 30 Boston Daily Advertiser and, ironically enough, in the May 19 Literary World, of which Duyckinck had regained editorship during 1848. The title page of Munroe's edition of A Week announced that the book also was being published simultaneously by George F. Putnam in New York, Lindsay and Blackiston in Philadelphia, and John Chapman in London. But this was, as Walter Harding has pointed out, simply Munroe's euphemistic way of announcing that those other publishers would carry a few copies of his edition in their stock.[45]

The damage that this episode did to Thoreau's reputation at the outset of his literary career seems obvious enough. When A Week finally appeared in print, it came into American culture by way of a publisher in no position to market or encourage reviews of Thoreau's book, and the result was a commercial failure that left him in considerable debt and, some have argued, shook his self-confidence. Yet if we approach this episode by way of Thoreau's ties with Duyckinck, its outcome seems both more compli-

---

44. *Correspondence of Henry David Thoreau*, 191. Robert Sattelmeyer, "'When He Became My Enemy': Emerson and Thoreau, 1848–49," *New England Quarterly* 62 (June 1989): 187–204, has argued that various developments surrounding the publication of *A Week* brought their relationship to crisis. That those developments included Emerson's explicit suggestion that Thoreau publish the book at his own expense, however, remains open to question. Given that this practice was commonplace in the case of relatively unknown or first-time authors, it seems unlikely Thoreau would have held Emerson even indirectly responsible for the debt he incurred.

45. Harding, *Days of Henry Thoreau*, 246–47.

cated and less disastrous than the traditional account allows. The commercial failure of *A Week* looks somewhat less abject if we recognize that Thoreau was to some degree simply a victim of bad luck. It is arguable that Duyckinck's fall from grace at Wiley and Putnam occurred at precisely the moment when otherwise he would have been in a position to add *A Week* to the widely circulated "Library of American Books" series without requiring Thoreau to bear the costs of its production. (Why Thoreau chose not to resubmit *A Week* for publication in that series in 1848 remains a mystery.) It also is important to notice here, however, that Thoreau did come to benefit from Duyckinck's cultural labors in other ways. His inclusion in Duyckinck's *Cyclopaedia*—where Thoreau was introduced as the author of "two of the most remarkable books" in American literature—has been mentioned already. After regaining his position as editor of the *Literary World*, Duyckinck also wrote a review of *A Week*, which, while expressing strong reservations about Thoreau's religious views, was generally admiring and respectful. It was also the *Literary World* that provided one of the few contemporary notices "Resistance to Civil Government" received at the time of its publication. (Although puzzled about why it had appeared in a volume titled *Aesthetic Papers*, the notice provided a fair summary of Thoreau's essay.) Finally, and perhaps most significant, it seems very likely that Duyckinck was, in 1854, the unnamed reviewer of *Walden* for *The Churchman*. We know that after disbanding the *Literary World* in 1852, he went on to write reviews for the Episcopal magazine, and in March 1854, six months before the appearance of *Walden*, had been officially announced as its literary editor. By the end of May of that same year, Duyckinck also was devoting much of his time to compiling his comprehensive anthology of American literature. Set side by side, it does not take much effort to see that the entry he would provide for Thoreau in *Cyclopaedia* represented little more than a slight abridgement and reworking of the anonymous review of *Walden* that had appeared the year before in *The Churchman*.[46] And as with the earlier review, the bulk of the *Cyclopaedia* entry consisted of excerpts taken from the first chapters of Thoreau's second book.

There can be no question, however, that the pivotal figure in the story

---

46. Miller, *Raven and the Whale*, 322; "Thoreau's Travels," *Literary World* (September 22, 1849): 245–47; review of *Aesthetic Papers*, in *Literary World* (September 29, 1849): 5. Later, in his own sketch on "An Account of Mount Saddleback," *Literary World* (August 30, 1851): 161–62, Duyckinck would compare his own ascent with Thoreau's account in *A Week*, commending the book as "filled with minute and delicate observations of nature." It may also be

of Thoreau's literary career during the years prior to the appearance of *Walden* was Horace Greeley. Important as they were, Duyckinck's reviews and notices can hardly be seen as parts of a determined effort to build Thoreau's reputation. Troubled by his unorthodox religious views, Duyckinck was perhaps never more than a grudging admirer of Thoreau's literary skills. (In the *Cyclopaedia*, he did describe *A Week* and *Walden* as "remarkable" yet only "on the score of a certain quaint study of natural history and scenery.") By contrast, Greeley was the figure who did more than anyone else to make Thoreau's name and writings visible in antebellum America, and it does not seem too much to say, in fact, that by the time *Walden* appeared, Greeley's efforts had already made Thoreau's name and ideas well-known to the tens of thousands of Americans who read the daily and weekly editions of the *New York Tribune*. Perhaps equally important, between 1843 and 1854, it was Greeley who also took it upon himself to serve as Thoreau's sponsor, agent, and coach—and it is hard to imagine that Thoreau could have found a more powerful and respected patron.[47]

The full story of the Thoreau–Greeley connection is rich and complicated, beginning in Concord in January 1843 with Thoreau—then curator of the Concord Lyceum—hosting a lecture by Greeley, and Greeley a few months later returning the favor by making several flattering references to Thoreau's contributions to the *Dial* in the pages of his newspaper, and thereby providing him with his earliest public notice outside of Concord. Their professional ties grew closer during Thoreau's stay in New York in 1843, when Greeley reprinted a long, seven-paragraph extract from "A Winter's Walk" in the daily and weekly editions of the *Tribune*. And during the years that followed Thoreau's return to Concord, Greeley continued to make space in the columns of this newspaper for reviews, excerpts, and reprintings of his writings, as well as occasional accounts of Thoreau's personal activities. It was Greeley, for example, in April 1849, who first brought public attention to views that Thoreau would later express in the opening chapters of *Walden*: in reporting the contents of "A History of

---

worth noting here that a circular letter asking Thoreau to send any material and information he would like to have noticed in his *Cyclopaedia* entry was mailed to him in May 1854, some three months before *Walden* appeared. See *Correspondence*, 326–27.

47. My account of Greeley draws primarily from Harding, *Days of Henry David Thoreau*, 151, 211, 212–14, 228–30, 239–41, 248–49, 282–83, 318–19, 330–31, 332, 341, 345, 393, 439; Lebeaux, *Thoreau's Seasons*, 59, 60, 89–94, 99–102, 105. Also see Fink, *Prophet in the Marketplace*, passim.

Myself," a lecture in which Thoreau had drawn from the first draft of *Walden*, the April 2 *Daily Tribune* brought to light a moralist intent on showing his contemporaries that there was more than the production of wealth in America's future.[48] It also was on Greeley's advice that Thoreau, in 1852, culled several passages from the penultimate draft of *Walden* for publication in the July and August issues of *Sartain's Union Magazine*— passages that Greeley in turn puffed with prepublication notices in the *Daily Tribune*. Finally, it was Greeley who used his considerable personal influence in helping place (as well as gain payment for) all but one of the articles Thoreau published between 1847 and 1855, thereby obtaining for him what Greeley told him was "the best kind of advertisement whether for a publisher or for readers."

Thoreau of course never came to be prolific as a "magazinist." He found himself deeply irritated in dealings with magazine editors who, in his view, typically took too much time in publishing and paying him for his work, and too many liberties in abridging and editing what he had written. Even so, Thoreau's close ties to Greeley show us it would be a mistake to see Thoreau as a writer who found himself in the position of rising or falling on the basis of his two books alone. For again it was Greeley who reminded him that, in the literary culture of their day, "You must write to the magazines in order to let the public know who and what you are." And by going all out in puffing, and in some cases republishing, Thoreau's articles (in addition to extracts from the *Dial* and *A Week*, extracts from "Ktaadn and the Maine Woods" appeared on the front page of the *Tribune* at roughly the same time the entire piece appeared in the *Union Magazine*), Greeley made Thoreau seem not only a more prolific magazine writer than he was; he made him a considerably more visible one as well. Or, put another way, as with Emerson, Greeley converted Thoreau and his work, more modest in quantity though it was, into items about which ordinary Americans were kept posted: the several articles and the two books Thoreau published over the course of twenty years Greeley in various ways made into the ordinary fare of popular culture, thereby adding the name "Thoreau" to the list of other serious American writers in his generation that Greeley

---

48. "Life in the Woods," *New York Daily Tribune*, April 2, 1849, [2]. Greeley's praise for the primacy Thoreau attached to living for "one's soul" would be quickly (and punningly) challenged by Timothy Thorough [pseud.], "How to Live by Mr. Thoreau's Example," *New York Daily Tribune*, April 7, 1849, [5], which was accompanied by an editor's reply to "Timothy Thorough," *New York Daily Tribune*, April 7, 1854, [5].

succeeded in making into what he called "daily information" of American life.[49]

Thoreau's reluctance to seize on some of the other opportunities Greeley made available to him should not be overlooked here. It is true that part of Thoreau was prepared to accommodate the demands of a new literary culture being built by figures like Greeley, and thus that an important aspect of his career played itself out in an institutional setting different from that which shaped Emerson's early reputation. But Greeley was of course in no position simply to impose his predilections on Thoreau. While he insisted that Thoreau was capable of having a successful and lucrative career as a "magazinist," Thoreau kept his distance, choosing instead to move in and out of the world of literary journalism as he pleased. (In February 1848, for example, when Greeley invited him to follow up his Carlyle essay with similar pieces on Emerson and Hawthorne, Thoreau declined.[50]) Moreover, while Greeley clearly gained some measure of Thoreau's affection and gratitude for his many services, their professional ties appear to have loosened considerably after 1854, the year in which Thoreau's literary career was in ascendancy, yet also the year in which he began to pull back from what his friend and patron had once spoken of as the project of being "known and talked about as an author."

For all its ebbs and flows, however, the primary points to keep in mind in understanding the historical significance of Thoreau's close connection to Greeley can be stated fairly simply. Like James T. Fields, Greeley was one of the great cultural entrepreneurs of antebellum America.[51] (He "listens

---

49. *Correspondence*, 232–33. One of the ideas that inspired the founding of the *Tribune*, Greeley later recalled, was "to embody in a single sheet the information daily required by all those who aim to keep 'posted' on every important occurrence." There can be no question that Greeley considered the activities and publications of American writers to be among such occurrences. See Horace Greeley, *Recollections of a Busy Life* (New York, 1868), 142.

50. Greeley also promised to publish the essays in the *Tribune* for $25.00 each, if Thoreau could not find a better offer elsewhere. Later, in March 1854, when *Walden* was being readied for the printer, Greeley urged Thoreau to collect and arrange his magazine articles, assuring him that he would even find a publisher. Thoreau again apparently had no interest in the project. See *Correspondence*, 173–74, 323–24.

51. Greeley of course played many other roles in antebellum culture. On his political identity, see Daniel Walker Howe, *The Political Culture of the American Whigs* (Chicago, 1979), 184–97; and for his complex role in supporting various antebellum reform movements, see Carl J. Guarneri, *The Utopian Alternative: Fourierism in Nineteenth-century America* (Ithaca, 1991), 32–33, 36–39, 42–44, 253–54, 259–60, 294, 296–97, 315–18, 373–74. Greeley awaits a definitive modern biography.

after all new thoughts and things," Emerson once said of him, "with the indispensable New York condition that they can be made available."[52]) Yet where we remember Fields as the figure who brought Duyckinck's work to fruition by establishing American literature as a distinct category in the cultural marketplace, Greeley pursued a parallel project in which Fields showed no interest—namely, making new literature more immediately available to the nation at large. While cultivating a popular image of himself as the "voice of the people," Greeley was at the same time intent on instructing them, and to that end he filled the pages of his newspapers with reviews of and excerpts from books and essays, as well as accounts of lectures, and more general cultural and literary gossip—all designed to draw attention to the activities and publications of native American thinkers and writers and thereby help to fashion, as Ann Douglas has put it, a democratic culture that would not have to apologize for itself.[53] Seen in this light, one way to summarize Greeley's role in establishing Thoreau's reputation might be to say that (again as he had done somewhat earlier for Emerson) he simply exercised his formidable institutional power within an emerging national culture to make a prominent place for Thoreau. Yet in another sense Greeley's chief service in Thoreau's behalf may have been less that he helped to market his name and writings to a national audience (although it bears emphasizing again that what the vast majority of Americans knew of Thoreau by the time of his death they almost certainly had learned from Greeley's newspapers[54]) than that he used his power to limit the full play of market forces in determining Thoreau's standing within antebellum culture. Greeley never offered Thoreau a professional livelihood and never managed to define any sort of national consensus regarding the significance of his writings, but he did provide him with something he took to be far more important: the publicity necessary to "make him an author" at a time when Greeley knew quite well the buying audience for the sorts of books and magazines in which Thoreau writings could be found remained low.

---

52. *Letters of Ralph Waldo Emerson*, 3:19–20. While Emerson never chose to make himself "available," Greeley, as we saw in ch. 8, regularly did so without his consent.

53. In exploring Margaret Fuller's career at the *New York Tribune*, Douglas, *Feminization of American Culture*, 338, has described Greeley's professed ideal as writing for the people "without pandering to them."

54. While testimonies to the results of these encounters are scant, it seems fair to assume that many have been lost or simply await recovery. Some doubtless will echo the awkward

Yet what light, more exactly, does all this shed on the contemporary reception of *Walden*? The widespread acclaim that greeted Ticknor and Fields's edition of the book during the last months of 1854, as we have seen, marked Thoreau's ascent into the ranks of acclaimed American writers. To this it can now be added that the successful reception of Thoreau's second book marked the culmination of a growing public knowledge of his name and writings that Greeley had been chiefly responsible for encouraging and sustaining during the 1840s and early 1850s. It is arguable, too, that the Thoreau–Greeley connection provides little-noticed evidence of the extent to which all of Thoreau's publications during his lifetime, including *Walden*, were initially integrated into the popular reading fare of antebellum Americans, not simply elevated into a position above it. Or, put another way, Greeley's many services to Thoreau (again as with those he had provided to Emerson) demonstrate the ways in which, during the antebellum period, new institutions of "popular" and "elite" literary culture might be said to have reinforced one another. For if it was the publishing machinery of Ticknor and Fields that finally confirmed Thoreau's status as a great American writer, it appears no less true that Thoreau's long-standing and highly visible association with Greeley had served to bring prestige to his name and writing well before he hooked up with Ticknor and Fields.

The lengthy prepublication notices of *Walden* that appeared in the *New York Daily Tribune*, *Semi-Weekly Tribune*, and *Weekly Tribune* of course provide another instance of Greeley's "publicity"-making efforts on Thoreau's behalf. But his services in this regard took at least two other forms that should be mentioned briefly here. In the first case, it was Greeley who served as catalyst in helping complete part of a task that Ticknor and Fields had begun in the summer of 1854, but then abandoned. Two months prior to the official publication date of *Walden*, Thoreau's publisher had attempted to secure a British copyright for the book by arranging for its simultaneous publication in London. Fields himself had left Boston by steamer with proof sheets of *Walden* on June 7, 1854, but never reached London, becoming so seasick en route that he was forced to leave

---

compliment of Benjamin Wiley, an American businessman who admired Thoreau's work, and in a letter of December 21, 1856, reported candidly: "Very few books I *read* but I like to look at the tables of contents the engravings & portraits of others. The N.Y. Tribune often has things of more than transient interest. . . . Their notice of 'Walden' introduced me to it." *Correspondence of Henry David Thoreau*, 459.

ship at Halifax and return home. The attempt to arrange for simultaneous publication continued by other means over the course of the summer, when Ticknor and Fields subsequently sent a copy of *Walden* to its London agent Richard Bentley, informing him that it was "no common book & is sure to succeed" and offering him the copyright for $100.00. Yet for reasons that remain unknown nothing came of this second effort either, and Ticknor and Fields chose not to send advance sheets or review copies to British periodicals, apparently fearing that positive reviews might lead to the pirating of the book by British publishers. A year after the appearance of *Walden*, however, in a letter expressing his surprise that there had yet to be reviews of *Walden* in any British periodical, Greeley would urge Thoreau to have Ticknor and Fields send review copies to three English magazines and a Scottish newspaper whose addresses he included in his letter.[55] At Thoreau's prompting, his publisher now launched a belated and apparently very modest effort to market and advertise *Walden* through its London agent. Three substantial reviews eventually appeared in British literary magazines over the course of 1856 and 1857. The best-known of these remains George Eliot's very positive appraisal in the January 1856 *Westminster Review*; the other two—which appeared in the *Critic* and *Chamber's Journal* (under the title "An American Diogenes")—offered more mixed responses, yet followed Eliot in providing generous selections from Thoreau's book.[56]

Perhaps somewhat more significant in building the reputation of *Walden* at home, however, were Greeley's occasional references to the importance of Thoreau's experiment in his own efforts to define cultural attitudes and ideals he thought to be characteristic of American life. We have seen one example of this already in the references to Thoreau's early accounts of his life at Walden Pond in the pages of the *Tribune*. Later, in the winter of 1853–54, Greeley offered a more extended account of the cultural significance of Thoreau's undertaking during the course of a lecture tour of cities in upstate New York and several midwestern states. Greeley would explain

---

55. *Cost Books of Ticknor and Fields*, 289; *Correspondence*, 380; Fink, *Prophet in the Marketplace*, 265.

56. [George Eliot], *Westminster Review* 65 (January 1856): 302–3; "America," *Critic* [London], May 1, 1856, 223–24; "An American Diogenes," *Chamber's Journal* 21 (November 1857): 330–32. As with the American reviews, excerpts reprinted in the *Westminster Review* and the *Critic* were drawn mostly from the two opening chapters; *Chamber's Journal* provided excerpts drawn entirely from later chapters.

to Thoreau in a letter of March 23, 1854, that while he had recounted the
Walden Pond experiment in some detail, he had not mentioned Thoreau
by name to his audiences, but then added quickly that his account of
Thoreau's experience—which he had cast as an important lesson for those
who mistakenly believed that, in America, economic success was the only
road to self-reliance—had "excited much interest and I have repeatedly
been asked who it is that I refer to." While Greeley himself did not go on
to say so, it seems very unlikely, given his many earlier efforts to promote
Thoreau's name and writings, that he then would have passed up such an
obvious opportunity to puff Thoreau's forthcoming book. It also is worth
noting here that extracts from Greeley's lecture on "Self-Culture" later
reappeared in print, in 1857, in *The Rose of Sharon*, the oldest of the many
literary annuals that attained such popularity in the antebellum period.
Here again there was no direct mention of Thoreau or *Walden*, yet once
more it seems unlikely that any reader of Greeley's essay familiar with the
literary news reported in the daily or weekly editions of his *Tribune* in
recent years would have failed to recognize the figure to whom he so flatter-
ingly alluded.[57]

5

The various strands of the story told in this chapter point to several conclusions. First of all, the simple model of success that has informed most
modern discussions of the publication and contemporary reception of *Walden*—one that assumes any book published in the antebellum literary marketplace could not have attracted popular attention without large sales—
can be dismissed as grossly unhistorical. Evidence taken from contemporary reviews, notices, and reprintings suggests quite plainly that during
Thoreau's lifetime *Walden* had a rich and complex cultural identity in
which America's emerging literary marketplace was involved at several
different levels. The evidence, to be sure, is not so overwhelming as to suggest that Thoreau's book came to form a centrally important item in the
popular reading fare of antebellum America. The simple reversal of an

57. *Correspondence*, 324–25; Horace Greeley, "The Bases of Character," in *The Rose of Sharon: A Religious Souvenir, for MDCCCCLVII*, ed. Mrs. Caroline Sawyer (Boston, 1857), 65–73, rpt. in *Critical Essays on Henry David Thoreau's 'Walden'*, 47–50.

enduring cliché, however, is not what I have in mind here. What I have tried to show is that during Thoreau's own lifetime *Walden*, despite its modest sales, quickly became visible in a complex array of institutions that defined the antebellum literary marketplace, and that the book was widely acclaimed as the work of a uniquely gifted writer, and that its appearance therefore served to elevate Thoreau into the ranks of those select few in America who had published writing of enormously and absolutely different value from that of other contemporaries.

Close study of the contemporary reception of *Walden* also adds weight to the view of scholars who find it misleading to approach Thoreau simply as a defiant critic of antebellum popular culture. His exaggerated reputation in this regard has been challenged by two recent commentators who, in somewhat different ways, assemble convincing patterns of evidence to show that Thoreau both understood and responded to the popular literary tastes of his day. In exploring Thoreau's reading from his matriculation at Harvard in 1833 to his death in 1862, Robert Sattelmeyer has demonstrated that he depended in many ways upon the popular press for the wide variety of subjects he came to address in his writings. It took someone widely familiar with the contents of antebellum newspapers, Sattelmeyer observes, to "compose the marvelous critique of the popular press in *Walden*, and the same holds true for many of his other targets, from the railroads to politics to the gold rush." Along this same line, David Reynolds has shown that Thoreau, as did other "great" American writers of his generation, both assimilated and transformed images and themes borrowed from now little-known or forgotten popular writings of the antebellum era. Approaching *Walden* as "trenchantly funny," Reynolds argues that the book represents "a Transcendentalist refinement" of central strategies that also informed the humor of antebellum radical democrats and urban humorists. Yet while these revised portraits of Thoreau correspond quite closely to the figure I have attempted to recover in this chapter, Sattelmeyer and Reynolds tip the balance somewhat more radically than I want to. It is true, as we have seen, that several contemporary reviews underscored the humor of *Walden*. Yet there is little evidence to suggest that Thoreau's adoption of American humorous language as a result made him "virtually indistinguishable from other humorists of the time." Ticknor and Fields was hardly in the business of publishing writers of popular humor, and we have no evidence that Thoreau himself took special pride in this side of *Walden*. It may also be true that Thoreau's broad and careful

reading of necessity rendered him a writer "profoundly affected by and implicated in his age."[58] Yet he was too, and perhaps more precisely, a deeply
ambivalent participant in antebellum culture. If Thoreau never turned his
back on his age, he of course never embraced it either—and certainly never
craved the general acclaim of his contemporaries. Seeing *Walden* as the
work of a writer who understood and benefited from the popular literary culture of his day, and recognizing that the book was something of a success as
well, hardly diminishes Thoreau's moral and imaginative achievement. Yet
once accomplished, the contemporary success of *Walden* was something to
which Thoreau himself apparently assigned no extraordinary significance.
When the first edition of *Walden* sold out in 1859, three years passed before
Ticknor and Fields published its small second printing of 280 copies, and
there is no sign that Thoreau thought his publisher ought to have made the
book more generally available.[59]

These conclusions also may be useful in pointing to some unexplored
questions concerning the impact that *Walden* and Thoreau's other writings would make on readers after his death in 1862. We still know relatively little about what became of Thoreau's reputation during the three
decades immediately following his death. At the closing of his famous
eulogy—which strangely enough did not choose to mention that Thoreau
had been a published author—Emerson observed that "the country knows
not yet, or in the least part, how great a son it has lost." During the four
years that followed, however, Ticknor and Fields moved quickly to fill part
of that gap in knowledge, and in the process make Thoreau appear to be
an even more productive author of books than he was—in 1862, reprinting
Walden and *A Week*, and between 1863 and 1866 publishing five new volumes that collected Thoreau's various reviews and magazine articles, as
well as some of his correspondence: *Excursions* (1863), *The Maine Woods*
(1864), *Cape Cod* (1865), *Letters to Various Persons* (1865), and *A Yankee in
Canada, with Anti-Slavery and Reform Papers* (1866). Still, as with the first
edition of *Walden*, while Ticknor and Fields saw to it that these posthumous volumes were widely reviewed, prices remained high and press runs

---

58. Sattelmeyer, *Thoreau's Reading*, x–xi; David S. Reynolds, *Beneath the American Renaissance: The Subversive Imagination in the Age of Emerson and Melville* (New York, 1988),
500–502.

59. Fink, *Prophet in the Marketplace*, 265, notes that Thoreau retained the copyright, and
Ticknor and Fields the sole printing rights for five years.

small, and little appears to have been done to make Thoreau's books available to the American reading public at large. What happened to Thoreau's reputation during the years when Ticknor and Fields and its two successors retained sole printing rights on his writings?

It is tempting to conclude that Thoreau's elegantly bound and costly "writings"—*A Week, Walden,* and his other posthumous volumes all varied in price between $1.50 and $2.00—for a time became the exclusive property of an affluent few who formed the self-proclaimed literary elite of America's increasingly hierarchical cultural order in the late nineteenth century. There may be some truth in that view, but how then do we explain the Thoreau who emerges from Henry Hardy's preface to the Boston Bibliophile Society edition of *Walden* in 1909, a writer revered in apparently equal measure within both "highbrow" and "popular" culture? Michael Meyer has suggested in this regard that Americans of all kinds made a pact with Thoreau in the 1890s—precisely the decade when his writings came into the public domain and immediately experienced dramatic growth in both production and consumption—as they first turned to "nature" as a tonic for the rigors of urban and industrial life, and in the process elevated him to the position of "nature writer" extraordinaire. Whether that now familiar view of Thoreau immediately came at the expense of other concerns he explored in his writings, however, needs more careful investigation. It is striking that in Britain, at exactly the same time, Thoreau gained cultural authority in rather different terms. Robert Blatchford's *Merrie England* (1895), one of the founding texts of British socialism, with sales of more than two million copies, began with the injunction that if prospective readers first read *Walden,* they would more readily understand his book, and noted that he slept with *Walden* under his pillow.

What events and circumstances during the 1890s evoked such different honorific views of Thoreau? And why, for that matter, would an "elite" figure like Henry Hardy, so obviously different from Blatchford in his concerns, be concerned to establish and popularize Thoreau's authority, even as he awkwardly acknowledged Thoreau's discontent with America's existing political and economic order? Were there contemporary American advocates of "the poorer classes" who thought *Walden* was saying something other than to make the best of misfortune? The inexpensive editions of the book widely available in Britain during the 1890s had counterparts in America. Who were their readers, and what happened to them in the process of going through Thoreau's book?[60]

Finally, a history of the publication and reception of the first edition of *Walden* may also be significant for those primarily interested in the questions of how and why Thoreau's book continues to maintain such authority in our time. For despite its relative lack of drama, the story of the initial reception of Thoreau's book reminds us forcefully that any effort to understand the cultural significance of *Walden* ultimately must include a full account of its actual historical fate. Commentators who have recently focused attention on the ways in which Thoreau himself was preoccupied with the interests of a popular reading audience have helped us see that *Walden* was, during the years of its composition, more deeply and complexly rooted in the American literary marketplace than was previously imagined. Yet they have done relatively little in helping us recognize and understand the equally important matter of the many unanticipated roles *Walden* has played within our cultural marketplace since its publication. Moreover, current studies of the intellectual and rhetorical demands Thoreau continues to make on readers appear only indirectly relevant to understanding the various historical identities the book has had since its publication. We will begin to find our way only as we more carefully establish and come to terms with the changing institutional settings within which the status of *Walden* has been debated and defined.

60. Meyer, *Several More Lives to Live*, 18; Hendrick, "Henry S. Salt, the Late Victorian Socialists, and Thoreau," 409–10; see also Buell, "Henry Thoreau Enters the American Canon," esp. 36–43. For a detailed listing of British and American editions of *Walden* published between 1886 and 1909, see Borst, *Henry David Thoreau: A Descriptive Bibliography*, 24–29.

Epilogue

It is handsomer to remain in the establishment better than the establishment, and conduct that in the best manner.
. . . I cannot afford to be irritable and captious, nor to waste all my time in attacks.

—Emerson, "New England Reformers"

A living dog is better than a dead lion. Shall a man go and hang himself because he belongs to the race of pygmies, and not be the biggest pygmy that he can?

—Thoreau, *Walden*

IN THIS BOOK I have tried to show that the writings and careers of Emerson and Thoreau cannot be separated from market practices and institutions in their own time; indeed, that to talk only of their opposition to the market, or of their alleged desire to escape its power, is to diminish the true complexity of their attitudes by ignoring the efforts each made to connect criticism to a larger conception of what was new and promising about antebellum American society. I have tried also to show that their attitudes were neither distorted nor unwitting reflections of economic developments they felt compelled to deny; that it is misleading to say their shared belief that America existed for the individual grew directly from "a set of breathtaking negations" of an economic order taken for granted by their contemporaries.[1] Emerson's and Thoreau's encounters with the market produced imaginative and philosophical results; their critical faculties were less engaged in the work of negation than in efforts to reformulate the ordinary language of the market and strategies of getting and spending commonly employed by other members of their society. The linguistic complexities of Emerson's essays cannot be fully understood if we fail to see that he often used the market's language to illustrate and embody values he cherished. His essays were not, strictly speaking, about the market, but that is why the frequent intrusion of economic language, illustrations, and preoccupations is so striking. The same holds true for much of *Walden*. The carefully detailed statistics in its opening chapter poked fun at the age's dominant penny wisdom, but they also served to identify Thoreau's spiritual quest in terms his contemporaries could readily understand—the accountant's ledger. Hence, the frequent contemporary identifications of Thoreau as a Yankee or American Diogenes.

Although Emerson and Thoreau were part of antebellum society, and not separate from it, they occupied a distinctive place. Modern literary critics and historians tend to exaggerate the radicalism of their views and their cultural isolation, but it remains apparent they thought of themselves, in part, as social critics who both gave voice to the common complaints of their contemporaries and clarified values that underlay those complaints. This meant, as I tried to show in part 1, that Emerson and Thoreau often assumed what Michael Walzer has defined as the role of a connected critic. Beginning with *Nature*, Emerson set out to question the economic myths and platitudes of his society at the same time as he expressed the aspirations of his contemporaries. The second of these projects was hardly possible had Emerson not been a connected critic, in the sense that he believed his contemporaries actually had aspirations that reached beyond the market order in which they lived, and that he could express those aspirations in the language of the marketplace itself. Much the same was true

---

1. Quentin Anderson, *Making Americans: An Essay on Individualism and Money* (New York, 1992), 36.

of Thoreau. However intense his quarrel with the "curse of trade" that afflicted Concord, Thoreau never got all that far from the place where he began. His cabin at Walden Pond was only a mile from the nearest neighbor, and only two miles from the center of town, to which he returned every day or two to catch up on local gossip that "taken in homeopathic doses, was really as refreshing in its way as the rustle of leaves and the peeping of frogs" (151). More important, his critical distance from his neighbors was the subject of intense thought and afterthought. Early in *Walden*, when Thoreau asked "What does our Concord culture amount to?" and answered that "our reading, our conversation and thinking are all on a very low level, worthy only of pygmies and manikins," one can suppose that his repeated use of "our" signaled that he included himself among the "pygmies and manikins." He also explained that he thought all antebellum Americans were culturally impoverished because "we . . . soar but little higher in our intellectual flights than the columns of the daily paper" (96–97). That is not all that Thoreau meant, however, and when near the end of *Walden* he asked rhetorically—"Shall a man go and hang himself because he belongs to the race of pygmies, and not be the biggest pygmy that he can?" (290)—one can suppose that here he meant to hold up *Walden* as an account of what one American "pygmy" had been able to make of ordinary circumstances.

We have also seen, in parts 2 and 3, that Emerson and Thoreau were not just interpreters of antebellum America's "market revolution," but participants as well. My reading of their antislavery writings in part 2 aimed to provide a deeper appreciation of how they assumed their roles as connected critics, and of how their views of the relationship between abolitionist sentiment and market values figured in their understanding of the most important and explosive policy issue of their day. Emerson and Thoreau, like most other abolitionists whose views they echoed, came to hate slavery more for what it did to Northerners than for what it did to black Southern slaves, although they were hardly blind to the inhumanity of slavery. Their primary task in speaking out against slavery, then, was to touch the conscience of Northerners, to remind them that continuing complicity meant they were falling short of their own recognized principles, including those that supposedly governed life in the economic marketplace. Emerson and Thoreau, again like other abolitionists, of course meant to apply these principles with a consistency and stringency that made their fellows uncomfortable. Yet their practical objective was not, in

Wendell Phillips's words, "to make every man a Christian or a philosopher." Forbearance qualified and alternated with stringency, precisely because Emerson and Thoreau saw themselves to be reasserting political and economic principles that informed the North's way of life. Emerson assumed this stance more confidently than Thoreau, who early on decided that the struggle to end slavery would lead to permanent political disunion. Yet in his own efforts to stir opposition to slavery, he too appealed broadly to the North's conceptions of justice and property. When Thoreau said that enforcement of the Fugitive Slave Law of 1850 had made all property in insecure, he wanted to remind Northerners that new legal protections for slavery now would allow them to know something of what it meant to be denied the right of self-ownership.

In part 3, I shifted ground somewhat to consider how Emerson and Thoreau themselves experienced the gradual but sweeping change the market brought to the production, circulation, and status of writing during the antebellum period. Here I invoked the "literary marketplace" not, as most commentators currently treat this issue, as another way of speaking about the rise of a new national culture that compelled "elite" writers like Emerson and Thoreau to accommodate themselves to the tastes of a mass reading public. I approached it instead as a set of heterogeneous and sometimes overlapping subcultures, and argued that the immediate historical importance of Emerson's and Thoreau's publications escapes us unless we make efforts to reconstruct the diverse and conflicting concerns of the culture they sprang from and helped shape. It was on this basis, too, I advanced the claim that, during the antebellum era, it was the literary marketplace that first connected Emerson and Thoreau to American society at large.

While I have not made many forward glances in this study, I think that at least one of the central themes in part 1 could be profitably pursued by American historians interested in exploring cultural practices fostered by the market in later periods. It regards Emerson's and Thoreau's shared habit of elevating or transforming the language of the market to articulate higher ideals and principles. While recognizing that over time the effects of the market have been multiple and contradictory, I cannot escape the feeling that troping the market's language has remained a characteristic way in which numerous subsequent American thinkers and social critics have tried to come to terms with its power. The reason for this, in my view, also does not seem difficult to explain: it appears that nothing is unsayable in market language, even if some things said will sound somewhat strange or dissonant.

Two brief examples will suffice here. William James's references in *Pragmatism* (1907) to the "cash value" of words and ideas are perhaps well known. But he also employed several other market metaphors to illustrate his positions—"All human thinking gets discursified," he wrote, "we exchange ideas; we lend and borrow verifications"—and I believe some work could be done on both James and Charles Peirce along lines I pursued in part 1.[2] Less noticed are the following passages from Martin Luther King Jr.'s famous "I Have a Dream" address before the Lincoln Memorial on August 28, 1963:

> We've come here today to dramatize a shameful condition. In a sense we've come to our nation's capital to cash a check. When the architects of our republic wrote the magnificent words of the Constitution and the Declaration of Independence, they were signing a promissory note to which every American was to fall heir. This note was the promise that all men, yes, black men as well as white men, would be guaranteed the unalienable rights of life, liberty, and the pursuit of happiness.
>
> It is obvious today that America has defaulted on this promissory note in so far as her citizens of color are concerned. Instead of honoring this sacred obligation, America has given the Negro people a bad check; a check which has come back marked "insufficient funds." We refuse to believe there are insufficient funds in the great vaults of opportunity of this nation. And so we've come to cash this check, a check that will give us upon demand the riches of freedom and the security of justice.[3]

Talk of "promissory notes," "insufficient funds," and "cashing checks" that "give us upon demand the riches of freedom" will sound strange to those who dissociate the market from struggles for individual self-determination and racial justice. But these sentences show King doing what Emerson and

---

2. William James, *Pragmatism*, in *An American Primer*, ed. Daniel J. Boorstin (New York, 1966), 724; see also 715–19, 722, 726–27 passim. Charles Peirce, "How to Make Ideas Clear" (1878), one of the founding texts of American pragmatism, also made some use of market metaphors. See *Writings of Charles S. Peirce*, vol. 3, 1872–78, ed. Christian J. W. Kloesel (Bloomington, 1986), 260, 275.

3. *A Testament of Hope: The Essential Writings of Martin Luther King, Jr.*, ed. James Melvin Washington (New York, 1986), 217.

Thoreau did so often: taking hold of market language and raising it to a higher pitch of intensity and imaginative power. For that matter, King's entire speech suggests that he, like Emerson and Thoreau, saw himself as neither peculiarly hostile to, nor alienated from, the society in which he lived, nor driven to use highly specialized or esoteric language to voice his hopes and complaints. King's dream was, in his words, "a dream deeply rooted in the American dream that one day this nation will rise up and live out the true meaning of its creed."[4]

One can object that in our time the language of the market typically has been used in much less admirable ways, to impede criticism and reform, or to encourage quests for individual realization that involve little more than material consumption.[5] But that objection hardly screens out the fact that substantial criticism of the market does not require us to abjure or renounce its language. Moreover, if the market, in some of its manifestations, has incarnated what is worst about the United States, I also see no reason to deny a possibility that King apparently recognized: its language can be transformed and elevated to hold the nation to its putative idealism. To recognize this possibility of course does not establish it as fact. Nonetheless, I would suggest that many critics of American society, beginning with Emerson and Thoreau, have known that failing to seize upon it would have put a perhaps unbridgeable distance between them and a society in which the market's language has long been one of our common languages.[6]

One final point. Even if one accepts the guiding notions of this book, they do not neatly resolve the question of our own stance regarding Emerson and Thoreau. What should our demeanor be in returning to their writings to contemplate the meanings of the market as we have come to know

---

4. Ibid., 219.

5. See T. J. Jackson Lears, "From Salvation to Self-Realization: Advertising and the Therapeutic Roots of the Consumer Culture," in *The Culture of Consumption: Critical Essays in American History, 1880–1980,* ed. Richard Wightman Fox and T. J. Jackson Lears (New York, 1983), 3–38. There is no evidence suggesting that either Emerson or Thoreau anticipated the dominant role that advertising would come to play in American society.

6. It seems plausible to say that Americans have had three long-standing common languages. The others, also visible in King's "I Have a Dream" address, are those of the Bible and of the Constitution. Sanford Levinson, *Constitutional Faith* (Princeton, 1988), 180–94, makes some broad points about the Constitution as a linguistic system that I think also hold true for the language of the market and repeat here.

them? Do we celebrate, affirm, and renew their loyally critical stances? If we answer "no," is it because we now have other approaches to the market that offer us better modes of cultural understanding? Or has the economic world in which we live engendered problems and possibilities inconceivable to Emerson and Thoreau—and thus disallow the possibility that on this issue it may be "handsomer to remain in the establishment better than the establishment"? Such questions invite a variety of responses. An answer made in good faith, however, surely depends upon one's ability to continue to approach their views with historically informed sympathy.[7] I have pursued that task in this book by confining my attention largely to particular meanings of the market I believe Emerson and Thoreau consciously held or experienced. My purpose, however, has not been to force a choice between mutually exclusive interpretations of Emerson and Thoreau: the "real" antebellum figures versus figures who have been variously interpreted (by critics and admirers alike) since their deaths. This is not a choice we have to make, and insisting on it would only impede efforts to understand the complicated and still disputed cultural legacies of Emerson and Thoreau. Whatever their intentions in discussing market practices and institutions, we cannot hope to comprehend fully the meaning and importance of those discussions in isolation from their results. Or, put another way, because Emerson's and Thoreau's own understandings of the market are not the only ones that count, my concern to avoid anachronism by no means prevents us from contrasting the meanings the market had for them with those it now has for us, which may be very different because we are free to view their economic world in light of our different experiences and concerns. The final point that I would stress, however, is that careful efforts to reconstruct the complex range of meanings the market has had for past actors such as Emerson

---

7. One problem with many contemporary accounts of Emerson and Thoreau (by literary historians "old" and "new" alike) is that they cast attitudes of disappointment and disapproval on the limits of their criticism of the market without making clear the specific historical circumstances under which that criticism might have evolved into more sweepingly "oppositional" stances. This is the main difficulty I see in Sacvan Bercovitch's recent reformulations of his views of Emerson and Thoreau in *The Rites of Assent: Transformations of the Symbolic Construction of America* (New York, 1993). Finding fault with Bercovitch on this score, however, in no way diminishes his value as the scholar who has done more than anyone else to draw our attention to the remarkable complexity of the literary results of Emerson's and Thoreau's encounters with the antebellum market.

and Thoreau remain the necessary groundwork for any such retrospective distinction. Indeed, as Thomas Haskell has insisted, only by scrupulously maintaining this distinction can we prevent our efforts to reenter the past for present purposes from becoming a bag of tricks we play on the dead.[8]

---

8. Thomas Bender (ed.), *The Antislavery Debate: Capitalism as a Problem in Historical Interpretation* (Berkeley, 1992), 238.

Index

Aaron, Daniel, 30, 149

Abolitionism/abolitionist movement, 79, 80, 81–82, 87, 107, 115–16; and belief in black inferiority, 91; class interest and, 83; Emerson and, xix, 78, 86, 90, 110–14, 198n. 30, 213, 220, 269–70; lack of success of, 87, 146; and market economy, 82–83, 85–88; origins of, 97; pragmatic side of, 89; reason for existence of, 82, 83–84; as religious struggle, 94; subgroups in, 128–29; Thoreau and, xix, 78, 86, 115, 116–29, 269–70

Abolitionists, 78, 81, 144–45; beliefs of, 96; and Fugitive Slave Law, 103–4, 106, 107; and Harper's Ferry raid, 135, 140, 142; and secession, 148; Thoreau as, 44; and writings of Thoreau, 233n. 15

Adams, John, 122

Alcott, Bronson, 14, 48

Allen, Gay Wilson, 105, 107

Ambivalence: in Emerson's opposition to slavery, 112; in Thoreau's attitude toward market, xi, 47, 52–54, 71–72, 133–34

America: cultural ideal of, in Emerson, 5n. 4, 31–38, 39–40; "newness" of, 72

American culture, xvi, 9, 39–40, 164–65; Emerson in, xx–xxi, 174, 180–81, 200–202, 204–7, 211–12, 218, 220–21; Emerson's influence on, 40–43; Emerson's vision of, 203; "high," 231; institutional organization of, 163; market and, 155–57, 162–63, 166, 168; printed matter in, 157–58; split between mass and high, 163, 169,
173; Thoreau in, xx–xxi, 59, 73–74, 174, 224, 259; *Walden* in; 227–29, 234–40; writings of Thoreau in, 254–55

"American Scholar, The" (Emerson), 7, 12–16, 23, 25, 32, 156n. 2, 178, 179, 210; as masterwork, 221

"American Slavery" (lecture series) (Emerson), 111n. 20

America's promise: Emerson's vision of, 5–12, 13, 41–43; slavery and, 80; Thoreau on, 72–73

Anarchism, in Emerson's opposition to slavery, 105, 107

Anglo-American market for books, 166–67, 215

Antislavery constitutionalism, 121n. 9

Antislavery movement, 94; Emerson in, 213; historical origins of, 92, 94. *See also* Abolitionism/abolitionist movement

Antislavery speeches/writings, 86, 89; of Emerson, 110, 111, 140, 143, 150–51; of Thoreau, 81, 113, 114, 115, 116, 119–22, 125, 129, 140, 143

Atlantic Monthly, 146n. 18, 151, 160, 225, 232n. 14, 247, 249

Audience, 163, 168, 173, 174n. 29; for writings of Emerson, 219, 220, 221. *See also* Popular reading audience

Bartol, Cyrus, 197, 218

Bercovitch, Sacvan, 5n. 4, 68n. 30, 273n. 7

Bible, 126, 165–66, 272n. 6

Index

Index

Teichgraeber, Richard F.
    Sublime thoughts/penny wisdom : situating Emerson and
Thoreau in the American market / Richard F. Teichgraeber III.
        p.   cm.—(New studies in American intellectual and cultural
history)
    Includes index.
    ISBN 0-8018-5000-2
    1. Emerson, Ralph Waldo, 1803–1882—Appreciation—United
States. 2. American litearture—19th century—History and
criticism—Theory, etc. 3. Thoreau, Henry David, 1817–1862—
Appreciation—United States. 4. Literature and society—United
States—History—19th century. 5. Authors and readers—United
States—History—19th century. 6. United States—Civilization—
19th century. 7. Canon (Literature)   I. Title.   II. Series.
PS1638.T44   1995
810.9′003—dc20
                                                    94-36088